W9-CDW-072

DISCARDED

Gift of

211

U72h

Urban, Wilbur Marshall
AUTHOR

Humanity and deity
TITLE

124553

DATE DUE	BORROWER'S NAME

211   U72h
Urban, Wilbur Marshall
Humanity and deity
124553

HUMANITY AND DEITY

By Wilbur Marshall Urban

BEYOND REALISM AND IDEALISM
THE INTELLIGIBLE WORLD
VALUATION
THE FUNDAMENTALS OF ETHICS
LANGUAGE AND REALITY

HUMANITY AND DEITY

by

WILBUR MARSHALL
URBAN

London

GEORGE ALLEN & UNWIN LTD

Ruskin House Museum Street

FIRST PUBLISHED IN 1951

*This book is copyright under the Berne Convention.
No portion may be reproduced by any process
without written permission. Inquiries should be
addressed to the publishers.*

PRINTED IN GREAT BRITAIN
in 11 pt. Baskerville type
BY PURNELL AND SONS LTD
PAULTON (SOMERSET) AND LONDON

PREFACE

I

IT HAS long been the desire of the author of this book to write on the subject of religion. But strong though the desire was, the feeling against undertaking such a task was still stronger. The greatness of the theme and the 'high argument' in which such a theme alone could be developed seemed to make any approach to it almost sacrilege.

The reading of many books on religion seemed only to add to this reluctance. In contrast to the greatness of the theme the efforts of the human reason to compass it seem pitifully weak. It is, as Kant said, 'wonderful what little minds can do with great issues,' and before the problems set by religion in the modern world who is there that does not know his mind to be small indeed? If, therefore, I have finally yielded to the temptation it is surely not because I am under any illusions as to my own powers or hope to contribute anything of great moment to a subject that has long engaged greater minds. It is only because there is that in the present situation which justifies any mind, however limited, in seeking to understand it and in hoping that in such understanding something may be contributed to the solution of this greatest of all issues. If the times are out of joint, there is also, perhaps, that in the very dislocation of our beliefs and the transvaluation of all our values which will enable us to see more deeply into the problem, and with this insight find means to its eventual solution.

II

It is patent to all observant minds that the situation in religion today differs in important respects from that of previous periods of western culture. The dominant attitude of the nineteenth century—to go no further back—may be described as a recognition of the values enshrined in religion—more especially of the Christian religion—independently of any 'creed,' or the cosmic and metaphysical basis of religion. An 'irreligion of the future,' to which many confidently looked, was felt to be wholly compatible with the very values which European religion had

124553

developed and enthroned. The 'magnificent structure of theology and philosophy which had endured for a thousand years is,' we were told, 'indeed gone, but the values themselves are still there.' All this is to a significant degree changed. The values themselves are now challenged and it is understood—at least by those who have any understanding of these issues at all—that, once detached from this structure, they cannot continue to live. God may be dead, but if he is, surely when we mouth the noble words, freedom, justice and brotherhood, we are, like Nietzsche's old man of the forest, merely continuing to mumble of things that are dying also.

In a second way the situation of religion in the modern world differs significantly from that of previous periods, namely with regard to the problem of the relation of religion to science. This problem has always been an important chapter in the philosophy of religion and doubtless will continue to be. The cumulative effect of the scientific world view, from Copernicus to Newton, created a tension between science and religion in the modern world, but with the Darwinism of the nineteenth century this tension has not only been intensified but taken on a novel form. If the physical sciences appeared to have eaten God out of the cosmos, the so-called anthropological sciences, based upon evolutionary naturalism, have, for many at least, finally eaten the God-like out of the human heart. Not only are our values themselves challenged, but the very existence of the human, as the bearer of these values, has for many ceased to be credible.

Formerly conflicts between science and religion arose out of seemingly unresolvable contradictions between the dogmas of religion and the pronouncements of science. Now the pronouncements of religion, with which our values in the past have been bound up, are held to be not so much false as, from the standpoint of science, intrinsically meaningless. Religion has become poetry—for many, as for Anatole France, a 'sorry sort of poetry'—and its pronouncements on nature and man essentially myth. Scientific naturalism has, from Comte on, always been the real enemy of religion in the modern world, but it remained for the new naturalisms and new positivisms of recent decades to give what is believed to be the *coup de grâce* to the entire notion of religious knowledge and truth—and finally to

6

relegate it completely to the sphere of emotion and fruitful illusion. For positivism belief in God has always been a 'presupposition purely human'; for modern positivism it is no longer even that.

All this has, for the time being at least, intensified the crisis of religion in the modern world, but it has also, perhaps, furnished the means for its eventual resolution. For this new scientific naturalism, having completely naturalized the intelligence of man, has not only denatured his values but, in a sense, his science also. If 'human' all too human, is applicable to the former it is applicable to the latter also. Our growing sophistication regarding moral and religious beliefs cannot ultimately leave our scientific beliefs untouched. There is a higher criticism of science no less than of religion. The new understanding of the limits of science has brought with it also a new understanding of its relation to other activities of the human spirit. A complete evaluation of the situation has not yet been reached, but it has at least gone so far as to justify new attempts at the solution of this perennial problem.

Humanity and Deity condenses in a phrase the problem of the modern world and therefore of this book. Is Divine existence credible? is a question which has been asked from time immemorial. It is only in our epoch that a still more fundamental question has been raised, one without which the former cannot be answered. Is human existence, as we have hitherto understood it, credible? Is this 'hybrid of plant and phantom' possible? Denial of Deity has long been the challenge which has led men to concern themselves with the philosophical problems of religion, but denial of integral humanity is the deeper issue which underlies the problem of religion today. It is becoming increasingly clear that the credibility of the one is somehow bound up with the credibility of the other. Certainly, the more God has been denied, the more man has been denied also. As men have ceased to give glory to God, so also, with all their vaunted glorification of man, they have insensibly held him in the greater contempt. The crisis of our time is to be found in the fact that men have tried to understand the one without the other. To understand man without God, and, that which is perhaps equally fatal, to understand God without man.

7

III

The crisis in religion has naturally produced what has been called a 'theology of crisis.' This theology is fully aware, perhaps more than any other form of religious thought, of the situation depicted in the preceding paragraphs. Above all, it is a theology of crisis in the sense that it has accepted the main premises of scientific naturalism which the developments of modern science have seemed to entail. It abandons all ways from man to God, direct or indirect, and knows only the ways of God to man. It accepts the dissolution of the theological and philosophical rationalism of the centuries and seeks to build both its life and faith on the firm foundations of a despair of all reason.

It goes without saying that a philosophy of religion so fully aware of the nature of the present crisis, and all that it implies, is of the utmost significance. Indeed it is just this *tour de force* —this violent turning of the spirit of man—that constitutes in part the challenge for the present work. The elimination of the rational, and of any notion of natural theology, from religion, the abandonment even of the practical reason of Kant, the last remnant of western rationalism, is a more significant phenomenon than many have realized. It is the reverse side of the scepticism and positivism of our epoch. It is tempting to say of this Neo-orthodoxy, as it has been called, that it is merely a highly sophisticated fundamentalism, but such a judgment would be as false as it is superficial. Actually it is one aspect— and a significant one—of modernism in religion, as modern as the tendencies in science and philosophy that have given it birth. The very humanistic naturalism against which it is in revolt has made of the theology of crisis a somewhat inhuman supernaturalism, but this is perhaps the sole form in which the present crisis in religion can find adequate expression. However deep our personal distaste for this *tour de force* itself may be, it is something for which we should perhaps be thankful, for it has at least revealed the superficialities of the preceding epoch and disclosed depths which so-called liberal religion had almost ceased to understand.

It is this very contrast—between a humanistic naturalism and an inhuman supernaturalism, between a narrow scientific

rationalism and an all-embracing irrationalism—which constitutes the challenge of the present time. This dilemma can be
met, if it can be met at all, only by showing that the premises
concerning nature and man, premises common to both, are
essentially false.

The essential thesis of both is that there is no way, either
direct or indirect, from man to God—no witnesses, either
natural or logical, to the Divine. For the one there is no way
from man to God at all, to the other there is only the way
from God to man. The challenge to this thesis—the reinterpretation and revaluation of the theistic arguments—of the 'ways
of the knowledge of God', constitutes the heart of our argument.
Not only, we shall maintain, is religion itself perennial in the
human heart, but that theology, both natural and revealed,
with which religion is inevitably bound up, is perennial also.
Not only are the human values which constitute the initial
datum of all religion eternal, but the theological and philosophical structures with which they are inseparably bound up
have elements in them that are eternal also.

That there are natural and logical witnesses for God constitutes then the central thesis of this book, but the argument
itself involves much more than this. A restatement of rational
theology involves also a restatement and revaluation of the
principles of reason presupposed. Not only is religion itself
nothing without a rational cosmic and metaphysical basis, but
religion, for the western world at least, is bound up with that
philosophia perennis which the genius of Greco-Christian thought
has developed through the centuries. In developing this theme
I have made use of material from previous books, *The Intelligible
World* and *Language and Reality*, but neither book is, I believe,
necessary to the understanding of the present work. The restatement and revaluation of natural theology must speak for itself.

It may seem overbold to attempt to maintain such a position
at the very time when the tide runs so strongly against it and
the facts seem so surely to belie it. The challenge to religion,
and to the philosophy which underlies it, is not confined to the
intellectuals but has become part of the communisms and
fascisms of the man in the street. And yet it is possible that
things are not wholly what they seem. Strong as these tendencies undoubtedly are, there are also, to the observant eye,

strong currents in the opposite direction. We like to speak of
the Christianity still latent in our culture, and, although our
faith may be exaggerated, these latent factors may be stronger
than we think. The almost universal challenge to our moral
and political values has driven men back to the historical
sources and the logical foundations of these values and, when
once driven back, they discover anew the Christian conception
of man that underlies them. As these Christian values are thus
latent, so also, we may hope, is that deeper rationalism of the
European tradition with which they have also been bound up.
Our human reason, maligned and denatured as it has been,
still survives, as the widespread revival of classical forms of
Christian philosophy attests. More and more the apologetics
for religion which grew out of the particular conditions of the
nineteenth century, and which were made obsolete by the
irrationalism of the twentieth, have given way to a new evaluation of human reason and with it to a revival of rational
theology.

IV

The spirit in which this book is written reflects, it is hoped,
the humility which the greatness of the theme must of necessity
engender. If little minds can, indeed, manhandle these great
issues, is it not the part of wisdom to be led in all things by the
minds which we know to be great? This book is written then
in the spirit of classical western theology and philosophy. It
assumes that the high argument in terms of which humanity
has continuously expressed the 'ways of the knowledge of God'
cannot in its essence be affected by the vicissitudes of time. It
is assumed that 'the classical is reality purified by time,' and
that the ways of thinking which have established themselves in
human discourse about that which is timeless will have in them
an element of the timeless also. Nor is there, I feel sure, a hidden
petitio principii in the expression, the minds that we know to be
great; for do we not know well enough who of all those who
have spoken of both human and divine things are really great?
Are they not those who have known that the two are bound by
a cord not lightly broken and that it is only when this bond is
acknowledged that we can speak significantly about either God
or man?

Descartes in his preface to the *Meditationes de prima philosophia* thought it 'not unbecoming' to commend his thoughts to the doctors of the University of Paris. He did so, I believe, not with any desire to set himself right with the powers that were, nor yet again merely to fall back upon the authority of the past, but rather in the sincere belief that, however radical one may be in his approach to these great issues—extending even to the principle of universal doubt itself—the things concerning which he was about to meditate, more especially, 'Of God: that he exists,' remain in principle untouched by the idiosyncrasies of any individual mind. Needless to say, the philosopher of the twentieth century cannot follow Descartes in the letter, either in his appeal to the doctors or in his particular restatement of the classical theistic arguments, but he can in spirit. He would, it is true, neither ask nor desire that *Nihil Obstat* should be printed at the beginning of his book, but he can at least hope that nothing will stand in the way of his orientation towards those great minds of whom it may be said that they are the masters of all who really know. It is in this spirit at least that this book has been written.

Although conceived through a period of years, the book itself has been actually written during a global war which threatens not only our common humanity but, humanly speaking, that very sense of the Divine without which man is not man. That it has been a welcome escape from things that will not bear thinking about I shall not deny. If for this reason it receive condemnation—as it probably will—I shall not be greatly disturbed. For who will doubt that escape from an almost universal and unbelievable human infamy is a laudable thing? In any case I have reached an age in which such considerations have little weight. On the other hand, it may not be merely an escape. It may be—who can tell?—that precisely now when humanity is at its lowest, there are many who are thinking about Deity—without Whom man as man is not. If

> Only by looking low ere looking high
> Comes penetration of the mystery,

may we not hope that man, having looked so low, perhaps into an abyss such as he has never glimpsed before, that, even now, he is secretly looking high again. If anything that men may write at this time serves merely to enable some to look again to the hills whence cometh their help and, having looked, still see that heaven and earth are full of His glory it is all that one can either desire or hope.

CONTENTS

Patri
Fide Simplici Parvulorum
et
Serena Intelligentia Veritatis
Mire Praedito
Quo Docente
Secreta Philosophorum
Indagare Didici

Chapter I

Religio Perennis *and* Philosophia Perennis.
God and Man in European Philosophy

I — A

'IN WANDERING over the earth you can find cities without walls, without science, without rulers, without palaces, without treasures, without money, without gymnasium or theatre, but a city without temples to the gods, without prayer, oaths and prophecy, such a city no mortal has yet seen and will never see.' The wanderer over the earth, of Plutarch's words, would doubtless, like Plutarch himself, be impressed by this fact—of the universality of religion. Should he reflect upon it and its significance, he would no longer be the mere traveller, or the mere historian and recorder of his observations; he would become the philosopher, and in his reflections we should have the germs of a philosophy of religion. Should he conclude, with Plutarch, that no mortal will ever see a city without these things, he would also have one of the themes of this chapter, *religio perennis*.

It is true he might come to another conclusion. He might come upon cities where the temples were deserted, where prayer and prophecy were half-hearted and where oaths were held in light esteem. He might conclude that religion was dying, that it perhaps belonged to the childhood of the race, and that for the prayers and prophecies of childhood would, in its enlightened manhood, be substituted a religion of science. Or he might come to still a third conclusion, namely, that precisely this devotion to truth is real religion and that, in Croce's words, it is the fate of religion to be dissolved into philosophy.

The traveller might come to any one of these possible conclusions and he would still be a philosopher. In his reflections would be the germ of a philosophy of religion. For each conclusion represents an attempt to understand religion and, having understood it, to evaluate it as a part or form of human experience. The two tasks of a philosophy of religion are understanding and evaluation; it is to the examination of these two conceptions that the present discussion is, first of all, committed.

B

The philosopher seeks, then, first to understand religion. If he were the mortal of whom Plutarch speaks he would have at least some of the presuppositions necessary to the understanding of the religion of any city into which he might go, for he himself comes from such a city, and a city without these things no mortal has yet seen. If he himself has never prayed, he has, nevertheless, seen and heard men pray and has some sense of what this peculiar form of behaviour means. He may despise the foolishness of prophecy, but he cannot have failed to catch something of the earnestness and conviction of those who feel themselves the messengers of the Divine Will. He may be cynical of oaths, but he at least understands something of those who can swear even to their own hurt and can be loyal even unto death. Let us suppose, however, that our traveller is a visitant from another planet, and that on this planet there are no temples to the gods, no prayers or prophecy or oaths. This 'visitor from Mars,' even though he possessed intelligence—a sort of mechanized intelligence, as it were—yet was wholly without a sense for that which moves men to pray and to prophesy, could never understand religion and could not, therefore, write a philosophy of religion.

The situation I am here supposing has been used with telling force by Sir Arthur Eddington in connection with a similar, although partly different, situation. The visitor from another planet arrives in London on Armistice Day. Suddenly at noonday all the traffic in the streets stops. He wishes to know the causes of the strange phenomenon. The scientist might explain the mechanical processes by which the cars are brought to a standstill; the physiological and anatomical processes by which the signal is passed from the eye or ear to the brain and from the brain to the hands which stop the cars; he might even explain in terms of a scientific psychology the processes by which the impressions and stimuli are sensed, attended to and pass into motor reactions—in short he might know all the causes of the phenomenon without having the least inkling of what it really meant. He might know a great deal *about* it, but not what it was *all about*. Eddington uses the illustration to point the moral of the limits of science—and scientific description—

and the moral he draws is both true and important. I wish, however, to use it to develop the notion of 'understanding.'

To understand the phenomena of Armistice Day it is necessary to enter into the ends and values to which these phenomena are related, but in order to enter into them, even imaginatively, it is necessary to share with those who celebrate that day certain presuppositions, human and moral; otherwise the meaning is wholly incommunicable. This illustration may serve to bring out two truths, both of which are basal to our entire treatment of religion. It is impossible to evaluate religion without understanding it and it is impossible to understand it without participation, in some form and in some degree, in the life of religion. If we cannot understand the ordinary behaviour of men without apprehending and acknowledging the values which alone give it meaning, it is still more certain that we cannot understand that extraordinary behaviour of religion— that prayer and praise which men call worship—unless we apprehend and acknowledge the transcendent values which give these acts their meaning.

C

Students of religion, as of many other manifestations of the human spirit, often try to assume the status of a visitor from another planet. This is described as objectivity. It is supposed that one can understand the human only by becoming non-human and understand religion only by becoming irreligious. This is sometimes called the 'scientific' standpoint and it is a standpoint often assumed in what is called the science of religion. I say assumed, for of course it is never really maintained. It is precisely one of the little ironies of the intellectual life that those who protest their objectivity loudest usually have an abundant share of prejudices and presuppositions, only they are not aware of them. But assuming that it is possible, is it desirable? Is it really the sort of objectivity which makes possible a real understanding? I think not. The objectivity required for a philosophy of religion—and it must of course be objective—is of a wholly different kind. It cannot exclude the element of 'understanding.'

'A philosophy of religion to be of any value', so A. E. Taylor tells us, 'must not come from the detached theorist, holding no

17

form of creed, but contemplating all; it must be the fruit of candid self-criticism on the part of men living the life they contemplate, each in his own way, but each alike ready to learn alike from the others and from the outsider.'[1] I should agree in principle with this but I should want to state it somewhat differently. A philosophy of religion to be of value must *ultimately* involve the contemplation of 'them all,' but such contemplation to be significant can proceed only from an initial understanding of one's own communal religion. A completely detached theorist, if indeed such be possible, might indeed know much about religion, but not what religion itself 'is all about.'

This much may, I think, be granted—and indeed has already been shown—but the question is just what such initial understanding involves and to what extent it requires the sharing of beliefs. The question thus raised is one which is in the forefront of much of philosophical discussion today. It may be put in this form. In order to understand a poet, a moralist or a religionist, is it necessary to believe the assertions which he makes, or is it sufficient, so to speak, to catch the emotion which he communicates? The question is raised primarily in connection with the poet. It is often maintained that in order to understand and appreciate his poetry it is not at all necessary to share in any degree the poet's beliefs, but merely to assume, for the moment, the emotional attitudes which his beliefs generate. Now I do not believe that we can understand the poet without sharing to some degree the presuppositions which create and determine the universe in which he lives and moves—and we shall have occasion to argue this point later.[2] If this is true in the case of poetry it is *a fortiori* true in the case of religion. We must to some degree at least share the life we contemplate if we are to understand it. But just how much must the philosopher share in order to understand, how much must he 'live the life he contemplates'? What form of creed must he hold? Now I do not propose to answer this crucial question here—in a sense the entire book is an answer to it—but merely to suggest the lines along which such an answer must proceed.

Strictly speaking, to the philosopher nothing human in religion should be alien. He should in a sense be able to live the

[1] *The Faith of a Moralist*, p. 23.   [2] Chapter xii, p. 400 ff.

life he contemplates in any of the great positive religions—yes, even of the most primitive forms of religion. But this is neither psychologically possible nor epistemologically necessary. There are many forms of religious behaviour and expression which, owing to the special conditions of race and stage of development, present insuperable difficulties to appreciation and understanding. The moral sense of man is, although not identical with the religious, yet so closely fused with it as to set definite limits to living, even in imagination, many forms the philosopher must contemplate. Again, even in what we call the more ethical religions there are significant differences in moral values reflected in the God-ideas, which constitute a bar to this sympathetic intuition. The differences of East and West are in this respect often unduly exaggerated, but they are real nevertheless. All this is true but constitutes no ultimate bar to understanding, for in order to understand the essence of religion it is necessary to live it only on the plane of the developed religious consciousness, on that level on which the values which religion embodies and expresses tend to become universal.

In illustration of this conception we may make use of a striking figure often employed in this connection. Religious experience is likened to a pyramid. At the base, which corresponds to the particular pronouncements of the different positive religions, we find great variations from race to race and from time to time, due to the varied natural conditions under which the religious experience finds expression and to the varied imagery and symbolism in which it is embodied. But as we pass from the base to the apex, we find less and less of the particular and more of the universal. When we reach the level of the great moral and religious geniuses—of a Jesus, a Buddha, or a Confucius—we find a striking unanimity and, as it were, completeness of communication.[1] To the question, then, how much the philosopher must share in order to understand, the answer is, at least in principle, simple. If he lives the life he contemplates on the highest level of his own religious tradition—on the level which expresses that which is highest and deepest in man, those values and beliefs which, in the first instance he alone can fully share—we may safely say that he understands religion.

[1] An especially vivid use of this figure is to be found in Aldous Huxley's *Those Barren Leaves*.

19

It is only, I believe, on the basis of such a postulate that any philosophy of religion is possible. We shall therefore, in the studies that follow, speak, in the first instance at least, largely in terms of the idiom developed by the European Christian consciousness, but we shall do so in full confidence that what is found essential there will, *mutatis mutandis*, be true of religion in general. We might, indeed, proceed upon the postulate, so largely determinative of the philosophy of religion of the nineteenth century, namely, of Christianity as the 'absolute religion.' I do not deny that there are grounds for such a view, but it is not necessary to resort to this, as it will seem to many egregious begging of the question; a more modest assumption is sufficient for the present purpose. There are many difficulties in the way of the application of even this postulate—and these will be considered when we come to its application in detail[1]— but they do not, I think, affect its validity. For when we come to the first and last things of which religion speaks, the categories of value and being in which such discourse is alone possible are in all times and all places ultimately the same.

II

The Dilemma of Religion: The Source of Religious Philosophy

A

Doubtless religion is eternal as Plutarch believed; nevertheless it is still true that religion is always on the point of dying. It is, as it were, always suspended between two worlds—one in which it is no longer at home and one not yet fully realized; and from this paradoxical position it can never wholly free itself. There is a dilemma at the very heart of all religion and out of this dilemma arise the chief problems of the philosophy of religion.

This dilemma may be stated in several ways. We may say that man finds it difficult to live without religion but he also finds it difficult to live with it. The individual man is born to a given positive religion. It is only in this concrete form that religion has any significant meaning for him. But precisely this

[1] Chapter viii, p. 256.

form, by virtue of its very concreteness, contains elements which he finds it difficult to accept. Nothing is clearer in the history of religion than this fact. It was little less than a stroke of genius when Nietzsche changed the famous line of the Psalm, 'Whom the Lord loveth he chasteneth' into the apparent paradox, 'Who loveth his God chasteneth Him.' For nothing is clearer than that the more seriously a man takes his God, the more critical he becomes of the imperfect images and ideas in terms of which the Deity is expressed.

This is one aspect of the dilemma of religion and, as thus stated, it arises out of the close relation of religion to the moral and value consciousness of man. But there is another form of the dilemma, one which rises out of the rational and intellectual side of man. In the words of C. A. Bennett, 'Religion cannot do without the supernatural, yet it cannot do with it, for the supernatural cannot be completely rationalized.' Religion may be, in its origins, non-rational and the supernatural may be expressed in non-rational form, but if man is to live with it, it must be the expression of what is highest and deepest in his rational nature also. It is, accordingly, the dilemma of religion on its intellectual side which has been the chief stimulus of the philosophy of religion. It is also, of course, the source of one of the main problems of such a philosophy, namely, the relation of religion to science.

B

This dilemma has made its appearance in all developed forms of religion, has exercised the greater minds throughout the classical period of Christian theology and philosophy and, as we shall see, contained in it the seeds of the modern philosophy of religion. Innumerable illustrations are available but I shall take only one, a typical illustration from Abelard.

In his remarkable Dialogue between a Philosopher, a Jew and a Christian, Abelard asserts that 'what is said of God in bodily form is not to be understood as the laity commonly do, corporeally and literally, but mystically and allegorically. By the height of the heaven above the earth is meant the sublimity (*sublimitas*) of the character of the future life rather than the site of any material heaven; and that Jesus should sit at God's right hand does not mean that he is to occupy a definite position in space (*localis positio*) but that he will enjoy an equality of dignity (*aequalis dignitas*). The bodily ascension of Jesus did indeed take place as reported, but it signifies "a nobler kind of ascension" (*melior ascensus*), namely, that which takes place within the soul of believers. Unlearned and simple men could not understand what was not presented in clear and pictorial form.'[1]

This attempt to 'rationalize the supernatural' is in every way both typical and enlightening, for it enunciates a principle of 'interpretation' which became a permanent part of classical theology. That what is said of God—his attributes and operations—cannot be said literally in the modes in which they appear in creatures, became a central part of the theology of St. Thomas. The difficulty in this, as in all forms of this principle of interpretation, is the retention of the literal, and the question of the literal and symbolic thus becomes a central problem of philosophical theology. For Abelard 'the bodily ascension did take place as reported,' although it signifies or symbolizes a 'nobler ascension'; and thus the retention of the 'historical element in religion' and the question of its significance becomes central in a philosophy of religion. For the historical involves the categories of space and time—the ascension must be in space—and to apply these categories of nature to the supernatural involves an 'interpretation' which no religion, on the higher levels of its development, has ever been able to avoid.

C

As the dilemma itself has appeared in all forms of developed religion, so also have similar principles of interpretation been formulated for its solution. There is scarcely any form which has not developed some doctrine of a twofold truth.[2] Christian philosophy has from the beginning revolved about this dilemma and has from the beginning also had some conception of 'the two truths, the one human and the one Divine.' The classical

---

[1] Quoted from Höffding, *Philosophy of Religion*, p. 47. Found in Petri Abaelardi, *Dialogus inter philosophum, judaeum et christianum*, ed. Rheinwald, Berolini, 1831, pp. 101 ff.

[2] An outstanding case is that of the theory of the Double Truth in Buddhism. Nāgāruna (about A.D. 125), called 'the greatest and foremost philosopher India has ever produced,' solved a similar dilemma by distinguishing between common-sense truth and higher-sense truth. I do not intend to suggest a complete similarity between the conception as developed in Christian and Indian philosophy, but merely to indicate that similar problems have led to similar solutions.

formulation is that of Albert and St. Thomas, not the form given it later by Duns Scotus.

There are two kinds of truth, although ultimately not contradictory, namely, truths of nature and truths of Grace. As St. Thomas says, 'the truth of the intelligible things of God is twofold—one to which the inquiry of reason can attain, the other which surpasses the whole range of human reason.' Reason can lead to certain truths of nature, but above these are supernatural religious and ethical truths which are not of nature but of 'Grace'—truths which are revealed and not discovered. The truths of Grace need not themselves be rationalized in order to be accepted. It is enough that reason show us the truths of natural reason and that the truths of revelation are not in conflict with the truths of nature but rather their fulfilment.

This solution of the dilemma was, in the main, satisfying to the dialectical mind of the late middle ages but, historically viewed, it was an impermanent solution. Having gone so far, men found it difficult not to go further, and thus the rift in the lute that finally destroyed the unity of scholasticism. It is not surprising, therefore, that Duns Scotus, generally held to be the most acute philosophical mind of the later scholasticism, was led to assert that theology is only a practical matter, aiming at salvation from sin and having to do with the will and not the intellect, each being right in its own sphere. This doctrine was conceived in good faith in order to give to dogma a claim untouched by reason which, in the form of modern science, had apparently become ever more inimical, but its actual effect was in the other direction. Reason was inevitably given an increasing scope and stringency and the consequence was that faith and theology became more and more a matter of will and feeling. Thus was prepared the way for the entire modernist movement, both catholic and protestant, with its inevitable tendency towards mere humanism.

It is no part of my intention to discuss this doctrine critically at this point, whether in its Thomistic or Scotistic form—that is a problem of later contexts—but merely to understand it and to show its relation to the dilemma of religion. It has, of course, never commended itself to what is called the healthy understanding of the plain man, for whom truth can be no more divided than could Solomon's child, or to the fundamentalist, theologian or scientist, for whom truth, to be true, must be 'true altogether.' But it is doubtful whether either the plain man or matter-of-fact theologian or scientist have really understood this very significant doctrine. What the scholastics realized is that the realm of nature and the realm of Grace are two different universes of discourse in which men speak different languages. When one is talking about creation and revelation, about sin and redemption, one is speaking in a language which is understandable within the realm of Grace but is not translatable into terms of the realm of nature and natural phenomena. As natural science, with its language and symbolism, developed, it became more and more clear that between it and the language and symbolisms of religion there is a yawning chasm which all the artifices of philosophy could not apparently bridge. Men came to speak, therefore, of two adequations of the same truth—the one human, the other divine. The two languages and symbolisms cannot be in ultimate conflict but must be in some sense complementary. That they are so the medieval philosopher sought to show in the thought idiom of his time. It is, however, equally a fundamental problem of the modern mind, for it formulates the problem of Humanity and Deity in what is, perhaps, its most fundamental form. This problem requires a similar solution, but one expressed in the philosophical idiom of the present. It is to this task that much of the present study is devoted.

D

It is this dilemma of religion which created the philosophy of religion and which sets its main problems today. The survival of religion in modern culture depends, humanly speaking, upon its solution. The classical solution with its attempt to find a middle ground has not, as we have seen in general, satisfied the modern mind and various other attempts at solution have naturally followed.

One of these is the 'Religion of Humanity' or naturalistic humanism. The essential of this view is that we should not seek to rationalize the supernatural but should exclude it from religion. In the words of one of its representatives, 'Until the supernatural is eliminated from the minds of men we shall not be able to comprehend the nature of religion.' We must assume that this represents a genuine effort to 'comprehend' or understand religion and is, therefore, in the terms of our definition, a type of philosophy of religion. This view found a classical expression in the positivism of Comte, with its religion of humanity, but it is a fundamental strain in all the pragmatisms and humanisms of the nineteenth and twentieth centuries. Comte's 'law of development'—from religion through philosophy to positive science—while not necessarily always taken in its literal form, nevertheless underlies a large part of our modern psychological and sociological thinking about religion. The idea of religion within the bounds of the human alone is the essence of all philosophies of religion built upon these sciences.

This is, I repeat, a genuine attempt at a philosophy of religion and at the solution of the dilemma which created its problems. To eliminate the supernatural is certainly one solution, although a drastic one, of what has become to many an unbearable dilemma. It seems also to be, abstractly considered, a possible one. It seems at least conceivable that the sense of the 'infinite' or the beyond which is the source of religion does not imply that man is a part of or related to an infinite being, but, as Feuerbach says, implies merely that 'man is a part of humanity and that the stirrings of the so-called infinite in him are merely the stirrings of humanity.' It is conceivable that the religious images or symbols in which man has clothed his sense of participation in humanity have great emotional and pragmatic value and that, until he is developed sufficiently to apprehend these relations directly and not indirectly through symbol, religion must be recognized as an essential part of human culture. This is a possible theory and cannot be lightly dismissed, but we may well ask whether it really understands religion. A theory which would solve the dilemma of religion in this way seems to 'naturalize' it, to use Dewey's words, only by denaturing it.

A second answer to this perennial dilemma is the so-called dialectical theology of Karl Barth and Emil Brunner. In contrast to the religion of mere humanity, we may, perhaps, call it the religion of mere Deity. It also tells us that we should not seek to rationalize the supernatural but eliminate the rational from religion. In principle at least, it says that until we eliminate all elements of the natural and the rational from religion we shall never understand its true nature.

At first sight this position seems to be the very antithesis of the preceding religion of humanity. In reality, however, it presupposes its existence and could not have arisen except on the soil of modern science and positivism. The elimination of the natural and the human rests precisely upon the same view of nature and of man as that held by scientific positivism. The negative aspect of the dialectical theology is the crucial point. The supernatural cannot in any sense be rationalized; religion cannot be grounded in human experience and reason, but only in God. But the reason for this is that man and his reason are *non capabilis*, for the mind and reason are precisely the natural products which modern science seems to say they are, only that for the dialectical theologian these facts are expressed in the language of religion, namely the worthlessness and sinfulness of man.

Now this also is a genuine attempt to understand religion and therefore a possible philosophy of religion. It has at least this advantage over the preceding one, that it has arisen out of the depths of a disillusioned experience which, in contrast to the superficial 'enlightenment' of the nineteenth-century positivism, represents a wholly different universe of discourse. It knows full well that to eliminate the supernatural from religion is to denature religion and to take all the meaning out of it. But we may also ask whether this is really a possible solution of the dilemma. For even if it were true that God and the world stand over against each other as absolute value and absolute worthlessness (or sinfulness), that religion cannot be grounded on anything human, but only on God—it still remains true that, if it is to be religion, God must be acknowledged and received by men. Granted that God is omnipotent—can, so to speak, break into human experience at will—it is still necessary that he be acknowledged as God and that these extraordinary ways of God should be justified to man.

These two efforts to solve the perennial dilemma of religion are typical of the modern mind which seeks to solve its problems by *tours de force*. Such solutions make a great effect but they cannot permanently satisfy the human mind. There must be some middle ground, and it is the finding of this which has, from the beginning, constituted the basal problem of philosophical theology. There can be no religion of mere humanity, but there can also be none of mere Deity. Doubtless man without God is not man, but it is equally true that, while God without man would still be God, he would not be the God of any city that man has yet seen or will ever see. He remains forever the 'Unknown God' which religion, precisely because it is human, has constantly sought to declare unto man. Such a declaration can, however, be only in the language of men, and we can know that this language speaks truly about Divine things only if between God and man there is a unique relation which makes of religion something at once human and Divine. It is with the nature of this relation that both philosophical theology and the philosophy of religion are ultimately concerned.

III

Philosophical Theology and the Philosophy of Religion

A

The philosophy of religion is essentially a modern phenomenon. Notwithstanding the omnipresence of religion in some form, noted by Plutarch, and the perennial reflections upon it by the wise men of all times and all peoples, as a distinct field of study it is a wholly modern creation. When, therefore, we speak of a philosophy of religion of a Plato, a Plotinus or an Aristotle, of a St. Augustine or a St. Thomas, what we are really doing is to read a modern notion back into these men. They had indeed a philosophical theology—for all of them philosophy and religion were inseparable, however differently they may have expressed the relation, while the modern notion presupposes their separation.

Philosophical theology is that truth of the intelligible things of God which the inquiry of reason alone can attain. It assumes that *ratio est capabilis* and that when faith inquires of the intellect it will get an intelligible answer. The philosophy of religion makes no such assumptions. There may really be no 'things of God,' and if there are, they may not be intelligible. The philosophy of religion would still be possible if there were no such truth. The only assumption it makes is that religious experience is a genuine, if unique, form of human experience which must be understood and evaluated.

The term itself, philosophy of religion, dates from the beginning of the nineteenth century and presupposes the background of the entire Kantian-Hegelian movement. Many are disposed to think of Hegel as its founder in that for him religion is one of the four fields of human experience to be interpreted and given a place in a total philosophy. The standpoint thus presupposed is clearly shown by a quotation from the *Encyclopaedia*. The beginning of all philosophical knowledge (*philosophisches Erkennen*), he tells us, is the acknowledgment (*Anerkennen*) of the four fundamental forms or types of human experience, namely the scientific, the moral, the aesthetic, and religious. And, he continues, philosophy consists in seeking the truth implicit in these fundamental forms. In so far as religion is concerned, then, the task of philosophy is the interpretation of the experience we call religious and an evaluation of it in its relation to other forms of experience.

A crucial illustration of this modern standpoint is the possibility of a philosophy of religion on atheistic premises. An outstanding example of such a philosophy of religion is, of course, that of Schopenhauer. For him, despite the fact that the world-ground is ultimately irrational will, the religious consciousness is genuine and of the utmost significance. Up to a point, Schopenhauer has a keen understanding of the phenomena of religion. Of the three ways of salvation—those of art, of morals and religion—the religious, with its denial of the individual will to life, with its altruism and asceticism, is ultimately the only radical way. With masterly skill he describes and evaluates the deliverances of the great religious geniuses of all time and comes to the conclusion that it is they who really know what it is all about. I am far from maintaining that this is either an adequate interpretation of the religious consciousness or a true philosophy of religion, but it is undoubtedly such a philosophy in our meaning of the term. There is involved, of course, the further question of whether religion itself is possible on atheistic premises—the question presented in its most acute form by Buddhism. This is, however, a question of definition of religion which forms in part the problem of the following chapter. Actually, however, phenomenologically, Buddhism still retains the element of the Divine. It seems to be very questionable whether, in fact or in logic, religion still remains when all notions of Deity are eliminated. Actually Buddhism as a religion —that is, in so far as it retains the fundamental religious modes of prayer and praise—does not eliminate it. If in some of its forms it does seem to do so, it becomes the supreme instance of that fate of all religion, according to Croce, to be dissolved into philosophy, and we are then no longer dealing with religion.

B

A definition of the philosophy of religion by Pringle-Pattison expresses this standpoint adequately. 'The philosophy of religion,' he tells us, 'investigates the nature of the religious consciousness and the value of its pronouncements upon human life and man's relation to the ground of things.'[1] This, it seems to me, is about what an initial definition should be. It also includes, as we shall see, all the main elements of such a philosophy and states its problems in a way which avoids begging questions which can be answered only in the course of the investigation.

The starting point is the investigation of the religious consciousness. It is characteristic of the modern spirit that it starts not with God, His nature and being, but with 'the meaning of God in human experience.' Thus it appeared for some time that the key to the understanding of religion must be in psychology and the so-called psychology of religion. This stage in modern thought may now be said to be passed. It is unnecessary to recall the reasons which are known to all. Enough to point out that it is part of a general reaction against psychologism in all spheres of the human spirit. It was, moreover, realized that psychology as a science, if indeed it be a science, proceeds upon certain naturalistic assumptions or postulates which *ab initio* beg the entire question of the nature and significance of the religious consciousness—even its reality as an autonomous form of experience. The movement from the psychological to the phenomenological point of view, which by its very method puts all such 'prejudices' in brackets, has been especially significant in the sphere of the philosophy of religion.

When I speak of the phenomenology of the religious consciousness I am referring not to any modern formulation of the 'phenomenological method'; I am using it rather in the sense

[1] See his article on the 'Philosophy of Religion' in the *Encyclopaedia Britannica*.

of Berdyaev, when, in speaking of philosophical theology, he says, 'an abstract metaphysic cannot exist, but a philosophy or phenomenology of the spiritual life is possible.'[1] Without agreeing with the denial of rational theology here implied, we may recognize that precisely such a phenomenology of the spiritual life is the initial step in a philosophy of religion, as was indeed recognized by Hegel. The acknowledgment of the religious as an original and fundamental type of human experience, in this sense of a religious *a priori*, is the essence of the phenomenological standpoint. In this respect *Phenomenologie*, even in the limited sense of Husserl, is wholly right. The essence of religion—its *Wesen*—is not to be got by any merely inductive study of psychological and cultural phenomena—these afford only the material. Man has a religious *Begabung*, and in this original intuition he possesses both the source of religious experience itself and the instinctive organ, so to speak, for the apprehension and understanding of all religious phenomena. In order to understand we must live, in order to live and to understand there must be this endowment, an *imago Dei*, an original intuition of what men call the Divine. Thus it is that, as we shall see more fully later, there is no form of philosophical theology which has not assumed either explicitly or implicitly this original intuition.[2]

C

Mere consciousness or awareness does not, however, alone constitute religion; it is rather the pronouncements of religion —on man and his relation to the ground of things—their interpretation and evaluation—that constitute the material of a philosophy of religion. The problem of such a philosophy is accordingly, in the first instance at least, this *interpretation*— the determination of what religion 'really says,' as distinguished from what it often appears to say.

What is said of God is said primarily 'in bodily form,' often in the crudest of physical language, and what is thus said, the philosophical theologian always knows is not to be 'understood literally.' If, however, it is not to be so understood it follows of necessity that it must be understood symbolically, and symbolism as a theological principle becomes a necessary part of philosophical theology. Something must, indeed, be said literally

[1] *Freedom and The Spirit*, English translation, p. 6.   [2] Chapter viii, p. 289.

of God, as St. Thomas held, and what this is becomes, as it did for him, one of the basal problems of philosophical theology. In any case what is said of God must always be in some way and in some degree interpreted. This is, to be sure, an issue upon which theologians differ, but there is no theology known to man that does not involve interpretation and has not developed principles of interpretation.[1]

The final problem of a philosophy of religion is the evaluation of the pronouncements of religion on man and on his relation to the ground of things. The problem of evaluation grows directly out of the problem of interpretation, for it is not until we know what these pronouncements really say that any judgments regarding their value are possible.

The word value is used instead of truth and thus the definition here also avoids begging questions which can be solved only in the course of the discussion. It is conceivable that these pronouncements might have value for life even if they were untrue or at least unverifiable. They might even have value if, when interpreted, they were found to say nothing, or were what certain logicians call pseudo propositions, useful fictions having merely emotive value. Again it might be possible to say, with Kant, that they are 'true,' but true only in a 'practical reference.' Yet neither of these positions is in the end possible, and neither has, I believe, really been held for long. Religious emotions and attitudes are ultimately inseparable from the pronouncements of religion and, being propositions, these can be ultimately valued only in the way any proposition is evaluated, namely in terms of truth value. Nor can this truth value be truth only in a practical reference, for to be true in this way they must ultimately be true in a theoretical reference also, as Kant in the end admitted. In other spheres, even in science, merely pragmatic and operational notions of truth may conceivably work, but when we come to religion, truth, to be true, must, as it has been said, be 'true altogether.'

Thus it is that, as in all developed religions, so in the philosophical theology of Christendom, the truth value of the pronouncements of religion becomes the basal problem. The 'ways of the knowledge of God' becomes the fundamental problem upon which all others hinge, and since knowledge and truth are

[1] Chapters vii and viii.

correlative terms, the problem of truth becomes central. It is not an accident, therefore, that practically every one of the classical Christian philosophers has written a treatise entitled *De Veritate*, or some variation of the phrase. Nor is it an accident that all have some conception of a twofold truth, one human and one divine, and that the relation of the two becomes for them a basal issue. All recognize that truth, like God, who is perfect truth, should be one and indivisible, but they also recognize that it must be 'multiple and diversified in its applications'; that while truth is adequation of thing and understanding, there are 'two understandings,' the one human and the other divine.[1]

It is this problem, more than any other, that has, from the beginning, forced the theologian to be a philosopher. What is called philosophical theology—'the truth of the intelligible things of God which the inquiry of reason alone can attain'— becomes of necessity the presupposition of the truth of the things of Grace. But the relation of religion to philosophy involves more than this. The pronouncements of religion—on man and his relation to the ground of things—without which religion is not religion, cannot ultimately be unrelated to the pronouncements of reason, pre-eminently those of 'science,' on these same issues, and their truth value cannot be ultimately unrelated to the truth value of the latter. It is at this point that the problems of theology merge into those of philosophy and at no time has any attempt to separate them been permanently successful. Religion to be perennial presupposes a perennial philosophy.

IV

The Appeal to Reason in Western Theology and Philosophy.
The Philosopher as Apologist for Religion

A

As religion is perennial in the human scene, so also is man's effort to understand and evaluate it. If, however, one understands religion at all—still more if, by virtue of that under-

---

[1] The truth notion in Christian theology and philosophy is the subject of discussion in a later context (Chapter ix, p. 324).

standing, he seeks to evaluate it in the life and spirit of man, he inevitably becomes, in some fashion and in some degree, an apologist for it. But to become such he must also become a philosopher, for only the philosopher can make the 'appeal to reason' which such apologetic presupposes.

The key figure of Abelard's dialogue is thus of necessity the philosopher. The presupposition of the entire dialogue—and this is true of all discourse about religion—is that Christian, Jew and pagan all share in the light of natural reason and it is to this light that the philosopher appeals. He, no more than anyone else, can understand religion without living the life he contemplates, but he cannot fully understand it without contemplating the life he and others live. Contemplation of the faith is always a function of reason. Even if, with Martin Luther, one should bid us 'know only Christ and Him crucified, for in such knowledge alone is justification of faith,' even then he would be constrained to say, also with Luther, that, apart from justification, when thou art disputing with others concerning the power, wisdom and majesty of God, 'then employ all thy wit and industry to that end and be as profound and as subtle a disputer as thou can'st; for then thou art in another vein.'[1] Then, indeed, is one in another vein, and when in this vein the believer becomes of necessity the philosopher. The dominant tradition in Christian apologetic is this appeal to reason. Thus the Fathers' way of dealing with pagans and unbelievers was not to demonstrate God's existence and nature as if they did not know Him at all, but rather to assume that they did and to purify and interpret their already existing conceptions of the Divine. In the main they did not uphold the pronouncements of the faith because they were absurd to the natural reason, but rather commended them to that very reason. The defence of the faith became ever more and more an appeal to reason. St. Augustine asked, Why should God disdain reason, His firstborn Son? and neither St. Augustine nor any other Christian philosopher has ever dared to disdain it.

B

European philosophy has thus, from the beginning, been predominantly religious even in pagan times. Plato and Aristotle,

[1] *Commentary on Galatians*, Chapter i, verse 3. English translation of 1575.

Leibnitz and Spinoza, Kant and Hegel, all in their several ways have shared in this apologetic. It was not merely that the Christian tradition was an essential part of the cultural complex in which these modern Europeans lived and thought; it was rather that the idea of God was something as real as the external world and the human soul with which the idea was connected in a 'metaphysical trinity.' For all of them any significant philosophy in the end becomes religious, and in the end, also, any significant religion becomes philosophical. An ultimate separation of the two—at least as far as the main stream of European philosophy is concerned—is impossible.

There is, to be sure, another tradition—that of scepticism and atheism—but in the main *philosophia perennis* has included and presupposed *religio perennis*. This scepticism and atheism arose in Greek thought primarily through the attacks of Xenophanes. What had been said of the gods had, from time immemorial, been said in bodily form, and it was this way of saying it—this anthropomorphism—that gave rise to the tradition of scepticism and atheism, which has been continuous to the present time. The only difference between the scepticism and atheism of the ancients and of the most modern positivist is that, whereas for the former the language of religion is 'human, all too human,' and cannot therefore be true, for the latter, because of this same human character, it is not so much untrue as meaningless. For him, as for Hobbes, the great nominalist and therefore sceptic, the knowledge of God is impossible because God is 'ingenerable,' and it is only of 'motions, generations and their effects,' or that which can be said in bodily form, that knowledge is possible. For the positivist, both ancient and modern, religion, as for Hobbes, 'has nothing to do with convictions'; it is not philosophy but only custom and law.

It was Plato who chiefly challenged the ancient scepticism and became the first great apologist for religion. It became clear to Plato and his successors that what is said of the gods is inevitably said in bodily form and is not to be understood literally and corporeally, but allegorically and mystically. It became clear also that the language of religion, if it is to be understood and interpreted, must be translated into the language of metaphysics. From his time on a distinction is drawn between

34

mythical and philosophical or natural theology, a distinction which becomes an integral part of philosophical theology. This did not, however, prevent Plato from understanding the significance of mythical language and his apologetic for myth is part of his greatness as a philosopher.

It was precisely because Plato thus *understood* religion and interpreted it in terms of reason that he valued it so highly and became the great apologist for it. Thus in the *Laws* he takes it for granted that a man should be secure in his religion, but he also maintains that no man can be thus secure who does not also possess the natural knowledge of 'science.' It is true that for Plato—and the whole European tradition—science meant something very different from that which most of us have in mind when we use the term today. It is true also that Plato's emphasis upon mathematics has led some to think that mathematical knowledge was for him the norm of knowledge. But after all, he thought of knowledge of the Good as the highest stage of science and those who would try to identify such knowledge with the knowledge of mathematics are welcome to the attempt. The 'science' through which men are to reach certainty about God is a science which includes the whole reason of man, and this reason, as Plato saw, is oriented towards the Good.

Plato sought to commend the 'religious' idea of God to the natural reason of man, identifying it with the philosophical idea of the Good. From Plato this conception passed over into the Academy and, through his pupil Aristotle, also into the Lyceum, and from both schools passed ultimately, through Neoplatonism, into the philosophy of the Christian world. The title of the sixth Ennead of Plotinus, The One or The Good, constitutes, in a sense, the culmination of this apologetic. With this passed into Christian philosophy also the idea of two sources of knowledge of the Divine, intuition and demonstration.

It is true that the two traditions, the Platonic and the Aristotelean, constitute in a sense the source of a significant bifurcation in Christian apologetic, leading to many misunderstandings between West and East and even in the West itself, but the appeal to reason is the same in both, and the rational or natural theology which resulted constitutes one continuous stream. From Augustine to Aquinas, the appeal to the natural light of

35

reason, to a reason enlightened because of its natural orientation towards the Good, is the essence of both traditions.

This is true not only of Christian theism, but of the entire European philosophical tradition, in which the theistic argument—in principle, a systematization of the apologetic of both Plato and Aristotle—is an inexpungable part. The rationalistic movement of the continent, more especially of Descartes and Leibniz, is from this point of view a continuation of this apologetic. Not only are the two elements, intuition and demonstration, present in all representatives of this movement but, as we shall see, the identity of the *ens realissimum* with the *ens perfectissimum*, of value and being, is the key to their understanding also. Of all these Leibniz, as we shall presently see, not only expressed this tradition most adequately but—and this is even more important—was fully conscious of the principles underlying this Great Tradition.[1]

C

It is often assumed that this relation of religion to philosophy came to an end with the eclipse of natural theology at the beginning of the nineteenth century. Quite the contrary is really the case. There was merely a change in the character of the appeal to reason made necessary by the dialectics of empirical and sceptical philosophy. The idealistic apologetics of the nineteenth century embodied this change, and was still an appeal to reason, although one different in significant respects from that of the eighteenth. Viewed in the perspective of the twentieth, this change is the significant thing and a proper evaluation of the apologetic which resulted becomes a basal problem for any modern philosophy of religion.

The eclipse of rational theology was itself due to a contraction of the notion of reason which the upholders of natural theology would never have recognized as reason at all. At the hands of Hume and his fellow sensationalists, it was reduced to experimental reasoning concerning quantity and number. Naturally, therefore, any 'volume of divinity or school metaphysics' was to be 'consigned to the flames.' For Kant this also was reason in its empirical and scientific employment—and for this reason these same books on natural theology, while scarcely to be consigned to the flames, had in a sense become outmoded, with

[1] Chapter iv, pp. 128.

36

the result that the entire 'appeal to reason' had to be couched in new terms. Reason having been 'reduced to a mere pittance of its former self,' as Kant as well as Berkeley realized, Kant also saw that the reason concerned with merely experimental reasoning about matter of fact or with abstract reasoning concerning quantity and number is no longer reason in all the fullness of its being as understood by traditional European philosophy.

This narrowing of human reason gave rise to that pseudo rationalism which rightly became the object of attack by the theologians and philosophers of the nineteenth century. The identification of reason with scientific method, in the two aspects described by Hume, could be met only by a new broadening of the conception. This both Kant and Hegel in their several ways attempted. Whether their attempt was successful or not is not the issue here; our concern is merely that of understanding it.

Kant's critique of reason in its various forms was really an attempt to evaluate it properly after the devaluation which it had suffered at the hands of a sceptical 'physiology of knowledge' as he called it. The purely empirical employment—that of science—Kant saw clearly could not lead us to God, but the practical, so he believed, could. Kant's apologetic for religion was therefore, in the first instance, a moral one, although far from the 'mere moralism' often ascribed to it. Nor is his supposed elimination of the theoretical reason quite the negative thing it is thought to be. True, he criticized the traditional formulation of the ways of the knowledge of God, but, as we shall see, he never denied that there is such knowledge, both of His existence and nature, but explicitly affirmed it in other parts of the total critique. It is true also that to the ideas of God and the soul he appeared to ascribe merely a regulative function, but, it is often forgotten, only with respect to the purely empirical employment of the understanding or science. Elsewhere they are more than regulative. While Kant's appeal was primarily to reason in its practical function and therefore to value, nevertheless he makes it clear that the reason in all its employments is oriented towards the Good, and that the theoretical reason has a 'value character' also. In sum, Kant's critique of reason was really an attempt at restatement—in what to many, to be sure, seem questionable terms—of the broader

37

notion of reason which the developing scientism of the time was threatening to displace.

Hegel, while accepting in the main Kant's broadening of the notion, went a step further. More particularly, he refused to accept the purely regulative value of the transcendent ideas such as God and the soul, with the result, as we shall see, of a reinstatement in a new form of the theistic argument of rational theology. The idealistic reconstruction or reinterpretation of the theistic proofs became, therefore, the main element in nineteenth-century apologetic. It is not a question, at this point at least, whether this reconstruction and reinterpretation is valid; the point is that it constituted the sole appeal to reason of many of the greatest minds of the nineteenth century.

The culmination of this 'idealistic' apologetic was the attempt of Hegel to 'rethink Christianity as the absolute religion,' an attempt which, as it has been said, 'is not encouraging.' However unsatisfactory this attempt may have been, it is highly significant, for it confirmed a fact which the entire history of European thought should have made clear, namely that there is no apologetic for religion which is not an appeal to reason, and secondly, once the appeal is made it must, in the end, include in some fashion all the elements of religion, dogmatic as well as rational. While a relative distinction between the two must be made, ultimately they are inseparable.[1]

The essential of the apologetic of modern idealism, in both its Kantian and Hegelian forms, is, however, its transcendentalism —its conception of human reason, as not only not derivable from nature, but as part of a reason which transcends nature. This transcendentalism was, it is often said, sometimes with scorn, but a translation of the supernatural into the transcendental. In a sense this is true. For, from the point of view of knowledge, the essence of supernaturalism is that the natural light of reason, by which man knows nature, self and God, gets its very light from that which transcends nature. The insistence upon transcendental elements in human reason, in both its theoretical and practical forms, not only continues this element in European philosophy but constitutes a challenge to mere naturalism at a point highly significant for both morals and religion. So long as one denies a complete 'naturalization of the

[1] Chapter v, pp. 155 ff.

intelligence,' so long as he recognizes in man a 'spiritual principle,' not derivable from nature, so long is the appeal to reason —to the *logos* in man—an appeal which constitutes the essential character of all Christian apologetics—still possible. If, on the other hand, man's intelligence is held to be but the product of the material forces of a merely 'circumstantial selection,' an appeal to such intelligence is vain.

The transcendental, as thus understood, is, to be sure, far from being the full equivalent for the supernatural of Christian philosophy. The transcendentalism of Kant, although in a sense a translation of the 'transcendentals' of medieval philosophy, actually left the problem in a highly dubious state. Apparently at least he took the transcendental out of the realm of being and transferred it to the realm of thought, but only apparently, I think. Be that as it may, transcendental idealism, in both its Kantian and Hegelian forms, never doubted that it was a genuine apologetic, not only for religion but even for Christian theism itself. And to anyone at all aware of the problem of humanity and Deity in the modern world there will be little doubt also. No one who views this modern idealistic movement against the background of the long story of European philosophy—and even more in the light of the developments of the twentieth century—can doubt that it continued in modern form the tradition of the appeal to reason which constituted the essence of the apologetic for religion.[1]

This transcendentalism reached its zenith, however, only to collapse, with results for western religion and culture not yet fully understood. There were various reasons for this collapse.

---

[1] In the *Critique of Pure Reason* (Kemp Smith translation, pp. 118–19), Kant has this to say of the medieval doctrine of the 'transcendentals.'

' These supposedly transcendental predicates of things are,' so Kant tells us, 'in fact nothing but logical requirements and criteria of all knowledge of things in general. . . . We have not therefore in the conceptions of unity, truth and perfection made any addition to the transcendental table of the categories, as if it were in any respect imperfect. All that we have done is to bring the employment of these concepts under general logical rules, for the agreement of knowledge with itself—*the question of their relation to objects not being in any way under discussion*' (italics mine). This is undoubtedly true so far as the discussion of the 'understanding' is concerned, but in the transcendental dialectic they become more than this, especially in the 'Canon of Reason.' Even in this mutilated form, however, Kant retained the element of transcendentalism, characteristic of traditional philosophy, and it is this, more than anything else perhaps, that makes his work a continuation of that philosophy.

An increasing sense of certain fundamental ambiguities and contradictions within the idealistic apologetic itself contributed to its downfall, but it was chiefly the result of wholly external causes—namely the complete naturalization of the intelligence which followed upon the application of Darwinian principles to the mind of man. With this widespread depreciation of reason, the idea of a spiritual principle in both nature and man, so natural to the higher levels of thought of the nineteenth century, became for the twentieth largely empty words.

The internal reasons for the collapse are not to be minimized. Immediately after Hegel's death, as everyone knows, there arose two conflicting tendencies and consequent interpretations, the one conservative, corresponding to a thesis never abandoned by Hegel himself—namely, that philosophy culminates in an apologetic for Christian theism—the other holding to the finality of the 'notion,' that is of the self-determining Absolute—culminating in pantheism—tendencies which served to lay bare certain ambiguities present in the position from the beginning. The apparently dialectical character of all rational theology, with its inevitable antinomies, made of Kierkegaard and his many followers the mortal enemies of Hegelian rationalism and led to that anti-intellectualism which is the fundamental note of all distinctively modern apologetics. But after all, the determining cause was the universal depreciation of reason which followed inevitably upon the complete naturalization of the intelligence of man. It became clear that such apologetic could be no longer an appeal to reason, but solely to feeling, and must take the form of a humanism which recognizes only a religion of humanity, or a form of supernaturalism which asserts a doctrine of extreme and exclusive revelationism which makes it a religion of mere Deity.

One can understand, and to a degree sympathize with, this violent reaction against the idealistic apologetic. In addition to its inherent ambiguities—indeed because of them—there developed in the English-speaking world, as well as on the continent, a version of idealism which could not be other than inimical to religion. It was held to be 'the fate of religion,' to use Croce's words, 'to be dissolved into philosophy.' Negative and sceptical elements triumphed in both Kantianism and Hegelianism and little was left to religion but a mere moralism or an arid intellectualism.[1] All this must be admitted, and yet to the unbiased mind this reaction must appear little less than tragic. It is not merely that this same transcendentalism was the one great opponent of the naturalism which threatened to overwhelm the latter half of the century. Not merely that to this idealism we owe interpretations and reconstructions of the theistic argument which formed the rational basis for religion of a large part of the intellectual world.[2] Even more fundamental is the fact that, strange as it may seem, it was in its essence a continuation of the apologetic of traditional philosophy.

This will be for many a hard saying, but it is nevertheless true. It might almost be said (*pace* the Neo-scholastics) to have restored some of the root ideas of scholasticism. For it takes God, not man, as its starting point; being, not sensation, as its initial option. God, or Absolute reason, becomes again the centre of the world and the subjectivism which followed from starting wholly from man, and the mere 'physiology of his knowledge,' was transcended in a conception which again connected the human with the Divine. In these respects, then, the idealistic apologetic was a continuation of the appeal to reason of traditional philosophy. However remote the *Deus philosophicus*, as thus envisaged, may have seemed to be from the *Deus vivus* of the anti-intellectualists that followed, it must still be remembered that for the former they were still really the same and that the language in which they expressed this great truth afforded to many of the finest minds of the modern world the only idiom in which it could be significantly expressed. One of the most devastating of life's ironies is the seeming fatality which drives the believer to join with the unbeliever in attempting to demolish all attempts made by reason to justify his belief.

[1] McTaggart's *Some Dogmas of Religion* and Bradley's *Appearance and Reality* have both had their part, not only in bringing about this dissolution, but in encouraging positivistic and humanistic views of religion. But over against these negations should be set the positive affirmations of a Pringle-Pattison, a Sorley and a Royce.

[2] This idealistic movement produced a number of restatements and reinterpretations of the theistic argument of which John Caird's *An Introduction to the Philosophy of Religion* may, perhaps, be taken as typical.

V

Twentieth-century Anti-intellectualism. The Appeal to Experience and the Rise of Value Theology

A

With the collapse of idealism, all distinctively modern apologetics, whether humanist or fundamentalist, really presupposes this depreciation of reason. In a sense it is a far cry from the original sin which for Tertullian had infected human reason from the beginning, to the struggle for existence which makes of our reason merely a means of adjustment and survival to an essentially irrational world, but the results for philosophy are much the same. The naturalization of the intelligence, together with the scepticism of reason which it engendered, combined to undermine the entire structure with which our values had been bound up, and all that was left was an appeal to feeling and the practical. The complete humanization of religion and the anti-intellectualism of religious thought became the dominant notes of the modern religious world.

An outstanding protagonist of this movement—at least in the English-speaking world—was William James with his appeal to religious experience in all its manifold 'varieties.' 'The mother-sea and fountain-head of all religions,' so he wrote in a letter to his son, 'lies in the mystical experience of the individual, taking the word mystical in a very wide sense. All theologies and all ecclesiasticisms are secondary growths presupposed; . . .' For this reason, 'they are also indestructible by intellectual arguments and criticisms.'[1] This latter sentence is the key not only to James' apologetic for religion (for despite the unsatisfactoriness of the religion for which he argues, it is still in the broad sense an apologetic) but also to the entire modern apologetic which followed. For his 'radical empiricism' envisages a unique form of experience, not really subsumable under either the outer or inner sense of traditional empiricism, and one therefore immune to the intellectual criticism based upon this narrow concept of experience. Natural and logical witnesses for God become superfluous.

[1] In a letter published by his son in the *Atlantic Monthly*, September, 1920.

A second form of this modern apologetic consists in an appeal to 'value' as against 'fact,' a form native to German theology since Kant. It too finds the fountain-head of religion in a unique experience and believes also that for that reason it is immune from intellectual arguments. The Ritschlian movement, denying in principle the appeal to reason, as embodied in natural theology, and accepting the narrow conception of 'fact' developed in modern science, and apparently sanctioned by the critical philosophy of Kant, left, so to speak, the world of fact and reason to 'science,' and founded religion upon experiences of value. The essential point, so far as the present issue is concerned, is the self-authenticating character of the intuitions of faith as embodied in revelation and developed in dogma. Ritschl's opposition to the rational and metaphysical element in theology was particularly directed against the apologetic of absolute idealism which for a time he had espoused, but it included an antagonism against all the speculative theistic proofs and the older scholasticism, both catholic and protestant, an antagonism which reached its culmination in the theology of crisis.[1]

This modern apologetic, in both its forms, is, I believe, but a temporary phase, a detour, as it has been said, away from the main road of Christian theology, to which there must ultimately be a return. It reflects, as it has also been said, an age desperately in need of an apologetic, a need so desperate in fact as to seem to justify even such appeals as these.

Its transitory character has, however, become increasingly evident. It has gradually been borne in upon men that such appeals have no meaning, to say nothing of cogency, except to those who are prepared to accept moral and mystical experiences at their face value—an acceptance which precisely the naturalization of man's spirit which gave rise to this type of apologetic has made increasingly difficult in the end. For man's intelligence, as so conceived, such an appeal is not so much invalid as meaningless, and modern positivism makes short work of this type of religious realism. Appeals to experience

---

[1] It is customary to find the sources of this movement in Schleiermacher, and this is in a sense justified. But there was in Schleiermacher, as a whole, much more of the rationalism of his predecessors than is ordinarily recognized. See on this point Richard Brandt, *The Philosophy of Schleiermacher*, 1941.

doubtless have their significance, but to have any significance at all, they must be supplemented by a new appeal to reason, and this appeal, it becomes increasingly evident, can only be in substance that of the traditional rational arguments, however novel in form the exigencies of the present require them to be expressed.

This detour, temporary although it of necessity was, has, nevertheless, not been without significance for the philosophy of religion. It has at least made us aware, not only that all appeals except to reason are in vain, but that even these are in vain unless the reason to which appeal is made is properly understood. A return to traditional forms of argument—and to the appeal to reason which they imply—is indeed inevitable when we realize that our values are inseparable from the cosmological and ontological propositions which they presuppose, but it is equally clear, I think, that the reason to which appeal is made cannot be that narrow conception which led to the destruction of the 'intellectual arguments.' An appeal to reason must include *an appeal to value as part of the essence of rationality itself.* The detour from the main road has again made us aware that this road which the great thinkers have travelled is a road illuminated by the natural light of a reason oriented towards the Good, the only road that can lead man to the being he knows as God.

B

It is for reasons such as these that, as R. F. Tennant recognizes, somewhat against his will perhaps, 'theology has increasingly derived its arguments from consideration as to values.'[1] Of the fact itself there can be no question—the important point is what these considerations of value are, and why they have entered so largely into theological argument.

This 'value theology,' as it has been called, has taken varied forms, some of them as unconvincing as the philosophies that gave them birth. To found religion upon merely subjective experience is not to make it immune to intellectual criticism, but rather to invite that criticism, especially at the hands of the psychologist. But this does not mean that considerations of value should not enter into theological argument, even the

[1] See his article on 'Theology' in the *Encyclopaedia Britannica.*

44

rational theology of the theistic argument itself. What these considerations are and how they enter into the argument it will be the task of later discussions to show in detail; here only one point need be made. Unless we start with values and their acknowledgement, as our initial datum, no argument for God's existence can get started at all. No discourse about God, I shall maintain, and therefore no arguments for His being and nature, which are but the development of that discourse, have any meaning, to say nothing of conviction, which do not presuppose, in those who thus discourse and argue, mutual acknowledgment of ultimate values. We may indeed, I believe, rise to the conviction of God from finite things, but I am equally certain that we cannot do so unless among these finite things— and indeed first among them—is man, with his consciousness of relative values and of the absolute perfection which they presuppose. Without the anthropological argument we cannot get started, although unless it includes the cosmological we shall not arrive.

It is therefore inevitable that all theological argument should appear to be an *argumentum ad hominem*, and in a sense that is true. Only to man—and to one who speaks the language of man—could any such argument be directed. To a sub-human intelligence, or to some dweller on a remote intellectual Mars, the argument would have no meaning. For those to whom the argument is directed would neither understand nor acknowledge the initial premises from which all such argument proceeds.

VI

The Problem of a 'Disinterested Theology.' Again the Human and the Divine

A

This character of theological argument—including rational theology itself—must, I think, be admitted, but with the admission does not theology become 'interested,' all-too-human in the sense which makes genuine objective knowledge impossible? I think not, for the type of argument involved—this *argumentum ad hominem*—is the only kind of argument possible in any field of human knowledge when it is concerned with 'first and last things.'

This is certainly true when men are driven to ultimate issues in what we call political philosophy. An argument for a democratic, as opposed to fascist or communist forms of the State, always rests, in the last analysis, upon an appeal to certain human values, acknowledgment of which is believed to be an essential part of the reason of man. We hold it to be self-evident that man has certain inalienable rights which, when analysed, go back to certain indisputable values. It is no less true that when anti-democratic forms of political theory argue against the democratic state, the entire argument is based upon a refusal to acknowledge these values and an assertion of others which are held to be higher than these—other values more fundamental than liberty and happiness, yes even than the life of the individual himself. Without acknowledgment of these initial valuations all argument falls to the ground. We may, it is true, as political 'science' tells us, examine forms of society and State as impartially as we may compare any forms of physical existence, but political 'theory' always involves the evaluation of one form rather than another and it is impossible to say that one is better than the other without an appeal to mutually acknowledged values.

All this would, I suppose, be admitted. But it is ordinarily assumed that there is one great exception to this general truth of 'the value character of the theoretical,' namely, physical science. Science appeals to facts, never to values; an apologetic for science is a contradiction in terms. This dogma of the disinterestedness of science has beguiled not only the man in the street but many philosophers also. Nothing can be further from the truth, and to dispel this illusion is one of the first conditions of a true understanding of the relation of science to religion.

Science appeals to facts, to be sure, but what it calls 'facts' is determined by a criterion (and a criterion is always a principle of evaluation) which is based upon a prejudgment as to what *shall be called* fact. Kant saw this clearly when he called this prejudgment a postulate of the understanding, according to which only that shall be called fact which is sensuously observable, existence itself being understood by science as

46

identical with the sensuously observable. This initial valuation appears still more clearly when the enlightened positivist recognizes this definition of the factual not only as a postulate but as a 'convention'—but by this very convention science explicitly disavows all interest in any other kind of fact.

As science is interested in only one kind of 'fact' so also it is interested in only one kind of understanding and 'explanation.' The famous dictum of Spinoza, *Neque ridere, neque flere, nec detestari, sed intelligere,* is an injunction shot through with a pathos all its own. We may indeed avoid the prejudices involved in smiling, detesting, lamenting reality, but how shall we avoid the prejudice necessarily involved in their repression? There are many things that we cannot understand at all unless we laugh with them that laugh and weep with them that weep—even detest the things that they detest. Evidently to 'understand,' as understood by science, is possible only by excluding *ab initio* other forms of understanding, and such exclusion is possible only by an initial valuation which itself cannot be justified by science. There is a fundamental value-centric predicament in all knowledge which science itself cannot escape.

Actually, as we shall see later, the entire development of modern science was made possible only by these initial valuations and by the exclusions which they necessarily involve. It rests upon the fundamental postulate that only such concepts shall enter into science which are resolvable into physico-mathematical terms. Our intellect has a natural bent towards the physical and the mathematical; that is what it wants and therefore what it, as 'science,' always finds. But having determined what it is in which it is alone interested and which it will alone accept as knowledge in its sense, science is scarcely justified in adding the footnote, this is what reality alone ultimately is. It can do so only by an *a priori* and exclusive valuation which *ab initio* begs the entire question at issue. All of which is of the utmost significance in any discussion of the relation of science to religion. For the basal assumption of much of that discussion is that knowledge to be knowledge must be disinterested and that this ideal is realized only in science. If, moreover, any concept of the limits of science enters into the discussion, it is important to realize that such limits are science's

47

own self-limitation as determined by its own fundamentally 'interested' character.[1]

Nor is science without its own apologetic. In the end the scientist must also seek justification for his own, often inhuman, activity, an evaluation of his own 'cognitive values.' In doing so he must either assert dogmatically, with Hume, the exclusive character of his own values or else look beyond science itself to something which justifies not only his own but all other activities and values of man. In looking beyond itself there is no place for science to look except to reason and to the ultimate values towards which all reason is oriented. The idea that science alone, of all the activities of man, is self-authenticating is not only sheer illusion but perhaps the most dangerous of the many to which modern man is subject.

B

The appeal to the dogma of the disinterestedness of science is then wholly fatuous. Still more fatuous is it, on these grounds, either to make scientific methodology a pattern for theology, or, still worse, to make science the basis of religion. There is a sense, to be sure, in which both may be disinterested—in the sense, namely, that both refuse to yield to individual desire. We believe, in any sphere, only in that which is independent of our individual desires, just as we believe only in that which is independent of our personal belief. Men have been willing to die for the glory of science, but so also have they been willing to die—even to be damned—for the glory of God. Indeed in this sense religion might be said to be more disinterested than science.[2] But disinterestedness in any ultimate sense—as

[1] Bergson saw this point clearly when, in his *Introduction to Metaphysics*, he argued for an intuitive metaphysic and for the limitation of science which it involves. He tells us that what such a metaphysic 'will lose in utility and rigour it will recover in depth of extension and meaning.' It is only in the former cognitive values that science and logic are interested, while metaphysic has other cognitive ideals and values. Now I am not, of course, accepting here either Bergson's implied criticism of the values of science—of utility and rigour, or of the values which he places higher—that is another story—but merely arguing for the recognition of the presence in scientific method itself of a prejudice which determines both its methods and its results.

[2] Einstein has, somewhat naïvely, expressed his disillusionment with science, in that, while religion and the Church stood out for ultimate human values, science and the universities yielded in large part to the pressures of National Socialism. He should scarcely have been surprised, for a progressive detachment of scientific

indifference to all values—is impossible and he who makes that claim is merely deceiving himself, even if he does not ultimately fool us.

But to return to the main issue, theological argument does indeed involve an *argumentum ad hominem*, but only in the sense that this is the nature of all argument concerning first and last things, including even the values of 'science' itself. If it is more apparent in theological argument than elsewhere it is only because, of all first and last things in which men are interested, 'divine things' are the more ultimate. Doubtless one would be wrong in supposing that without going out of ourselves and by an appeal to the human alone, God could be easily and certainly known, but one would be equally wrong in thinking that without this knowledge of ourselves and of the values of which we are the bearers and which make us what we are, we should ever rise to the knowledge of God at all. Here an *argumentum ad hominem* becomes an *argumentum ad rem*. For man, with all he is and hopes to be, is an essential part of the 'thing' to which appeal is made. Moreover the reason that makes the appeal is human reason, with all that that implies. It is neither reason reduced to the stature of animal intelligence, nor expanded to the measure of the Divine. If it were the first it could not argue to first and last things at all; if the second it would claim to see these things as God sees them and in its vanity destroy itself.

All of which brings us to the main theme of this chapter— God and Man in European Philosophy. One thing stands out with extraordinary clearness, namely that in the main they have never been separated. Humanity and Deity, like the inside and the outside of the curve, like the mountain and the valley, are apart from each other unthinkable. Implicit in European philosophy from the beginning, it was finally made explicit in the distinctively Christian doctrine of an analogy of being between the Creator and the creature, between the human and the Divine. It is only from perfections, conditioned by the way in which they appear in creatures, that we can rise to that Unconditioned Perfection which from the beginning has been the essential or 'formal' principle of Deity. On the other hand, it is only by an appeal to that which is highest and deepest in man

activity from the values which give it ultimate significance has been an outstanding characteristic of recent decades.

49

—to reason in this fuller and deeper sense—that we can be led to acknowledge that Unconditioned Perfection to which our human attributes are ascribed. Without an appeal to reason in this sense there is no way, direct or indirect, to God. It is this truth that forever makes impossible a religion of mere humanity, but, by the same token, it also makes impossible a religion of mere Deity. This is the 'moral' to be drawn from the story of European philosophy.

Chapter II

The Language of Religion: The Word of Man and The Word of God. The Essence of Religion

I — A

IN THE preceding chapter we discussed the problems of a philosophy of religion without making it clear what the thing religion is which all this discussion is about. We defined the philosophy of religion without defining religion itself. This must have seemed a grave oversight and one which should be immediately rectified. It was not, however, an oversight but rather deliberate intention—an intention for which, it seems to me, there are the best of grounds.

'Most books on the philosophy of religion try,' as William James says, 'to begin with a precise definition of what its essence consists of.' But he also points out that 'the fact that they are so many and so different from one another is enough to prove that the word "religion" cannot stand for any single principle or essence, but is rather a collective name.' It is not necessary to accept this excess of nominalism in order to recognize what he calls the 'futility of definition.' There have been many definitions of religion, but they are all felt to be unsatisfactory. They are inevitably too broad or too narrow. Either they are the former and say nothing, or they are the latter and what they say excludes that which is for many the very heart of religion. It is, however, the narrow definitions which are pre-eminently fatal to the philosophy of religion. The essential function of definition is to set limits, and the moment one does this an element of exclusion is inevitable and tends to vitiate the entire discussion that follows. 'The theorizing mind,' as James insists, 'tends to over-simplification of its materials and this over-simplification is bound to result in onesidedness and dogmatism.' Even James himself did not wholly escape this fatality of definition. For when he asks us 'arbitrarily to take religion as the feelings, acts and experiences of individual men in their solitude, so far as they apprehend themselves to stand in relation to whatever they consider divine,' it is indeed at first as only arbitrarily that it is taken, but this 'postulate' tends to pass into an unquestioned premise, to the virtual exclusion of the communal element in religion, with the result that in the end the entire issue is more or less begged.

It may be said that if we do not begin with definitions we shall be in the predicament of not knowing what it is that we are talking about. I am not sure that this is not as it should be, and that this predicament is not a good starting point. It is possible to know too much as well as too little at the beginning of the discussion of so fundamental a thing as religion. But I should be disposed to insist that we do know well enough what we are talking about, for a city without religion no one has ever seen. Our most fundamental knowledge, as a distinguished mathematician has recently reminded us, is always of the undefined. The things we know best—life and love—are not only hardest to define but, in any ultimate sense, indefinable. Of the thing we call religion—so closely related to both life and love—this is pre-eminently true. The universes of discourse in which religion may be meaningfully talked about are so many and so varied that no single definition is either possible or desirable. Doubtless, both anthropologist and psychologist may define it for their own special purposes, but in other contexts such definitions become little less than absurd.

B

It was, therefore, I repeat, no oversight that we discussed religion without defining it. It is equally with deliberate intention that we now begin our discussion, not with a definition of religion, but rather with the phenomena of religion themselves. We shall begin with the *expressions* of the religious consciousness —and with these expressions, moreover, in a special form— namely, *the language of religion.*

We might, to be sure, begin with the non-linguistic forms of expression—with temples, statues, ceremonies, dances, etc.— in short, with forms of behaviour which we might designate as religious. There is, indeed, a sense in which cult is more fundamental in religion than the theologies which have developed around it. But I very much doubt whether we should know what the temples, statues, etc., are all about unless there were the prayer and prophecy of which Plutarch speaks. The only form of behaviour—if we may call it a form of behaviour at all

—that is in any sense an adequate expression of meaning is language; and it is only through the language of religion that we can hope to get to the heart of religious experience and to the essence of the thing we call religion.

As a matter of fact, all investigations of the religious consciousness actually start with language. William James's *Varieties of Religious Experience*, when closely examined, is really a comparative study of the language of religion—the language of the confessors, saints and mystics—that unique and extraordinary language which, as we shall see, marks off religion from any other form of human activity and expression. The documents which James interprets in the main with understanding are, indeed, as he says, personal documents and, as such, often contain descriptions of subjective states which constitute material for the psychologist in the usual sense; but precisely the language of these documents, when more closely examined, discloses the fact that the very words in which the individual experiences are expressed are already conditioned by references, both over-individual and over-social, to a transcendent object which no psychology, by the very nature of its postulates and methods, can either understand or describe. I should be disposed to go so far as to say that James's method is not psychological at all, but rather phenomenological in the sense of our previous discussion.

These facts—about the actual methodology of the study of the religious consciousness— embody a principle which is fundamental for the entire succeeding study. We shall call it the inseparability of intuition and expression. The classical expression of this principle is that of Croce, developed in his aesthetics. In his well-known work, entitled *Aesthetic or General Linguistic*, he enunciates the principle of the 'identity of intuition and expression,' maintaining that intuition is impossible without expression. Formulated mainly in connection with aesthetics, he extends it to the entire range of human intuition and its expression. This principle has two aspects of importance for our ensuing studies. On the one hand, one does not first intuit or present an object to himself and *then* find linguistic or other forms with which to express it; the expression is rather constitutive of the intuition itself—otherwise expressed, all immediacy is 'mediated immediacy.' In the second place—and it is this

53

aspect which is most significant for our present purpose—the only way to understand any intuitive experience is through the language, the terms and categories, in which that experience is expressed. More generally speaking, the only way to determine being or reality at all is in those forms or categories in which statements about it are possible.

This principle is, to be sure, constantly and emphatically denied, but I agree with Croce that such denial is always founded upon certain equivocations and errors. It is undeniable that we can think with geometric figures, algebraic signs and ideographic symbols—in short, without any words—but we forget that these are also languages, and that if we seek to communicate what we think we cannot do so without resorting at certain points to ordinary language.[1] But while we maintain the essentials of Croce's thesis we must be careful to avoid an error in his theory which not only vitiates much of his aesthetics but has baleful effects throughout his entire philosophy. Knowledge is indeed bound up with expression, but there is no expression without the correlative, understanding. Communicability is not an irrelevant *addendum* of expression—even in the aesthetic —it is the very heart of it. And what is true here holds equally for all regions of intuition and knowledge. The doctrine of presentational immediacy—or knowledge by simple acquaintance, without any element of expression and 'description', of a hypothetical form of knowledge in which we merely have or possess the object—is pure myth. This does not mean, as is sometimes assumed, that the element of immediacy in knowledge is denied, but that all immediacy is mediated—that, to use an expression of Cassirer, the inseparability of intuition and expression is an *Urphenomen*. All knowledge, precisely in so far as it is knowledge, is bipolar in character, including elements of both intuition and representation. In so far as religious experience is also knowledge, it constitutes no exception to this principle. It is, to be sure, often maintained that the mystical experience is one of pure immediacy. Of that, however, we could never know, for to be known it must be expressed and when it is expressed it can be only in the language and symbols of the native religion of the mystic.[2]

[1] B. Croce, *op. cit.*, p. 23.   [2] Chapter xiii, pp. 437 ff.

II

The Language of Religion: Religion and Poetry

A

The key to the nature of religion is to be found, then, in its expression—more especially in the language of religion. When this language is examined one thing stands out with undeniable clearness, namely its poetic character. To employ for a moment one of the barbarisms of logical positivism, 'the protocol language' of religion is the language of poetry. This protocol language—the deliverances of the great saints and mystics, but also the forms of expression of cult and worship—is, like poetry, emotional in character, but it also has other aspects which show its kinship with poetry and distinguish it from the language of common sense and of science—namely, its intuitive and figurative character.

These facts have led to the attempt to understand religion as *merely* a form of poetry—an important tendency in the present-day philosophy of religion. This identification of religion with poetry has been aptly expressed by Santayana in his well-known statement in *Poetry and Religion*. They are, he tells us, 'identical in essence and differ merely in the way in which they are attached to practical affairs. Poetry is called religion when it intervenes in life and religion poetry when it merely supervenes upon life.' Now I do not believe this to be a true statement of the relation, but we may at least accept it as a starting point of our analysis.[1]

Certainly there is great similarity, if not 'identity of essence,' of religion and poetry. This is seen in a certain community of language. The cry of the psalmist, 'All flesh is grass,' is equally poetic and religious. The simile, 'as the flower of the field, so it flourisheth,' is both poetic figure and religious insight. Finally, the dramatic 'the wind bloweth over it and it is gone and the place thereof shall know it no more' is a highly poetic way of stating a fact of tremendous religious import. It is immediately clear what it is that constitutes the similarity. Both are, in the first instance at least, highly emotive forms of language and

[1] *Op. cit.*, Preface, p. v.

both have the characters of intuitive and metaphorical representation which are intrinsic to poetic language as such. But more than this—the *vis poetica* is present in all language that is 'alive,' only in the language of religion it is heightened and deepened in a unique way. It is, so to speak, poetry transposed to another scale, a scale so transcendent that to call it any longer poetry, in the ordinary sense of the word, is to stultify both poetry and religion.

B

We have been considering phrases and sentences which are both religious and poetic. Let us now consider the language wholes in which these phrases and sentences are found. We may describe them respectively as the lyrical and dramatic modes.

By lyrical language in religion I understand the form of hymn or psalm or prayer—any form in which the worshipper or devotee addresses the object of his devotion. As it appears in the literature of religion, it includes the Hebrew psalms, the Vedic hymns, the hymnology of the various religions, from the hymns to Dionysus in the Dionysian mysteries to the *Veni Creator Spiritus* and *Ave Maria* of Christian devotion. Prayer includes magical incantations, 'empty repetitions,' and the exalted dignity of the Stoic prayer to Zeus or the so-called high-priestly prayer of Jesus. The emotive element in religion is here at its highest. Exaltation and depression, love and hate—the entire gamut of human emotions finds expression in the language of devotion. But all these emotions have a peculiar tone quality which has been described as the sense of the 'holy.' This quality varies all the way from the grovelling awe of the primitive to the 'Holy, Holy, Holy' of the *Sanctus*, but it is the same religious mode (or sentiment) which in all cases informs and permeates them. The songs or hymns of religion are, as a well-known Christian hymn expresses it, 'songs of love and praise.' They are expressions of love, but of love *divine*, all loves excelling. They are expressions of praise, but of that peculiar praise, as in the *Gloria in excelsis*—which ascribes glory to God in the highest— to that plenitude of reality which in philosophy can be called by no other name than the *ens perfectissimum*.

The language of religion is then evocative. But it is also invocative. It evokes feelings but it also invokes objects. Invocation of spirits, of saints and angels, and of the Godhead itself—is of the very essence of religion, and distinguishes its language from that of poetry. Poetry itself may invoke objects but when it does so it is a 'little remainder' of religion—as invocation of the muses—or it tends to pass over into religion. Invocation involves not only the existence of higher powers, but also by the very fact of invocation, powers that intervene mightily in life. The 'stories' of these interventions can, in the nature of the case, be only in dramatic form.

The second fundamental type of religious language is, accordingly, the dramatic. By the dramatic mode I understand primarily the language in which the acts or 'operations' of Deity, whether in time, or before all worlds, are expressed. It is therefore primarily the language of 'myth' from which the original symbolism of all positive religions is derived. It is, of course, needless to say that in using the term myth I am employing it in a purely phenomenological sense, without any implications as to truth and falsity. It is our term for the dramatic and therefore 'anthropomorphic' way of rendering the events of nature and history in contrast to the physico-mathematical way of science. In this sense there is a mythical element in all religion; the problem being what it is that the categories of the myth symbolize and express.

C

In his recent Frey Lecture, entitled *Science and Drama*, C. Lloyd Morgan describes this type of language in an interesting and suggestive fashion. His main contention is that there are two radically different ways of describing and understanding the world: that of science, which, broadly speaking, consists in framing wider and wider generalizations based on observation and experiment; and secondly, that of drama, which seeks to understand and describe in terms of the agencies and activities to which objects and events are due. His contention is that, although radically different, the two ways are not antagonistic, but rather complementary. Finally he holds that no adequate account of what happens in human life, the central home of action and drama, is possible if relations of the mental type and the dramatic way of rendering them are left out.[1]

Insistence upon the existence and necessity of these two languages and of the two types of intelligibility to which they correspond, is the burden of Lloyd Morgan's contention. The primacy

[1] *Op. cit.*, p. 21.

of the dramatic type is, on the other hand, argued by H. B. Alexander. In a suggestive article which in many ways parallels that of Lloyd Morgan, he further insists upon the necessity of the dramatic categories in science. A cosmology, he tells us, is always action and has, of necessity, a dramatic character. 'Upon drama, then, even our natural science has depended and does ultimately depend for its sense of rationality.'[1] Upon this latter point we may suspend judgment for the present, although it is my own view that, properly understood, the statement is profoundly true. The primacy of dramatic language in all meaningful and intelligible discourse follows from the fact that our 'sense of rationality' includes not only 'necessary connections' —not merely patterns of connections—but, in the last analysis, reference to ends and values. But this is not the point to be emphasized here. It is rather that no intelligibility in the sphere of the human, and in the relations of the human to whatever higher powers there be, is possible which is not expressed in language of this type.

D

The primary forms of the language of religion are then the lyrical and the dramatic. But there is an aspect to all religious language not exhausted in these two. We may call it theological language.

The religious hymn, psalm or ode invokes objects, but it also ascribes predicates or qualities to those objects: 'Holy, Holy, Holy, Lord God *Almighty*.' Religious myth and drama picture —and, as we shall see, in developed religions 'symbolize'—the activities of these objects; but they also assert, either explicitly or implicitly, certain relations of the divine object or objects to the world and to human life. It is these assertions—together with the development of their implications and relations, the one to the other—that constitute theology.

The language of theology, so we shall maintain, constitutes an extension of the language of religion and retains the dramatic character inseparable from the language of religion. The study of theological language in its details belongs to another context,[2] but an illustration will make the main point clear. For

[1] H. B. Alexander, 'Drama as a Cosmic Category,' *The Philosophical Review*, March, 1930.
[2] Chapter iii, pp. 86 f.

religious belief, God exists and has certain attributes and characters; for theology the question is the grounds for that belief and for the ascription of these characters. For religious belief, God became man; for theology the question is why God became man. The two classics of Christian theology, the *Proslogium* and the *Cur Deus Homo* of St. Anselm, seek to answer these questions. Unless, as we shall see, the language in which these questions are answered retains the dramatic character of the language of religion, it really does not answer them at all. Theological language, like the language of metaphysics with which it is necessarily connected, contains, of course, elements which are not poetic, but its basal symbolic form still remains dramatic; otherwise it would lose all touch with religion. The discourse about God which we call theology could never be in purely mathematical form for it would then not be talking about God at all but about 'something else.'

Theology, as we shall see, involves a certain kind of translation of the language of religion into terms of greater generality. But with all its generality this language retains its dramatic character. The hymn beginning, Praise to the Holiest in the Heights is said to be excellent theology—and it is—but that is solely because the theology which is thus embedded in the hymn has not lost its 'poetic' character. If the language of theology were like that of mathematics no such translation into poetry would be possible. The thesis here maintained involves, of course, the entire question of the relation of the dramatic to the metaphysical—a point to be considered fully in its proper place. Here our sole point is that the language of theology is no exception to general principle that all religious language, to be religious, must share the characters of the language of poetry.

III

Religion as Numinous Poetry. The Numinous and the Holy

A

Our examination of the language of religion, both devotional and theological, has disclosed certain marked similarities between poetry and religion, but also certain significant differences. We may distinguish the language of poetry from that of religion by describing the latter, in the terms of Rudolf Otto, as numinous poetry. According to the well-known thesis of *The Idea of the Holy*, the religious consciousness is a unique form characterized by the sense of the numinous, which he describes as the *mysterium tremendum*, the wholly other, the Holy or Sacred; and the devotional language in which this sense is expressed is described as numinous poetry.[1]

Of the notion of the numinous itself it may be said that had it not been formulated by Otto it would inevitably have found expression in some form in the philosophy of religion of the last decades, for it represents, as no other term possibly could, the uniqueness of the religious consciousness which is the characteristic note of the period. It may therefore be welcomed for two reasons. In the first place, for its phenomenological significance. Examination of the religious consciousness for its own intrinsic quality—one which cannot be reduced to any other mode—shows us that this quality can be expressed only in such terms as the sacred and the holy. In the second place—and this is perhaps of equal importance, it emphasizes not only the uniqueness of the religious consciousness but also of that to which this consciousness refers. This, I agree with A. E. Taylor, is 'the sure and certain kernel of Otto's famous conception, however much there may be to correct in Otto's own elaboration of his thought.' No amount of criticism, however justified in other respects, will shake the central position, that it is this immediate recognition of the numinous, the wholly other or transcendent, in persons, things and events which is the root of worship and so of religion.[2]

The notion of numinous poetry is developed by Otto in Appendix II, in which illustrations are taken from Hindu, Jewish and Christian hymns and liturgies, but important aspects of the phenomenon are treated in Chapter IX, entitled 'Means of Expression of the Numinous.' Here non-linguistic media of expression—of the arts, and more specifically music—are studied with insight and understanding. He distinguishes between direct and indirect expressions of the numinous, the distinction corresponding roughly, although not completely, with

[1] Rudolf Otto, *The Idea of the Holy* (translation), Oxford University Press, 1923.
[2] A. E. Taylor, *op. cit.*, Volume II, p. 187.

the preceding distinctions between linguistic and non-linguistic means of expression.

Of the indirect means of expression, music is, as Otto rightly recognizes, the most potent. But not even music, as he tells us, 'which else can give such manifold expression to all the feelings of the mind, has any positive way to express the holy.' This is true even of the most consummate mass music which can give utterance to the holiest, most numinous moment in the Mass—the moment of transubstantiation—only by sinking into stillness, and no devotional element in the whole mass approximates in impressiveness to this 'keeping silence before the Lord.' He finds it instructive to submit Bach's Mass in B minor to the test in this matter. Its mystical portion is the *Incarnatus* in the Creed and there 'the effect is due to the faint whispering, lingering sequence in the fugue structure, dying away pianissimo. The held breath and the hushed sound of the passage, its weird cadences sinking away in lessened thirds, its pauses and syncopations and its rise and fall in astonishing semitones, which render so well the sense of awe-struck wonder—all this serves to express the mysterium by way of intimate rather than forthright utterance.'[1] Commenting further on the mass, Otto continues, 'And by this means Bach attains his aim here far better than in the "Sanctus."' This latter is indeed 'an incomparably successful expression of Him whose is the power and the glory; an enraptured and triumphant choric hymn to perfect and absolute sovereignty. But it is very far distant from the mood of the text that accompanies the music which is taken from Isaiah vi, and which the composer should have interpreted in accordance with that passage as a whole. No one would gather from this magnificent chorus that the Seraphim covered their faces with two of their wings.' Without wishing to enter into any controversy regarding the adequacy of the *Sanctus*, more particularly the question of its expression of the mood of the text, we may be permitted to point out that precisely because it is 'an incomparably successful expression of Him whose is the power and the glory,' it is also an inimitable expression of the *thelogia gloriae* which together with the *thelogia crucis* constitute the two fundamental elements, not only of Christian thought, but of Christian worship also.

---

[1] *Op. cit.*, pp. 72–3.

No one who has heard the B minor Mass will, I think, question for a moment what is here said about the *Incarnatus*. All of the mystery as well as of the transcendent significance of the phrase, 'and was made Man,' finds expression in Bach's tones, but this superb 'intimation' would be impossible except as the music were joined to the 'forthright utterance' of the words. I must therefore take issue with those who say, with Vossler, that 'religion depends only indirectly on language, not directly; for music, architecture and painting, dancing and gestures are of similar and often even of better service. It can frequently dispense with the mediation of language.'[1] If religion can at times dispense with the mediation of language, as it undoubtedly can, it is only because the means of expression which it then finds have already been associated with the word, and it is the meaning which this association gives it which is not only conserved but enhanced.

Only in the forthright utterance of the word is adequate expression here possible, although here, as elsewhere, completely adequate expression is not possible. Of the central and supreme Christian sacrament it has been said 'it is a simple piece of symbolism to express a number of spiritual ideas too great for ordinary language. It shows forth directly, so to speak, something which words could express only weakly and indirectly.' True as this seems at first sight, it really contains a paradox. The symbol expresses something too great for words, yet if we ask what these things are too great for words, we find that they are 'spiritual ideas.' If then we ask what these ideas are we must either remain silent or give them verbal expression. However it may be historically and genetically, logically it is true that in the beginning was the *word*.

This does not in the least affect the principle of the historical primacy of cult, the essential truth of which we have recognized, but it does affect the question of the logical primacy. It is true that, generally speaking, 'ritual was evolved long before belief.' The language of the primitive is visual and his communication behavioural. He thinks with his eyes rather than by articulate sounds and he communicates with effective rather than with verbal symbols. Nor does it affect in the least the truth that the 'root feeling of primitive religion is arrived at through the

[1] *The Spirit of Language in Civilization*, Chapter iii 'Language and Religion', p. 25.

investigation of ritual.' It is, however, in the ritual *language*, rather than in the accompaniments of tones and gestures that the essence of religion can be apprehended if it can be apprehended at all. Here, as elsewhere, it remains true that among all signs and symbols it is the word alone to which adequacy of expression is ultimately to be ascribed. Those who set cult over against creed have been unduly impressed by behaviouristic and emotive theories of religion and forget that all liturgies are themselves embodiments of creed.

B

To call the language of religion poetry—even numinous poetry—is, however, possible obviously only on the basis of a philosophical conception of poetry at once much broader and more fundamental than that in ordinary use. This larger conception of poetry is, however, generally acknowledged. Even the dictionary definitions, although they define poetry first of all as metrical composition, invariably add as a secondary meaning, 'imaginative composition whether in prose or verse.' It is in this sense that Coleridge in his *Biographia Literaria* insisted that the true antithesis of poetry is not prose but science. S. Alexander is entirely right in accepting this as the fundamental antithesis and is equally sound in maintaining that the contrast runs throughout all the arts.[1] The characters which make language poetic are in principle the same as make the other media of artistic expression aesthetic.

Poetry is then not a special language, but rather a character of all language that is *alive*—that has not been devitalized for the purposes of science. Croce has expressed this truth in the following words: 'Man speaks at each moment like the poet, because, like the poet, he gives expression to his impressions and feelings. It does not matter that this is done in the tone of ordinary conversation of familiarity, for there is not the slightest distinction between this and the other forms that are called prose, prose poetry, narrative, epic, dialogue, drama, lyric, or song. And if the ordinary man will not mind being regarded as a poet, which he is because of his humanity, the poet may not

---

[1] S. Alexander, *Beauty and Other Forms of Value*, Chapter vi. It is interesting that in his well-known lecture on *Literature* John Henry Newman takes this same position.

take it amiss that he is coupled with ordinary humanity; for this relation alone explains the power of poetry on all human minds in the narrow and in the highest sense. If poetry were a special language, "a language of the gods," human beings would not be able to understand it.'[1] If poetry is not a special language—of the gods—neither is it a special language of the 'poets' in the narrow sense, although that special language, like the special language of science, has its own technical interest and significance. The poetry of which we are speaking—the *vis poetica*, is something inherent in all natural language. It is present in the primordial construction of the world, as we know it, and is that which not only makes the relation of religion to poetry fundamental, but also makes myth the original source of all significant religious symbols.

To say that the language of poetry is 'emotive,' and that therefore that of religion is merely emotive also, is not only to misunderstand religion but poetry also. I think it can be shown, and I shall attempt to show, that this theory stultifies not only the religious but the poetic consciousness also. The poet catches something in reality which the scientist misses, and this something is not merely felt but also known.[2]

Numinous poetry is the supreme expression of a power shared by all forms of poetic language—to convey the sense of things which lie in the twilight zone between the finite and the infinite —a sense of things which the language of science cannot express. Like all poetry it refers to that which is highest and deepest in us, but it has another quality, namely, a transcendent reference to that which is beyond all we can desire or hope—a quality which has the power not only to suggest the infinite, but to lift man out of the finite into the infinite. For these reasons men have often identified not only religion but philosophy with poetry. 'Explicit statements about reality itself,' we are told, 'don't convey very much unless they too are written poetically, and it is for this reason men have said beauty is truth and truth beauty.'[3] This is in so far true that many have cried with F. Lange, 'Plato would not see, as Kant would not see, that the intelligible world' (of religion and metaphysics) 'is a world of poetry and that it is precisely in this fact that its value and

[1] B. Croce, *Foundations of Aesthetics*.   [2] Chapter xii, pp. 400 ff.
[3] Aldous Huxley, *Time Must Have A Stop*, p. 250.

worthiness consists.' Plato would not see it, nor would Kant, of course, for it simply is not true. The fact that there are statements about ultimate reality which do not convey much unless they trench on the language of poetry does not at all mean that the realities about which these statements are made belong solely to the world of poetry.

C

That the language of religion does communicate something which is not expressible in any other type of language is, of course, a commonplace to all religiously-minded people. As Lavinia says in Shaw's *Androcles and the Lion*, 'Religion is such a great thing that when I meet really religious people we are friends at once, no matter what name we give to the divine will which made us and moves us.' Such communication is possible with the widest variety of ideas and names, not only because they express a common emotion, but because the names have a common reference. What this reference is is the problem of the philosophy of religion, but the fact of communication itself and the possibility of translation of one language into another are outstanding facts of the phenomenology of religion.

These facts are in themselves important, but even more important are the implications of the facts. Religion may, indeed, be defined arbitrarily as 'certain acts and experiences of individual men and women in their solitude' and this definition has, of course, its element of truth but it is not in solitude that the 'truth' of religion is ultimately known, any more than the truth of any other form of experience. The fact, therefore, that religious experience, including the peculiar quale that makes it religious, is thus communicable, affords at least the presumption that there is a religious universe of discourse—a beloved community of all faithful people—in which not only are genuine meanings communicable, but one in which there are also pronouncements—on man and his relation to the ground of things —which are mutually acknowledged and of which the truth may be confirmed and verified. This is, however, a problem for later contexts.[1]

The language of religion, then, communicates something not expressible in any other type of language and therefore not really sayable in the conceptual language of science and philosophy.

[1] Chapter ix, pp. 316 ff.

Otto is doubtless right when he tells us that the numinous 'resists all expression in rational conceptual terms,' but there are, as he also tells us, 'conceptual equivalents,' such as the supernatural, the transcendent, the infinite, etc. Such terms 'appear to give positive attributes and thus to divest the mysterium of its original negative meaning and turn it into an affirmation,' but this, he holds, is not really so. On the side of conceptual thought, at least, this is nothing more than appearance, for it is obvious that they are merely negative. 'But on the side of feeling content,' he holds, it is otherwise; that is in very truth positive in the highest degree, though here too, as before, it cannot be rendered explicit in conceptual terms. It is through the positive feeling content that the concepts of the transcendent and supernatural become forthwith designations for a unique 'wholly other' reality and quality, something of whose special character we can *feel* without being able to give it clear conceptual 'expression.'[1] It may well be that for this unique and positive character of religious experience no completely adequate expression in conceptual or rational terms is possible— that is, of course, the meaning of the futility of definition, but it does not follow that because the meaning is not completely expressed in *such terms* it is not expressible at all. In any case it is, as we shall see, precisely to these conceptual equivalents that we must ultimately turn to give expression to the essence of religion, for essence is expressible only in conceptual terms.

D

Despite the profound similarity of poetry and religion, the religious man, whether plain man or theologian, denies that this similarity means identity of essence, and in this denial he is completely justified by the critical philosopher. This refusal does not rest upon any superficial distinction between poetry and prose. Nor does it rest upon any naïve depreciation of poetry as merely emotional expression to which the notion of truth is not applicable—poetry, as we shall later seek to show, does give us truth. Our contention is rather that the religionist also catches something which the poet in the ordinary sense, no less than the scientist, misses. It is this something which shines out in all religious language which makes of it a unique language

[1] *Op. cit.*, p. 30.

and symbolic form, an expression of reality not possible in any other idiom.

With this we may see, if not the complete falsity, the grave inadequacy of the statement of the relation of religion to poetry with which we started. Identical in essence, they differ, we are told, only in their relations to life, poetry being religion when it intervenes in life and religion poetry when it supervenes on life. Actually poetry, which is in no sense religious, may intervene mightily in life and constantly does so—the patriotic song or drama is a case in point. There are times when such poetry intervenes in life even more powerfully than the language of religion. It is not mere intervention in life that constitutes the differentia of religion, but rather the unique character of the intervention. The *vis religiosa*, that power which makes the language of religion intervene so mightily in life, is the sense of the Holy, of the 'wholly other' which it expresses and communicates.

The intervention in life which differentiates religion from any other form of human experience and expression, is then that unique intrusion which men find it possible to describe only in terms of revelation. Religion catches something which neither poetry nor science can apprehend, but it catches it only because it is there—only because that which it apprehends and communicates is a disclosure, not only of that which is highest and deepest in us and in the nature of which we are a part, but even more, because in the same act of revelation there is shown forth that which so transcends both man and nature as to be beyond anything that either the language of poetry or science can express. This the language of religion embodies and thus the word of man becomes the Word of God[1].

'A divine sentence,' we read in Proverbs, 'is in the lips of the King.' And sentences which have the quality of divinity, the numinous quality which makes of the language of men also the language of God, are in the lips of all those who have revealed the ways of God to man. There is no speech nor language where their voice is not heard, and none in which some sentences of the divine locution are not found. How the word of man can also be the Word of God, how divine revelation is possible, are basal questions for any philosophical theology; only one point

---

[1] See Chapter xi, pp. 407 ff.

need be emphasized here. The divine presence in the words themselves is assumed by all theories of revelation however varied. In the 'inspired' language itself is disclosed something of that plenitude, that fullness of being, which men everywhere recognize, as the essence of Deity.[1]

IV

The Essence of Religion. Again the Problem of Definition.
The Numinous and the Infinite

A

The results of the preceding studies have, I think, justified our approach to religion and the religious consciousness through its expressions—more especially through its language. In this language itself—in both its spirit and its form—there is a unique character of quale which marks it off significantly from any other form of human language. The denial of the identity of essence between religion and poetry, or any other form of human activity and expression, raises again the question of what the essence of religion really is.

This essence resists, as we are told, any expression in rational or conceptual terms, but there are conceptual equivalents which, while not exhausting its meaning, yet enable us to discuss its nature in that rational universe of discourse known as philosophy. Such equivalents being conceptual, their discovery is possible only on the higher levels of religion and religious experience. This is the fundamental postulate of any philosophy of religion. No one would, I suppose, seek the essence of science, or of any other significant human activity, on the primitive levels out of which it has developed. To see the essence of science in primitive magic would, as everyone sees, constitute a veritable caricature of science. Is it likely that a similar procedure with regard to religion is any less a caricature?

This principle seems, at first sight, to be in contradiction with our previous descriptions of religion and its expression, and the authority of Otto appears to lend weight to this view. In his

[1] These questions will be further discussed in an appendix, 'How can the Word of Man be the Word of God? How is Divine Revelation Possible?'

introductory chapter to *The Idea of the Holy*, Otto points out that 'the philosopher must be on his guard against an error which would lead to a wrong and one-sided interpretation of religion.' This is the assumption that 'the essence of deity, and therefore the essence of religion, can be given completely in the rational attributions essential to the theistic conceptions of God and especially that of Christianity.' It is, he points out, 'not an unnatural misconception but none the less seriously misleading.'[1] This is undoubtedly true, but a still more serious error may be made in the opposite direction, namely, in stripping off these rational attributions and going back to the non-rational and non-moral. Only when we understand the higher can we understand—often with the profoundest pathos, the lesser goods for which men pray and the lesser gods to which their prayers are raised. If, however, we seek to understand the higher in terms of the lower we shall not only caricature the higher but, by a curious fatality, fail to understand the lower also. There is, I believe, no real contradiction in a conception of religion which finds its character in the numinous but its essence in the value of the Holy, as indeed Otto himself makes clear.

The force of these considerations is increasingly realized by the philosopher but finds special emphasis in Bergson's philosophy of religion. The essence of religion, he tells us, is to be found not in primitive mentality but only on the highest levels of religious experience. He himself goes to the Christian mystics, who constitute for him the experts in religion and whose pronouncements in the sphere of religious knowledge should be accepted just as those of the physicists are in the sphere of physical knowledge.[2] One may indeed question, as we shall later, this extreme evaluation of the mystics as also his interpretation of the mystical experience at certain points. Still more might one question, perhaps, his identification of religion, as thus interpreted, with the metaphysics of *Creative Evolution*. But the principle itself is unquestionable, and its application makes of his philosophy of religion as outstanding a work in this field as is his *Creative Evolution* in the sphere of metaphysics.

[1] *Op. cit.*, p. 2.
[2] *The Two Sources of Morality and Religion*, New York, Henry Holt, 1936.

69

B

The methodological principle just formulated, is, I repeat, the assumption, explicit or implicit, of all significant philosophies of religion—even, I believe, of those which in the end seek completely to naturalize and humanize religion. There are various ways in which it has been formulated, but it finds explicit expression in Höffding's philosophy of religion, one, moreover, which will be especially useful in our present study. 'The core of religion—at any rate according to the hypothesis that we have been led to adopt' (so writes Höffding), 'consists in the conviction that no value perishes out of the world. This faith appears in all popular religions, *but especially in the higher forms in broad and easily recognizable features*';[1] and further in the same context, 'in its *innermost essence* religion is concerned not with comprehension but with the valuation of existence,' and that religious ideas express the relation in which the actual existence, as we know it, stands to that which for us invests life with its highest value (italics mine).

There can be little question, I think, that when the philosopher contemplates religion, as it is lived on the higher levels of human experience, he must also, like Höffding, find its essence in the 'evaluation of existence,' and that when he examines the 'religious ideas' of which Höffding speaks he will also find that their 'innermost core of meaning' expresses precisely the relations of existence to value. I have chosen Höffding's statement not because it is a wholly adequate expression of the essence of religion—in certain respects, as we shall see, it leaves much to be desired—but because it emphasizes the principle enunciated and applies it in a way inevitable for modern thought. For, as there is a sure and certain kernel of truth in the conception of the numinous, however much there may be to correct in Otto's development of his thought, so also there is, as I believe, similarly an incontestable kernel of truth in Höffding's conception of religion as 'belief in the conservation of values' however much we may find to criticise in his elaboration of his fundamental thesis.

The concrete expressions of the religious ideas of which he speaks are indeed very varied, and, in so far as their imagery

[1] *The Philosophy of Religion*, p. 6.

is concerned, have their source in the original symbolism of the myth, as the studies of the following chapter will make clear. But it is possible, speaking generally, to describe them as the dramatic ideas of creation and consummation, sin, redemption and salvation, categories belonging uniquely to religion. I shall venture to state them in summary fashion in the three great ideas of God, grace and the eternal life—ideas which, as A. E. Taylor has shown, constitute 'the three inter-connected themes from which all the great religions have been built up,' by which he means of course the great *developed* historical religions. 'In Buddhism, Mohammedanism and Christianity the variations on these themes differ widely—one religion may give special prominence to one of these themes, another religion to another, but all three are to be discerned as fundamental in any religion which has proved on a large scale its power to govern the hearts and minds of humanity.'[1]

Examination of these three great 'interconnected themes' shows them to be really variations on one still more fundamental theme, namely, that of the relation of the Good to being or, in Höffding's terms, of value to existence. God as the *Valor valorum*, to use a medieval phrase, grace as the self-diffusing good, the essence of Deity, and eternal life, which involves the conservation in being of values—of all that which invests our life with the highest meaning and significance. The God-ideas refer to values—that is the sure and certain kernel of truth in Höffding's analysis. But the values to which they refer, while, in the first instance, that which is highest and deepest in us—otherwise they would have no significance—ultimately refer to that which is beyond anything in us, and to that without which the heights and deeps in us would not be understandable. The values to which they refer, the qualities of deity, are, at least on the higher levels of religion, perfections in a supereminent and absolute degree. The essence of man as religious is, as Feuerbach tells us, man's sense of his own finitude, and thus the precariousness of his own values, but this sense presupposes, even as the condition of its being sensed at all, the sense also of the infinite. This infinite presents itself in various forms, according as we proceed from the lower to the higher levels of religion, but in one form or another it is always there as an essential part of the religious

[1] A. E. Taylor, *The Faith of a Moralist*, Volume II, Chapter i. p. 2.

consciousness, and it is this that Höffding does not adequately recognize.

As Höffding expresses inadequately the content of the religious ideas, so also, his critics hold, he expresses inadequately the nature of our beliefs regarding the relations of these values to existence, namely, the axiom of the conservation of value. The moral (or value) consciousness, so they point out, is never satisfied with mere conservation, or with the *status quo*. It demands perfection, for the reason that the values themselves get their significance through the presupposition or coimplicate of the perfect. The demand which the religious consciousness makes always includes the demand for the increase of value, and it is finally of values as fully perfected that it postulates conservation.[1] All this is true, but the inadequacy is to be found at a still more fundamental point. For the religious consciousness, in its highest development, postulates an identity of value and being—before all time and beyond all time—for this consciousness the *ens perfectissimum* and the *ens realissimum* are one. On the lower levels of religion, doubtless, the primary religious belief may be expressed in terms of the axiom of conversation. Here it is the primitive goods of life which men seek and for the mere preservation of which they implore divine aid. But this scarcely expresses man's belief regarding the relations of value to existence on the higher levels of religion. Here, too, men 'thank God for their creation, preservation, and for all the blessings of this life,' but they thank him 'above all for the means of grace and for the hope of glory.' On the highest levels, however, they thank him 'for His great glory.' It is the glory of God—the infinite perfections for which the name of God stands—for which they praise him, and only secondarily for the hope of glory which they shall ultimately share with him.

It is impossible, I believe, to express the essence of religion— the inmost core of meaning of the religious ideas themselves, of our beliefs concerning the relation of value to existence, without recourse to this 'formal principle of Deity,' namely the idea of the infinite. For, in the words of Wordsworth, our very

'being's heart and home
is with infinitude and only there.'

[1] W. R. Sorley, *Moral Values and The Idea of God,* p. 179.

Infinitude is even a better expression than the infinite for the principle of Deity. It is not only poetically more significant; it has also significant relations, in form as well as spirit, with the notion of plenitude, which, as we shall see, is the true infinite of religion—that fulness of being which, in order to be really our being's heart and home, must be the infinite of a 'value theology.' Not the skeletal infinite of, let us say, mathematics, but the infinite clothed upon by all the perfections of the finite.

It is sometimes maintained that the use of the term infinite by Christian theologians as the 'formal principle of Deity' involves a confusion of two meanings of the term. Thus when St. Thomas says that the being of God is called infinite because it is pure, self-subsistent, he is using the term simply to imply non-limitation by other self-subsistents; and to pass from this notion of infinitude as self-subsistence to the notion of plenitude, with its connotation of an 'omnitudo' of all qualities, however incompatible, is not only a change in meaning but a change from sense to nonsense. There are, no doubt, these two meanings of the term, and their close connection is inevitable, for God's infinity and his perfection are both identical with his essence, but I do not think that they are ever confused. The pure being of which St. Thomas speaks is, as we shall see, not vague and indeterminate, but is *ab initio* identified with the sovereign Good. Being and the good are for him convertible;[1] it is therefore supremely rich and active. Nevertheless there is, as we shall also see, a genuine problem here, namely, whether the two conceptions can be thus related, whether, in other words, there are not, as it is charged, one God but two.[2]

But to return to the main issue—the essence of religion is inexpressible without resource to the infinite. This is true even in the case of those philosophies which, in the end, seek completely to humanize and naturalize religion. Like Feuerbach, we may argue that this sense of infinitude does not imply that we are part of or related to infinite being, but merely that man is part of humanity and the stirrings of the so-called infinite in him are merely the stirrings of humanity. Similarly Bertrand Russell, in his article on 'The Essence of Religion,' finds that this essence is man's sense of the 'quality of infinity.' The things which have this quality of infinity 'seem to give an insight

[1] Chapter vi, p. 211.   [2] Chapter iv, pp. 138 ff.

73

deeper than the piece meal knowledge of our daily life.' To the question whether belief in God is necessary to the birth of this infinite life, and therefore to the essence of religion, he too answers in the negative. Like Feuerbach, he also denies that belief in God is necessary for the religious consciousness; he too speaks of religion as 'consciousness of the life of the whole' and of 'that inexplicable sense of union which gives rise to compassion and the unhesitating service of humanity.'[1] With this humanistic interpretation of the sense of the infinite we are not here concerned—that is the problem of a later chapter—our only point here is that even for the humanist and atheist it is impossible to express the essence of religion except in terms of the finite and the infinite.

All expressions of the religious consciousness—at least on its higher levels—bear out this account of the essence of religion. Prayer and praise, its two direct expressions, presuppose it. The recognition of power, goodness, beauty and sublimity call forth in all men admiration and imitation, but when they appear in the excessive form men call Divine they evoke worship and praise. Prayers seek to bring into being in human life these transcendent values or to conserve them when thus realized. But prayer is really not prayer unless it presupposes the acknowledgment of the infinite perfection—in both goodness and power—which the values, to be thus realized and conserved, presuppose. Without this initial datum of the infinite neither form of expression or religion is understandable, and to one who had not this sense of the infinite the essence of religion could never be really shown.

This is the essence of religion as expressed in the Christian consciousness, and without it Christianity collapses into mere moralism or mere philosophy. The hymn to the Holy Trinity expresses all this perfectly:

> Holy, Holy, Holy, Lord God Almighty
> All thy works shall praise thy Name in earth and sky
>   and sea . . .
> Only Thou art holy; there is none beside Thee
> Perfect in power, in love and purity.

Christian theology is in this sense inevitably a value theology. *Tu solus sanctus!* 'This sanctus,' so we find Otto warning us,

[1] The Essence of Religion, *Hibbert Journal*, Volume XI, No 1 October 1912.

'is not merely "perfect" or beautiful or good, though being like these concepts also a value, objective and ultimate, it has a definite perceptible analogy with them. It is the positive, numinous value or worth, and to it corresponds on the side of the creature a numinous disvalue or unworth. . . . *Tu solus sanctus* is rather a paean of praise which, so far from being merely a faltering confession of the divine supremacy, recognizes and extols a value precious beyond all conceiving.'[1] All this is true—and until its truth is recognized there is no understanding of the essence of religion. But it is also true that it is precisely the definite, perceptible analogy with our human values that alone makes possible either apprehension or acknowledgment of this value 'precious beyond all conceiving.' This is, as we shall see, the essence of classical Christian theology and its answer to the question of humanity and Deity.

C

The foregoing account of 'the essence of religion' is, we have maintained, inevitable when we contemplate the life of religion on the higher levels of religious experience. Nevertheless this 'value theology,' whether in the form presented by Höffding or in any other form, has been the object of the severest criticism in recent theological and philosophical literature. Not only, it is charged, are such 'definitions' merely psychological and thus completely humanize religion but in so doing they substitute value for being and become but a part of the 'mere moralism.' which followed upon the modern criticism of rational theology.

These charges, it must be admitted, are not without a certain force, so far, at least, as some forms of value theology are concerned. Indeed Höffding describes his own definition as 'psychological', and, as we have seen, tells us, falsely I believe, that religion has to do not with the comprehension of existence but its evaluation. This criticism, however, while applicable to some forms, is not applicable to those for which the value is not psychological but metaphysical, and of which the essential thesis is the inseparability of value and being. On the other hand the essence of religion cannot be separated from man's consciousness of value without losing its meaning. The initial *datum* of all religion is the acknowledgment of value, and, as we shall see, from this all religious thought proceeds.

[1] *Op. cit.*, pp. 53, 54.

The point I am trying to make comes out clearly in Heidegger's attempt to divorce the notion of *Sorge* or anxiety from all conceptions of value and to make of it a purely metaphysical concept unrelated to emotive and ethical experiences. Introduced first by Kierkegaard in a wholly religious context, Heidegger has extended it to the metaphysical, to characterize man's sense of his own finitude. In thus making it metaphysical the attempt is also made to distinguish it completely from all notions of value. One can, indeed, agree with Heidegger that, as he says, 'the term has much more than a merely emotive or ethical significance—that it is the description of a fundamental metaphysical situation' yet even so it is hard to see how the notion of anxiety has any meaning at all if it is separated wholly from the notion of value. Of his use of the word *Sorge* Heidegger writes as follows in his *Kant und das Problem der Metaphysik*:

'The word itself is not important, but rather all-important is the understanding of that which the analytic of existence seeks to express by the word. If one takes the word *Sorge* in the sense of an ethical philosophical evaluation of human life instead of as a term for the description of the structural unity of finite transcendence of existence, then all falls into confusion.'[1] No one would deny, I think, that if the word were limited to a wholly ethical meaning, all would fall into confusion, but it is just as certain, I think, that if it were divorced wholly from its ethical significance, the word would become meaningless. The condition of the term anxiety being given a metaphysical significance is a metaphysic in which value and being are inseparable.

It is clear, I think, that value theology, when properly understood, is neither a mere moralism nor a mere psychologism. Men do indeed often find the essence of religion solely in its moral value, and the significance of religious beliefs solely in their character as necessary postulates of morality. They frequently argue that since on the higher levels of religion its primary datum becomes increasingly its moral content, therefore its essence is exhausted in morality, and that this essence would remain even if the values were divorced from the cosmological and metaphysical beliefs with which the values are bound up. Men do, indeed, often find the essence of religion wholly in its emotive value—that it is found not in comprehension but in

[1] *Op. cit.*, p. 11.

feeling and that on the higher levels the sense of infinitude refers not to God but to humanity of which the word God is merely an emotive symbol. But neither of these misconceptions is inherent in value theology itself, but are both in fact refuted by the phenomenology of the religious consciousness, for which no conceptual equivalent for the numinous itself can be found which does not include the formal principle of the infinite.

The foregoing objections to any value theology are, to be sure, but part of a more far-reaching criticism which challenges the entire modern approach to religion through experience, or, more specifically, through 'the meaning of God in human experience.' All such definitions, it is charged, are merely subjective and psychological. In contrast to these, traditional definitions have always been objective—have revolved about God and not about man.

The definition of St. Thomas, we are told, brings out vividly this contrast. 'Religion,' he writes, 'denotes properly a relation to God. For it is to Him we ought to be bound as to our unfailing principle, to whom also our choice should be resolutely directed as to our last end; and whom we lose when we neglect him by sin and should recover by belief in him, believing in him and confessing our faith.'[1] No one would, I suppose, deny that this is what religion actually denotes in the Christian community and that if religion is denatured by removing the God-idea, it loses its meaning within that community. I think also that a theologian within this community when he speaks of the essence of religion must mean this also. And yet even he, in so far as he is a philosophical theologian, will take to heart the warning of Otto not to identify the essence of religion with theistic conceptions of God and that, *prima facie* at least, to do so is seriously to beg the question. He will, therefore, have ultimately to go beyond his own community and seek for the 'meaning of God' in *all* human experience. But however narrow or wide the range may be it is this meaning that he must seek, and there is no place to which he can go for that meaning except to experience itself.

This is, I believe, what the philosophical theologians have always done. For St. Anselm the meaning of God is the idea of a being than whom a greater cannot be conceived—a meaning which, as he believed, could be found in all human experience,

[1] *Summa Theologica* II, II, 81, 3, i.

even that of the fool, and from this initial datum all further thought and discourse about God proceeded. This is no less true of St. Thomas. At the close of each of the ways of the knowledge of God, or of the proofs for God's existence, he concludes (and this conclusion is the very nerve of his argument) 'and this is what men mean by God.' If you ask him what God is, he will, to be sure, answer in the words of God to Moses, 'I am that I am,' but this is the numinous language of revelation and as philosopher, he does not hesitate to translate them into words which have meaning in the natural and rational experience of men. Religion, indeed, denotes properly a relation of man to God, but what the word God itself connotes is something which can be known only by an interrogation of that which is highest and deepest in man. When this interrogation is made it is found that an answer to the question can be made only in terms of a value theology which identifies the most real being with the highest good. This as we shall see, St. Thomas, no less than St. Anselm, actually did.[1]

V

The Problem of Definition and The Dilemma of Religion

A

It is impossible, of course, to define religion in all the fullness of its being—as it is impossible to define its unique object, God, in all the fullness of His being. All definitions tend to be either too broad or too narrow. In the interest of understanding religion and of evaluating it truly one is tempted to give that name to anything that is great in human life, to any experience in which man is, so to speak, at his highest pitch. On the other hand, a sense of its very greatness may lead to such a feeling of its uniqueness that to give this name to anything and everything, is not only to make the term itself meaningless, but to degrade and to denature the object for which it stands.

The temptation to define religion too narrowly is very great. In the attempt to understand religion and to value it properly one is tempted, not only to insist upon its uniqueness among the spiritual activities of men, but also upon the particularities of his

[1] Chapter v, pp. 178 ff.

own specific religion which make it for the believer the transcendent thing it is. To one who lives the faith—and only to such an one is it wholly understandable—it is *the* faith that is lived, and such living faith can never be divorced from the concrete and historical elements which make it living.

The temptation to define religion too broadly is, however, equally great. Not only is the magnanimous philosopher disposed to say with Plutarch that a city without religion no man has ever seen, but also that no one has ever seen a wholly irreligious man.

He will want to say with William James that religion is concerned with 'man's relations to whatever he considers divine or even of the highest value'; with Douglas Fawcett that 'religion is attachment or devotion to the most useful or perfect reality present or seeming to be present to experience';[1] or perhaps with others, 'an emotion resting on a conviction of a harmony between ourselves and the universe at large.' He will want to say these things and it is an irenic impulse, not only of the noblest humanism but of the deepest religious understanding, which moves him thus to speak—the same impulse which led the earlier Christian writers to speak of the nobler pagan as *Christianus naturaliter*. For he knows that religion must not only be lived but, if it is to be lived worthily, it must also be contemplated, and contemplation inevitably leads us to the universal.

In his attempt to express the essence of religion the philosopher is always faced with this dilemma. Indeed it is but one aspect of that more fundamental dilemma of religion itself from which, as we have seen, all philosophy of religion inevitably arises. The only possible solution is that one shall be able to say, not 'either-or,' but 'both-and.' Such a solution is, I believe not only possible but even necessary if religion is to be adequately understood and properly evaluated. I shall not attempt to state that solution here—indeed, being part of the dilemma of religion itself, it can be formulated only as part of the solution of the larger problem. Instead I shall conclude with the consideration of a point in which this dilemma of definition becomes a serious stumbling block to a philosophical understanding of religion.

In the preceding chapter we spoke of the possibility of a philosophy of religion on atheistic premises. This involved, however,

[1] Douglas Fawcett, *Oberland Dialogues*, p. 106.

the further question whether an atheistic religion is itself possible, the question presented in its most acute form by Buddhism. Now I suppose we must assume on the authority of the most competent scholars of both East and West, that Buddhism in some of its forms is atheistic.[1] We must assume also, I suppose, that when, as it has been said, 'the Christian and Buddhist monks understand one another and salute each other across the street,' despite the apparent paradox, this also is significantly true. Nor is the situation as paradoxical as at first sight seems. They understand each other, doubtless, because the fruits of the spirit are in all righteousness, but even more because the spirit that moves them both is acknowledged as the same infinite spirit, whatever name they may give it or, perhaps, if they give it no name at all. In actual Buddhism, as in all religions that have proved on a large scale their power to govern the hearts and minds of humanity, the three great interconnected themes—God, grace and the eternal life—are still there, however they may vary from the same themes as they appear in Christianity. It is perhaps in the God-idea itself that the divergence is greatest. We may, indeed, say with Mc-Taggart, 'by God I mean a being who is personal, supreme and good,' and we might add with him, 'all these characteristics are implied in the word God in western theology.'[2] Even so, we can scarcely demand that this is what it must mean in every context in which religion is defined. Even in Christian theology 'person' has been thought of as a symbol in which the being of God is only inadequately expressed. The ideas of supreme being and sovereign good are, however, I believe, always present in every form of religion, as is also, I believe, the identity of inseparability of the highest good with the most real being. In this is the essence of religion—at least for the philosopher.

[1] Professor Junjiro Takakusu is probably only partly right when he tells us (*Philosophy—East and West*, p. 85), 'Buddhism is atheistic—there is no doubt about it.' This is true of some forms, but not of all. When, moreover, he adds, 'The Buddha did not deny the existence of gods (Devas) but he considered them only as the higher grade of living beings, also to be taught by him,' he adds something which makes all the difference in the world. We are told that, when questioned about the first cause or principle, the Buddha always remained reticent. But reticence is not downright denial and since he did not deny the existence of gods, the conditions for the primary attitudes of religion, prayer and praise remained a constituent element in religion.

[2] *Some Dogmas of Religion*, p. 3.

Chapter III

Religion and the Mythical Consciousness: The Myth as the Material of Religious Symbolism

I—A

THE *vis poetica* is present in all genuine religious language; to lose it is at the same time to lose the *vis religiosa*. This does not mean that religion is identical with poetry, but rather that in the language of poetry—more especially its dramatic character—there is something indispensable to the expression and understanding of the religious consciousness. From this fact follows a second problem which must now engage our attention, namely, that of the relation of religion to myth. What we now call poetry is but a 'little remainder,' as it were, of a way of intuiting reality, which was once universal—and consequently the problem of the relation of religion to poetry leads directly into that of its relation to myth. Moreover, the original symbolism—*der ursprünglicher Symbolismus*, as Nietzsche calls it—out of which the symbolisms of religion develop, has its origin in the myths, cosmic and heroic, in which the primary experiences of the race have found expression.

The problem of the myth has thus always been fundamental in philosophical theology and some philosophy of myth in all types of philosophy of religion. The identification of religion with myth by the Greek rhetoricians and sophists, led to scepticism, and in later classical times men sought to distinguish between mythical and natural theologies, the former meaning acquaintance with the gods and their doings, the latter the interpretation of the meaning of the myth. As against the rhetoricians and the sophists, Plato developed what is, perhaps, the first critical conception of the myth—which became a commonplace of the western tradition, both pagan and Christian. His own 'recourse to the myth,' as against its unintelligent treatment by the sophists, arose primarily out of his recognition of it as a stage of knowledge itself, but even more fundamentally out of his recognition of the fact that it is the only type of language in which the world of 'becoming' can be expressed at all. Unlike the structures of logical and mathematical knowledge,

81

which persist in identical determinateness, this world *becomes*, from moment to moment, and of this there can be no representation except in the dramatic language of myth.

The problem of the relation of religion to myth presents itself in another form in the modern philosophy of religion. With the development of physical science came first the affirmation of its autonomy and finally of a dominance which excluded from the realm of knowledge all forms except that of 'positive' science. The essence of positivism in all its forms, in so far as the problem of religion is concerned, is the identification of the religious with the mythical consciousness—the original source of both philosophy and science. The 'three stages' of Comte's theory constitute the premise, explicit or implied, of all theories of the pragmatic and humanistic type. Religion is *identical* with the mythical. Philosophy is either wholly or partly still in the mythical stage, while science has completely outgrown it. The transcendence of the mythical means the transcendence of the religious also, and the thesis of 'the irreligion of the future,' in one form or another, is always a necessary element in this theory. For the modern critical philosopher, however, this treatment of the myth is no less unintelligent than that of the rhetoricians and sophists.[1] As Plato and Plotinus sought to rescue the myth from them, so the more humane and magnanimous philosophers of modern times have sought to rescue it from the manhandling of the positivists. They, too, recognize the naïve assumptions underlying this theory, as well as the misconceptions of both religion and science to which it inevitably leads.

This unintelligent conception of the myth consists primarily in the positivistic contrast of science with myth. It is indeed the character of the myth that it represents 'forces' in personal and quasi-personal forms and as performing supernatural and superhuman functions. But—and this is the important point—the forces are not the 'forces of nature' in the scientific sense at all; they are the forces of *reality* before reality has been transformed by the formation of a concept of nature as opposed to super-

[1] Ernst Cassirer's second volume of his *Die Philosophie der Symbolischen Formen*, entitled *Das Mythische Denken*, is in every way the most significant, as it is also the most thorough, treatment of myth in modern philosophy. His critique of the positivistic conception of myth in the closing chapter, especially pp. 290 ff., is in every respectdefinitive.

nature. Reality is represented in forms which we now, in contrast to the symbolism of science, call 'anthropomorphic,' but these forms are not 'projections' into nature, but rather the primary way of apprehending nature in so far as it is immediately given. But there is a further sense in which this contrast is unintelligent. For science itself, as we shall see, unless it be taken in the truncated form of the positivist, has its dramatic and mythical elements also. The mythical, then, is neither merely a primitive form of mentality to be outgrown, nor a wholly provisional form of expression to be dissolved, but a symbolic form, having its own principles and structure and representing in its own way an aspect of reality not otherwise expressible.

B

As defined in the dictionaries, and as ordinarily understood, a myth is 'a story, the spontaneous product of unreflective and uncritical consciousness in which the forces of nature are represented in personal or quasi-personal forms and as performing supernatural and superhuman functions.' With this definition has ordinarily gone a dyslogistic meaning of myth which practically identifies it with fiction. This is, however, neither the classical nor the most modern and critical conception, but rather the product of the Enlightenment and of modern positivism.

One of the latest to protest against this conception is the well-known Russian theologian Nicolai Berdyaev. 'It is high time,' he writes, 'that we stopped identifying myth with invention, with the illusions of primitive mentality, and with anything, in fact, which is essentially opposed to reality. For that is the sense which we give to the words "myth" and "mythology" in ordinary conversation. But behind myth are concealed the greatest realities, the original phenomena of the spiritual life.'[1] In this protest Berdyaev reflects not only the modern philosophy of myth but also the attitude of more critical modern theologians towards the mythical element in religion. Some comment upon his own formulation of this protest will afford a preliminary to the understanding of this attitude.

The illustrations used by Berdyaev are the myths of Prometheus and the Fall of Man. They 'symbolize, in a sensible manner

---

[1] Nicolai Berdyaev, *Freedom and the Spirit*, New York, 1935. See especially Chapter ii, entitled 'Symbol, Myth, Dogma.'

and on the natural plane, certain events in the moral or spiritual
life of man and of the relation of his life to nature.' But the
great nature myths—with their pictures of man's origin and
destiny—represent no less surely the greatest realities—the
original phenomena of the spiritual life. For they too symbolize
in a sensible manner the metaphysical presuppositions upon
which the spiritual life of man depends.

That the myth expresses or embodies something *original*—
something not only temporally but logically primary in experience and knowledge—is recognized as the first element in any
critical theory of the myth. The primary way of apprehending
things is neither that of common sense and practice, nor of
science and analysis. These are later forms developed for special
purposes of manipulation and control. The original phenomena
are the immediate intuitions of the 'living' and the 'becoming,'
and it is these intuitions that the dramatic language of myth
expresses and that 'mythical thinking' develops. It is these
original phenomena, the 'presences' in nature which, as Whitehead tells us, the poets have remembered when science has forgotten them, which make, as we shall see, the concept of nature
developed in science neither the nature of man's original intuition nor of his more mature philosophy.

The primary experiences are said to be the original phenomena of the *spiritual life,* and if the notion of spirit is properly
defined, there is, perhaps, no better term. The appropriateness
of the term is immediately evident in the case of the myths which
symbolize the universal moral experiences of man, but the term
is also applicable to the nature myths. The spiritual life of man
includes, not merely his 'moral' experiences in the narrow sense
of that word, not only the experiences of his own life, but also of
its relations to the cosmos in which that life is lived. These
relations also can be expressed only in the dramatic form, and for
such expression the language of the myth is essential.

It is, however, with the third element in the statement that the
critical conception of the myth finally appears. The mythical
form of expression is neither illusion nor fiction, but embodies or
'conceals' the greatest realities. The myths, whether historical or
cosmic, are formed on the sensuous and natural plane—otherwise
they could not be original—but their reference (their symbolic
reference on later stages of thought and experience) is to that

which transcends the sensuous and the phenomenal. The moment, however, the notion of the real, as opposed to the unreal, truth as opposed to fiction and illusion, are introduced we have entered the realm of philosophy. It is with this problem, then, that the philosophy of myth *eo nomine* is especially concerned, and to this philosophy we shall now turn.

II

The Critical Conception of the Myth. The Philosophy of Mythology

A

The philosophy of mythology is a product of the nineteenth century, more especially of what is called the Romantic movement. The protagonist was Schelling who, in his *Philosophy of Mythology*, opened up for the modern world a new conception of myth which, in contrast to the naïve intellectualism of the Enlightenment, gave to it a fundamental place among the forms of human experience and its expression. In principle it is an extension of critical position of Kant and was, perhaps, already implicit in the *Critique of Judgment*.

The essential of Schelling's position is that myth is 'a necessary moment in the process of the self-unfolding or self-development of the Absolute.' In so far as religion is concerned, the mythical conceptions of the gods—the dramatic polytheisms of the nature religions—were necessary stages in the development of the rational and ethical monotheism which constitutes developed religion. But in so far as it is a necessary stage in the development of the Absolute, the mythological process, with its forms, has not merely a religious but a universal meaning, for it is the universal process in which the world itself is apprehended and expressed. According to Schelling, one cannot deny historical truth to the myth for the process in which it develops is itself a true history, a real process. Just as little can one deny its 'physical' truth, for nature itself is just as truly a construction, a necessary stage in the mythological process as a whole.[1]

This philosophy of mythology was the beginning of the modern critical conception of the myth. The critical element

[1] *Philosophie der Mythologie*, neunte Vorlesung, S. 216.

consists in its insistence upon the 'truth' of myth, both historical and cosmological (or physical). As a necessary moment in the development of the Absolute, it was thus accorded an objectivity not recognized in the philosophies of the Enlightenment. But this theory has its uncritical elements also. In so far as myth is viewed merely as a stage, although a necessary stage in the self-development of the Absolute, it is inevitable that its fate, as well as the fate of religion with which it is so closely connected, should be to 'be dissolved into metaphysics,' as in the later development of idealism in Croce. On this view, the myth is indeed no longer subject to the criticism of a narrow positivism, as fated to disappear before the rising sun of 'science,' but it is subject to a more subtle form of rationalism in the eyes of which it is fated to be dissolved into metaphysics. A really critical view finds it necessary to deny both conceptions of its ephemeral character and to insist upon its permanent place as an original and necessary way of intuiting reality. That myth, thus understood, must be interpreted, and that such interpretation requires a metaphysical idiom is beyond question, but while it is not exactly true something in reality like it must be true.

B

One way in which this critical philosophy of myth has been stated is by distinguishing between transitory and permanent myth—between that part of mythology which is derived from pre-scientific thought and which must necessarily be sacrificed in a scientific age and the permanent myth in every great mythical heritage. 'The mythical categories express the organic character of reality as opposed to the mechanical. Scientific descriptions of reality always tend to a mechanistic interpretation of it. The facts of organic growth can be comprehended and described only by mythically transferring the inner unity of the human consciousness (where unity is directly experienced and apprehended) to the external world. A certain amount of primitive myth is always involved in this process (its analogy to animism of primitive mythology is apparent). But it is also permanent myth in the sense that it is permanently valid, since reality is actually organic and not mechanical in its processes.''[1]

[1] Reinhold Niebuhr, 'The Truth in Myths,' an essay in the volume *The Nature of Religious Experience*, 1937.

I shall not dispute the relative value of such a distinction although I should want to express it somewhat differently. For neither the nature of the reality which the mythical 'categories' express, nor the real ground of their permanent significance is, to my mind, adequately expressed. It is not merely the 'organic' in contrast to the mechanical that the myth symbolizes and expresses—although this is an important part of it—but much more 'the original phenomena of the spiritual life'—the ultimate inseparability of value and existence which makes them at once both original and spiritual. Moreover—and this is a still more important point of difference—the dramatic language of the myth and its categories are not permanent in religion *as myth*, but rather as a necessary symbolic form in which religion—itself not myth—is alone expressible. Above all, I should, therefore, dispute the relation of myth to religion as envisaged in this theory, namely, the identification of religion with permanent myth. It is this identification which brings with it such expressions as the 'creation myth' and the 'Christian myth' which, permanent though they may be, are still myth. The view which I should maintain is that myth and religion are fundamentally different in essence, as I shall attempt to show. Myth simply furnishes the material for religious symbolism, for only the dramatic language of the myth can provide the appropriate symbols for the content of religion. There is, as we shall see, all the difference in the world between those two conceptions of the relation of myth to religion.

C

Uncritical philosophies of myth are characterized, as we have seen, by a naïve contrast of myth with science. The concept of the three stages of Comte is the major premise of them all. Science gives us truth, myth fiction. When, however, the myth is studied from the standpoint of language, and as symbolic form, so simple a contrast as this is found to be no longer tenable. Science itself, in so far as it speaks a dramatic language—and at certain significant points it must speak that language—has its mythical aspect also.

The idea of the 'myths of science,' strange as it may seem to the ordinary man, is one which is entirely familiar to critical and sophisticated science. Thus C. D. Broad speaks of the myths of science and Sir James Jeans speaks of the 'fables with which we deck our mathematical equations.' By myth in this sense is understood two things: (a) all those elements of science which retain the dramatic language—with its categories of substances, forces, energies, etc.—survivals, as it is held, of a pre-scientific, animistic level of thought; and (b) all those cosmologies and cosmological propositions which, being pronouncements about the universe as a whole, transcend empirical phenomena and are therefore, in the nature of the case, empirically unverifiable. It is evident, I think, that a critical philosophy of science must recognize mythical elements in this sense in the language of science. As we have seen, cosmology is always action and that the language of any cosmology must be dramatic in character. Our sense of rationality in science also depends ultimately on drama. The only question is whether these mythical elements should be excluded from science, as the extreme positivist maintains. Our answer would be that if science is to include cosmology at all, the idea of the 'myths of science' cannot be wholly excluded. In any case, it is wholly uncritical to contrast myth, when properly understood, with science and a critical view of their relations becomes of the utmost importance when we come to the discussion of the relation of religion to science.[1]

III

The Myth as the Material of Religious Symbolism:
Ursprünglischer Symbolismus

A

An essential part of the critical philosophy of myth is that the myth is symbolic of spiritual realities, moral and metaphysical. In that the myth 'conceals' these greatest realities, these original phenomena, it becomes, on the later and more developed stages of religion, the material of religious symbolism.

The notion of symbolism as an essential part of religion is characteristic of the later stages of all positive religions, and the notion itself will be discussed later under the head of 'Symbolism as a Theological Principle.' This constitutes an essential

[1] Chapter x, pp. 357 ff.

chapter in any philosophy of religion, but before the significance of this aspect of the problem can be understood it is necessary to determine the relation of religious symbolism to myth. The primordial religious symbols—the original symbolism as Nietzsche calls it—is mythical in origin; in other words, the myth provides the material of religious symbolism.

The mythical origin of most of the primary symbols of religious expression is historically beyond question. Even the most spiritual symbols of the most moralized religions have their source in the womb of the unconscious out of which the myth and its symbols have been born. The most exalted idiom of theology, no less than the language of purest devotion, makes use of this treasury of the ages. The chief sources of religious symbolism are, then, the great nature or cosmic myths and the historical or hero myths. Let us then start with this distinction between nature and human nature.

For the purposes of simplification (we are interested here only in illustration of a principle) we may single out two great classes of nature myths, the sun myths and the life myths. Our justification for so doing is found in two considerations: (a) their practical omnipresence in all mythology and religion, and (b) their contribution to the spiritual symbolism of all developed religions.

The wide diffusion of the worship of the sun and of sun myths has been questioned, as for instance by Frazer,[1] but it is probable that the solar implications of many myths have been obscured by the luxuriant overgrowth of lesser images. In any case, the worship flourishes in all nations that have achieved a certain degree of civilization and certainly enters into the symbolism of all the higher religions, the point in which we are mainly interested. The sun with its powerful rays, its warmth and light, its life-giving qualities, becomes a natural symbol for the creating and eliciting power. Moreover, the contrasts bound up with it, light and darkness, power and weakness, life and death, spirit and matter, good and evil, become a natural vehicle for the expression and embodiment of moral and other value contrasts as they develop in the life of man.

[1] *Worship of Nature*, Volume I, p. 441.

B

As the sun is the most appealing and significant centre for the mythical organization of external cosmic experience, so the life functions, more particularly the sexual, afford the most powerful centre for the organization of internal experiences. Hunger and self-preservation may be more fundamental drives or instincts, but sex, 'the burning glass of the will,' as Schopenhauer called it, is that which focuses and organizes our inner experiences. There is reason to believe that the worship of fertility, and the sex symbolism which goes with it, is indigenous to all agricultural and grazing peoples. The agriculturist, in order to live, must give life; and his highest ideal, his value of all values, is fertility—fertility of plant and animal, and of the human family itself. His deity becomes the Life-Giver, the life giver in both male and female form. Whether, as in some types of social organization, the relation of motherhood is singled out and the symbol of the Great Mother is dominant; or in other forms the notion of fatherhood is supreme, is immaterial; both become natural and appropriate symbols in which to envisage the *mysterium tremendum* from which our being comes, as well as the 'infinitely holy' to which love and devotion aspire.

In primitive religions of certain types the sexual act may be connected with the general productive and reproductive processes of nature, and not only represent in some fashion these forces and processes but also in some magical way affect and control them. Thus ritual acts of a sexual character are born. Lifted out of their merely human context, they are given a transcendent reference and, like other acts such as washing and the common meal, become dramatic representations of a supernatural world, and ultimately the source of one of the most important fields of religious symbolism.

The religious or numinous quality almost universally attributed to sex and the sexual act in primitive forms of religion, has its origin both in the mystery of procreation and in the excessivity of the joy of sexual union. It is a commonplace of comparative mythology and religion that the worship of sex and the sexual symbols which go with it has, in its earlier forms at least, nothing of the prurient or vicious which later appears in more sophisticated forms, and it is even questionable whether, with all their abominations, the latter lose entirely this numinous quality. Even in those religions which have been purified from the abominations of the sexual idolatries of Baal, Ashtaroth, etc., this sacred character of procreation with its transcendent reference remains. Thus in the religion of Islam there is still adoration of sex and the sex act itself is looked upon as a form of prayer and praise. Thus we find Mohammed saying: 'and Adam saw that coition was good in that it gave the man as well as the woman inexpressible joy and it also made of the man the active principle, the creator, the completer of the divine procreative will.' Again we read in El-Ktab, 'Coition, O man, is the greatest and holiest song of praise—the highest desire of man and his companion for primitive unity and the paradisical joys.'[1]

The Christian religion, despite its revulsion against pagan sexual idolatries—indeed precisely because of this revulsion— emphasizes the transcendent significance of the sexual act. It is not only that God himself said, be fruitful and multiply, and made of man the completer of the Divine creative will; it is still more that it has always recognized in the love of man and woman a shadow or symbol of Divine love. Lifted out of the mere world of nature into that of Grace, they, the man and woman, become, as St. Peter wrote in his epistle, 'heirs together of the grace of life.'

The language of love is thus the constant and universal vehicle for the expression of religious experience—the symbolic form in which the highest and deepest in man is expressed. Nor need we ask why this is so; the wonder would be if it were otherwise. All love, it has been said, seeks eternity, and it is only natural that the highest love should be 'Love Divine, all loves excelling.' The transcendent reference to the infinite being present in all love, it is only natural that religious experience should find its symbols in those human loves which are thus excelled. Nevertheless, while sex symbolism remains, even in the higher mystical forms, an indispensable vehicle for the expression of oneness with the Divine, the very conditions of its origin and development set one of the chief barriers to mutual understanding and communication on the lower levels of the various positive religions. These difficulties are not to be

[1] Quoted from *Magica Sexualis*, by Dr. Emile Laurent and Professor Paul Nagour, English translation, 1934, p. 265.

minimized—even in the Christian religion the erotic language of many of the mystics is frequently embarrassing to their fellow believers—but this does not in the least affect the principle that it is only in this language that the deepest realities of the spiritual life can be expressed.

C

We have been examining the nature myths, both cosmic and 'vital,' as the source of the original symbolism of religion. These myths are, however, paralleled by those taken from human nature and these are often fused with the former. As the cosmic myths are the significant centres for the mythical organization of external cosmic experience, and the life myths for *internal* volitional experiences, so the hero is the significant centre about which historical and racial experience is organized. The great Aryan myth of Prometheus represents or symbolizes in a sensible manner, and on the natural plane, certain events of the spiritual life of man and of his relation to nature. The same may be said of the Dionysian myth which, on the higher levels of religious development, and interpreted allegorically and mystically, became, for countless souls, the expression of the greatest realities of the spiritual life. These realities are precisely those evaluations of existence, those intuitions of the relations of our values to existence which, as we have seen in the preceding chapter, constitute the initial data of all religion and determine its inmost essence.

The essence of man as religious is the sense of his own finitude and of the precarious nature of the things he prizes and loves, and with which he therefore identifies his own being. This implies also the sense of 'infinitude, his being's heart and home.' Sin and separation from the Holy or from the principle of perfection is, as an original phenomenon of finite existence, in the first instance, physical or metaphysical rather than moral, 'original' rather than derived. The most significant of the historical myths are, accordingly, those which deal with these original phenomena—of sin and salvation. They are the stories of man's fall and man's redemption—stories of the saviours of mankind and, as saviours, they are, and indeed must be, embodiments or incarnations of the Divine.

It is unnecessary to emphasize the prevalance of the notion of the God-man in all the great positive religions and analogous expressions of the notion in the most varied historical settings. 'Pagan Christs,' to employ the title of a book by J. M. Robertson—the Egyptian Horus, the Hindu Krishna and Buddha, the Persian Mithras, the Mexican Queztzalcotal, the Phrygian Attys—all embody in legendary or mythical form an original phenomenon of the spiritual life, a mythical form which later becomes a primal category of developed religious experience. Moreover, 'the old story of Prometheus crucified in the Caucasus is repeated in all the crucifixions of the young incarnate divinities of India, Persia, Asia Minor and Egypt.'[1] As the result of modern research it seems necessary to say that there is scarcely a single element of Christian imagery and symbol for which a parallel in heathen mythology cannot be found.[2]

Nevertheless, the theologian is wholly justified in his refusal to permit the notion of the Incarnation in Christian thought to be identified in *essence* with these mythical forms, just as he is justified in refusing to allow the identification of religion with poetry. Similarity of form does not mean identity of essence. The essence of religion is to be found only on the higher levels of religion and of the religious consciousness and can be expressed only in conceptual equivalents. A philosophy of the Incarnation, such as that developed in the classics of Christian theology, is, as we shall see in the following chapter, in a different universe of discourse from that to which these primitive myths belong. The incarnation, as there understood, presupposes a cosmology and an ontology infinitely remote from the primitive 'philosophies' with which the mythical forms are bound up.

D

The significance of the foregoing paragraphs obviously does not lie in their value as an account of mythology. As such they are doubtless sketchy, if not wholly inadequate, although in this over-simplification I have, I hope, avoided saying anything untrue. Their significance lies wholly in showing how myth provides the material of religious symbolism. The myth, with its *Ursprünglischer Symbolismus*, provides a fund of imagery which can be more or less consciously and religiously used as representation of Deity (*imago Dei*). Light (as in the Creed: God of

---

[1] Eduard Norden, *Die Geburt des Kindes*, Leipzig, 1924, p. 305.
[2] J. P. Lundy, *Monumental Christianity*, p. 393.

God, *light of light*); love (as in the hymn, 'Love Divine, all loves excelling'); fatherhood, motherhood—these are not in any sense arbitrary symbols, but intrinsic to the spiritual life itself. The sun, with its unearthly radiance, becomes easily a symbol for another light that never was on land or sea, that light which lighteneth every man that cometh into the world. Sex love, its heights and its depths—its horrible darkness and its blinding light—is never wholly alien to that creative love of which Plato no less than Christian theologians and philosophers discourse. The primitive worshipper and the Christian saint are, and should ever remain in this respect, 'brothers under their skins.'

Sir James G. Frazer closes his last chapter of *The Golden Bough* with this 'Farewell to Nemi':

'The place', he tells us, 'has changed but little since Diana received the homage of her worshippers in the sacred grove. The temple of the sylvan goddess, indeed, has vanished and the King of the Wood no longer stands sentinel over the Golden Bough. But Nemi's woods are still green, and as the sunset fades above them in the west, there comes to us, borne on the swell of the wind, the sound of the church bells of Aricia ringing the Angelus. Ave Maria! sweet and solemn they chime out from the distant town and die lingeringly away across the wide Campagnan marshes. Le roi est mort, vive le roi! Ave Maria.'[1]

This passage, like all things which concern that which is highest and deepest in us, can be read in two ways—either forward or backward. When we cry Ave Maria we may believe that our salutation is really to the sylvan goddess who dwelt in the sacred grove. But we may also believe that those worshippers who saluted her in Nemi's woods were really in their hearts worshipping something yet to be. For myself, I prefer the latter reading, for if, as we maintained in the preceding chapter, the essence of religion becomes explicit only in its higher forms, then we may understand the earlier by the later, but can never understand the later in terms of the earlier. In any case we have here a supreme expression of the principle of the indispensable myth of which we shall speak later.

[1] *The Golden Bough*, The Macmillan Company (abridged edition), 1940, p. 714.

IV

Mythical Images and Mythical Categories: The Mythopoeic Infinite.

A

Myth, we have seen, furnishes the indispensable material of religious symbolism even on the highest levels of religious intuition and its expression. It is important, therefore, that the relation of myth to symbol should be made clear and that, in so doing, the religious symbol should be differentiated from other forms of symbolization.

It is the general character of all symbols, whether scientific, poetic or religious, that 'ideas or images are taken from the narrower and more intuitible regions of experience and used as expressions for more ideal and universal relations which, because of their pervasiveness and ideality, cannot be expressed directly.'[1] By the more intuitible regions of experience are here understood, of course, in the first instance at least, sense intuition and the imagery derived therefrom. When the poet cries, 'Gather ye rosebuds while ye may,' what he means to say is, enjoy all sweet and pleasant things while enjoyment is possible. When the scientist speaks of lines of force, what he actually means to say is that these 'lines' stand for or symbolize, as Clerk Maxwell fully realized, certain ideal relations. So it goes throughout the field of scientific symbols, as we shall later see.

But these symbolic ideas and images are taken not merely from the outer sense intuition but also from the inner intuitions of the life of feeling and emotion which, in contrast to the abstractions of reason which men call science, have the character of poetry. Of these the love and hate which for the early Greek physicists expressed in the only way intelligible to them the attractions and repulsions which, as it seemed, constituted the inmost core of becoming, is the outstanding example. Survivals of a pre-scientific mythical consciousness, as they may be thought to be, something of them still remains in any philosophical cosmology that 'can be made to march,' as witness the philosophies of a Schopenhauer or a Bergson, or even of a Hegel or a

[1] H. Höffding, *Philosophy of Religion*, New York, Macmillan, pp. 77 ff.

Whitehead. Cosmology can be expressed only in dramatic language and there is no such language which, in the last analysis, does not involve symbols taken from the inner life of man.[1]

Religious symbols, as Höffding points out, are also taken from these more intuitible domains, but, according to him, they differ from those of art and science in a significant way, in the first instance, at least, in the character of the regions of intuition from which they are taken. These he describes as 'the great fundamental relations of nature and human nature—light and darkness, power and weakness, life and death, spirit and matter, good and evil, love and hate, etc.' This undoubtedly describes a relative difference between religious symbols and those of ordinary poetry and of science. The great myths, both cosmic and historical, from which the material of religious symbolism is taken, represent, indeed, a much deeper layer of human experience than the images employed by the symbolisms of art and science, and it is for this reason that myth is the original symbolism from which the later forms are derived.

This distinction of intuitible material is important but it does not go to the heart of the matter. Speaking of the religious symbol, Récéjac writes, 'not all the images with which thought

[1] It is one of the outstanding paradoxes of human ideation—and one often commented upon—that, whereas our knowledge of the external world proceeded by means of metaphors and symbols taken from the vital and the mental, our knowledge of the inner or spiritual world seems to have proceeded in an opposite direction by means of metaphors taken from the world of the bodily and sensible. The situation is, however, really not so paradoxical as it seems. The primary way of apprehending and expressing reality is the dramatic; the pre-scientific or mythical consciousness knows only this type of symbol and category. The physical language of science was made only later to manipulate the bodily object and it was only a matter of time that, with the perfection of this instrument, it should be transferred analogically to knowledge of the vital and mental, interest in which arises late in the ideational life of man. Human knowledge, it appears, proceeds necessarily by a fundamental dialectical movement between the two intuitible domains. It is as though the human spirit, having exhausted the one way of knowing, turns for new vigour to its opposite. The language and symbolism developed for the knowledge of the inner world soon shows its ineptitude when applied to the manipulation of the external, but it is no less true that the physico-mathematical language and symbolism developed for the manipulation of 'things' soon shows a similar ineptitude when it seeks to express the things of the spirit. A 'double symbolism' thus seems inevitable if reality is to be really known and expressed, and the relation of these two symbolic forms, the one to the other, becomes a fundamental problem of both science and philosophy. See on this point my *Language and Reality*, pp. 524 ff.

clothes itself properly bear the name of symbols if we contrast them with the representations by which the Absolute shines out in consciousness.' It is the unique reference of the religious symbol—to the absolute, the infinite, the *mysterium tremendum*, the wholly other—whatever the conceptual name we may choose to give it—which distinguishes, in principle at least, the religious symbol from all other forms of symbolization. As it is this reference which gives to the language of religion its numinous quality, so it is this same reference which distinguishes the religious symbol from all other symbolic forms such as those of art and science. It is for this reason that, as Höffding also rightly holds, 'the symbols of religion, considered epistemologically and not psychologically, differ from the metaphysical symbol only in that its figures are more concrete, richer in colour and more toned with emotion'—are in short similar to the poetic symbol. It is for this reason also that, as we shall see in the following chapter, the language of religion is inevitably translated into the language of theology and that when this language is examined it is seen to be the language of metaphysics also.

B

The original symbolism provided by the myth includes not only intuitible images but *categories* of intuition also—not only images and representations in which 'the absolute shines out in consciousness' but also the categorical forms in which alone the 'absolute' can be symbolically apprehended and expressed. Any adequate account of the relation of religion to myth must contain an account of what are called the 'mythical categories.'

In the myth all the categories of human experience are already present, but they have their unique form and structure. Space, time, number, causality, all have different meanings from those which they have in science, and constitute a symbolic form with its own immanental principle and structure. An adequate understanding of this symbolic form and of its relation to religion and metaphysics would require some such detailed study as one finds in Cassirer's *Das Mythische Denken*, the second volume of his *Die Philosophie der Symbolischen Formen*. It must suffice for our present purpose to single out certain special points which have direct bearing upon the development of the main theme of this chapter.

The primordial language of religion, as of the myth, is spatio-temporal. What is said of the gods is always said in bodily form, although not ultimately to be so understood. But it is not always sufficiently realized that the spatio-temporal language thus employed is not the later spatio-temporal language of science. The space-time forms of consciousness of the myth embody and express a form of consciousness in which physical dimensions and dimensions of value have not yet been differentiated, and which make therefore these mythical categories the natural form for the expression of the relations of value to existence.[1]

Few chapters in comparative mythology and religion are more enlightening than those which deal with their spatio-temporal imagery and their symbolic function in religion. The cosmic myths all presuppose a world picture in which there is the earth, that which is above and beneath the earth—heaven and earth and hell. All men, writes Aristotle, believe that there are gods, and all—barbarians as well as Greeks—assign to the Godhead the highest place. Cosmic myths also presuppose a world picture in which there is beginning and end. All men, Aristotle might also have said, believe that there are gods, and all barbarians as well as Greeks assign to the Godhead the first and the last place. As the religious consciousness located the Godhead in space so also it located it in time. As it gave to the gods the highest place so it gave to them the longest lives. The theogonies, indeed, envisaged that which was before the gods, and also, in many cases, that which comes after them—the *Götterdämerung*, the twilight of the gods after which comes the dark. But on the higher levels time itself is transcended and the religious consciousness cries: 'From everlasting to everlasting Thou art God.' Eternity becomes the time form of value.

Actually it is time rather than space that constitutes the basal form of the myth. The 'echte Mythus,' as Cassirer rightly points out, 'begins not only with demons and gods, but at the point at which these forms are described as having an origin, a becoming and a life in time.'[2] For the mythical

---

[1] For the details of this comparative study the reader may be referred to certain lectures in Edwyn Bevan's *Symbolism and Belief*. Lectures II and III entitled 'Height,' and IV and V on 'Time,' contain a wealth of material and a sureness in its evaluation and interpretation possible only to a scholar with the long list of excellent studies in the world's religions already to his credit.

[2] Ernst Cassirer, *Philosophie der Symbolischen Formen*, Vol. II, p. 132.

consciousness time itself has no 'why'; it is rather the why of things themselves. The past has no why; it is a *regressus ad infinitum*. The same is true of the future; it is a *progressus ad infinitum*. On the other hand, the myth seeks 'to put a stop to time' for, as it is felt, 'time must have a stop.' It is out of this tension between the finite and the infinite—most intensely felt in the tension between time and eternity—that the mythopoeic imagination develops its categories of beginning and ending, of ultimate origination and ultimate destiny—its mythical cosmologies and eschatologies. Despite this primacy of time, space and time are ultimately inseparable, and they remain so throughout the entire development of religion. Transcendence of time as well as of space is the *sine qua non* of any interpretation of what is said of God, for to speak of him as in time, no less than in space, means to speak of him in bodily form. The allegorical and mystical interpretation of which Abelard speaks involves this transcendence. It is, as we shall see, precisely the mystics, of all times and all places, who have realized most fully this inseparability of space and time. They have known instinctively how ruinous for the spiritual life is the triumph of the category of time no less than that of space. They, more than all others, make use of the categories of the myth only to transcend them.[1]

C

It is out of the tension of the temporal and the timeless that the mythopoeic imagination develops its categories of ultimate origination and ultimate destiny. Like the forms of space and time with which they are closely connected, these categories represent a form of consciousness in which existence and value have not yet been separated and which, therefore, by the very fact that they are thus 'dramatic,' make man's relation to the ground of things intelligible.

The idea of creation, it is said, is a 'typical mythical category.' Primitive myth speaks of God making man out of clay and of breathing into him the breath of life, but although the imagery of the primitive myth may be discarded, the idea of creation remains and retains the insight given by the primitive intuition of the myth. It is the source of all our notions of intelligible causation—for no notion of causation is intelligible which does

[1] Chapter xiii, pp. 453 ff.

not relate our life and the world in which our lives are lived to
an original source which makes them meaningful to us. The
same is true of the category of ultimate end or consummation.
Primitive myths speak of 'heavens' in which all we love and
prize is not only conserved but gloriously enhanced—and
these heavens are painted in the crudest of colours both
cosmic and moral; but when the primitive language and
imagery are discarded the original intuition remains, for the
idea of consummation is as necessary to intelligibility as that of
creation. It is not—we are here insisting—the categories of
creation and consummation which are themselves mythical;
they are, as we shall see later, necessary and permanent
elements in the life of reason itself, but solely the imagery in
which these categories of necessity found their original expression. As religion itself is not myth, either ephemeral or permanent, so the categories of rational theology are not mythical
although they may be expressed in the original symbolism of the
myth.

The historical myths, no less than the cosmological, furnish
categories which differ in principle from those of 'science,'
categories which, as we shall see, have no meaning in secular
history.[1] Typical categories in this sphere are the notions of the
fall of man and of his redemption and restoration through the
mediation of saviours. The fundamental category here is that of
incarnation which, as we have seen, has analogous expressions
in the most varied historical settings. The essence of all these
'historical categories,' together with the category of revelation
which is always a part of them, is the breaking through into
space and time of that which is beyond space and time. Since
the space and time of myth are not the space and time of history,
the historical elements of religion are not history in the secular
sense and the mythical language in which they are symbolized
is significantly called *Urgeschichte*.

Of the categories characteristic of the historical myths that of
the miraculous is in many ways most significant. That by which
the God-man is always known is the 'wonder of his ways.' He
not only speaks as never man spake, but acts in ways that are
more than human. What the belief in miracle really illustrates
is the persistent tendency of the human mind, to which the

[1] See Chapter viii, pp. 267 f.

concept has from the beginning been familiar, to expect that the unexpected will attend the acts of men through which God discloses Himself as a sign. The imagery in which this expectation expresses itself is inevitably taken from the myth, but the expectation itself survives all change in imagery and becomes an essentially religious category of which the mythical is but symbolic. The full meaning of the miraculous, as a religious and not merely mythical category, cannot be understood until we have examined its role as a fundamental category in the "historical element" in religion, but enough has been said to indicate the fundamental difference between the sign and the thing signified in this mythical category also.

The 'mythical categories,' both cosmological and historical, are then permanent elements in religion, not *as myth*, but as an indispensable form in which the non-mythical is expressed. Without this form the essence of religion cannot be expressed, for only in such symbolic idiom can the tension between the finite and the infinite, which is the essence of the religious consciousness, be embodied and shown forth.

D

The 'essence' of religion, as we have seen in the preceding chapter, is man's sense of infinitude, 'his being's heart and home.' If, therefore, myth is to furnish the material of religious symbolism, even on the higher levels of religion, the infinite must be already present in some sense in the mythopoeic imagination itself. If the myth is, in Schelling's terms, a necessary stage in the development of the Absolute, however these terms be understood, the Absolute itself must be present implicitly in the myth. In this sense mythology is symbolization of the infinite. Our first problem is then the nature of the mythological infinite or the 'idea' of the infinite as it functions in the mythopoeic imagination.

There is, so to speak, a primitive infinite, a primordial form, which springs directly out of man's sense of his own finitude. Out of the limitations of our finite desires and the unsatisfactoriness of their satisfactions springs the sense of infinitude. It is all important that we should understand this primitive infinite. To do so we must go back to the concept of the numinous as developed in the preceding chapter. The conceptual equivalents in which it is expressed are, as we have seen, all negative; while apparently positive they are so only in appearance. But—and this is the important point—'on the side of feeling' it is otherwise. Here there is positive feeling content and it is through this that our conceptual equivalents—the transcendent, the supernatural and the infinite—become forthwith designations for the 'wholly other,' something whose special character men can feel without being able to give it clear expression. This we may call the primitive or primordial infinite.

It has been attempted, notably by Jung, to explain the idea of God as infinite on the basis of the infinity of repressed desires of the *libido*, and in his analysis of Meister Eckhart's mysticism, Jung explains his idea of God in this way. But, as Professor Tillich has pointed out, the category of the infinite cannot be derived from the immediacy of the vital urges. The *libido*, however strong, is always finite. This is undoubtedly true, but this does not mean that the finite desires, as expressed even in the desires of sex, may not, like all forms of finitude, presuppose the infinite. The essence of man as religious is his consciousness of his own finitude and nowhere, perhaps, is that consciousness more persistent, as some of the greatest of the saints have realized, than in that urge towards 'physical' union men call love. There is a psychological sublimation of our desires, but there is also an ontological sublimation of our perfections, and chief among those perfections, conditioned though they be by the way in which they appear in creatures, is precisely this capacity for oneness with other beings which men call love. Love of God and love of man are indeed different, as all things human and divine are; but he who will make them wholly different will scarcely understand the one or the other.

The primordial infinite of which we have been speaking may be described as the principle of *excessivity*; in the words of the Apostle, it refers to that which 'exceeds all that we can either hope or desire.' This primordial infinite sets going a dialectic of the religious consciousness which, in the end, brings it to the highest levels of religious experience and thought. The primitive sense of excessivity passes into the negative infinite; of all phenomenal things men say, that it is not, that it is not. But this negative always presupposes a positive, and the *mysterium tremendum*, because of its very excessivity, passes through negation to a

Waynesburg College Library
Waynesburg, Pa. 15370

positive infinite. The excessivity is thought of not as wholly other, negating all finite predicates, but rather as an inexhaustible 'fulness of being' which includes the finite, and can, therefore, to some degree at least, be known by the finite. It can, therefore, be *named* only by applying the finite perfections of the creature to the fulness of being in an absolute or supereminent degree.

This is the 'good infinite,' which, in contrast to the bad infinite of mere negation, constitutes the formal principle of Deity. It is not the naked, skeletal infinite of mathematical manipulation, but one clothed upon by all the richness of experience, the *valor valorum* of Christian theology. The infinitude which is our being's heart and home is of our very heart because it is thus primordial, and has its roots deep in the unconscious life of man; it is our ultimate home because, through the principle of negation, it creates a house not made with hands, eternal in the Heavens.

It is, however, with the primordial or mythopoeic infinite that we are now concerned. This primitive infinite, present from the beginning in the mythical consciousness, creates an original symbolism of the infinite which, precisely because it is original, remains of necessity the material of all religious symbolism, and leads therefore to a fundamental principle of all philosophy of religion, namely, the principle of the indispensable myth. In order to understand this principle it is necessary to understand also how the myth thus symbolizes the infinite and thus from the very beginning expresses in its way that which we have seen is the very essence of religion.

V

The Symbolization of the Infinite and The Phenomenon of Distortion.

A

All symbols, that is all images taken from intuitive domains and applied to other domains of experience, require that the intuition shall be moulded so that there shall be some distortion of the intuition if it shall represent symbolically or indirectly that which itself is not immediately intuitible. 'Distortion' is a technical term for a phenomenon which appears in all forms of symbolization. Used primarily in connection with art and the aesthetic imagination, it may be extended to all fields in which symbolic representation plays a role, the scientific and religious as well as the artistic. The moulding of the intuition which results from its reference to the infinite serves to distinguish the religious symbol from all other symbolic forms and also to connect it with the mythopoeic imagination from which it springs.

The principle of aesthetic distortion is a commonplace in all theories of art. Essentially it consists in the fact that for a literal copy of an object is substituted a variant which, precisely by its variation, suggests or symbolizes an 'idea' other than itself and not otherwise expressible. Such substitution is not necessarily conscious. Indeed, it should rather be said that in the highest forms of the aesthetic imagination, the variation is, properly speaking, not substituted at all, but rather takes place in the very intuition itself.

An outstanding case of such distortion is the overemphasis or underemphasis of the lines of the human form—overemphasis of the curves and masses of the breasts and buttocks on the part of the 'primitives', and more self-consciously by modern primitives such as Matisse, or the underemphasis of the same curves and masses by the pre-Raphaelite painters and their more sophisticated modern followers. It seems more than likely that when the natural primitives overemphasized buttocks or breasts to express physical fertility it was wholly unsophisticated—the distortion was part of the intuition itself. For the modern 'primitives' it is thoroughly self-conscious and sophisticated. It is also possible that when the early Christian artist underemphasized the lines of the female body it was done more or less unconsciously. For the modern pre-Raphaelites it is thoroughly self-conscious and sophisticated. In either case, however, it is in the interest of expressionism. For a literal copy is substituted a variant which by its very variation suggests or symbolizes an idea other than itself, namely, spirituality or fecundity, as the case may be.

This distortion is, then, a deviation from the 'real' in the sense of a literal copy of the real. As such, these deviations are lies, to use an expression of Van Gogh, but these very lies are, as he also truly says, 'more valuable than the real values.'[1] Properly speaking, these deviations are not lies, for they take place in the intuition itself and intuition as such cannot lie. The literal copy of the real with which they are contrasted is itself only a selection from the varied aspects of the 'real' made for practical purposes of manipulation and control. It is only when these deviations are judged from this limited point of view that art may at all be said to tell its little lies, but even then it tells them in the interest of a great truth. On the other hand, science itself makes its own deviations from the real of sense perception for its own special purposes. It is only when one ascribes to these symbols and symbolic forms exclusive value that the one unforgivable lie is told.[2]

B

The phenomenon of distortion, with the moulding of the intuition which it involves, takes place in all the arts, but it is in religious art that it takes on the special character of the symbolization of the infinite which constitutes the essential character of the religious symbol. It is therefore to religious art that we must look primarily for the functioning of the primordial infinite.

In his account of the 'expressions of the numinous in art,' Otto recognizes this moulding of the real immanent in the intuition, although he does not use the term. 'The Madonna of ancient

[1] *The Letters of a Post Impressionist*, p. 23. 'Tell Seurat,' Van Gogh wrote, 'that I should despair if my figures were correct. Tell him that if you take a photograph of a man digging in my opinion he is sure to look as if he were not digging. Tell him that I think Michelangelo's figures magnificent, even though the legs are certainly too long and the hips and pelvis bones a little too broad. . . . Tell him that it is my most fervent desire to know how one can achieve such *deviations from reality* [italics mine] such inaccuracies and such transfigurations that come about by chance. Well yes, if you like, they are lies; but they are more valuable than the real values.' It is this last phrase that especially demands our attention, and contains the whole essence of the aesthetic symbol. What then does valuable here mean? It means for Van Gogh—and it must mean the same for every artist—that precisely by these deviations certain aspects of reality are apprehended and expressed which could not be otherwise shown forth.

[2] It is for these reasons that some philosophers of art object to the use of the notion of 'distortion' and would banish it from the idiom of aesthetic criticism. This seems to me as unnecessary as it is undesirable, for the fact that the moulding of the intuition takes place in the intuition itself implies that the term distortion has not such unfortunate implications. On the other hand, there is no term to take its place, to express adequately that 'moulding' of the intuition by which alone these deviations from practical reality, the very essence of art, can be described.

Byzantine art attracts the worship of many Catholics more than
the tender charm of the more human Madonnas of a Raphael.
Durgâ, the great Mother of Bengal, whose worship can appear
steeped in an atmosphere of the profoundest devotional awe, is
represented in the orthodox tradition with the visage of a fiend.'[1]
This 'blending of appalling frightfulness and most exalted holiness,' as Otto describes it, presents indeed to the imaginative
understanding a barrier which is to many insuperable, but to the
philosopher, to whom nothing human is alien, it is precisely this
phenomenon of distortion which above all affords the key to an
understanding of the symbolization of the supernatural or
infinite.

The religious symbol thus symbolizes the supernatural in
various meanings of the term. It may represent the supernatural in the sense of that which is contrary to nature. Thus,
when Hindu mythology and art represent the infinity of the
divine activity by the figure of a god with innumerable arms
and legs, we have, indeed, an unnatural distortion of nature,
but one which the imagination finds necessary in order to
symbolize that excessivity which is the necessary character of the
infinitely other. Such distortion is indeed a 'fiction', but it is
never felt as such by either artist or worshipper, for it is apprehended not as a picture but, whether consciously or unconsciously,
as a symbol; and as such, its deviations from the 'real' are truly
'more valuable than the real values.' But there is another and
equally important sense in which it may represent the supernatural or Divine—in the sense, namely, that it takes the human
and natural itself and so moulds it as to make it attributable to
the Divine. Here, too, there is an element of distortion in the
technical sense of the word. In art, in so far as it is religious, this
moulding is ever present, as seen in the conventional art of
Egypt and the primitive art of the Greeks. In Greek art it finds
its epitome, perhaps, in the majestic statues of Zeus and Athena.
In Christian art—to which was added an Hebraic sense of the
sublime not felt so much perhaps by the Greek—the epitome of
such distortion is perhaps to be found in Michelangelo's pictures of creation in the Sistine Chapel. One may, in looking upon
them, feel that the ancient Hebrew rule against representing
Deity at all should never have been abandoned, but surely, if

---

[1] *Op. cit.*, p. 64.

God is to be pictured at all, it can be only by such moulding of the human as the genius of Michelangelo achieved.

C

Both the fact of distortion itself and the peculiar nature of the distortion were clearly recognized by Hegel in his philosophy of religion. In his doctrine of the religious symbol the dialectical movement which he sought to establish between the oriental, the Greek, and the Christian religions undoubtedly led to the forcing of the varied and manifold expressions of the religious imagination into a narrow procrustean bed, but it also served, as theory often does, to disclose significant facts.

The 'fantastic shapes,' which, as Hegel said, 'attracted the imagination of the orientals' were for him a distortion for the expression of the infinite. More particularly, the zoomorphism of these religions is a case in point. The body of a lion with the head of a man and the wings and feathers of a bird represents in the first instance, doubtless, an attempt to render abstract attributes in sensuous form. In like manner it seems probable, as the result of recent studies, that the figure of the Sphinx is an attempt to combine the ideas of royalty (power) and wisdom. But there is more to it than this. Studies in animal symbolism, what we have called zoomorphism, make it increasingly clear that the deeper significance of animal symbolism lies in the fact that the more than human (super-human), character of its objects is expressed in the sub-human direction. These forms do not correspond to the idea, but it is precisely this *Unangemessenheit* which suggests the excessivity of the object, that is the object which the symbol does not reach. To the Greek mind—at least the more rational side of the Greek mind—this type of distortion was, according to Hegel, more or less repugnant. It is true that more recent views of Greek religion emphasize the dark and Dionysiac side of life and its closer relation with the 'oriental.' Nevertheless, on the whole, it is rather the *human* body that serves as symbol of the Divine. It 'appears to them as a nobler symbolism than that of the barbarians who discover in animal shapes the image of the divine.' But here also there is distortion in a wider sense, a moulding of the intuition in the direction of the 'ideal.' The point to be emphasized here is that on the higher levels, where grandeur and sublimity replace mere terror and dread, there is a moulding of the intuition and the phenomenal no less than in the latter.

The 'fantastic shapes' which were so repugnant to Hegel and which he believed, perhaps too readily, were equally repugnant to the Greeks, are now much more understandable to us than formerly. The fantastic shapes of more primitive religions—a fetish or a dance mask, a piece of negro sculpture or a Shiva picture—all have acquired in the last decades new meanings. In them are expressed depths of reality which had for long escaped our understanding, but which had subconsciously always been present and had never ceased to determine our being. Distortions of organic form are now seen to be 'expressions' of the organic and vital. The organs of the will to life and of the will to power such as hands, feet, teeth, eyes, and the organs of procreation, such as breasts, thighs, sex organs, are given in these fantastic shapes a violence of expression which we no longer find merely fantastic, but rather significantly demoniac—an expression, so to speak, of the infinite in reverse. Whatever be the source of our renewed sense for, and delight in, the demoniac— whether it be the constantly increasing violence and irrationality of our own life, or the equally increasing element of irrationality in our science and philosophy, or perhaps both—the fact remains that we now have an understanding of, and even delight in, these forms formerly not possible. However bad it may be for our souls, it is at least good for our minds, for it has made possible an understanding of the depths as well as the heights of human experience not possible in more superficial periods, and to that extent, perhaps, a greater understanding of religion itself.[1]

There is, however, another side to the story—that of 'nobler symbolism' of which Hegel speaks. Here also there is distortion, but in the direction of the 'ideal infinite'; here also the bodily forms are moulded but, so to speak, in the opposite direction. These ideal distortions also express the fulness of life, but the life

[1] The revival of demonology in some form in all critical periods of human culture is an outstanding fact of history. If we are to believe the reports, the so-called 'black mass' is an outstanding illustration of the functioning of the infinite in reverse. Doubtless, from one point of view its blasphemies, and their accompanying sexual orgies, are fantastic expressions of the repressions of the sexual instinct, but it is much more than that. It is indeed the infinite in reverse—a reversion to the unconscious out of which as an amoral reservoir there comes that which is both good and bad.

of the spirit. The iconography of Christian devotion, more especially of the Son of God and of the Mother of God—although it, too, as moulded by the hands of more primitive worshippers, often approaches the fantastic and the grotesque—in the main represents that nobler symbolism which, as Hegel believed, constituted the expression of the 'good infinite.'

This process of moulding does not, however, stop with the bodily shapes of man. On the higher levels of religion it extends to the mental and spiritual and seeks so to transform our natural human perfections as to make them properly applicable to the Divine. The 'perfections' we find in the universe and in ourselves are applicable to God also, but to be so they must first be 'moulded.' Indeed the very stages involved in such analogical predication reveal the nature of the process. There is the stage of negation—negation of the imperfections which inhere in these predicates as characteristic of creatures; and secondly the stage of ontological sublimation, for God's manner of possessing them is truly 'supereminent and sublime.' I am, of course, far from saying that this is all that there is to the principle of analogical predication as developed in Christian theology—what it further involves will appear in a later context[1]—I wish merely to emphasize its character as involving symbolization of the infinite, and the genetic relation of this principle to the symbolization present in all forms of the religious consciousness.

D

The moulding of the intuition, together with the processes of distortion characteristic of the mythopoeic imagination, are present unconsciously in the intuition itself and thus stand out in marked contrast with the more sophisticated symbols and allegories which appear in the later artistic creations of the religious consciousness. We may, indeed, speak of 'an immanental law of the mythopoeic imagination.'

Immanent in the mythical consciousness itself is the 'idea of the infinite' of the tremendous mystery of the infinitely sacred or holy—call it what you will—working in and moulding the intuition. It may work below the human, creating the fantastic shapes, both animal and human, of which Hegel spoke, or it may work beyond the human, creating the ideal shapes of the

[1] Chapter vii, pp. 226 ff.

more developed ethical religions. This idea of the infinite, or later of perfection, is not, however, merely a predicate of an already given God-idea, it is the essence of the God-idea itself. It is, so to speak, the kernel about which the pictures and symbols crystallize. In other words, it is, if we use the terms with care, the very essence or quality of deity, or, as the theologians say, the 'formal principle of Deity' itself.

The point I am making is of great importance and will become increasingly significant as our understanding of religion proceeds. It is the doctrine of an 'original intuition of the Divine,' of a religious *a priori*, a doctrine equally significant for the phenomenology of religion and for the problem of religious knowledge. When the philosopher says, I have in my mind the idea of the infinite, of a being than whom a greater cannot be conceived, doubtless the images in which the Absolute shines out in consciousness have their origin in the most lowly processes of the mythopoeic imagination, but the 'idea' itself which these images symbolize is another matter. How he has it in his mind, and just what the idea is, is a problem for later consideration. Some original intuition of the Divine is, however, as we shall attempt to show, a necessary part of any tenable theory of religious knowledge.[1]

VI

The Mythical Element in Religion. Allegorical or Symbolic Interpretation

A

Recognition of the mythical element in religion is always presupposed, if not explicitly asserted, in all philosophies of religion. Every theology distinguishes some part, however small, of its material as mythical in this critical sense. Among the 'stories' which form the material of exegesis there are always some of this character. This was true of the religious philosophers prior to the Christian era, of the theologians and philosophers of classical Christian thought itself, and of all modern theologians whether orthodox or liberal, theistic or humanistic. Indeed it might almost be said that it is precisely those theologians who make most of the Word of God, as contrasted with the word of man, among

[1] Chapter ix, pp. 289 ff.

others, the so-called Barthians—who recognize most explicitly the mythical and symbolic character of stories such as those of the creation and of the fall. We have here to do, as they would say, with no ordinary matter of history but rather with what may be called *Urgeschichte*—a timeless story which has to do with the original phenomena of the spiritual life. It follows, therefore, that some philosophy of myth is a necessary part of all philosophical theology and some theory of the interpretation of the myth a part of any philosophy of religion.

The notion of allegorical or symbolic interpretation has, from the beginning, been an essential part of Christian philosophy. When Abelard spoke of allegorical as opposed to literal interpretation, he was but expressing a constant element in the Christian tradition. Höffding points out how it was a great relief to Augustine in his youth when he was told that the corporeal expressions used of God in the Bible might be understood metaphorically and not literally, and how later in life he had no scruples in stretching allegorical interpretation as far as it would go whenever he found something in the teachings of the Church from which he would otherwise derive no spiritual sort of value. Within the Church also he did not hesitate to distinguish between a more spiritual understanding (*serena intelligentia veritatis*) and a more literal one (*fides simplex parvulorum*).[1] The simple faith of the little children was never annulled by this more serene insight of the intelligence—indeed it was always an essential part of that insight to include an understanding of the simpler faith—but that did not in the least affect the truth that, as in Abelard's words, there is a *melior ascensus*, so, in general, there is a better way of interpretation.

I have used the terms allegorical and symbolic interchangeably, and in a sense this use is justified, as our examination of the myth as the material of religious symbolism has shown. Some writers, however, as for instance Croce, have distinguished between the notion of the symbol and that of allegory. 'The symbol is a synonym for the intuition itself'—in our terms not separable from the intuition—whereas 'allegory is the exposition of an abstract concept, art or religion aping science.'[2] That this

---

[1] *The Philosophy of Religion*, pp. 183-4. See also on this aspect of mysticism, Chapter xiii, pp. 452 ff.
[2] B. Croce, *Aesthetic*, English translation, p. 34.

distinction has a certain force we need not deny. Allegory, especially in its later and more sophisticated forms, does indeed often become an exposition of abstract concepts in intuitive language —but this is not its primary character. There is, doubtless, a relative distinction between symbol and allegory but the difference is found elsewhere. For the myth is also synonymous with the intuition itself—mythical construction works directly in the intuition itself—and, in so far as the myth is taken as an allegory, its interpretation retains its relation to the primary intuition.

The question of the nature of allegory and of its relation to symbol is so important as to merit further consideration. In discussions such as that of Croce two aspects of allegory are, I believe, not sufficiently distinguished. I shall call them allegorical presentation and allegorical interpretation. In the case of the former the allegory is, indeed, as Croce says, 'the exposition of an abstract concept.' The moralities of the middle ages are characterized by the exposition of the abstract virtues in intuitive form; the more modern and Protestant morality, *Pilgrim's Progress*, is an exposition of the abstract theological categories of sin, salvation and grace in intuitive form. But allegorical interpretation moves in the opposite direction. It starts with the mythical intuition and expands or interprets the symbol in ideal or spiritual terms. Allegory has been defined as extended symbolism and as such we may view it in the present context.

Allegorical or symbolic interpretation is one stage in the fourfold method of interpretation which became classical in Christian theology. It had reference primarily to the 'moral' truth of the Bible stories and their application to humanity as a whole. This 'translation' of the language of religion into the idiom of moral theology has been a constant character both of the preaching and teaching of the Christian Church; and was viewed as a necessary step to a still higher stage of interpretation called the anagogic, the leading of the mind to things above, from the seen to the unseen, from the temporal to the eternal. But this was only one aspect of this allegorical mode of interpretation. The sacred cosmologies and eschatologies, these 'stories' of first and last things, are also symbolic, symbols not only of the truths of human life, but of that larger life of the cosmos without which human life is unintelligible. The great cosmic myths, therefore, when thus understood and interpreted, provide the categories which constitute the idiom of metaphysics.

Symbolic interpretation, in this broader sense, is therefore present in all developed religions, and we may probably say that precisely such interpretation is itself a criterion of development. In India, some seven or eight centuries before the Christian era, the mythical ideas of the gods and their activities were superseded for wide circles of people by the idea of God as an immaterial reality behind the manifold appearances of the world. Before Christianity came into the world it had come to be a familiar doctrine among the Jews that all this kind of language was figurative, poetic metaphor. Among the Greeks and Romans all the chief schools of thought came finally to recognize the allegorical character of the old theology. Thus the Christian thinker found such symbolic interpretation of the mythical language of religion completely established and took it up into Christianity as a principle of theology. Philosophical theology has, accordingly, from the very beginning, included in its apologetics an *apologia* for the mythical element in religion. It seeks to explain to the learned the *fides simplex parvulorum*, but it seeks also, in so far as it is possible, to help the simple to understand the more serene *intelligentia veritatis* of the learned. The main problem of the philosophy of religion still is, as it has always been, properly to understand and to evaluate these two aspects of religion—to find sound words in which to express the essential oneness of these two aspects of religious truth.

The significance of this principle of interpretation may be further illuminated if we make use of von Hügel's expression, 'the thing element in religion.' The language of religion, like any other language, is primarily a language of things rather than of ideas, essences and of what men call the 'spirit.' Now, as von Hügel rightly sees, nothing is more certain than that we must admit this element in religion, just as 'we must admit the obtrusive element and power of things somewhere in our lives. If we do not admit it as a means it will grip us as our end.'[1] It is only when this language of things is recognized as a means of communication of spiritual realities which transcend such expression that we shall escape the grip of these things on our soul. Either we shall have a literalism which eventuates in the soul-

[1] *The Mystical Element in Religion*, Volume II, p. 375.

destroying absurdities of fundamentalism or we shall have a liberalism which generates an equally soul-destroying fictionalism, one which ends in excluding all religious language as meaningless. It is between the Scylla and Charibdis of this dilemma that religion always has and, in so far as one can see, always must pursue its dangerous way.

VII

The Relation of Myth to Religion: 'The Indispensable Myth.'
The 'Truth' of Myth

A

We can now see why the thoughtful theologian should protest against the 'identification of myth with invention, with the illusions of primitive mentality, and with anything in fact as opposed to reality.' Why he should also hold that 'behind the myth are concealed the greatest realities, the original phenomena of the spiritual life.' To take any other standpoint is greatly to misunderstand both the nature of myth itself and also the very spiritual realities which it is the function of the language of religion to express.

It is clearly impossible to make any study of religion without determining its relation to myth and cult. The further we follow the content of the religious consciousness to its beginnings the more it is found impossible to separate it from the mythical consciousness. If one does attempt to separate the 'intuitions of faith' from the mythical language and categories in which they are expressed, one has no longer religion in its actual historical and objective nature, but merely a shadow picture and an empty abstraction. Nevertheless—and this is the point often overlooked —despite this inseparable interweaving of the content of myth and religion, they are far from being identical. Neither in form nor in spirit are they the same.

Religion is no more mere myth than it is mere poetry. It is indeed the peculiar character of the religious consciousness that it recognizes this difference. The religious consciousness shows itself precisely in this changed attitude towards the mythical picture of the world. It cannot do without this world, for it is in the mythical consciousness that the immediate intuition of the meaningfulness of the world is first given. Nor can the religious consciousness express its deepest insights without using the language of myth and employing the mythical categories, as all times and all peoples have discovered. But while they have discovered this they have also discovered something else—namely that the myth has acquired a new meaning and function; it has become symbolic. Religion makes use of sensuous pictures and signs but at the same time knows them to be such.

Every religion, in the historical sense, comes to a point in its development where this distinction must finally be made. Until it does so it cannot be called religion in the phenomenological sense. This is the reason that the essence of religion can be found only in the higher forms of religion; it is the reason also that symbolism as a theological principle becomes an indispensable element in all developed theology. In so far as the general question of the relation of religion to myth is concerned it is sufficient to emphasize the fact that while the myth is indispensable to the religious consciousness it is not identical with it. Let us then turn to a consideration of this notion of the 'indispensable myth.'

B

Ever since Forberg and Lange there has grown up the notion of the indispensable myth, and this principle has finally been established as fundamental in the philosophy of religion.

In the first place, it is indispensable psychologically. Comparative religion has made it clear that the basal myths—both of nature and of man, of creation and salvation, are practically omnipresent in all religions. Even the theological dogmas of the Christian religion—the ideas of a Triune Godhead, of an Incarnate Saviour, of the Virgin Birth, of the Sacraments and of the Communion of the Saints have their pagan prototypes. The modern study of primitive religion shows that every one of these beliefs is or has been held in some part of the pagan world quite independently of Christian influence. When after the shock of the first discovery of these prototypes the Christian scholar explained them as 'God-implanted ideas' he was merely expressing in his theological language the principle of the indispensability of the myth.

But the principle of indispensability has a deeper foundation than this. It is, as we have seen, wholly impossible to separate religion from myth, for if we attempt to do so we have left merely a shadow picture and an empty abstraction. Myth is indispensable for the reason that it is only from the language of myth that the primary symbols can be formed and only in such language that its deepest insights can be expressed. As it is in dramatic language alone that the *vis religiosa* can find expression, so it is only in the mythical categories, connected with that language, that the original phenomena of the spiritual life can be expressed. We may go even further than this and say that it is only in such language and such categories that any meaningful account of nature can be given—of nature at least in so far as it is the background of human life and drama. Plato did not fall back upon this language as an imperfect pre-scientific form, to give way ultimately to mathematical symbols and forms of expression. It represented rather a clear recognition on his part of the essential limitations of this later language and of its inability to express the world of living and becoming.

This interpretation of the notion of the indispensable myth must obviously be clearly distinguished from that other interpretation to which reference has already been made. This other view, it will be recalled, rests upon a distinction between pre-scientific, and therefore transitory, myth, and the myth which is permanent and therefore identical with religion. The former has yielded and must continue to yield before the concepts and explanations of science; the latter does not thus yield because it expresses truths which the language and symbolic form of science cannot express. Religion is identified with this permanent myth. Religion is not myth, whether transitory or permanent. The religious consciousness, to be religious, must distinguish itself fundamentally from the mythical. There is all the difference in the world between saying that religion is myth, however permanent, and saying that it is the indispensable symbol for the expression of non-mythical truth. If this difference is not wholly clear, it will become so, I think, when we come to the interpretation of the pronouncements of religion—the historical, cosmological and metaphysical propositions which constitute the basis of religion.[1]

[1] Chapter viii.

C

This thesis of the indispensable myth raises one of the most fundamental, as it is one of the most difficult problems of the philosophy of religion, namely, that of the 'truth of myth,' for nothing can be indispensable which is not in some sense true. No critical philosophy of myth can escape some formulation of the nature of this truth.

To the uncritical the very notion itself is repugnant. How, it may be asked, perhaps indignantly, can we express truth in terms of that which we know to be untrue? How can the religious consciousness, when once the distinction between religion and myth is clearly seen, continue to use the mythical language, no longer literally true, as true expression of its deeper realities? Can it do so without self-stultification? How can the scientific or philosophical consciousness, when once the mythical images and categories have been transcended, continue to speak of the 'truth' of these products of primitive mentality without doing violence to all our hard-won 'scientific' criteria of truth and reality?

But surely it must be clear by now that this is a wholly false statement of the situation. We cannot, of course, express the 'truth' in terms which we know to be wholly untrue, but we can express it in terms that we know are not literally true—and what is more, we are constantly doing so in science no less than in art and religion. The essential character of the symbol is that it contains both truth and fiction. If it were wholly fiction it would not be a symbol for it would stand for nothing. If it were wholly true it would not be a symbol but a literal representation. We may use that which is not literally true for the expression of deeper truths and 'more real values'—and indeed we cannot avoid doing so, even in science. It is therefore commonly said that the myth is false if taken literally, but true if taken symbolically, or, as Gilbert Chesterton liked to put it, 'not literally true, of course, but only really true.'

The question of the truth of myth can obviously not be answered in any satisfactory form until we have examined the entire question of the nature of symbol and symbolic truth— the myth being the material of religious symbolism. This is the task of a later chapter but this much can be said as the outcome of the present discussion. The element of truth in myth must be 'really true,' not truth put in quotation marks as is commonly the practice. The assumption underlying this way of speaking is, of course, that it is science alone which gives us literal or real truth and that therefore the criteria of truth developed by science are the only criteria. Both of these assumptions of an uncritical philosophy of science we shall find to be untrue. Science itself is not literal representation but a symbolic form, constructed for a specific purpose and which has validity or truth only with reference to that purpose.[1] There are other purposes, and therefore other activities, of the human spirit, and for the realization of these other forms of representation other symbolic forms are necessary, including even that original symbolism which the myth alone can provide.

It is customary for those who uphold in one form or another the notion of the truth of myth to comment upon the famous saying of Plato on this point, and with some such comment this chapter may be appropriately brought to a close. I do not say, writes Plato, speaking of the myth of the Demiurge, that this is exactly true, but something like this must be true. A complete *adaequatio intellectus et rei*—and from the beginning some correspondence between idea and thing has been essential to the notion of truth—no one would ascribe to the myth whether we find it in religion or science; but something like it must be true. What, then, is it in the myth which compels us to say that something like it *must* be true and what is this something which is like the myth?

To the first of these questions our answer is in principle already given. It is the dramatic character of the language of myth, by which the living and the becoming alone can be expressed, which compels us to say that any language by which reality could be ultimately expressed must have this character, that in reality itself there is something corresponding to the myth. To the second question, however, the answer is not so easy. In saying that in reality there is something like the myth we have, to be sure, said that this something is itself dramatic, otherwise the language of myth would not represent or express it, but this does not take us very far. In fact, it takes us only so far as to land us in serious difficulties. Even if the answer is not

[1] Chapter x, pp. 344 ff.

wholly circular, surely this dramatic element in reality is like the dramatic language of the myth only in certain respects. True, men speak of the drama of creation, and the stories of creation are of a highly dramatic character; they also speak of the drama of salvation and of the consummation of all things, and the stories in which these notions are expressed are also of a highly dramatic character; but they too are recognized as symbolic of something which the stories themselves are only partly like. What then is this something?

No direct answer to this question can, I believe, be given. If it could, Plato would no longer use the myth and as a philosopher, he would see in the language and symbolism of the myth merely temporary surrogates for that which could be better expressed in the abstract language of science and philosophy. True, Plato recognized that the basal form of the myth, the 'echte Mythus', is time, and time was 'the moving image of eternity,' but this is poetry and does not constitute a direct answer. Only an indirect answer is, I believe, possible. The dramatic language of religion can, I believe, be translated into the idiom of philosophy without losing the *vis religiosa*. This language of philosophy cannot, perhaps, say just what the reality is that the myth is like, but it can interpret the language in terms of higher generality and thus enable us to understand what it really says. This is, I believe, the path which theology in any developed religion has taken, and indeed must take. It is moreover that which Christian theology, both dogmatic and rational, has pre-eminently done. How it has done so the following chapter, entitled 'Language and Logic in Theology,' will, I hope, make quite clear.

Chapter IV

Language and Logic in Theology: The Critique of Dogmatic Theology

I — A

THE PRIMARY forms of the language of religion are the lyrical and the dramatic. It is impossible to express the religious consciousness directly except in the form of prayer and praise. He who can neither pray nor sing is not only religiously inarticulate, but finds himself inhibited at the very sources of religious experience. There is, however, a more indirect form, the dramatic. The language of the great myths, whether cosmic or heroic, is always dramatic in the sense defined. Indeed the drama itself, in its narrower sense, is historically a product of the myth, the play in its primitive form being a representation of divine acts, in connection with the worship of the gods whose life and acts are celebrated. Thus all religious cult is primarily dramatic in character. It 'celebrates' and 'shows forth,' in imagery and symbol, the mighty works of gods and men.

In a sense the dramatic expression of the religious consciousness is more fundamental than the lyrical and is presupposed by it. The gods are praised, not only for what they are but for what they have done—for their wonderful works for the children of men. It is for these reasons that the historical element in religion is fundamental and the myth provides the indispensable material for the symbolic expression of this element. As religion is not myth, whether permanent or transitory, so theology is not 'myth rationalized,' as is sometimes said. It merely makes use of the language of the myth as the necessary symbolic form in which its reasons are expressed.

The relation of the language of religion to that of theology has already been stated in a preliminary way. The religious lyric, hymn, psalm or ode, invokes objects, but it also ascribes predicates and qualities to these objects. Religious myth and drama picture and, in developed religions, 'symbolize' the activities of these objects, but they also assert, either explicitly or implicitly, certain relations of the divine object or objects to the world and to human life. It is these assertions, together with the development of their implications and relations, the one to the other, that constitute theology proper. When this character of theological language is properly understood, it is seen immediately that it is, and indeed can be, but an extension, *in the first instance at least*, of the dramatic mode of expression characteristic of religious experience itself. If it should lose the *vis poetica*, it would lose the *vis religiosa* also.

Speaking of the language of theology, an English theologian writes as follows: 'The language of religion in its beginnings is poetic, symbolic and pictorial. It registers primitive reaction to experience in crude mythological images. With the stage of reflective thought more general concepts appear constructed from wider generalizations of experience, individual, social, and historical, moral and rational. Yet *these wider concepts for the most part retain traces of earlier mythological forms and imagery.* [Italics mine.] A third stage is reached in which scientific observation and rational reflexion develop an abstract terminology of their own which has a different genealogical descent from that of religious terminology proper.'[1] No one would, I suppose, dispute the truth of this account of the first two stages —certainly it corresponds in principle with our own account— but the description of the third stage in the development of theological language, with its 'abstract terminology,' leaves room for doubt.

This terminology, it is said, has a different genealogical descent from that of religious terminology proper. This is in part true, but only in part, as we shall presently see. Christian theology was, indeed, made possible only by the translation of the language of religion into the metaphysical idiom of Greek philosophy, but there is the further question of the nature and origin of this idiom. It is true that it came in part from Greek 'science,' more particularly the mathematical, but the main elements in this terminology consisted in the translation of the language of Greek religion into terms of greater generality and thus the metaphysical idiom itself remained dramatic in character. It was solely because of this that the Christian religion found it possible to translate the language of its own experience

[1] L. S. Thornton, *The Incarnate Lord*, p. 12.

into the language of a philosophical theology which should retain the *vis religiosa*.

Theology is discourse about God. If we are to talk about God at all it must be in language appropriate to the universe of discourse in which our conversation takes place. The ancient dictum that there is no thought without language is essentially and profoundly true—and any denial rests upon misunderstandings and equivocations—but the truth of this dictum implies a further truth, namely, that it is only in language appropriate to our discourse that any significant thought can be carried on. If it be a mark of intelligence to understand to what things mathematics may and may not be applied, this is but one aspect of a more general philosophic truth—that the only way to determine being or reality at all is in those forms or categories in which meaningful statements about it are possible.

B

Theological thinking includes two aspects or phases which we may describe as thinking about God and thinking from man and nature to God. These correspond to the well-recognized divisions of dogmatic and natural theology. Thinking about God—His nature and His acts—takes place within a universe of discourse already determined by the presupposition of the existence of God and belief in Him. This universe may be conceived as established by revelation, but its prior determination is already presupposed. Thinking to God, on the other hand, always proceeds from man and nature either logically, from some *a priori* intuition, or empirically, from the things that are seen to the things that are unseen. One of the main problems of philosophical theology has revolved about the relation of these two theologies.

In the earlier centuries of Christian thought the two were not clearly distinguished. Neither St. Augustine nor St. Anselm found it necessary to make the sharp division which later reflection seemed to demand, and Anselm at least has often been chided for his 'neglect.' It was only later that this distinction became, so to speak, the working theory of Christian theology and philosophy. The doctrine that 'the truth of the intelligible things of God is twofold, one to which the inquiry of reason can attain, the other which surpasses the whole range of human

reason,' enunciated by St. Thomas,[1] became the authoritative
position of classical Christian theology. Theology has insisted
upon this difference but it has also always maintained that the
two ways are intimately connected. Thought is integral and
indivisible as is the 'truth' towards which it is directed. There
must therefore be some 'organic' relation between what man
can find out about God through his reason, and what only God
can make known to him, otherwise there are 'two Gods,' the
deus vivus of revelation and the *deus philosophorum* of reason. On
the other hand, distinctions between the two kinds of truth are
equally necessary, otherwise one or the other of these two notions
of God must be eliminated, to the ultimate impoverishment if
not actual stultification of all religious thought and discourse.

The problem is really more difficult than appears at first
sight. How—so runs a question which is inevitably asked—
if philosophy, of which natural or rational theology is a part, is
simply the work of human reason, can there be a specifically
Christian theism? How account for the difference between the
natural theology of an Aristotle and an Aquinas? There is one
answer to the question which, while appearing to be an answer,
is on reflection little more than verbal and formal. Abstractly,
we are told, they are indeed autonomous, but concretely they
are not. While in principle there is a certain limited knowledge of God accessible to the human reason alone, actually in
practice it is only in the light of revelation that human reason
can function adequately and obtain, even within its own
limits, a knowledge of God free from error. Man's natural
powers, so we are told, are themselves so weakened by sin that
even his natural knowledge of God is clouded and distorted.
Grace not only supplies perfections which transcend those
possible to nature, but also restores nature to its proper integrity. But surely this is to give away the entire case for natural
theology, for it is the entire point of such a theology that the
existence and nature of God is known—up to a point at least—
by pure reason alone; and if this is so, must it not be the
natural light of reason given to every man, not a reason which,

[1] I *Cont. Gent.* Another formulation is found in the *Summa Theol.* (I, q. 1, art. 1):
'It was necessary for man's salvation that there should be knowledge revealed by
God, besides philosophical science built up by human reason . . . because man is
directed to God as to an end which surpasses the grasp of his reason.'

even if thus 'restored,' has been changed by Grace from its natural character into something else? One can not follow the argument of reason wherever it may lead and at the same time insist upon knowing beforehand where the argument will come out.

All this does not mean that we deny either the fundamental organic relation between the two theologies or their relative independence. It simply means that we must state both aspects of the relation in a different way. This is possible, however, only after we have studied the language of theology in both its dogmatic and rational form. It is the language of dogmatic theology or divinity, and with it the type of thinking involved in that language, which constitutes the first problem of this chapter.

II

Theological Thinking as Dramatic. Fides Quaerens Intellectum.
The Dramatic and the Axiological

A

As illustrations of the language of theology we have already suggested the *Cur Deus Homo* and the *Proslogium* of St. Anselm. In the first faith inquires of the intellect why God should have become man; in the second it inquires whether there is any God to become man. Let us begin with the answer to the first question and by an analysis of the argument seek to understand its character and its form.

The object of the *Cur Deus Homo* is to search for the reasons of the Incarnation. That God did become man is, for Anselm, a fact of the religious order—a dogma accepted on faith. The problem is to understand the fact. It is, as he says, *fides quaerens intellectum*, and it is the reason alone that can give understanding.

The Incarnation, according to St. Anselm, necessarily follows from the need of redemption. Sin is an offence against the majesty of God. In spite of his goodness, God cannot pardon sin without compounding with honour and justice. On the other hand, he cannot revenge himself on man for his offended honour; for sin is an offence of infinite degree, and therefore demands infinite satisfaction; which means that he must either destroy humanity or inflict upon it the eternal punishments of hell. Now in either case, the goal of creation, the happiness of his creatures, would be missed and the honour of the creator compromised. There is but one way for God to escape this dilemma without affecting his honour and that is to arrange for some kind of satisfaction. He must have infinite satisfaction because the offence is immeasurable. Now in so far as man is a finite being and incapable of satisfying divine justice in an infinite measure, the infinite being himself must take the matter in charge; he must have recourse to substitution. Hence the necessity of the Incarnation. God becomes man in Christ; Christ suffers and dies in our stead; thus he acquires an infinite merit and the right to an equivalent recompense. But since the world belongs to the Creator and nothing can be added to its treasures, the recompense which by right belongs to Christ falls to the lot of the human race in which He is incorporated: humanity is pardoned, forgiven and saved.

'Liberal theology' has largely repudiated this particular way of thinking. It is said to be too legalistic and to bear the stamp of the spirit of chivalry and feudal customs which inspired and conditioned it. With these aspects of the argument we are not here concerned—although I am inclined to believe that it contains an abiding element of truth which will survive the softness of any temporary sentimentalism. Our problem is rather the more general one of the type of argument involved and of the kind of 'reasons' it embodies. Any theory of the Atonement—any answer to the question, why God became man, would I think, involve reasoning of this same general type. In this universe of discourse only such language is appropriate, for here reasons can be only of this character. Moreover, the element of 'necessity' in the argument is 'moral' or, as we shall express it more generally, axiological. Granted that there is a God, and that his character is such as described, then the Incarnation follows necessarily. Between such attributes as honour, justice and equity, when attributed to Deity, and the forms of action which they entail, there subsist relations of such a character that a revelation of God in man necessarily follows. But the fact that the thinking here is of necessity axiological does not exclude the fact that it is also logical. The sheer logic of Anselm's *Cur Deus Homo* is as much a part of it as is the logic of the *Proslogium*. In both, as we shall see, and indeed in theological argument wherever found, whether in dogmatic or rational theology, the same problem of the relation of the logical to the axiological is fundamental.

B

Illustrations of this type of thinking could be taken from all forms of religion which have developed far enough to have a theology. If this were a study of comparative theologies, it would be pre-eminently desirable to take them from Jewish, Mohammedan or Hindu sources also. It is, however, with the general problems of the philosophy of religion as defined that we are concerned and here European theology will prove more helpful.

The question of St. Anselm, why God became man, is paralleled by questions of a similar character: Why did God create the world? and Why did He create it as it is? and the answers all display the same kind of thinking. An illustration from Averroes is of special significance for it brings out clearly the principles of axiological thinking. Averroes writes, 'Why did God create more than one sort of vegetative and animal souls? The reason is that the existence of most of these species rests upon the principle of perfection (or completeness). Some animals and plants can be seen to exist only for the sake of man, or of one another; but of others this cannot be granted, e.g., of the wild animals which are harmful to men.' (*Metaphysics*, tr. Horten, p. 200.)[1] That God did create such a variety of things is the *fact* with which the argument starts, a fact which may be known either by revelation or inference. To the question Why? the answer is, and indeed can only be, in terms of ends and values, for only such reasons can have any meaning here. Anthropomorphic language may be translated into axiological terms of a more general character—'the principle of perfection or completeness'—but the thinking itself never loses its dramatic and axiological character.

Why did God become man? Why did he create the world of

---

[1] An important source book for the study of the language of theology is *The Great Chain of Being*, by Arthur O. Lovejoy, Harvard University Press, 1936. This and several other illustrations are taken from this work. Page references will be made in the appropriate places. The present quotation is found on p. 82.

creatures with all their manifold variety and apparent purpose-lessness? But we may also ask, 'Why did God—the very essence of perfection and completeness (including self-sufficiency)—*create at all?*' The problem of creation itself exercised the minds of the theologians from the beginning. It is most interesting and enlightening to see how St. Thomas answered it. His answer is in principle that God *must* create—not to be sure, by any external compulsion, but by an axiological necessity that springs out of his very nature as the principle of the Good. In speaking of the love of God, St. Thomas writes: 'Love which works good to all things, pre-existing overflowingly in the Good . . . moved itself to creation, as befits the superabundance by which all things are generated. . . . The Good by being extends its goodness to all things. For as our sun, not by choosing or taking thought, but by merely being, enlightens all things, so the Good . . . by its mere existence sends forth upon all things the beams of its Goodness.'[1] Here it is said, 'the phraseology of the primitive Christian conception of a loving Father in Heaven has been translated into the Platonic idiom.' In a sense this is true, and of the nature of such translation we shall have more to say presently: here the point is that, although it is a translation, the original dramatic and axiological character of the primitive phraseology is retained in the translation. So far as our present problem is concerned, once the identification of God with the Good is made, creation necessarily follows. For it is the nature of the Good, by *merely being*, to extend its goodness to all things.

C

This way of thinking, and the 'translation' which it involves, is, I think, implicit in all classical theology, and, indeed, in traditional European philosophy as well, for which the primacy of value is the cardinal principle. It is native to the entire Christian tradition. But it was equally the natural idiom of the entire rationalistic movement of the seventeenth and eighteenth centuries. From this period I will choose only one figure, but that an important one, namely, the philosopher Leibniz, who, it is well known, was as much at home in theological as in mathematical reasoning and to whom it was wholly natural to name the name of God.

[1] A. O. Lovejoy, *op. cit.*, p. 68. The passage is found in *De div. nom.*, IV, 10.

The work of Leibniz most typical in this respect is his famous Theodicy. This book, written in French, has the title *Essais de Théodicée sur la Bonté de Dieu, la Liberté de l'Homme et l'Origine du Mal* (1710). The chief topic is again the goodness of God and what necessarily follows from that goodness. One passage will indicate both the nature of the presuppositions and the way of thinking in this famous book.

'If the will of God did not have as a rule the principle of the best, it would either tend towards evil, which would be worst of all, or else it would be in some fashion indifferent to good and evil and guided by chance. But a will which always allowed itself to act by chance would scarcely be of more value for the government of the universe than a fortuitous concourse of atoms, with no God at all. And even if God should abandon himself to chance only in some cases and some respects . . . he would not deserve to be wholly trusted; he would act without reason in those cases, and the government of the universe would be like certain games, half a matter of chance, half a matter of reason.'[1]

Commenting on this passage Lovejoy tells us that 'Leibniz was continuing the tradition of Platonic rationalism in theology.' This is doubtless true, but the significant point is that Leibniz is fully conscious of the axiological character of the argument. For him the sufficient reason of anything must always have reference to ends and values. Any explanation that really makes the world intelligible, in an ultimate sense must be of this character. This view is implicit in all Leibniz's writings but it receives explicit recognition in two of his most characteristic works.

In the *Principles of Nature and of Grace Founded on Reason*, he tells us, 'Thus far we have spoken as pure *physicists*; now we must rise to *metaphysics*, making use of the *great principle,* usually little employed, which affirms that nothing takes place *without sufficient reason*, that is to say, that nothing happens without its being possible for one who should know things sufficiently to give a reason which is sufficient to determine why things are so and not otherwise.' When, however, we examine this principle as understood by Leibniz we find it to be fundamentally axiological in character—the principle of perfection. This is even clearer in

[1] *Op. cit.*, p. 167.

his famous essay *On the Ultimate Origination of Things.* Here he makes it quite clear, not only that the issue of a 'first cause' is wholly independent of time and temporal causality, but that God's causality is expressible only in axiological terms.[1]

The significance of Leibniz in this connection cannot be exaggerated. Not only does he recognize explicitly that all intrinsic intelligibility is axiological in character, but that the theistic argument itself is necessarily of this type—a point of great importance for our later interpretation of that argument. Here our only point is that for him 'sufficient reason' or intelligibility always implies 'considerations of value.'

III

Theology and Dialectic. The Logical and the Axiological

A

An examination of these typical illustrations discloses elements common to them all. In the first place, they are all dramatic, in the sense that in answering the question why, the answer is always in terms of motives or reasons (not causes) which are humanly understandable or intelligible. In the second place, the thinking is always finalistic, in the sense that the premise of the argument is always in terms of the goal of creation and the purpose of the Creator. In Leibniz's terms, which, as we have seen, are typical of the axiological way of thinking, 'the will of God has as a rule the principle of the best.' Theological thinking is necessarily finalistic in this sense for the reason that all ultimate reasons, all intrinsic intelligibility, can be expressed only 'in terms of aim at value.' The relation of this axiological

---

[1] 'Even by supposing the eternity of the world,' Leibniz holds, 'we cannot escape the ultimate extra-mundane reason of things, that is to say, God. For in eternal things, even if there be no cause, there must be a reason, which for permanent things is necessity itself, or essence. But for the series of changing things, if it be supposed that they succeed one another from all eternity, this reason is the prevailing of inclinations which consist not in necessitating reasons, of an absolute metaphysical necessity the opposite of which involves a contradiction, but in inclining reasons. These inclining reasons are the superiority of the good over the bad in things that come to pass. The balance or preponderance inclines the will of God, without absolutely necessitating it, to create these contingent things.'

necessity to logical necessity thus becomes a basal problem of all theology.

The fundamental character of this problem can be seen from the fact that it is precisely at this point that the most devastating form of the dilemma of religion appeared in Christian thought and has continued throughout its entire history. Logic or dialectic is the very heart of Christian theology, as the preceding illustrations abundantly show. On the other hand, this same dialectic seems to generate contradictions and antimonies which appear to make of the dogmas of religion something illogical and unintelligible. This dilemma appears, of course, in one form or another, in all religions which have reached the stage of a theology, but in Christianity and for the western world it found clearest expression in the continuous opposition of the *deus vivus* to the *deus philosophorum*. The ancient battle of Lactantius against the God of the philosophers has been constantly revived—in the battle of Duns Scotus for the 'God of willing' as opposed to the 'God of being,' in the battle of Luther for the living God of the Scriptures against the God of the scholastics, and in the battle of Kierkegaard and his congeners against all dialectical theology. The dialectical element in theology seemed to the believer to threaten the 'integral' character of faith and led to a violent reaction against all dialectic in religion which continues with unabated virulence to the present day. The relation of the logical to the axiological thus becomes the fundamental problem of theology, whether dogmatic or rational, and constitutes a necessary prolegomenon, not only to all theology, but to all philosophy of religion.

B

All thinking, to be thinking at all, presupposes logic. Logical form is so woven into all our speech that it is impossible to utter a phrase, much less to form a sentence, without throwing it into logical form. Logic is not only the mould of thought but, in an important sense, a condition of all intelligible expression. As such, all thinking, to be thinking at all, involves the relation of ground and consequence or the logical principle of implication. It is axiological when the principle of implication involved, the 'following from,' is, as we have seen in preceding illustrations, determined by the principle of the Good or value. In this sense all theology is 'value theology'—not only the thinking carried on in the sphere of Divinity, or dogmatic theology, with which we are primarily concerned in this chapter, but also in natural or rational theology which will engage our attention later. What then, so our problem runs, is the 'necessity involved in those cases in which the 'following from' is determined by the 'principle of the Good,' and what is its relation to logical necessity?

In the first place we must distinguish between formal and material implication. Formal implication is independent of the material of thought, for it is woven into all our speech. It can apply equally well to men, geometrical figures, to gods, demons, unicorns or what not. It is indeed sometimes said that logic can no more admit a unicorn than can zoology, for logic is concerned with the real world, although with its more abstract features. This can, however, scarcely be true, for if it were logical form would not be woven into all our speech. Meaningful discourse is not concerned solely with the 'real world,' so called, the world of sense, but with things in heaven and earth not dreamed of in this philosophy.

Formal implication being involved in all thought and speech is, accordingly, involved also in all intelligible discourse about the good or value. It is therefore not with formal but with the type of material implication involved in axiological thinking that we are now concerned.

Material implication is traditionally divided into physical and moral—Aristotle speaks of the 'moral syllogism.' The nature of material implication in the sphere of physical reasoning is clear enough. The proposition that Socrates is a man and is not mortal is materially as well as formally false. It is materially false because of certain physical characters which make man and immortality incompatible. But there is also another type of material implication and it is from this, in the last analysis, that all axiological thinking gets its cogency. Socrates could not flee the hemlock without compounding with honour, and if he could not it was because there were other characters, in this case non-physical, which made flight and honour incompatible. Similarly, if, in the reasoning of Anselm, God cannot pardon sin without compounding with honour and justice, it is also by an analogous necessity arising out of the ultimate nature of the Good, with which in the argument God is identified. It is true that the necessity is only analogous, for what is said of the good,

conditioned by the way in which it appears in creatures, cannot
be said without limitations and reservations of that Sovereign
Goodness which is God. But it can be said, and it follows that
this necessity and its relation to the formal necessity which we
call logical, becomes the fundamental problem underlying all
theological thinking. It involves, moreover, as we shall see, the
problem of the relation of logic to language, for it is out of the
character of the language of theology and of its relation to the
language of religion that the entire problem arises.

C

Christian theology consists, we have seen, in the answer to
certain questions and the answers to these questions follow from
a primary identification of the idea of God with the idea of the
Good. Whatever is implicit in the notion of the Good is true of
God, for Goodness by its very being expresses itself necessarily
in certain ways. In this sense, and this alone, God is bound by
the Good, which is his very essence, and He cannot do that which
is contrary to his nature. The principles of identity and contradiction are thus fundamental in our thought about God and
theology, as discourse about God, must of necessity be dialectical.

But this raises, as we have seen, the problem of logic and theology in a crucial form. For if the theologian appeals to logic, so
also does the critic of all theology. 'Epicurus said: Either God
wishes to hinder evil and cannot, or He can and does not. If He
wishes to and cannot He is impotent; if He can and does not
wish to, He is perverse.' So Boutreaux quotes him with glee in
Anatole France's *The Gods Are Athirst*, and, turning to his friend
the monk, cries, 'If He does wish it and can, why does He not?
tell me that father.' To which the monk retorts, 'There is
nothing more contemptible than these difficulties you raise.
When I look upon the reasoning of infidels I seem to see ants
piling up a few blades of grass as a dam against the torrent that
sweeps down from the mountains . . . what you quote from
Epicurus is foolishness because God is arraigned in it as if he was
a man with a man's moral code. Well, sir, the sceptics from
Celsus down to Bayle and Voltaire have cajoled fools with such
like paradoxes.' *Sancta simplicitas!* the sophisticated logician will
say—and it was doubtless as such simplicity that it was meant
to be taken in Anatole France's kindly if ironical presentation—

and yet, with all its simplicity, it is, I am inclined to believe, the right answer to the sceptic. In any case, it is in principle the answer implicit in Christian theology from the beginning and given classical expression in Thomas Aquinas.

St. Thomas is in no doubt as to the applicability of logic to 'divine things,' but such application, he tells us, is dependent upon the 'unequivocal character of the divine predicates.' If, as he points out, 'nothing were said of God and of creatures except by pure equivocation, no argument could be made from creatures, whereas the contrary is evidenced by all who speak of divine things.'[1] Terms must be unequivocally predicable of God for 'the use of equivocal terms hinders the continuity of the argument.' Logic is then applicable to God, but the condition of any valid application is that what is predicated of God, His power, His goodness and justice, should be God's not man's. If we argue from man to God equivocally, we shall indeed arraign Him as though he were a man, and shall be landed in precisely those paradoxes which the believer finds so contemptible. The laws men call logical are indeed applicable to all things, including the divine, but it does not at all follow that our human application of them, conditioned always by the way thought appears in us creatures, is equally absolute.

I should not wish to improve upon this formulation of a master theologian, and yet a good deal of water has run under the bridges since this ancient formulation, and it is possible that we may find in modern thought certain glosses which may make this classical principle, as well as the answer to Epicurus which it implies, less difficult of acceptance than it has often appeared. It concerns the relation of language to logic, or of the concrete material of thought embodied in language, to the formal principles of all thought—a problem much in the foreground of present-day philosophy.

Logical form is, indeed, woven into all our speech, but it is equally true that the two are so interwoven that it is impossible to separate completely the logical form from the speech in which it is embedded. Logic, too, is conditioned, at least in its application, by the language with which it is bound up. One need not go so far as to say that logic is merely 'the rules developed for the manipulation of our language,' but we shall do well to

[1] See on this point, M. C. D'Arcy, *Thomas Aquinas: Selected Writings*, p. 151.

recognize that the application of logical rules is also conditioned by the way in which they appear in the experience and language of creatures. The principles of contradiction and excluded middle are doubtless applicable to all thought—about divine no less than human things—but the manner in which they thus function is not always fully understood.

It is commonly supposed that two propositions, simply as propositions abstracted from all discourse, contradict each other, and that by examining them simply as propositions one can determine whether they do or not. This current doctrine is, I believe, wholly false and rests upon a serious misunderstanding. One way of pointing out this misunderstanding is that of Collingwood. 'A proposition,' he tells us, 'always has reference to a question to which it is an answer. No two propositions can contradict each other unless they are answers to the same question. In other words, it is the 'question' which constitutes the 'supposition' of the universe of discourse in question.[1] Just as propositions have meaning only in the universe of discourse which gives them their meaning, so contradictions between such propositions have meaning only within the universe of discourse determined by the questions to which they are the answers. More technically stated, this misunderstanding arises from the false assumption that propositions are 'entities,' and have both meaning and subsistence wholly independent of discourse or context. Now a proposition is always a proposal and cannot be anything else without losing its character as a proposition. It has its 'existence' or subsistence only in discourse. To the question, Do propositions exist? the answer can be only *in some universe of discourse*. In order, therefore, that this relation of contradiction may arise between two propositions they must be in the same coherent system or universe of discourse and when abstracted from this system have no such relation to one another.[2]

These considerations we shall find of major importance throughout our discussions—not the least in connection with the relations of science and religion and the supposed contradictions between their pronouncements—[3] here we are

---

[1] R. G. Collingwood, *An Autobiography*, Oxford University Press, 1930.

[2] For a fuller discussion of this same issue see my *Language and Reality*, Chapter vi, 'Language and Logic', p. 269.

[3] Chapter xi, pp. 330 f.

concerned solely with their implications for theology and what it says about divine things. The questions to which theology or divinity seeks to give answers—about God, His nature and His acts—have meaning solely within a universe of discourse established by the supposition of God's existence and His identification with the Sovereign Good or the principle of perfection. How this presupposition is established—whether by intuition or demonstration, or by both—is here beside the mark. But granting the validity of this universe of discourse, in it the divine predicates are, as St. Thomas says, predicated unequivocally and, being so, logical argument about about them is possible. It is when men take them equivocally, as though the answers given to questions about the divine are such as would be given about the human, that God is arraigned as though he were a man. If they are taken equivocally, if we pass from the human to the divine without 'ontological sublimation' of the predicates, our pronouncements will inevitably develop contradictions, and we shall have all the consequences which the thoughtful theologian deplores.

We are frequently told that 'we are not to look for a special logic of religious thinking, that logic is logic wherever it occurs.' Doubtless there is a sense in which this is true—in the sense namely that the logical form woven into all our thought is the same wherever it occurs. But surely it is also true that this same logic, in so far as it is conditioned by the way language appears in creatures, is not applicable directly to divine things. 'The will to create a universe,' writes McTaggart, 'includes the law of contradiction. Could God create a man who was not a man?'[1] This Anatole France's monk would doubtless find contemptible. I do not think that it is, but is it not a rather foolish way of stating the fundamental truth of the ontological character of logic? One recoils from such a way of speaking not because logic is inapplicable to our thought about God but rather because one realizes that no system of human categories, bound up as they inevitably are with human language, can adequately describe the eternal being of God. It is this feeling which has led men of the deepest insight to insist upon what is called the metalogical in religion and theology. In the twelfth century the humanist John of Salisbury wrote a book called *Metalogicus*

[1] J. M. E. McTaggart, *Some Dogmas of Religion*, 203.

which, as Gilson wisely remarks, 'records an experience which may well be our own.' This experience had taught him 'the manifest conclusion that, while logic furthers other studies, it is by itself lifeless and barren, nor can it cause the mind to yield the fruit of philosophy except the same conceive from some other source.' What these sources are, is, of course, the fundamental question of any theory of knowledge, of religious no less than scientific. But whatever the source—and this is the problem of a later chapter[1]—the fact remains that the source of religious knowledge like that of all knowledge, is metalogical, and that logic has neither the right nor the capacity to pronounce on either the nature or validity of this source. The contrary assumption is, as we shall see, the source of much of the misunderstanding and scepticism of our time.

IV

God and The Good in the Greco-Christian Tradition.
A Modern Critique of the Great Tradition

A

In the preceding section we have become familiar with a type of thinking that is not only natural to the religious mind but inevitable if the mind is to think religiously at all—that is about God, His nature and His acts. The principle upon which this thinking proceeds, the 'principle of perfection,' as Leibniz calls it, was predetermined by the Greek philosophical tradition. The identification of God with the Good in Christian theology was made possible by the assumption, either explicit or implied, of the ultimate inseparability of the good or value and being. This is the major premise of all Greek thinking.

The primary source of the identification of God with the Good is of course Plato. The two sources are the *Republic* and the *Timaeus*. If we are to assume that the doctrine of the *Timaeus* is at all reconcilable with that of the *Republic*—to which it is presented as a kind of supplement—then the Idea of the Good of the Republic, the ground and source of all being, and the Creator who figures in the *Timaeus* are one and the same. The

[1] Chapter ix.

details of myth of the *Timaeus* and most of the characteristics and activities ascribed to the Demiurgus, cannot, of course, be taken literally—nor, indeed, have they ever been so taken by most of the followers of Plato, ancient or modern—but who can doubt that the strain in Plato's thought presented by this myth was for him an element which could not be excluded from his philosophy as a whole, that he felt that while it was not exactly true, something like it must be true?[1]

The interpreters of Plato, in both ancient and modern times, have endlessly disputed over the question whether the idea of the absolute Good was for him identical with the conception of God. Stated thus simply the question is, as Professor Lovejoy rightly says, meaningless, since the word 'God' is in the last degree ambiguous. But 'if it is taken as standing for what the Schoolmen called the *ens perfectissimum*, the summit of the hierarchy of being, the only completely satisfying object of contemplation and adoration, there can be little doubt that the idea of the Good was the God of Plato and there can be none that it became the God of Aristotle, and one of the elements or "aspects" of the God of most of the philosophical ideologies of the Middle Ages and of nearly all the modern Platonizing poets and philosophers.'[2] With all this I should agree up to a point, but only up to a point. The word God is indeed ambiguous because of its origin in the poetic and dramatic language of religion and of the inevitably symbolic character of that language, but I should maintain, in opposition to Lovejoy, that the translation of the language of religion into that of theology and philosophy takes place without loss of meaning, and that it is not ultimately ambiguous. It is the postulate of the essential identity of the two notions which constitutes the initial premise

[1] There are three possible interpretations of this situation: (*a*) that the figure of the *Timaeus* is simply a figurative personification of the idea; or (*b*) an emanation or subordinate divinity, through which the world generating function of the Absolute and Perfect One was exercised; or (*c*) what Lovejoy holds to be more probable, the view that two distinct strains in Plato's thought are here fused and the resultant conception then given a largely figurative expression. The latter is, I agree, the more probable interpretation. But if so, the very fact that there are these two strains may be taken as an indication of the necessity, in Plato's mind, of retaining the *vis poetica* and the dramatic character of theological language—the same necessity which he felt regarding the retention of the myth for the saying of the things that count.

[2] *Op. cit.*, p. 41.

and the necessary condition of the possibility of all theological thinking, and it is the truth of this postulate which I shall seem to maintain in the ensuing argument.

B

The translation of the dramatic language of religion into the Platonic idiom, a tendency already present in Greek philosophy, becomes dominant in Christian theology. The Good as *ens perfectissimum*, as self-sufficing perfection, was, so Lovejoy continues 'by a bold logical inversion converted into a Self-Transcending Fecundity.'[1] A timeless and incorporeal One became the logical ground as well as the dynamic source of the existence of a temporal and material and extremely multiple and variegated universe. The proposition that, as it was phrased in the Middle Ages, *omne bonum est diffusivum sui*, here makes its appearance as an axiom of metaphysics and, what is more significant for our present purpose, the axiom from which all axiological thinking, as we have described it, proceeded. In so far as Christian theology was concerned, this 'inversion' seemed possible 'without the notion of Self-Sufficing Perfection losing its original implications,' those implications upon which all theological thinking depends. It seemed possible also without the notion of God losing the *vis religiosa*, the dramatic and anthropomorphic character which alone makes it the object of religious devotion. It has been constantly maintained, however, that this is impossible, and that there is, in consequence, a fatal contradiction at the very heart of all Christian theology, that the identification of God with the Good involves antinomies of both practical and theoretical import, antinomies which destroy Christianity not only as a way of thought but as a way of life also.

Here then we come to the very heart of the theological problem, for it is to this supposed contradiction between perfection or self-sufficiency and activity, including creation, that all the specific antinomies involved in thinking about divine things ultimately go back. Lovejoy holds that the contradiction is insoluble and in examining this contention we shall take his own formulation of the issue as the starting point of the discussion.

Lovejoy states this irreconcilable conflict thus: 'God was the

[1] *Op. cit.*, pp. 48 f.

idea of the Good, but He was also the idea of Goodness; and although the second attribute was nominally deduced dialectically from the first, no two notions could be more antithetic. The one was an apotheosis of unity, self-sufficiency and quietude, the other of diversity, self-transcendence and fecundity. The One God was the Goal of the "way up," of that ascending process by which the finite soul, turning from all created things, took its way back to the immutable Perfection in which alone it could find rest. The other God was the source and informing energy of that descending process by which being flows through all the levels of possibility down to the very lowest.' In all this, we are told, there is a fundamental contradiction between two irreconcilable conceptions of the good or value. Theoretically this contradiction did not greatly trouble the medieval mind, we are also told. For the notion of the coincidence of opposites (*coincidentia oppositorum*) in the Absolute was an essential part of all medieval philosophy. But this discrepancy was, he holds, not merely between two abstract ideas but also between two practical attitudes. Here a conflict between two irreconcilable concepts of the good or value is a more serious matter. The final good of almost all western philosophers for more than a millenium 'consisted in some mode of assimilation of, or approximation to, the divine nature, whether that mode were defined as imitation, or contemplation or absorption. The doctrine of the divine attributes was thus also, and far more significantly, a theory of the nature of ultimate value and the conception of God was at the same time the definition of the objective of human life. The Absolute Being, utterly unlike any creature in nature, was yet the *primum exemplar omnium*. The God in whom man was to find his own fulfilment was then not one God but two.'[1]

If Christian theology contains at its very heart this fatal contradiction then indeed that great structure which has endured for a thousand years is not only now seriously compromised but has been so from the beginning. So also is the Christian life which from the beginning also has been lived on the postulate of the identity of the 'two Gods.' That it does not contain this contradiction I shall now attempt to show.

[1] *Op. cit.*, p. 82.

C

The fundamental issue is, of course, theoretical, as all fundamental issues are, but let us begin with the practical aspect which Lovejoy finds so serious. Now that there is an element of paradox here, as in all practical striving, I am ready to admit, for life itself is paradoxical. None the less it seems to me that nothing is clearer than that the entire story of Christian life and piety constitutes in principle a reconciliation of these two opposites. I do not mean that every individual believer has been able to reconcile completely contemplation of the Perfect Being with devotion to the God of Goodness, and the expression of this devotion in works of mercy and of love. But the great saints and mystics have, and it is precisely this which constitutes their outstanding significance for the philosophy of religion.[1] Moreover, I hold it to be a fundamental principle that wherever there is a reconciliation of opposites in life, there is created the presumption that they are reconcilable in theory also. It is this which, as I believe, and shall attempt to show, philosophical theology has been able to do.[2] For the present, however, we are concerned wholly with the theoretical issue as formulated by Lovejoy—the supposed contradiction between two irreconcilable conceptions of the good or value.

The issue, as thus stated, involves the entire question of the nature of value and, as such, belongs to what is known in modern philosophy as value theory or axiology *eo nomie*, and it is therefore in terms of the modern analysis of value that, in this context at least, the challenge must be met. The assumption which underlies this charge of contradiction between the two ideas of value is that the good or value is an essence in the same sense as the other Platonic essences, such as geometrical ideas, the nature of which is just to be. This assumption is, I believe, quite false. I do not believe that Plato himself, even in the *Republic*, identified the Good with this notion of essence. The famous passage in which objects of knowledge are said to derive from the Good the gift of being known and which ascribes to the Good not only 'dignity' but 'power,' seems to belie such a notion. But with this question of interpretation I am not concerned, for if Plato did identify the Good with the

other essences he was certainly wrong. An adequate phenomenological analysis of value shows, I think, that it is *toto genere* different from the other essences. In the idea of the Good is
contained, as part of its very nature, precisely this 'power'
which makes it translatable into Goodness, for as essence it
includes the element of oughtness or ought-to-be which involves
the tendency to realization.

This is scarcely the place to retell the long story of modern
axiology, of which this phenomenological analysis is an outstanding feature.[1] It must suffice for our purposes to call as
witness one who has a unique place in this story, namely,
Nicolai Hartmann.[2] The distinction between value and other
essences is one of the main points of his analysis. The 'ideal'
ought-to-be, as he calls it, is not something added to value but
something without which value itself cannot be thought. In
man this ought-to-be becomes obligation or ought-to-do, and
man is probably the only part of nature in which this form of the
ought appears, but the ought-to-be is the essence of value itself.
Like Plato, he tells us that value is a power, a power which
causes existence to strive beyond itself (*es tendiert über sich
hinaus*) which marks it off from the other essences. But to our
amazed distress he tells us, almost in the same breath, that
'values have no power, that power belongs solely to the human
will'—a contradiction which, as it seems to me, not only
vitiates much of his argument, but has tragic significance for
his entire philosophy. This contradiction runs throughout his
entire treatment of value. He recognizes the active principle in
value in so far as the bearer of value, man, is concerned; also
that teleology as the necessary time-form of value, is an
essential part of reality as it expresses itself in man, but he
denies it to the cosmos as a whole. To ascribe value and
teleology to the cosmos means for him 'the metaphysical
humanization of the cosmos,' and thus necessarily the 'moral
annulment of man.' That both these contentions are untrue, I
profoundly believe, as I shall later attempt to show.[3] All that I

[1] See my chapter on Axiology in *Twentieth Century Philosophy*, edited by D. D.
Runes, 1943.
[2] Nicolai Hartmann, *Ethik*, English translation, Volume I, pp. 272 f., Volume
III, pp. 219 ff.
[3] Chapter xii, pp. 423 f. See on this point also N. O. Lossky, *Value and Existence*,
p. 147.

am concerned with here is that an adequate phenomeno-logical analysis of value shows it to have this 'power,' as Plato had already said, which marks it off from the other essences.

D

All of which means—to return to the problem from which this technical analysis started—that, so far at least as philosoph-ical conceptions are concerned, there is no irreconcilable conflict between the two ideas of the Good such as Lovejoy asserts underlies Christian theology, and consequently between the religious and philosophical conceptions of God. When, therefore, Christian theology converted the idea of the Good into the idea of Goodness and embodied this active principle into the axiom *omne bonum est diffusivum sui*, it was merely saying explicitly what was implicit in the notion of value as such. In other words, it translated the 'loving Father in Heaven' into the language of the philosopher without loss of the original *vis religiosa*. Two names are, indeed, given to God, but they refer not to two gods but one.

The foregoing critique of the basis of all Christian theology was stated in the technical terms of abstract philosophy; our reply to it was necessarily couched in these technical terms also. But the issue, as we have already seen, is far from being a merely technical matter, important as this aspect of the question is. This supposed contradiction was not only between two abstract ideas but also between two practical attitudes, between the God of religion and the God of philosophy. It is therefore not only from the theoretical but also the practical point of view that the foundations of dogmatic theology have been increasingly attacked. The champion of simple piety also becomes the critic, and often the enemy, of theology. In the name of what he calls vital religion he, too, often tells us that the God of prayer and praise and the God of theology are not one God but two. Of the two forms of attack, that of piety is, if anything, the more inimical to true religion. The sceptical philosopher may be met in the lists of reason and may, con-ceivably, be overcome in the battle of dialectic; the champion of piety, on the other hand, cannot be met at all, for there is no common ground. One finds this attack where one least expects it. It is something of a shock to hear an Anglican dean assert that 'the *Deus philosophicus* is not the God and Father of our Lord Jesus Christ' and that 'we cannot believe in the Deity who emerges from their [the schoolmen's] logic, not because He is too high, but because he does not in reality sustain the Christian values.' On the contrary, so I believe, only such a deity can really sustain these values.[1]

V

The 'Critique of Dogmatic Theology.' The Relation of Dogmatic to Rational Theology

A

Dogmas, writes William James, 'are secondary products, like translations of a text into another tongue.'[2] In this he is in principle right, but everything depends, as we have seen, upon a true understanding of the tongue into which the intuitions of religion have been translated. Theology involves, indeed, the translation of the lyrical and dramatic language of religion into the idiom of conceptual thought, but it is because this idiom retains the *vis religiosa* that such translation is possible. This is, however, denied by the opponents of dogmatic theology we have now in mind. When, we are told, we forsake the language of religion, the mode of address of prayer and praise, thought ceases to be 'integral' and breaks up into dialectic. Theology, as Kierkegaard says, 'can never be anything else than dialectical.' Theological thought, being thus dialectical, is refracted by logic into contradictions and antinomies; involving, as it does, the application of our human and phenomenal categories to the Divine, such thought is necessarily antinomical and destructive of religion.

Of this general standpoint there are many protagonists in the modern world. I choose for our present purpose Leo Tolstoy and his famous *Critique of Dogmatic Theology*. When, after his conversion from atheism, as recorded so vividly in *My Confession*, he sought to return to the religion of his fathers he undertook an extensive study of the Christian theology as developed in the Orthodox Church, the result of which was his famous *Critique*

[1] Dean W. R. Matthews, *God in Christian Thought and Experience*, p. 104.
[2] *The Varieties of Religious Experience*, p. 431.

and a 'creedless' religion as embodied in his still more famous book, *My Religion*. In every respect an extraordinary book, the *Critique*, like the *Confession*, displays all the inimitable powers of imagination and expression which make of Tolstoy the unsurpassable genius he is.[1]

The Preface to the *Critique of Dogmatic Theology* is at once one of the most pathetic and most terrible of all confessions. 'I read and studied these books,' he writes, 'and here is the feeling which I have carried away from that study. If I had not been led by life to the inevitable necessity of faith; if I had not seen that this faith formed the foundation of the life of men; if this feeling, shattered by life, had not been strengthened anew in my heart' (My Confession) . . . 'if there were within me only the faith of which theology speaks (taught to believe) I, after reading these books' (on dogmatic theology), 'not only would have turned atheist, but should have become a most malignant enemy of every faith, because I found in these doctrines not only nonsense, but the conscious lie of men who had chosen the faith as the means for obtaining certain ends.'[2]

We need not concern ourselves over-much with the charge that in these doctrines he found the conscious lies of evil men. It is entirely understandable that the charge of insincerity should bulk large in the thought of one who had had Tolstoy's experiences with the Russian Church. It is also possible that he did not wholly understand the motives of those against whom the charge is, perhaps, somewhat lightly made. Our main concern is with the general standpoint which he represents. 'I intended,' he writes, 'to go to God and I found my way into a stinking bog.' To the theologians he cries: 'Go yourselves to your father, the devil . . . You are not speaking of God, but of something else.' Of the particular dogmas he writes, 'I found these doctrines nonsense.' In the very extravagance of this language we feel the full force of a current of thought and feeling which, although present in Christianity from the beginning, has been gathering momentum in these latter days.

---

[1] Leo Tolstoy, *My Confession: Critique of Dogmatic Theology*, translated from the original Russian by Leo Wiener, Dana, Estes and Co., Boston.

[2] *Op. cit.*, p. 94.

B

You are not speaking of God but of something else! As made by a man such as Tolstoy, himself deeply religious, the charge is not to be treated lightly. Now that such a charge is true—that the God of religion and the 'God' of theology are not one God but two—is of course possible, but certainly highly improbable. On the face of it, it seems absurd to say that when men such as St. Augustine, St. Anselm and St. Thomas used the very language which Tolstoy deplores, they were talking not about God but about something else. The theological classics examined by Tolstoy are, to be sure, those of the Orthodox Eastern Church, but the type of theological thinking involved, and the language employed, are in principle the same as those of the theologians of the West. When faced with an obvious absurdity such as this we can only ask how was such an absurdity possible?

The motives which led Tolstoy to these extraordinary assertions are fairly plain. 'If,' he tells us, 'he had not been led by life to the inevitable necessity of faith,' if, as we are further told, he had not found God in the deepest experiences of his own life, and found that faith confirmed in the life of the simple peasant, he would have become, through reading the theologians, the enemy of every faith. Tolstoy wished, therefore, to protect the God of simple piety from the manhandling of the theologian, with the result that little more is left of religion than moral pathos, and all that remains of the God of religion is the loving Father in Heaven whom, as he believed, the simple peasant alone understood.

Tolstoy made here, I believe, the same fundamental blunder of which he was guilty in his equally devastating critique of the language of poetry in *What is Art?* He appealed to the simple intuitions and unspoiled understanding of the peasant in order to rule out the poetry of Shakespeare and then, by a magnificent irony, found that the very play against which he chiefly railed, *King Lear*, was not only wholly understandable, but reduced all the peasant listeners to tears. So it is with the great dogmas of religion. It is not without significance that in the entire magnificent Russian liturgy it is the singing of the *Credo* that appeals most to the Russian peasant. One has only to read deeply in the *Critique* to realize how little understanding Tolstoy had of the language of theology, but, which is more to the point, of the language of simple piety itself.

What is true of Tolstoy is true also, I believe, of all who follow this line of criticism. But these critics of theology make a still more fundamental blunder. For surely if what they say of the God of theology is true it is even more true of the God of religion. If the former refers to nothing and is therefore meaningless, surely, on their own premises, the 'loving Father in Heaven' is without reference in this sense and has wholly emotive significance. In other words, the argument proves too much, and it is passing strange that they do not see it. If we go thus far with Tolstoy and his way of thinking, surely we must go a step further. When we are talking about the loving Father in Heaven, no less than when we are talking about the Perfect Being of the theologians, we are talking about nothing.

This is, to be sure, a position somewhat widely maintained, and has been explicitly formulated by a group of philosophers known as logical positivists. For them all religious terms are empty words, have no meaning (in the strict sense of the word) because they refer to nothing. The view we are considering is clearly distinguished by its upholders from that adopted by atheists and agnostics. For 'it is characteristic of an agnostic to hold that the existence of God is a possibility in which there is no good reason to believe or disbelieve; and it is characteristic of an atheist to hold that it is at least probable that no God exists. But the view that all utterances about the nature of God are nonsensical, so far from being identical with, or even lending support to, either of these familiar contentions, is actually incompatible with them. For if the assertion that there is a god is nonsensical, so is the assertion that there is not.'[1] In short, any talk about God is 'blab blab' to use the elegant terms of one of the more irresponsible representatives of the position.

Now that this extreme position is also possible—although surely less possible than the preceding—cannot be denied; but surely it is highly improbable. *Prima facie* the opposite is the case. It is so contrary to all the apparent facts of human experience that we are bound to ask how it could have entered into the mind of man to assert so paradoxical a thesis.

[1] A. J. Ayer, *Language, Truth and Logic*, Chapter vi, 'Critique of Ethics and Theology,' p. 174.

We know well enough, of course, how it has come about. It is one of the more challenging applications of the so-called 'logical analysis' of language and of the semantics which logical positivism propounds. What this positivism really says is that what is said of anything—that is if our discourse is to be meaningful—must be said in bodily form. Only physical language is significant, and this is so because for any word to have meaning it must refer to a sensuously observable entity. Obviously there is something very wrong in any criterion of meaningfulness that makes unmeaning not only the language of religion but of a large part of human discourse, for the argument is equally applicable—and indeed is so applied—to all ethical and aesthetic terms. This is, of course, not the place to go into the problem in detail—it would involve a critical examination of the so-called 'logical analysis' of sentences and propositions upon which this theory of meaning rests, and ultimately, of course, the entire problem of the relation of logic to language—it must suffice for our purposes to suggest the main source of the error, for it raises an issue fundamental not only to religious but to all knowledge.

No one questions, of course, the initial assumption upon which this extraordinary thesis rests, namely, that for words to have meaning they must have determinate reference. Propositions which have no such reference are really pseudo-propositions and, being neither true nor false, are, strictly speaking, meaningless. What is questioned, not only by the protagonist of religion but by any critical philosopher, is the dogmatic assertion that, to be determinate, reference must be solely to physical or sensuously observable entities. What the positivist is here doing is to take a criterion of meaning which scientific method has postulated for its particular purposes and extend it arbitrarily and uncritically to all forms of experience and knowledge.

The error involved in this procedure—and it is an egregious one—arises in the first place from a misunderstanding regarding language itself. In order that a word may have this determinate reference, and therefore meaning, it is not necessary that the reference be to a physical object. It is true that in the primary universe of discourse there is always such a referent in the physical environment, common to speaker and hearer, and it is that which, in the first instance, makes meaningful

147

communication possible. But this is not necessary and, in fact, the words employed in the major part of human discourse have ceased to have this physical reference. From this initial misunderstanding of language arises a second. In order that a word may have such reference it is not necessary that it shall be univocal. It may have a double reference, first to the primary object to which it initially refers and secondly, by analogous predication, to a second object which it symbolizes. It is in fact this very dual reference which alone makes possible the development of language, and with it the entire spiritual life of man. No linguistic expression is meaningless or non-significant in the sense that it wholly lacks a referent; the task of philosophical analysis of language is to find out what the referent really is. In sum, the criterion of meaning, of a meaningful proposition is that it is communicable.[1]

But these erroneous conceptions arise from a still more fundamental misunderstanding, namely, as to the nature and function of logic, of a piece with the misuse of logic already examined. Appeal is made to what is called the logical analysis of language. It is assumed, rightly, of course, that until a 'fact' is enunciated it does not enter into the sphere of communicable and verifiable knowledge, and since logical form is woven into all our speech, the sentences in which it is enunciated are subject to logical analysis. But it also assumes, and here it is in error, that logic instead of being the mould of thought also has the right and power to determine the material of thought. Asserting that logic is concerned with the 'real world,' it also claims to determine by logical analysis what real here means—which is a metalogical, not a logical problem at all. Logic cannot cause the mind to yield the fruit of knowledge unless the mind conceive from some other source.

But to return to the specific problem out of which this technical discussion arose, surely to say that religious utterances are nonsensical is to fly in the face of all the facts. Nor does it mitigate the absurdity of the position to say that religious words have emotive meaning but yet refer to nothing. It can be shown that they cannot have even this meaning without some reference, however vague, to some object, and without pre-

---

[1] For a fuller development of these points see my *Language and Reality*, especially Chapter v.

148

supposing some judgment or assumption of the existence of the object.[1] Of one thing we may be sure, namely, of the truth of the ancient dictum that we cannot talk about that which is not. We may, of course, be mistaken as to the mode of existence of the object of our discourse—we may think that we are talking about one thing when we are really talking about another. We may also be mistaken as to the mode of existence of the object of our discourse—even in physical science men sometimes suppose that a thing exists in the sense of being sensuously observable when it does not. But all this does not alter the fact that whatever the universe of discourse, when men understand one another they are never talking about that which is not.

But if this is true something else is equally true. If the language of religion is meaningful, so also is the language of theology. The argument which makes the language of theology meaningless makes the language of religion meaningless also. Tolstoy and similar critics of theology would, of course, deny indignantly this *argumentum ad absurdum*, but it is difficult to see how they can avoid it. They would insist upon the meaningfulness of the language of religion in a more than merely emotive sense, but when we ask them *what* it means, to *what* this language really refers, the answer can be only in terms of higher generality and involves the translation of this language into that of theology. Far from it being true that when we talk the language of theology we are not talking about God but about something else, it is rather the case that we do not know what we are really talking about—what religion 'really says'—until we do translate the language of religion into that of theology, for it is the latter language alone that makes the former ultimately intelligible. Our quarrel with Tolstoy, and those of like mind is, then, not that they demand sincerity and meaningfulness in religion but with their naïve view of what constitutes the sensical and the nonsensical—not with their championing of the faith of the simple, but with their failure to understand what it is to which that faith is really directed.

C

The second reason for the critique of dogmatic theology is the charge that when the language of religion is translated into the

[1] *Language and Reality*, Chapter v, especially Section vii.

concepts and propositions of theology the latter develop contradictions which make of them logical nonsense. In this Tolstoy follows the beaten track long trod by the sceptics and with which we are already familiar. His critique of the notions of an omnipotent God, of predestination and free will, of the doctrines of the Incarnation and of the Trinity, differ in no significant way, except perhaps in a certain terrible naïveté, from these classical criticisms.

The so-called metaphysical attributes of Deity—those deducible from the concept of God as *ens perfectissumum*—are, of course, for Tolstoy, as they were for William James, of no practical significance, even if they were faultlessly deduced and a coercive logic led us to accept them.[1] When we used them we should be talking not about God but about something else. But far from being thus logically deducible they are, when brought before the bar of logic, mutually contradictory and wholly incompatible. He concludes his examination of these attributes with the following question: 'This disclosure of the essence of God in himself and in his essential properties is finished. What is there in it? He enumerates the contradictions generated by the application of various predicates to an infinite absolute being; but the chief contradiction he finds in the statement that God is both comprehensible and incomprehensible! We have thus, he tells us, the beginning of the logical nonsense which, as he had said, would, were it not for faith, have driven him to hatred of all religion.

Still more does this logical nonsense appear in the central dogmas of specifically Christian theology. Of the dogma of the Incarnation he writes that the 'words' in which the dogma is defined 'are a series of contradictions.' The notion of the God-man is itself for this theology a fundamental contradiction, for the attributes already ascribed to God and the attributes ascribed to man are incompatible. But the contradictions, he tells us, become intolerable when the union of the two is expressed in the language of Greek metaphysics. 'Two essences and one hypostasis,' he cries, waxing both sarcastic and indignant over the application of such grotesque technicalities in the discourse we call religious, without, perhaps, understanding very well either the necessities which gave rise to the terminology or its meaningfulness to those who use it.

[1] See in this connection, *The Varieties of Religious Experience*, pp. 445 ff.

All this becomes even clearer when we examine his criticism of the dogma of the Trinity. Of this he writes: 'it is impossible to believe that God, my good Father (according to the teaching of the Church), knowing that my salvation or perdition depends upon my comprehension of him, should have expressed the most essential knowledge about himself in such a way that my reason which he has given me should not be able to comprehend his expressions. . . . No, if it were so God would have given me such an intellect that $1 = 3$ would have been as comprehensible as it is impossible now.'[1] Of the details of the criticism it is unnecessary to speak; they differ in no important respect from those with which the so-called rationalistic criticism of the dogma have long made us familiar. Here again we have rather to ask how a mind as penetrating as that of Tolstoy should have shared such banal misunderstandings of the nature of theological dogma.

The underlying motives are indeed the same as led him to defend the 'good Father in Heaven' of the simple peasant from the manhandling of the theologians. But something else of importance enters into the picture at this point. It was, as he makes it clear in *My Confession*, 'reason reflecting upon life' that led him to the necessity of faith, if his own life and that of which it is a part were to be meaningful or intelligible. If, however, it is reason properly understood that led him to God, it was impossible for him to believe that this same God, to whom he was thus led, should not be comprehensible to his intellect or reason. He believed himself to be justified in excluding all ideas of God not thus comprehensible by the intellect and he became the malignant enemy of every faith that proposed ideas of God which were not thus intelligible.

Here again our quarrel with Tolstoy and with those of like mind is not with their demand that the things of God be intelligible, but rather with their naïve misunderstanding of what intelligibility and comprehensibility here mean, not with their demand for reason in religion but that their conceptions of reason are so limited and naïve. It is really the old question of the axiological and the logical over again and of the role of logic when applied to divine things. If Tolstoy and the many who follow his way of thinking do not actually arraign God as

[1] *Critique of Dogmatic Theology*, p. 187.

though He were a man (although fundamentally, I think, in their hearts they always do) they certainly apply the categories of our human logic, conditioned by the way in which they appear in creatures, as though these categories exhausted the eternal essence of God.

One cannot, of course, deny a certain sympathy even with this naïve demand for an intelligible God—the source of all criticism of dogmatic theology from Arius to the present day. In all this Tolstoy is but expressing the feeling of Channing when he was moved to exclaim: 'Trinitarianism, instead of teaching an intelligible God, offers to the mind a *strange combination of hostile attributes* [italics mine], bearing plain marks of those ages of darkness when Christianity shed but a faint ray and the diseased fancy teemed with prodigies and unnatural creations.'[1] With the demand for intelligibility itself the philosophical theologian need not quarrel—faith will always seek understanding of the intellect, however men may caution us against it—the entire question at issue revolves about the criterion of intelligibility. On this very point Earl Balfour has something of significance to say. 'Had Arius,' he writes, 'succeeded, he would have inflicted irremediable impoverishment on the idea of the Godhead which was essentially embodied in the Christian life. The truths for which Athanasius contended gave reality and life to the worship of millions of pious souls who were utterly ignorant of the controversy of Nicea. The paradox of the Christian life consists in the power of this idea, transcending our own powers of understanding, to lift man out of the finite into the infinite.' Transcending our powers of understanding? In a certain sense yes; in the sense namely that the dogma of the Trinity or any other dogma can never be completely rationalized; for it is the very condition of such rationalization that the supernatural shall be denatured and become part of the natural. But in another sense no. To the extent that this idea has this power of lifting even the simplest soul from the finite into the infinite it also lifts him into the 'place of understanding,' for to understand one's self and one's own finitude one must also apprehend the infinite which his finitude presupposes. Here also Tolstoy and those of his way of thinking

[1] 'Unitarian Christianity most favourable to Piety,' *Works*, Boston 1875, p. 390.

have misjudged the capacity for understanding of the simple peasant.

D

We have been examining Tolstoy's defence of the 'living God' against the manhandling of theologian and philosopher. It is well to see this pietistic critique of dogmatic theology in the naïve and passionate form in which Tolstoy expressed it. But this same critique is found in principle in the most sophisticated forms of the religious thought of the present, especially in those influenced by the significant work of Sören Kierkegaard. We may therefore with advantage turn briefly to the more philosophical critique of the Danish theologian and philosopher.

For Kierkegaard, as we have seen, theology cannot be anything else than dialectical. When we forsake the mode of religion, of prayer and praise, for the mode of theology, theological reasoning not only breaks up the original experience into contradictions, but the insoluble antinomies thus generated serve but to reveal the abyss of alogical meaning which is for him the ground and source of all religious experience. The 'paradox of reason' of which Kierkegaard speaks, corresponds in principle to the paradoxes which Tolstoy finds in the God-ideas of the theologians and which turn him from this God to the God of religion.

Naturally intensely religious, Kierkegaard, like Tolstoy, also finds the same difficulties with the official theology and religion of his Church. For him, too, religion is primarily a matter of personal decision, necessitated by the dreadful alternatives of life. When one reads his *Either-Or*, his *Stages on the Way of Life*, and, above all, *The Concept of Anxiety*, one knows himself to be in the same spiritual atmosphere as in Tolstoy's *My Confession* and *On Life*. But while the approach is similar and the spiritual atmosphere of the same passionate intensity, the logic of the criticism is even more devastating and the 'subjectivity' of his 'existential thinking' even more self-conscious and uncompromising than anything found in Tolstoy. He is for this reason the chief inspiration of the most modern form of faith philosophy which has set its face against all rational elements in theology whether natural or revealed.

As for Tolstoy, so also for Kierkegaard, the 'paradox of reason' appears pre-eminently in the dogma of the Incarnation as he makes clear in his *Philosophical Fragments*. The union of the two essences—God as unchangeable and absolute with man as becoming vanquished and suffering—what thought can grasp such a union? It cannot any more for Kierkegaard than for Tolstoy. Nor should any one expect that it could. If by reason one understands reasoning about the objects of religion abstracted from the universe of discourse in which they have meaning, and transferred uncritically to a purely naturalistic universe in which they have no meaning, insoluble antinomies are inevitably generated. If by objective truth one understands only the truth of nature, then indeed are they beyond truth and falsity in this sense and 'subjectivity is truth.' But then, as Kierkegaard would doubtless admit, morality so conceived is equally paradoxical and the truth of freedom also mere subjectivity. It is indeed impossible for thought in this sense to grasp such a union as that of God and man and no form of theology ever has, I think, claimed that it could; but it does not follow that such union is unintelligible.

But we may go even further than this. Like the first argument of the critics of theology this second proves for Kierkegaard, as it did for Tolstoy, entirely too much. For the paradoxes of reason thus exploited by the irrationalist do not appear solely in connection with any special dogma, whether of the Incarnation or the Trinity, but are present from the beginning in every image of God, whether the loving Father in Heaven of religion or the God-man of the theologian. The term fatherhood when applied to God is, when taken literally, the fruitful source of logical nonsense also. We can only conclude that men who think in this fashion do not realize the full implications of their own position; or, if they do so, they do not say all that they think. For if we go this far, surely we must go a step further, a step which will, I think, involve us in a virtual atheism.

This point is of such transcendent importance for our entire argument that it must be stated with the greatest care. Kierkegaard, we are told, 'was the first' (in modern theology and philosophy) 'to break through the closed system of the idealistic philosophy of essence,' the philosophical idiom of Greco-Christian theology—in other words, more significant in the present context, the first to break completely with the principle of objectivity embodied in the system on which western theology, both natural and dogmatic, was based, and to fall back upon the principle of subjectivity as the ultimate ground of religion. All objective approaches, it is held, seemed, as the result of the dialectical character of theology, to lead to atheism. Indeed, those of this way of thinking are willing to say, with Professor Tillich, that, 'in the face of an objectively existing God, atheism is right.' But surely if ever there was a case of an argument proving too much this is that case. For myself, I do not understand what a God who does not objectively exist really can be. I am, of course, aware that the terms objectivity and existence require interpretation but that is a far cry from the denial of all existence involved in this position. It is not without significance that the philosopher Heidegger, the original inspiration of whose thinking was in large part Kierkegaard, finally reaches complete atheism. The 'philosophy of existence,' so he maintains in *Sein und Zeit*, requires a 'destruction of classical philosophy' and, as soon appears in the development of his theme, the destruction of *philosophia perennis* involves the destruction of *religio perennis* also. All of which makes it clear that between dogmatic and rational theology there exists an intimate bond which cannot be severed without the ultimate destruction of both. To this problem—of the relation between the two—we must therefore again turn.

VI

Dogmatic Theology and Rational Theology.
Kritik aller Theologie.

A

The theme of this chapter is, in terms of a critical philosophy, the question, How is dogmatic theology possible? The 'Critique of Dogmatic Theology' we have been examining says it is not possible. Our answer to this has been that *it is possible if religion itself is possible*—that the language of theology is as meaningful and valid as the language of religion of which it is the translation and explication. But is religion itself possible? Is the existence of God, the God about whom both religion and theology speak—itself credible? The question How is dogmatic theology possible? is bound up with the further question, How is rational theology possible?

The title of the section on rational theology in Kant's *Critique of the Pure Reason* is entitled 'Kritik *aller* Theologie.' What Kant saw clearly is precisely this fact, that the two theologies are of one piece and that the critique of the one involves the critique of the other. If there are contradictions which make nonsense of man's pronouncements upon God's nature and attributes, similar contradictions and antinomies make nonsense of the God idea itself. But while it is true that the two theologies do hang together, and that if they do not continue to do so they will (humanly speaking!) hang separately, there is, after all, a sense in which they are separable, a sense in which rational theology is not only autonomous but, logically speaking, ultimate.

The underlying postulate of all thinking about God, His attributes and His acts, is, as we have seen, the identity of God with the Sovereign Good, and of the inseparability of the latter from being. What then is the basis of this postulate? It has its source either in some direct intuition or in a reasonable belief based upon rational 'demonstration,' or, as I believe, and shall later attempt to show, in both.[1] Even revelation cannot, of itself and alone, guarantee this presupposition or postulate of theological discourse. The existence of God and a necessary relation of God to man are logically prior to any particular revelation, and this existence and this relation can be shown forth only by reason. From all of which it becomes clear that the two forms of theology constitute an organic whole; but just as certainly as they are thus integrally related, they are also functionally separated, for the one is logically prior to the other. With this we are brought to the issue with which the discussions of this chapter began.

I have no desire to minimize the difficulties of the problem as there pointed out. Unless the two theologies are continuous and organic, we have not one God but two. On the other hand, unless the appeal to reason is actually to reason alone, the entire question is begged. Nevertheless I am inclined to believe that the developments of this chapter make possible a clearer understanding of the problem and perhaps point the way to its

[1] Chapter ix.

eventual solution. I shall simply state the relation as I conceive it, leaving its further validation to the following chapter.

The two theologies are continuous and organic because ultimately both speak the same language. The continuity of the language of divinity or dogmatic theology with that of religion has now been made plain; this continuity extends also, I believe, to the language of rational theology. Both speak the same axiological idiom and the problems of the relation of the logical to the axiological are, *mutatis mutandis*, the same for both. If rational theology spoke a wholly different idiom from that of revealed religion then there would indeed be not one God but two. This the classical theologians have always realized. If Plato and Aristotle spoke a wholly different language from the Christian, their God would not be the God of the Christian. On the other hand, if Plato and Aristotle, to say nothing of thinkers more widely remote from us, could not achieve a reasonable belief in God independently of the images and symbols of a particular revelation, then it would be impossible to show that the God whom these others 'ignorantly worship' is one with the God whom the Christian seeks to declare.

This the founder of the Christian religion Himself fully understood, and it is a pity that so many of his followers lack this understanding. Jesus made his appeal in the words, 'Ye believe in God, believe also in me,' and not in the form Ye believe in me, believe also in God. The latter is doubtless for many minds the psychological order, but it is certainly not the logical order. It is only when we believe in God, the Sovereign and Eternal Good, as the ground and goal of our human existence that we can believe in His own concrete revelation of that Good. It is only if we know *that* God is and *what* He is, whether through intuition or reason or both, that we can acknowledge a revelation as divine. The historical pronouncements of religion presuppose the cosmological pronouncements of religion, and the latter the ontological; the *Cur Deus Homo* presupposes the *Proslogium* as Anselm fully saw. To the further development of this theme we shall now turn.

Chapter V

Natural and Logical Witnesses for God: The Classical Theistic Argument and the Critique of Rational Theology

I — A

I THINK it is clear by now that theological thinking—thinking about God, His nature and His acts—is, and in the nature of the case must be, axiological in character. The only type of reasons that have meaning in this universe of discourse are of this kind. This was obvious in the case of the *Cur Deus Homo*. If there is a God and if He did become man, the only possible answer to the question Why? is in these terms. But is there a God to become man? Is there a God and can we know that He is? Is there a genuine theological universe of discourse at all? St. Anselm asked this question also and in the *Proslogium* we have a classical expression of the kind of thinking by which men have tried to answer it.

That God became man is for theology a fact of revelation, but even that 'brute fact' can to a certain extent be made intelligible. Granted that there is a God who is identical with the principle of perfection human reason is capable, to a degree at least, of showing why, by reason of His very nature, He should reveal himself in the created world in human form, but the fact that there is a God, and that he is of this character, must be capable of being shown by natural reason alone; otherwise all our thinking about God is a huge *petitio principii*. It is true that Anselm begins the *Proslogium* with a prayer that the natural reason may be enlightened that it may proceed aright, but the *argument itself* must make its appeal to that natural reason, enlightened or unenlightened, which is given to every one that cometh into the world.

Thus when the Vatican Council decreed that the existence of God could be demonstrated by pure reason alone it crystallized and, so to speak, institutionalized, a position which was not only practically necessary but was also the inevitable outcome of centuries of philosophical reflection. That, despite widespread repudiation, this position is, when properly understood, in its essentials sound, seems to me to be beyond question. But it must be equally clear, I think, that the proposition that the existence of God can be 'demonstrated' by 'natural reason' depends both for its significance and its truth on the meanings given to the two notions, natural reason and demonstration, for it is upon these meanings that everything turns. The notions may be so understood as to express fundamental truth; they may also be so interpreted, as they have been by critics of the theistic argument, as to be wholly false.

B

Natural reason, it seems quite clear, meant, for those who used the term, precisely what the term natural suggests, namely, that 'instinctive', unabashed use of reason in which man's whole nature, as a rational being, functions integrally—not the abstract and artificial thing it has come to mean so largely in the modern world. Reason in this sense was never abstracted from its native and intrinsic reference to the Good or value to which it is by nature oriented. When, therefore, a 'rationalist,' in this original and undiluted sense, says we know by the 'light of natural reason' that there must be a being to which we can give the name of God—when he says he knows by this light that the cause or ground must contain eminently all there is in the effect, that *ex minime maximum non fit*—it is reason in this sense that he means, not that mere residue of its former self to which, as Berkeley says, the 'minute philosophers,' even of his own time, had already reduced it.[1]

It is equally clear, I think, that demonstration meant for these 'rationalists' of the Greco-Christian tradition something quite different from what it means to many of us today. For these believers in the natural light of reason it meant just what the word in its first intention signifies, a 'showing forth'—that to a rational being, in the sense previously defined, it could be *shown* that the being to which we give the name of God exists. It is quite clear, I think, that for St. Augustine and St. Anselm— and even for St. Thomas, as we shall see—this is just what it meant. According to their view, in contrast to many modern

[1] *Alciphron, or The Minute Philosopher.* The minute philosophers, according to Crito, are 'a sort or sect which diminish all the most valuable things, the thoughts, views and hopes of men; all the knowledge, notions and theories of mind they reduce to sense; human nature they contract and degrade to the narrow, low standard of animal life and assign us only a small pittance of time instead of immortality.'

thinkers, the natural knowledge of God is not a matter of a mechanical autonomous reason, but one which presupposes the practical moral life. Now I shall not deny, of course, that many of the proponents of natural theology have at times spoken as though demonstration here were like demonstration in mathematics, which seemed to them, not knowing its true nature, the ideal of reason in every sphere. But this was not the true inwardness of this traditional rationalism—even, as we have seen of a Descartes and a Leibniz. It is not even true of Spinoza who belies it with every breath he breathes. The appeal to reason as mathematical or quasi-mathematical demonstration is but the outer shell of an appeal to reason in this deeper and more fundamental sense.

Demonstration of the existence of God means here, then, that which it alone can possibly mean, namely, the showing forth to any one who understands the meaning of the name God— to any one who lives in the moral and spiritual universe in which the problem alone has meaning—the necessity of the Divine Being. It does not mean that to a 'visitor from another planet'— to one who had neither the idea of God nor the necessary conditions of understanding it—whose mind was merely a machine for grinding out syllogisms—any such necessity could be shown. That would be ridiculous.[1]

All of which leads us to a conclusion which, at first sight, will appear to many as repugnant as it is paradoxical—namely, that the type of thinking with which we are concerned in rational theology is, while logical, axiological also, and that the general relations between the logical and the axiological are, *mutatis mutandis*, the same here as those developed in the preceding chapter. This is, from one aspect at least, the basis of the organic relation between religion, with its dogmatic theology, and the rational theology which it presupposes, suggested in the preceding chapter.

I shall not attempt to defend this thesis at this point—the entire story of rational theology, as we shall presently see it developing before our eyes, must constitute its proof—but there are certain glosses which make it seem less paradoxical. One of them has been offered by William James and, properly understood, is not without significance.

[1] See on this point, Chapter i, pp. 16 ff.

In his chapter in *Pragmatism* entitled 'Some Metaphysical Questions Pragmatically Considered,' he points out that questions such as the existence of God and the freedom of the will have no meaning except in what he calls their 'prospective reference'—that is their reference to ends and values; 'their sole meaning,' so he puts it, 'is their meliorism.' Viewed retrospectively, such questions are irrelevant. It makes no difference to the facts whether one or the other of the possible hypotheses is true. However false some of the inferences he drew, namely, that the question of the truth or falsity of such metaphysical propositions is one merely of pragmatic value, and that questions of destiny can be separated from questions of origin, his main contention is, I believe, sound. For he saw clearly that considerations of truth and falsity in connection with such metaphysical propositions cannot be separated from 'considerations of value,' that consequently the latter must enter into any argument concerning these issues, and therefore into any argument concerning the existence of God. It may be, of course, that if this is so this entire rational theology is a huge 'rationalization,' determined wholly by the desires and spiritual exigencies of man—as indeed, on one view, all religious thought is. It may be that all theistic argument really begs the question, is solely an *argumentum ad hominem*, and moves in a circle, as is so often maintained. All this may be true—and these are questions which must be raised and answered in their proper place. Here the question is solely one of interpretation—of determining the true inwardness of this great body of religious thought. This question can be answered only by retelling the story of the theistic argument in western thought and culture, and to this we must now turn.[1]

---

[1] For a fuller discussion of James's position on this point, see my book *The Intelligible World*, pp. 217 ff.

II

*The Story of the Theistic Argument. The Ways of the
Knowledge of God*

A

The story of the theistic argument is in a very real sense the
story of western European philosophy itself. The argument is
a formalization of certain basic elements in the metaphysics of
both Plato and Aristotle, but given a unity, as well as religious
significance, by their development in the context of Christian
thought and experience. The 'Five Ways' of the knowledge of
God, as formulated by Aquinas, constitute the systematization
of these elements. Not only, however, is this argument bound
up with the origins of western thought: it is also about the fate of
the argument that western thought largely revolves.

In the first place, it was carried along as an essential part of
the *corpus philosophicum* of continental rationalism. Descartes,
Spinoza and Leibniz, to speak only of the greater lights, all had
their special formulations of these great proofs. It never entered
into the minds of any of them to question the meaningfulness of
the language they were using or the cogency of the arguments
they developed. The reason for this is that they were all
'rationalists.' They knew, or believed that they knew—by the
light of natural reason—certain necessary principles from which
the argument proceeded. It is true—and this point must be
emphasized for its bearing upon later questions—that this
'light of natural reason' did not always shine unambiguously
when it came to the question of what it revealed concerning the
nature of God. Among these rationalists there were not only
theists but pantheists and deists. But on the central issue all were
at one. For all of them there were both 'natural and logical
witnesses for God.'

The story of the theistic argument—of its rise and decline—
is not only the epitome of European philosophy but, in a very
real sense, of European culture itself. So convinced was the man
of the Enlightenment of the enduring character of this structure
—with which all his cultural values were bound up—that he
thought it possible to abandon entirely—as superfluous, if not

actually inimical *impedimenta*—all the dogmas of Christianity or any other positive religion without affecting the values themselves. The Christian theist became a mere deist, often a wholly pagan deist. It is not strange that from this point on this structure itself began to crumble and the story becomes one of gradual dissolution of the argument. The light of natural reason began to wane and with its waning went the vision of the Divine. Finally it seemed possible to say with Julian Huxley that for the modern man 'the whole magnificent structure of theology and philosophy which had endured for a thousand years is now gone.'[1]

B

Hume's *Dialogues on Natural Religion* may for our purposes be taken as the turning point in the story. Into the mouths of the characters of the dialogue, their author puts all the classical arguments. One maintains the *a priori* argument, another the empirical point of view for which the argument from design can be the only possible one. In still another we have a quite modern figure—one who discards all the rational arguments and falls back on an irrational faith. But the real point of the entire dialogue, its true inwardness, is the change in the notion of reason that underlies the argument, and the consequent abandonment of the classical conception of natural reason in all its forms. If in our notion of reason we are to include only abstract reasoning concerning quantity or number, or experimental reasoning concerning matter of fact or existence, it requires very little intelligence to see what happens, not only to 'Divinity' but to humanity. For when man's reason is thus barbarously reduced to a pittance of its former self it becomes in the end as powerless to deal with that which is really human as with that which is divine.

It is at this point also that Kant's famous critique of all theology, including rational theology itself, came upon the scene. Kant, the all destroyer, to use Heine's epithet, is supposed to have demolished the entire rational basis for this way of life and thought that had endured for a thousand years. It is true that Kant did not so consider his own work. He believed rather that he was putting this value-charged scheme of thought on a firmer basis. Whether rightly or wrongly, he believed him-

[1] Julian Huxley, 'Will Science Destroy Religion?' *Harper's Magazine*, April 1926.

self to have opened up to us a more spacious world of human reason—one in which not only the starry heavens above but the moral law within, are equally parts of a rational world order and in which the latter, even more than the former, constitutes the true witness, both natural and logical, for God. So central is this for all that follows that it is of the utmost importance that we should have a true view of what his position really was.

Kant's problem at this point is precisely the fundamental problem of all theology, whether supernatural or natural, namely, the relation of the axiological to the logical. For him the relation is expressed first of all in the contrast of the practical with the theoretical reason and the elevation to primacy of the former. Reason, according to him, may be applied in various ways—indeed he speaks of 'various employments of the reason,' the empirical, the theoretical and the practical. The issue of God's existence is primarily one of the practical reason—certainly not of the empirical merely, nor of the merely speculative, although, as he makes it clear, the speculative is not without its place in the argument as a whole. But in the interpretation of Kant at this point all depends upon the meaning of the 'practical.' 'By the practical,' he writes in the *Critique of Pure Reason*, 'I mean everything that is possible through freedom.'[1] And we learn, both here and in the *Practical Reason*, that freedom is definable in terms of determination by the idea of the Good, and the obligation that springs from it. But for Kant—and this is an aspect of his thought that is often forgotten—the ideal of the highest good is not only the determining principle of the practical, in the narrow sense of the moral reason, but of all activities possible through freedom, including the activities of pure reason itself. We may describe this as the axiological element in the *Critique of Pure Reason*, and the recognition of its presence there affects vitally not only the Kantian philosophy as a whole but, as we shall see presently, in an especially significant way our interpretation of his critique of rational theology.[2]

[1] *Critique of Pure Reason*, translated and edited by Norman Kemp Smith, p. 632.
[2] This axiological element in the *Critique of Pure Reason* is worked out in the part of the book entitled 'Transcendental Doctrine of Method,' more particularly in what he describes as the 'Canon of Pure Reason.' According to Kant, reason in all its forms—in all its various types of employment, empirical and speculative or dialectical—is guided by an ideal or norm. The formulation of this norm he describes as the 'Canon' of pure reason. He defines such a canon as 'the totality

However justified the above interpretation may be—and I myself believe that it alone gives us the real Kant when all the relevant facts are taken into consideration—it is certainly not the Kant of our present story. To him has been accorded the dubious honour of having finally given the *coup de grâce* to the magnificent 'rationalization' which had endured for a thousand years. In order, therefore, to discover the significance of this critique it is necessary to see just what this rational structure really is and just how the critique is supposed to have destroyed it.

III

The Ontological Argument: The Logical Witness for God

A

The reasons men have given for believing in God have been formulated in what are called the 'proofs' for the existence of God, or, briefly, the theistic argument. Of these proofs the Platonic or ontological argument is in a sense the most significant, for it constitutes what, in a dialectical or logical age, men believed to be the 'logical witness for God.'

It is significant, in the first place, for the reason that it is the argument which springs naturally and inevitably from the very nature of theological thinking as described in the preceding chapter. The initial assumption of this thinking is the identification of God with the Highest Good and the identification of the *ens perfectissimum* with the *ens realissimum*. What is more inevitable and natural than that the argument for the existence of God Himself should start from this point—that the identification of the Good with Being, the very basis of all theological thinking, should be first validated? This is what the ontological argument attempts to do.

But it is significant for the following reason also. The fact that

---

of the principles of the proper employment of the reason.' Now a canon or norm can be established only in the light of some ideal or ultimate end of pure reason —in short only in terms of some value notion. This Kant recognizes in his statement that 'the ideal of the highest good is the determining ground of the end of pure reason itself.' Thus, for Kant, the principle of the primacy of value holds for the theoretical no less than for the moral reason. The theoretical reason itself is oriented towards value.

man has in his 'mind' an idea of God at all, the idea of the most perfect being as Anselm expresses it, has seemed to many highly significant, if indeed not something of a miracle. This fact may lead to reasoning of the following character. Whence could this idea possibly have come? Could I have made it myself, could it be factitious, in Descartes' terms? Surely no possible accumulation of impressions from without could give rise to the consciousness of the infinite. There seems to be no other source of the idea than the Infinite Being Himself to whom it witnesses. This line of argument was made classical in Descartes' *Meditations*. It is, to be sure, not the ontological argument itself but is closely related to it. The ontological argument is so significant precisely because it starts with an idea unique among all other ideas, and it is this uniqueness which constitutes the key both to the understanding and evaluation of the Platonic argument.[1] All this becomes abundantly evident when we examine the argument in the classical form in which it is enshrined in the *Proslogium*.

B

The Anselmian formulation of the argument starts with a highly dramatic situation—the appeal even to the fool. 'The fool has said in his heart there is no God.' But in the very fact of denial—if the denial is to be significant—he knows *what* God is —in other words the notion of God has meaning. It is with this idea of God—which even he who denies God has—that the argument begins. I have, then, this idea—than which a greater cannot be conceived. But this idea must include existence or being; otherwise a greater could be conceived, which is contrary to fact; therefore God exists.

Thus the argument runs, and if ever sheer logic witnessed to anything, it seemed to the proponent of the argument—as well as to many others who followed him—that it witnessed to God. It doubtless seemed an unimpeachable syllogism which enforced conviction.

The argument found, however, as it was bound to do, a critic immediately in Gaunilo, a monk of Marmoutiers, who in the

---

[1] It has been said, wittily I suppose, that the so-called Platonic argument is not found in Plato himself. This is in a sense true, for certainly, as formalized in medieval thought, it is not found in Plato or Neoplatonism. But if not in the letter surely in the spirit, the very essence of Platonism is there.

seclusion of his cell anticipated, as was also inevitable, the trans-cendental dialectic of Kant. Gaunilo emphasizes the difference between thought and being and points out the fact, which scarcely needed to be pointed out, that we may conceive and imagine a thing and yet that thing not exist. We have as much right to conclude from our idea of an enchanted island in the middle of the ocean that such an island really exists. Strange as it may seem, the weight of opinion, even in Christian philosophy, has been that this is a valid analogy and that the implied criticism of the ontological argument is justified. Even St. Thomas is sceptical of the argument and, although including it in a sense among the ways of the knowledge of God, accorded it little force. But it is the Kantian dialectic which is supposed to have finally made clear the real character of the argument as well as its fundamental fallacy.

If, as supposed, Kant finally destroyed the entire scheme of theistic thought, it is because he is believed to have demolished once for all the ontological argument. For it was Kant's con-tention that this argument is presupposed by all the other argu-ments for the existence of God. If it is sound, there might be good reason to conclude that the other arguments are cogent. If it is not valid—and Kant believed that it was not—then all the structure of 'rational theology' falls to the ground. It is true that in criticizing the various arguments, the cosmological and the teleological, he took cognizance of other difficulties in their reasoning, but his final argument always consisted in showing that the argument in question presupposes the ontological argu-ment. In showing the fallacies of the latter, the cogency of the other arguments was destroyed. This is, of course, the real issue of the entire Kantian critique of rational theology. Kant was, I believe, right in the first of his contentions and wrong in the second. Indeed I should be bold enough to say that his position here is really inconsistent with his own premises.

Kant accepts, as the initial assumption of all theology, the identification of the idea of God with the Sovereign Good, of the *ens perfectissimum* with the *ens realissimum*. He saw clearly that without this initial datum the other arguments for the existence of God could not proceed. He pointed out that the so-called empirical arguments alone could at best lead only to a finite being, never to the Perfect Being with which the theological consciousness had identified the God of religion. The so-called empirical proofs really presupposed the ontological as their initial datum. But is the ontological argument really 'proof?' Is it really a logical witness for God?

To this question Kant gave a negative answer and for many that well-known answer has been final. There is no logical or *a priori* argument for God's existence, for there is none for the existence of anything. By deductive logic one can proceed only from essence to essence, never from essence to existence. And Kant clinched his criticism with the famous illustration in which he points out the abysmal difference between the dollars in my mind and the dollars in my pocket. But is the answer final? I think not. The constant revival of the argument and its reinterpretation in modern thought suggests at least that actually the critique has not been convincing, and the reason for this seems to be, as many have felt, that the criticism does not touch the nerve of the argument.

I do not believe that it does. For the argument, despite its appearance, does not deduce existence from essence. What it says is that in the case of God essence and existence are the same—which is precisely what all Christian philosophers, including St. Thomas, have always said. To separate them is essentially contradictory. More specifically, separation of the notion of the *ens perfectissimum* from the *ens realissimum*, of the Sovereign Good from Being, is indeed a contradiction, but a *contradictio in adjecto*. If, moreover, we should apply to God that kind of existence which, as Kant rightly saw, cannot be deduced from essence we should not be talking about God at all, but about 'something else.'

It is natural, but really quite unnecessary, to grow indignant over Kant's trivial illustration of the dollars, one which was quite unworthy of him. For he knew, if Gaunilo did not, that the idea of the blessed isles and of God are two quite different things, and if so still more the idea of God and the idea of the dollar in the pocket. What is assumed in both cases, to put it more technically, is that existence means the same thing in these two wholly different universes of discourse. Now Kant had really already answered his own dialectic. In discussing the 'empirical employment of the understanding' he made it quite clear that the definition of existence as that which is sensuously observable is merely a postulate—made solely for this employment of the understanding and not applicable elsewhere. To apply the notion of existence applicable in only one employment of the reason to all, was to be guilty of a provincialism really foreign to Kant's whole way of thinking and which he himself corrected, although imperfectly, not only in the *Critique of the Practical Reason* but, as we have seen, in the *Pure Reason* itself. For he made it clear that the determining ground of reason in its totality is the idea of the highest good, the *ens perfectissimum*, and to be thus the determining ground it must have being or existence.[1]

C

It is frequently said that the ontological argument, in the form given it by Anselm, is a rather clumsy attempt to put in a syllogism a type of argument which is of another character, namely, axiological. Among the first to realize this was doubtless Lotze, who said of it that 'this is obviously a case where an altogether immediate conviction breaks through into consciousness: to wit the conviction that the totality of all that has value —all that is perfect, fair and good—cannot possibly be homeless in the world or in the realm of actuality, but has the very best claim to be regarded by us as imperishable reality. This assurance, which properly has no need of proof, has sought to formulate itself after a scholastic fashion in the above-mentioned awkward argument.'[2]

This statement, while in part true, is scarcely an adequate expression of the modern axiological interpretation of the argument. Indeed Lotze recognized its inadequacy at certain points. But it goes directly to the heart of the matter, for it at least recognizes that the condition of all intelligibility and rationality—in any ultimate sense—is precisely this inseparability of value and being, or in Thomistic terms that value and being are convertible. But does this constitute a logical witness for God? Is it a 'demonstration' to our 'reason' that that to which we give the name of God must be? All depends, of course, upon our notion of logic and our conception of its relation to the

[1] As is well known, Hegel and many of the greatest thinkers after Kant did not find his critique convincing. See in this connection the paper by William Ernest Hocking, 'The Ontological Argument in Royce and Others,' in *Contemporary Idealism in America*, 1932.

[2] *Philosophy of Religion*, p. 10.

axiological. For my own part I think it is. I am quite sure that
God cannot be demonstrated by a syllogism, but I am equally
certain that the syllogism is not the whole of logic. I have never
been able to see why this immediate and quite incorrigible
conviction of which Lotze speaks is not a conviction of reason.
Nor am I able to see why the denial of this inseparability of
value and being does not involve a fundamental contradiction
and why the recognition of this contradiction does not constitute
a logical witness for God.

The point I am making here—and with it the entire significance of the ontological argument is involved—is expressed by
Gilson when he describes the ontological argument as the
'initial datum' of the other proofs.[1] Faithful to the Thomistic
tradition, he denies to it, of course, the character of a proof, but
gives it a much more significant rôle when he calls it the initial
datum of all the others. For what really is the difference between
saying that this argument is a logical witness for God and that
it is the initial datum of all the other proofs that witness to Him?
What is the difference, except one of words, between saying
that it is the initial datum of these proofs and, with Kant, that
it is presupposed in the empirical or *a posteriori* proofs? For
myself I see no difference. In any case, as initial datum, it is
required for the interpretation of the other proofs. To these we
shall now turn.

IV

The Natural Witnesses for God: The Cosmological Arguments

A

The denial of any *a priori* argument for God led to the exclusive emphasis upon the 'empirical' proofs for the Divine
existence. In the *Summa* St. Thomas asks the question, 'How
God is known to us,' and the answer consists in the enumeration
and systematization of the ways in which nature witnesses to
God. He did not wholly deny the logical witness for God of the
Platonic argument, but it is the arguments from nature which
are really cogent, for 'the invisible things of Him are known

---

[1] *The Spirit of Mediaeval Philosophy*, p. 60. The entire chapter in which this
conception is developed is worthy of careful study.

from the things that are made.' Of these the first three have been called cosmological, as distinguished from the anthropological, and it is under this term that we shall consider them.

Now doubtless these proofs can be described as a formulation of the natural witnesses for God. Doubtless also they are in a sense *a posteriori* or empirical. We do find in nature finite causes, and the natural reason, in the sense defined, argues 'naturally' to a first cause. We do find finite motions, and the natural reason argues to a prime mover. We do find in nature apparent adaptations of means to ends, and the mind naturally argues from design to the designer. But this is really not the issue involved. The question is rather that which was raised by Kant, namely, whether they are *wholly empirical*, whether without the initial datum of the principle of perfection, the things that are seen, in nature and in man would lead us to infer the existence of a perfect being—an all-wise, all-powerful and all-good God. Kant thought not, and for this reason he held that there are no purely empirical proofs for the existence of God—that, in other words, the so-called empirical proofs presuppose the ontological as their initial datum.

Kant's point is clear enough—and, to my mind, as convincing as clear. From *purely* empirical premises no inference is possible to anything but a purely empirical or phenomenal object, and therefore no inference to the God postulated by theology. We could at best argue to a finite and limited god—which would be not God, but 'something else.' Unless we take as our initial datum some intuition of the Divine, as embodied in the ontological argument, we cannot reach the God of religion and theology. The crucial point, of course, is the question of the possibility of the extension of the empirical employment of the reason to that which by definition transcends the possibility of experience, in the sense of empiricism, or, as Kant puts it, 'the applicability of the categories to God'—more especially the causal category in the two forms of efficient and final causality. This extension has been denied ever since Hume and it is precisely this denial that is the source of the dissolution of natural theology in its old form. If reason is reduced to merely empirical and mathematical employment and if intelligibility, as understood by 'science,' consists exclusively in necessary connections among phenomena, then, indeed, all books on

Divinity, including rational theology, should be cast into the flames. Kant, it is supposed, also denied outright this principle of intelligible causation and the applicability of the categories to God. This is such a complete misrepresentation of his actual position—indeed so contrary to his own statement—that clarification of this point is the first condition of the development of our own general thesis. I shall first quote Kant's own words on this point, a passage from the *Critique of Judgment*.

It is a 'General Remark on the Application of the Categories to God.' 'The alleged contradiction,' Kant writes, 'between the possibility of a Theology asserted here [in the preceding paragraphs] and that which the critique of the speculative reason said of the Categories—viz., that they can only produce knowledge when applied to objects of sense, but in no way when applied to the supersensible—vanishes if we see that they are here used for a *cognition* [italics mine] of God, not in a theoretical point of view (in accordance with what His own nature, inscrutable to us, may be) but simply as a practical—in order then at this opportunity to make an end of the misinterpretation of that very necessary doctrine of the Critique . . . I add here the following elucidation.' The rest of the passage, in which the possibility of natural theology is maintained, is too long to quote *in extenso*. It must suffice to bring out his main point and its bearing upon the causal argument. Kant takes up specifically the argument to the first mover. He points out, first of all, that if I apply a phenomenal category such as motion to a supersensible being, namely God, the category cannot be applied *literally*. Thus if I think of him as *first mover*, I must abstract from all spatial and temporal elements involved in the notion of motion and the notion can therefore no longer give us knowledge in the sense of empirical science. Nevertheless the categories are applicable to God. We cannot, of course, operate with them. He holds then that 'a cognition of God and of His Being (Theology) is possible by means of the properties and determinations of his causality merely thought in him according to analogy, which has all requisite reality in a practical reference though only in respect of this.'[1]

The importance of this passage can scarcely be exaggerated. The categories *are* applicable to God; a cognition of God and of

[1] *The Critique of Judgment* (translation of J. H. Bernard) Sections 89 and 90.

His being (Theology) is possible, by means of the 'properties and determinations of his causality.' It is true that he recognizes that this knowledge is analogical and involves a symbolic use of the notions of motion and cause—the symbolic element is recognized in all theology, even natural theology—*but it is still knowledge*. In fact, Kant is really merely extending the principle of the *analogia entis* to include the theoretical as well as the moral categories. It is true also that he adds that, while it has 'all requisite reality' it is 'only in a practical reference.' But all depends, as we have seen, on what Kant means by the 'practical', and it means for him, as we have also seen, the axiological. What Kant is really saying here is that what the Critique of the speculative reason said of the categories was applicable only to the employment of the empirical understanding and not to other employments of man's reason. That when the true significance of the magnificent structure which theology and philosophy had built up is really understood it remains unaffected by this critique.

But, to return to the main issue, surely Kant is in the main right. As God cannot be demonstrated by a syllogism, so equally it is impossible that he should be demonstrated wholly *a posteriori*. There can be no wholly empirical verification of God's existence, that is verification by His effects, because we must first know that they are effects—and that which is still more significant—effects of a certain quality, or a unique quality from which we could infer a unique Being. This unique quality can, however, be known only if we have in our minds already an intuition of perfection in terms of which this quality can be determined. Kant, then, is surely right in denying that the empirical categories may be extended *literally* to God. 'God's causality,' of which he speaks, is not the causality of nature, although from this causality in nature and in man God can surely be known. If He can be thus known it is, however, only by virtue of the first principle of all knowledge of Divine things, namely, the witness to the Divine in the heart of man. We are thus led to the 'anthropological' argument as the primary approach to God.

V

The Anthropological Argument: The Argument from Values.
Intelligible Morality

A

At the close of each of the cosmological arguments St. Thomas says—of the first cause, of the prime mover, etc.—and 'this is what men mean by God.' It is, however, only when we come to the fourth argument, from 'degrees of being or goodness' to perfection, that we arrive at what men *really* call God. The heart of the Thomistic argument is then the fourth 'way.' We experience degrees of good—distinctions of more or less, of better or worse—and from these we argue to the Perfect Good presupposed by them.

'Among beings,' so the argument runs in the *Summa*, 'some are more and some are less good, true, noble, and so on. But more and less have a meaning only in so far as things approximate in the quality under consideration to that which possesses the quality in the supreme degree, which has all of it there is, we might say. And this being that possesses the quality in the supreme degree must be the cause of the occurrence in other beings in lesser degree . . . Therefore,' concludes St. Thomas, 'there must also be something which is to all beings the cause of their being, goodness and every other perfection: and this we call God.'[1]

This argument may also be described as *a posteriori* or empirical in a sense. If we did not 'find' these degrees of good among existent beings there would be no starting point for inference to the Sovereign Good. But here, no more than in the case of the causal arguments, is experience alone the sufficient basis for such an argument. To be cogent, it must have as its initial datum knowledge of the perfect being which the degrees of being presuppose. Here too is presupposed that unconquerable conviction that if being is denied to perfection it is no longer the idea of perfection itself.

There has, accordingly, been some dispute among Thomistic scholars as to whether the fourth argument does not presuppose

[1] *Summa Theol.* I. q. II, art. 3.

the ontological and constitute a 'lapse into ontologism.' Some maintain that, unlike the others, the argument from degrees is conceptual in appearance and in some way ontological—in other words, 'a concession to ontologism.' Others, while admitting that the sources of the proof point to this—namely, St. Augustine's text praising the Platonists for their recognition of a supreme principle in view of the degrees of beauty, etc.—yet insist that we must not conclude from this that it is ontological in character and insist that it can be brought back to the properly Thomist point of view of moderate realism.[1] I should not like to say that this argument is a *form* of the ontological, but I should say that the ontological is the initial datum of this, as of the other proofs. It is true that the argument here also does not deduce the existence of the maximum good from the mere concept of goodness, but it does imply that we should not know the imperfectly good without its correlative or co-implicate, perfection. I do not believe that the charge of ontologism can be escaped unless there is implied in the Thomistic system the activity of intuitive as well as discursive reason.

B

It is at this point that the specifically anthropological or 'moral' argument, as it is called, enters into the value-charged scheme of thought. In this scheme the moral argument constitutes but one aspect of the general argument from degrees of good, but an aspect which, as we shall see, is determinative.

Among beings that are more or less good there are human beings and in a nature characterized by degrees of value there is human nature. But of all the beings which make up this world it is man alone who, so far as we know, is the conscious bearer of values. Doubtless every created being has its own good but, so far as we know, man is the only being who knows, even imperfectly, his own good and is conscious of the obligation which arises from that knowledge. For this reason, if considerations of value are brought into the theistic argument at all, the primacy of the anthropological and, with it, of the practical reason, is necessarily involved. But there is more to it than that. This primacy is necessitated also for the reason that it is only the

[1] On this question see E. Gilson, 'Quinquae Viae' of St. Thomas, 'Thomisme' 83, *Quatrième Preuve*.

knowledge of degrees of more or less of good *in us* that enables us to apprehend and understand such degrees in the being without us—it is only the inner scale which gives meaning to any conception of an outer scale, or *scala naturae*. It is not necessary to deny such an external scale independent of ourselves, and I would be the last to deny it—indeed, as I have argued elsewhere, there is such an objective scale; my only point is that it is through the interior scale alone that the external scale can be known—only from the anthropological can we pass to the cosmological.

Attempts are constantly made to formulate such a *scala naturae* in wholly naturalistic, non-human terms—in these latter days largely in terms of the evolutionary concept. It is said that it is just ' a fact of natural history that higher forms of existence have been imposed upon lower, and the lower developed to form the material of the higher, and it seems reasonable therefore to assume a continuity of degrees of meaning and value and a progress towards perfection.' But there is a serious misunderstanding here. It is not a fact of natural history abstracted from its relations to the human at all, for natural history as such there is merely transformation of forms, degrees of complexity, not value. If we put man higher than the amoeba it can be only on the assumption that the meaning of higher and lower is given intuitively in the experience of man. It is always possible to retort to such a scale that ' the amoeba has not been consulted'; but I do not believe that we need consult the amoeba, for 'he' does not live in a universe of discourse in which such a question has any meaning. My only point is that any *scala naturae* is necessarily anthropomorphic in the sense that it cannot even be apprehended without acknowledging the primacy of the anthropological. One need not deny such an objective external scale, although there are patently serious difficulties in constructing one, owing to our lack of insight into the nature and activities of non-human creatures—my only point is that the interior scale is and must remain the key to the external order and that, while moral and metaphysical perfection are not to be confounded, they are also not to be completely separated.[1]

[1] For further discussion of the scale of being, see *The Intelligible World*, pp. 440 ff. and my article in *Contemporary Idealism in America* entitled 'Idealism and the Philosophy of Spirit.'

A. E. Taylor speaks of ethics as 'a proper approach to theistic belief.'[1] It seems to be assumed that this is only one among other possible approaches and that consequently we might conceivably have the faith of a physicist or of a biologist. In my view there is no such thing as the faith of a physicist except as the physicist is a moral being, no faith of a biologist except as he is more than a biologist—in short a human being with all that that involves. I do not mean that Mr. Taylor himself would suggest anything else. I wish merely to emphasize the fact that the moral approach is not only a proper one, but also that, except upon the assumption of the primacy of such approach, no other is possible. This is, as we shall see, far from saying that the others are superfluous; they are, indeed, as we shall see, implied in the axiological approach.

It is not surprising, then, that Descartes should have thought that 'without going out of ourselves God may be more easily and certainly known than the things of this world.' Certainly God cannot be known if we go wholly out of ourselves—such self-alienation would be complete alienation from God also. On the other hand, Descartes was surely mistaken that God could certainly be known if we remain wholly within ourselves. Such self-preoccupation would be equally alienation from God who reveals himself, not only in that which is highest and deepest in us, but equally in that which is highest and deepest in the world —not only in the moral law within, but in the starry heavens above. God can be truly and fully known only in *all the things that are made*. Without the cosmological we should never arrive at a true knowledge of God, but without the anthropological we should never get started at all. In this sense the anthropological approach is primary. In exposition we may start with either argument, but in actual thought both are implicitly present from the beginning and constantly complement one another throughout.

[1] *The Faith of a Moralist*, Chapter ii.

VI

The Axiological Character of the Thomistic Argument as a Whole

A

The French theologian, Father Garrigou-Lagrange, tells us that the five arguments of St. Thomas are nothing more than philosophical refinements of one broad general proof that is actually used unreflectively by the most untrained people. The driving force, the 'principle of this general proof' is the following:

'The greater cannot arise from the less' condenses in effect into one single formula the principles on which our five general proofs rest: becoming can emerge only from determinate being; caused being only from uncaused being; the contingent only from the necessary; the imperfect, composite and multiple only from the perfect simple and one; order only from an intelligence. The principles of the first three proofs place in relief especially the dependence of the world upon a *cause*, the principles of the last two insist upon the superiority and perfection of this cause; all of them can be summed up in this formula: 'The greater does not arise from the less; only the higher explains the lower.'[1]

I think there is no question that the 'natural' reason as we have defined it argues in this way. Nor is there any question that the driving force of the argument, as summed up in this formula, is 'demonstrative' in the sense also in which we have defined 'demonstration.' The real issue is the interpretation of the formula and what the true inwardness of the principle of the general proof really is.

Everything turns, it will doubtless be admitted, on the meaning of the terms greater and less, higher and lower. No one supposes, of course, that they are to be taken in their original undefaced spatial imagery. It is, as we have seen, because originally the spatial and the axiological categories were not separated that these relations can be applied analogically. Their meaning is then axiological. It is true that Leibniz, voicing, as no other modern philosopher has, the essence of the classical tradition on this point, tells us that 'moral goodness or perfection

[1] *Dieu, son existence et sa nature*, English translation, I, pp. 252 ff.

178

is not to be confounded with metaphysical perfection or greatness'—and this is undoubtedly true—but it is just as certain that
while they are not to be confounded, they cannot be completely
separated. If *ex minime maximum non fit* is truly a necessity of
thought it is so only because the necessity is fundamentally
axiological. The determinate being from which alone becoming
can emerge, the uncaused cause from which finite causes alone
can be derived, are thus ultimate because there is 'more' in
being than in becoming and this 'more' is always understandable only in terms of value. In sum 'the principle of this general
proof' of which the French theologian speaks is essentially
axiological. It is value-charged from the beginning, because from
the beginning our reason is itself oriented towards the Good.

The objection is often made to the Thomistic argument that
it offers us, not a genuinely religious, but merely a 'value-
free,' cosmological notion of God. That Aquinas combines the
notion of absolute value with this cosmological notion when
actually there is no ground for the combination, and we have
here really to do with two wholly different universes of discourse.

Such an objection proceeds, however, from a misunderstanding of St. Thomas. It assumes the modern disjunction between
the sphere of value and the sphere of being, a disjunction which
did not exist for him. I agree, therefore, with von Rintelen when
he writes as follows: 'We must agree with the critic when he
says that an absolute causality and finality of God does not
alone bring us beyond the cosmological and ontological standpoint. But St. Thomas insists also on viewing God from the
standpoint of absolute intrinsic value as the very presupposition
of his being the ground and end of all.' He rightly concludes
that the 'concept of God of the Angelic doctor' is not open to
these criticisms. Translated into the terms of our discussion, this
means that the Thomistic way of thinking is axiological from
beginning to end. For St. Thomas there is not this contrast of
the existential and the value sphere as in the thinking of the
present—for him value and being are inseparable. I am,
accordingly, in agreement with von Rintelen when he further
writes: 'The concept of God is then not to be derived monistic-
ally out of the ontological cosmic unity, but rather in a special
degree out of the qualitative sphere of the value contents. This
Deity would then be (with Baeumker) the *ratio essendi* of all

values which are grounded in the ultimately subsisting Goodness and Holiness. This concept is not idealistic in the epistemological sense, nor merely a regulative idea, but a concrete divine form of absolute perfection and actual fulfillment of all potential good. . . . From this standpoint every reality of the universal value hierarchy can be related and the principle *Omne ens inquantum ens est bonum* can be applied to all being.'[1]

The theistic argument, as thus interpreted, finds its place therefore in the general movement of European thought for which, as we shall see, the primacy of the axiological is its determining character. Of this general movement we shall have more to say when we come to the discussion of the relation of religion to science in contemporary philosophy; here we are concerned solely with the relation of the theistic argument to European philosophy as a whole.

VII

The Driving Force of the Theistic Argument. Consilience of Proof. Probability and Intelligibility

A

One feature common to all modern interpretations of the theistic argument deserves special attention. All agree that it is not a collection of separate proofs, each of which has its own force apart from the others, but constitutes rather a systematic whole of inference in which the arguments mutually support one another; they constitute what is called consilience of proof.

'The proofs for the existence of God,' we are told, 'are not to be regarded singly and separately as if each constitutes an independent demonstration by itself. Rather are they to be taken cumulatively. We are not to suppose that the cosmological proof establishes a First Cause, the teleological proof an intelligent Designer and the moral proof a good and just Lawgiver. In fact, the cosmological argument merely leads up to the question whether the ultimate cause of the orderly and intelligible system we call nature can be anything short of an intelligent and

---

[1] Fritz Joachim von Rintelen, *Philosophia Perennis*, Volume II, pp. 966 ff. On this more ultimate question see also von Rintelen's *Der Wertgedanke in der Europaeischen Geistesleben*, especially pp. 219 ff.

purposive will. And as the cosmological argument serves to introduce, the moral argument completes the teleological argument. In short the traditional arguments are simply aspects of one complex and cumulative argument. The intelligibility of the natural order to human reason, the fitness of the natural environment for life, the course of organic evolution as a whole, the adaptiveness of natural beauty to our subjective faculties and the reality of moral values in human life rooted in nature— all of these evidences seem to suggest 'an intelligent Creator designing the world as a theatre for rational life.'[1]

This emphasis upon the 'cumulative' nature of the evidence is of great importance, but it also raises certain questions, the answers to which have an important bearing upon the entire problem of natural theology and of the true inwardness of the theistic argument. The first of these questions has to do with the cumulative nature of the argument and with the inward drive which makes it thus cumulative; the second with the character of this consilience of proof, as it is called, which its cumulative character creates.

The moral argument, we are told, *completes* the entire movement of thought. This, I think, hardly describes the situation as it actually is. It is questionable whether there would ever be this movement of thought at all, if the value consciousness and its implications were not there from the beginning to set the entire process in movement. This is, of course, the contention of the proponents of moral theology as the primary approach to Divinity, and of the moral argument as the heart of all theistic argument. But there is more to it than this. If, I should insist, there were not from the beginning the moral or value consciousness of man, with its co-implicate of perfection and of an *ens perfectissimum*, the movement of thought which we call the theistic argument would never get started at all. To a mind for which this were not an *a priori*, an initial datum, the meaning of God Himself would be doubtful; certainly the arguments for his existence would lack this cumulative force.

This interpretation of the cumulative character of the theistic proof determines likewise our conception of the consilience of evidence. As ordinarily stated this consilience means increase of probability, and as applied to the 'theistic hypothesis,' as it is

[1] F. R. Tennant, *Philosophical Theology*, Volume II, Chapter iv, p. 105.

called, this hypothesis commends itself to us as the most reasonable or *probable* explanation of the data of experience, even if it is not scientifically demonstrable. The question we shall have to ask is what the terms reasonable and probable mean in this context. Surely they can scarcely mean what they are supposed to mean in the context of scientific knowledge.

The notion of consilience of proof is derived, I suppose, in the first instance at least, from the sphere of circumstantial evidence. When the 'facts' or circumstances supporting a theory begin to accumulate, there is a consilience of evidence and the probability of the truth of the theory increases, so to speak, not arithmetically but geometrically. This notion of consilience is then applied to the more far-reaching scientific hypotheses, regarding, not specific facts, but more general concepts and theories. Of these the biological theory of evolution is often taken as an outstanding example. The various lines of evidence, the anatomical, physiological, etc., are consilient in the sense that they mutually support one another and attain thus, if not complete demonstration, at least a degree of probability which is said to be 'overwhelming.' From this a transition to more far-reaching cosmological and metaphysical hypotheses becomes easy and natural, and among such hypotheses, we are told, is the theistic, the cosmological and anthropological arguments presenting a consilience of evidence which, if not absolutely convincing, has also, as we say, a high degree of probability.

All this sounds reasonable enough, but presents, on closer inspection, a problem the difficulty of which is not always sufficiently appreciated. With this gradual transition to more and more far-reaching hypotheses and theories, the meaning of the notion of consilience of proof, and with it that of probability, undergoes a subtle but most significant change.

Even in the sphere of 'science' this change is patent. The biological theory of evolution of species by natural selection is one thing; a theory of universal or cosmic evolution is quite another. The former is empirical and the consilience of proof is also empirical; the latter since it is evolution of the whole, is metempirical, and no consilience of empirical evidence can verify such a proposition. This is true, as we shall see more fully later, of all cosmological propositions of science, such as evolution or devolution of the universe. Not only are such

Waynesburg College Library
Waynesburg, Pa. 15370

pronouncements in principle unverifiable empirically, but they are not even probable in the sense that empirical propositions are said to be. When now we pass from scientific hypotheses, however far-reaching, to more metaphysical hypotheses, such as the theistic, not only is all this *a fortiori* true, but the change in the notion of probability reaches a point at which, so to speak, this quantitative difference passes into a qualitative, and constitutes a transition to a wholly different order of meaning. With this change comes, therefore, a significant change in our notions of probability. It is quite generally recognized by those who, like Tennant, apply the notion of probability to the so-called theistic hypothesis, that probability here means something significantly different from that which it has in science.

B

The notion of probability, in the widest sense of that term, presents a difficult and puzzling philosophical problem which is recognized by all philosophers, and for which, as I believe, no satisfactory solution has yet been found. The mathematical theory of probability is based upon certain statistical assumptions; and when these assumptions hold, the meaning of probability is simple and the problem set is a wholly technical one of mathematical development. But the notion of more or less probable is meaningfully used where the idea of statistical theory is not applicable; and it is at this point that the meaning of *more or less* and of the notion of probability itself becomes a problem.

Even in the scientific universe of discourse this is true. When, for example, we consider, as we certainly do, the probability of some scientific conjecture as to the internal constitution of the stars, we seem to be influenced by some analogy which it is very difficult, if not ultimately impossible, to convert into an appeal to any definite statistical fact. Still more is this true of pronouncements on the past state of the cosmos or any prediction of a future state. When physicists tell us that the universe is 'running down,' or 'building up,' such pronouncements are influenced also by analogical lines of reasoning which, just because they are concerned with the cosmos as a whole, cannot be reduced to statistical fact. Such pronouncements of probability are not amenable to logical and mathematical handling, for probability, in order to be so treated, must be defined as a relation between sets of propositions—no proposition is probable or improbable in itself—and there seem to be no sets of propositions into which propositions about the universe as a whole can be thus set in relation. Thus the notion of probability, even here, has insensibly but significantly changed in our hands. How shall we describe this more fundamental probability?

It is sometimes called intuitive, as contrasted with calculable probability, and is considered to be the support of the latter.[1] Even in physical science there is a notion of probability which it is impossible to convert into an appeal to relations between sets of propositions, still less into any definite statistical fact. Thus, purely theoretically, as has often been pointed out, the verification of a scientific hypothesis by a single case might be an accident. It might be an accident that the displacement of the perihelion of Mercury given by the Einstein theory of gravitation, is exactly forty-three seconds of arc, and so just the same amount as that which the astronomers have inferred from their observations independently of the theory, or it might be an accident that the spectral lines of glowing substances, so far as they have been observed, have exactly the regularity expressed by Bohr's formula. But the physicist does not believe that; indeed the absurdity seems so absurd that no one would seriously take it into consideration. This is undoubtedly true, but it is precisely this fact that shows that there is a more ultimate notion of probability which constitutes the support of the calculable. The situation described is *antecedently* so improbable as to be intrinsically unintelligible and therefore absurd. The issue becomes clearest when we ask what is the basis of the probability which we are forced to ascribe to the postulates that underlie all knowledge and ultimately to the whole body of knowledge relative to which the probability of specific beliefs is assessed, since, *ex hypothesi*, there can be no more ultimate postulates, nor a more ultimate body of knowledge, to which it may be referred. Surely we have here come upon a meaning of probability which escapes all expression in logical and mathematical terms. One may quarrel with the term intuitive, which is, without doubt, highly ambiguous, but, after all, what is such antecedent and intrinsic probability or improbability but intuitive in some sense?

---

[1] Arthur Balfour, *Theism and Humanism*, pp. 189 f.

C

Those who speak of probability in connection with the theistic argument are, of course, not unaware of this situation. They acknowledge, as does Tennant, that purely logical or calculable probability is not that with which we are concerned in life, and it is obvious that it cannot be that with which we are concerned when we apply it to an hypothesis such as the theistic which is essentially an ultimate pronouncement upon human life and its relation to the ground of things. This intuitive probability is felt to include an element which can only be called 'moral,' although the notion of moral probability here has a much wider meaning than as used in jurisprudence. In the cumulative argument for theism it is, it is held, the moral argument which not only completes the movement but that without which it would never get started. It is reasonable to suppose that the probability which accompanies this cumulative evidence is in this broad sense moral also. The intrinsic intelligibility with which the more ultimate notions of probability are identifiable, seems to include an axiological element.

Men speak of conceptions or theories as being antecedently probable or improbable—even in science, as we have seen. It is antecedently so improbable that the single fact which verifies an hypothesis should be a chance coincidence of events that men refuse to entertain it. But certain larger conceptions of life and the world are thought to be antecedently so improbable as to be intrinsically unintelligible or absurd. Thus to the philosopher of old the very idea of an organism as merely a fortuitous concourse of atoms—that the parts, let us say of a gazelle, came together by chance—seemed so antecedently improbable as to be the dream of a drunken man, and as such intrinsically unintelligible. On the other hand, to another way of thinking, the idea of a creative *fiat*, of a Great Mind ordering the atoms in such a way as to bring into being the organism, seemed so anthropomorphic as to be antecedently improbable and in principle intrinsically unintelligible. It is not a question here which, if either, of these notions of antecedent probability and improbability is right, but merely that in both cases some notion of intuitive or intrinsic probability is assumed.

There are apparently two different meanings attached to the

notions of rationality and intelligibility, and therefore to the
notion of probability when used in this way; the question is
whether they are wholly opposite and contradictory. According
to the first notion, rationality demands the highest degree of
simplicity and clearness in any account of things. This is
attainable, however, only by the reduction of the complex to
the simple, and intelligibility in this sense consists exclusively in
simplicity and lucidity of relations. This is the ideal of intelligibility in science for which rationality consists exclusively in
necessary connections; the fact is no longer isolated and is
therefore intelligible. Rationality in the second sense demands,
however, the highest degree of meaning in any account of the
universe which it will accept as intelligible, and since meaning
when analysed is seen to have reference ultimately to ends and
values, intelligibility in this sense involves purposive or quasi-
purposive significance. Since, however, such significance is
realized only on the higher levels of being, intelligibility in this
sense means understanding of the simple in terms of the more
complex, of the lower in terms of the higher. The difference in
these two notions is obvious; the question is whether they are in
contradiction. I do not think that they are, as I shall attempt
to show in a later context.[1] In any case it is this second conception of reason and intelligibility that is assumed in classical
rational theology. If in this theology the notion of probability
is employed, it can only be one which finds its place in a value-
charged scheme of thought.

Yet probability, even in this second sense, seems to be
scarcely the concept really applicable to belief in divine things.
Even if belief in God were belief in an hypothesis, established as
any hypothesis regarding finite things is established—which of
course it is not—even then it would not have the kind of conviction which belief in God, to be significant, must have. Kant
seemed to have sensed this fact and to have expressed it in an
extraordinarily forceful way. An hypothesis or postulate in the
realm of scientific or theoretical reason, so he tells us, is only for
the purposes of explanation. From the standpoint of life and
practice it does not matter much whether I make the postulates
of Euclidian or non-Euclidian geometry. The hypothesis that
light is corpuscular or undulatory is important for scientific

[1] This will be developed in detail in Chapter xi, on 'Science and Religion.'

186

knowledge and the practical control of light, but it is a matter of indifference for life in its moral aspect. The role of a postulate in the practical life of morality is a wholly different matter. Here, as he says, 'a postulate is a requirement of practical reason, it is based on a duty, that of making something, the highest good, the object of my will so as to promote it with all my powers. In which case I must suppose its possibility and consequently all the conditions necessary thereto, God, freedom and immortality.' Kant goes on to point out that, whereas belief in the sphere of science is not necessary, and even sometimes not desirable, faith that is rational faith is necessary in the realm of practice.[1]

Despite these obvious facts, men will doubtless continue to speak of belief in God as a reasonable hypothesis—of the probability of that hypothesis and of the improbability of atheistic theories, and it would be sheer pedantry to insist that they should not. We may, however, be forgiven for seeking to point out what they should really mean when they use such terms. It has been said—and the saying has been widely quoted—that we would not be satisfied with probable friends; how should we then be satisfied with a probable God? Now I should not wish to press such a fortiori argument too far, for no theologian, and much less a philosopher, could allow that the universe of discourse in which we speak of our earthly friends is quite the same as that in which we speak of God, but there is an element of truth that cannot be gainsaid. A probable God, in the sense of a probable hypothesis, would not be God at all, but 'something else,' at best a part of the finite world which men in their ignorance called God. If a man once becomes aware of the real significance of the facts of the moral life, he is in little danger of reducing the postulates which make these facts intelligible to the level of mere speculation and probable hypothesis. Still less is he in danger of doing so if he once becomes aware of the real significance of the facts of the religious life; if he has once known what worship is— the experience of genuine prayer and praise. The *Deus vivus* can never be merely a probable god, and when the relation of this god to the *Deus philosophicus* is rightly understood it becomes clear to him that the latter cannot be a merely probable god either.

[1] *The Critique of the Practical Reason*, section viii.

VIII

The Theistic Argument in Present-day Culture.
Restatement and Reinterpretation

A

The story of the theistic argument as we have attempted to outline it—its long maintenance in the *corpus philosophicum*, both ancient and modern, and its apparent later dissolution, could result only in one of three things. Either it should pass out of men's thought as a gigantic 'rationalization' of the human mind, magnificent but pitiful, and give way to outright atheism; or, secondly, it should disappear and religion remain as a world of imagination and poetry, beautiful and in a sense significant, but without any relation to reality, a virtual atheism; or, finally, it should be interpreted as a temporally conditioned statement of a line of thought which, in its essentials, is of perennial value and validity.

The first two positions have been accepted by many modern thinkers. It is often held by sincere and forthright minds that the 'theistic hypothesis' is one in which men ought not to believe because there is 'no shred of evidence for it.' This is a possible position, but one which it is difficult to maintain. To the unbiased mind it seems more than improbable that the greatest minds of all time should be the victims of a progressive and systematic illusion. It is possible, but it is not a conclusion that a responsible thinker would care to accept. The second position seems much more reasonable. The God-idea has a meaning— for man's emotional and practical life. His attempt to rationalize that idea and belief, while as a rationalization a failure, has nevertheless a significance—if not as argument, still as poetic embodiment of socially valuable ideas. Apparently a much more generous and humane position, really it is not, for it merely fixes man in his illusions, and here, as elsewhere, perhaps, one may be cruel only to be kind. Neither of these positions, then, has seemed wholly acceptable to the great body of thoughtful men. It seems much more likely that the criticisms of these arguments which brought about their dissolution affect the form in which they were stated rather than their substance, their temporal conditions, not their perennial character.

'Nothing is more striking in modern philosophy of religion,' writes Professor Hoernlé, 'than the shift of emphasis from proofs for the existence of God to the effort to understand and appreciate religion.' . . . These proofs, 'divorced from their basis in religion, through which alone the very word "God" has any vital meaning, become ingenious pieces of dialectics, easily riddled by counter dialectics, and enabling the critics of religion to argue that a scheme of faith and conduct, built upon foundations so flimsy, has no claim on the allegiance or even respect of reasonable men. Far otherwise is the result if we approach God through religion rather than through an argument about the existence of God.'[1] Again we are told that 'these proofs, when presented in their traditional garb, stalk about with the unsubstantiality of ghosts,' and it is these ghosts—of Plato and Aristotle—that the truly religious man must finally learn to lay.

This general attitude, although far from being universal in modern philosophy, is widespread enough to be considered a typical modern attitude. That it should be maintained by those who hold that all discourse about God is meaningless except in an emotive sense is understandable. That it should also be held by many who still talk about God and his relations to nature and man, as though such discourse were significant—by those who still use the language of religion and theology—is harder to comprehend. To talk about God without reasonable grounds for believing that there is an object to which our discourse refers is, perhaps, possible for the ordinary believer, but not for the philosopher, and such reasonable grounds can be none other than the kind of reasons which have been embodied in the classical arguments. It seems, then, more than likely that the modern criticisms of these arguments affect the form in which they are stated rather than their substance, their temporal conditioning rather than their perennial character. It is this thesis—the third of the possible modern positions—that we shall seek to maintain. To maintain it involves, however, a restatement and reinterpretation of the theistic argument in terms which, while not truer, perhaps, are more congenial to the modern mind. It is to this task that the following chapter is devoted.

[1] *Studies in Contemporary Metaphysics*, pp. 294 ff.

Chapter VI

*Natural and Logical Witnesses for God (continued): The
Axiological Interpretation of the Theistic Argument*

I — A

A<small>N</small> EXAMINATION of the traditional theistic argument showed
us that while it was often misunderstood by those
who used it, it is fairly clear what its true inwardness has always been. Whatever it appears to be, actually
it always starts with values as its initial datum. On the surface
the ontological argument appears to be merely logical and not
axiological and the cosmological and teleological arguments
appear to start from value free facts, but closer examination
shows that this is really not so. If it were the argument would
lead, not to the God of religion and theology, but to something
else. It is insight into these facts which has increasingly led
theology to derive its arguments from considerations of value.
Unless one accepts the traditional argument in a wholly un-
modified form, or else asserts an apprehension of God so
personal and direct that the question of any other witness need
not even be raised, the argument is bound to take this form.

I choose for our initial consideration a peculiarly vivid and
illuminating illustration of this approach taken from an
article by Bernard Shaw in the *New Republic*. 'It was,' he
writes, 'thinking on intelligence, honour and beauty that
brought me to God. I cannot accept any theory of the universe
that makes these impossible.' Here we have the nerve of the
argument in its simplest form and one immediately apprehen-
sible by every one, even when more technical forms of statement fail either to make themselves understood or to convince.
Values are the initial datum of the argument—not only honour
and beauty, the moral and aesthetic, but those of intelligence
and reason, and therefore the entire scientific universe which
our reason builds up. It denies emphatically that these values
'are there,' in all their meaning and validity, independently of
any view of the cosmos we may hold; there *are* theories of the
universe which make them 'impossible.' It is this that Shaw,
after many vagaries, as he himself confesses in the preface to

Back to Methuselah, finally came to see. It may be, of course, that he ought not to have been brought thus to God, but the fact is that he was and that many others have followed the same path. It may be that the God to whom he was brought is scarcely He to whom thinking on these things should have actually brought him—Shaw himself listened too readily to the twentieth-century mythology of the finite, struggling God—but the fact remains that for him, as for many, the belief in Deity in some form alone made humanity intelligible.[1]

The more technical form of the argument merely expands and makes more definite this initial insight. It is the 'broad, general proof' of which Garrigou-Lagrange speaks and of which, as he holds, the Thomistic arguments 'are nothing more than philosophical refinements.' The greater cannot arise from the less; only the higher explains the lower. It is unnecessary to repeat here our analysis of this general proof; it is sufficient to recall that it is a value-charged argument throughout and that it has no meaning unless higher and lower are given an axio-logical significance.

That this is the heart of the entire theistic argument Nietzsche also saw with unexampled penetration. It is, as he calls it, the 'typical prejudice' by which the metaphysicians of all time can be recognized. 'How could,' so they ask us, 'anything originate but of its opposite? Such a genesis is impossible; whoever dreams of it is a fool. Things of the highest value must have a different origin, an origin all their own. In this transitory, seductive, illusory, paltry world, in this turmoil of delusion and cupidity, they cannot have their source. But rather in the lap of being, in the intransitory, the concealed God, in the thing-in-itself—there must be their source and nowhere else.'[2] Nietzsche is undoubtedly right in seeing in this the 'typical' presupposition of all religious philosophy. Whether it is also a 'prejudice' is another matter—indeed one of the fundamental issues of this chapter.

[1] I have used this illustration for a special reason for, as Hesketh Pearson, in his *G.B.S., A Full Length Portrait*, rightly says, the outstanding character of Shaw is 'his understanding of the religious temperament.' In view of the application of his mordant wit to many forms of religious expression, this may seem strange, but a deeper study of Shaw's work as a whole, I think, shows this to be essentially true.

[2] *Beyond Good and Evil*, Chapter i.

B

This then is the type of argument we have to understand and evaluate, but in order to do so we must be quite sure in our minds what the argument really is. There is a very common interpretation of it which I believe to be wholly false. We must therefore first state quite clearly what it is not.

The argument here, it is maintained, is that belief in God as the necessary ground of values gives satisfaction to a fundamental form of human exigence. 'We desire that the universe surrounding us should in some way care for values; that these should not be merely a mode of feeling which happens to have been developed by the accidents of the evolutionary process in a species of creatures crawling about on this planet; that they should represent the essential ground of things behind the phenomena; that the course of the universe through time should be such that the Spirit, for which values subsist, should be eternal and triumphant, in spite of the apparent perishability of all material things. What is put forward as the rational ground for believing in God is always some form of the argument that belief in God satisfies this exigence, this desire.'[1]

Now I believe this to be an essentially false statement of the argument. I do not deny, of course, that such desire is present in all those who are interested in rational grounds for such a belief at all. I cannot well envisage the type of mind that could find the fate of values significant at all unless it *did* desire their realization and conservation, any more than I can envisage a mind that would be interested in finding a rational pattern in the universe unless it valued such a pattern of relations and desired to find it. But it is not the desire that constitutes the exigency in either case, nor does the presence of such desire affect the cogency of the argument, unless the desires unconsciously and surreptitiously affect the argument in a way they should not; axiological thinking is not wishful thinking. There is indeed a desire which the belief in God satisfies, but it is not at all of the character represented. It is the demand for intelligibility—the same demand that makes itself felt in any form of really rational procedure, for it is the very nature of reason that anything with which the mind concerns

[1] E. Bevan, *Symbolism and Belief*, pp. 365 ff.

itself shall be made intelligible. The fact that that with which the mind here concerns itself is values—and their place in reality, in other words their cosmic significance—does not in the least affect the general character of the demand for rationality.

It is therefore difficult to understand what certain theologians can possibly mean when they criticise the argument from values as 'interested' and demand what they call a disinterested theology. They seem to think that our interest in human values, and in their conservation, somehow invalidates the cogency of any argument from them to God as their ground, whereas man is no more interested here than at any point at which the reason is brought into play, the scientist being no less interested in his particular values than the theologian. The motive for this criticism is, we are told, 'the subordination of man's values to the Divine values,' the substitution of a theocentric for an anthropocentric philosophy of religion.[1] Doubtless religion to be religion at all must be theocentric—any merely humanistic interpretation of religion ends in denaturing it completely—but only God is completely theocentric, only He could, so to speak, start from Himself alone. Man is for ever caught in a value-centric predicament which he cannot escape and should not attempt to if he could—neither by a religion of mere humanity nor one of mere Deity.

II

The Essentials of the Axiological Argument:[2] *The Demand for Intelligibility*

A

We have seen what the axiological argument is not. Let us now see what it is and seek to formulate it in a way in which it may be subjected to critical examination. It may take two forms, although in essentials they are one: namely, the argument from values and the argument from meaning. Before

[1] H. Richard Niebuhr, 'Value Theory and Religion' in *The Nature of Religious Experience*, pp. 93–116.

[2] For the sake of brevity we shall hereafter speak of the axiological argument, always remembering, however, that it is the axiological interpretation of the traditional theistic argument that we have in mind.

examining them separately let us see them in their relations, as two aspects of one fundamental and integral movement of human reason.

What is put forward as the rational ground for believing in God, so the false way of stating the argument informs us, is always some form of human exigence, and that therefore God must exist. Now belief in God does indeed satisfy human desire—and a very fundamental one at that—but it is the demand for intelligibility. It is precisely this which makes the argument *rational*.

Man finds himself in a 'world' in which he is 'concerned' with many things. Indeed it is precisely this concern which, as the 'existential' philosophers like to tell us, is the essential character of the human situation. This concern is, in the first place, with life and with the means of life—that the goods of life may be enhanced and conserved. But life has no ultimate meaning except as it is the 'good life,' and the means of life no significance unless, as instrumental values, they presuppose ultimate and intrinsic values. It is for these, the transcendentals, goodness, beauty and truth, that man as a thinking being is ultimately concerned. They are there—even the complete mechanist and naturalist, in so far at least as he is also a man, must acknowledge them—the question is 'how' they are there, how they are possible.

It is at this point that the argument from meaning enters in and that the argument from values and that from meaning are seen to be in essentials the same. The question whether the world has a meaning resolves itself into the more ultimate question whether values are realized in the world and when realized conserved. Is the world such as to make this realization and conservation possible?

This is the demand for intelligibility or rationality which constitutes the true inwardness of the theistic argument. The denial of meaning in the world constitutes what Tolstoy calls 'the fundamental contradiction of human life.' The essence of human life is the seeking for the Good—this seeking alone gives it meaning, and the denial of fulfilment or realization would constitute the denial of life. Now it may be, as we shall see, that this contradiction is fundamental to human life and constitutes a vicious circle of existence—in the life of the

individual, of society and of the cosmos itself—but even if it
were so, this contradiction would bring out clearly the relation
of the argument from value to the argument from meaning
which is all with which we are here concerned.[1]

B

The argument from values starts then with the initial acknowledgement of the intrinsic values—of beauty, honour and
intelligence—upon which the goods of life depend for their
significance; with the initial assumption that the values are
there. Without this acknowledgment and this assumption, the
argument itself has no meaning. As genuine values, however—
and that is the initial assumption—they are unintelligible,
'impossible,' unless they have their origin and consummation in
a being religion calls God.

The starting point of the argument is then, I think, indubitable or, if not absolutely so, at least of sufficient certitude to
constitute the initial datum of the argument. But even granting
this, it does not at all follow, it will be said, that to be 'possible'
these values must be made intelligible, and to be intelligible
they must have their ground and goal in God.

It is often maintained—and at first sight it seems true—that
their mere 'existence,' even in this objective sense, no more
demands that they be made intelligible than does the mere
existence or subsistence of sense data. We simply have them;
they are there and that is all there is to it. It is sheer nonsense to
say that any theory of the universe can make them other than
they are, still less impossible. Now this would, I suppose, be
true if, like sense data, our values were simply given; if they
came to us simply as objects of intuition and contemplation.
But that, as we have seen, is precisely what they are not.[2] They
come to us with the character of 'oughtness,' and that character
is intrinsic to their very nature. Not, it must be added, the oughtness of moral obligation alone—that is merely a secondary or
derived ought—but that more fundamental 'ought-to-be'
which is phenomenologically part of the nature of value as
such. The good is, as we have seen, different from other
essences in that in the 'ought-to-be' which is part of its essence

[1] Leo Tolstoy, *On Life* English translation, pp. 239 ff.
[2] Chapter iv, pp. 140 f.

as such, is the drive to realization, a power to go out beyond itself. Out of this arises the secondary or moral ought-to-do, the demand which the values make upon us. It is this exigence of the Good, in its metaphysical no less than its moral aspect, which gives rise to the demand for a 'rational' basis for values, for a conception of the world itself which shall make them 'possible.'

This analysis of value is, I believe, fundamental for the argument of the present chapter. The demand which the values make upon us is an essential part of our experience of reality and is therefore a demand of reality itself upon us, as the bearers of value. But this demand, to be intelligible, carries with it rational demands which the bearers of these values may make upon reality. This necessary correlation is, from one point of view, the demand for intelligibility which constitutes the burden of the axiological argument. 'Every one,' writes Baron von Hügel, 'who believes fully in anything at all, be it the obligation to truthfulness, in the more than utilitarian worth of his wife's or daughter's chastity, even in the more than empirical worth of natural science, believes that these things are part of a moral order' and, as he continues, 'in the more than human character of this order moral.' Now I think that this is true, and I think also that any one who does believe in these things— even in the more than empirical worth of science itself—must also believe in the more than human character of the value order presupposed. But suppose he does not acknowledge this character of our values? Then I do not believe that there is any form of argument that will convince him of the existence of God, for the idea of God itself has then no meaning. Without this acknowledgment, the argument would never get started, although unless the argument includes the cosmos as a whole it would never arrive. Science itself presupposes the more than merely empirical worth of its cognitive values and to deny this presupposition is as fatal for science as it is for morals.

It is true that since any argument for God involves the prior acknowledgment of intrinsic values it is to that extent an *argumentum ad hominem*, and the validity of such an argument is one of the issues we shall have to meet. Here our sole concern is with the drive of the argument. Elsewhere I have tried to express its force in the following way. If the demand of which we have spoken lies in the nature of values as such, and if further the fulfilment of that demand is necessary to give meaning or intelligibility to our entire life of volition as determined by values, then only a world in which finality, in the sense of 'increasing purpose,' and conservation of values, in the sense of an 'imperishable goal'—in short a world such as it is conceived by religion—would be intelligible to our reason and in any sense tolerable to our feeling. A theory of the world which denied these presuppositions of intelligibility would be an intolerable world. I also maintained that, in an ultimate metaphysical context, unintelligibility and intolerability are one and the same thing.[1]

This form of argument easily lends itself to caricature and it has been so degraded by McTaggart. He calls it a *reductio ad horrendum* and describes it in the following words: 'Unless a certain dogma is true the universe will be intolerably bad—either intolerably miserable or intolerably wicked—and therefore the doctrine must be true.'[2] Surely criticism of this kind is as superficial as it is gratuitous and beneath the dignity of the magnanimous philosopher. But even more than this, it fails utterly to grasp the real nerve of the argument. It is but another illustration of that false interpretation which sees in the argument merely the satisfaction of human desire. The argument does not say that a belief is true because the opposite would make the universe intolerably miserable or wicked. What it really says is that the belief is true because the opposite would make the universe, *as we actually know it*, 'impossible.'

The question may indeed still be asked, Why should the world not be ultimately unintelligible in this sense? Are there not many who seem to find it quite tolerable, although for them it is an utterly senseless world? Now I would not deny, of course, that this is apparently so. Psychologically 'one can get used to anything, even to hanging.' But our point is that it is not a psychological matter (of desire), but a necessity which is purely logical or axiological. This men finally learn through bitter experience, as did Tolstoy. In *My Confession* we are told

---

[1] *The Intelligible World*, Chapter x, pp. 334 ff.

[2] J. M. E. McTaggart, *Some Dogmas of Religion*, p. 82. This is but one sample of the manner in which both dogmas and argument are caricatured throughout the book.

how he continued to find certain 'drops of honey' pleasant on his tongue even after a valueless and meaningless world had become intolerable in this sense. But he had both psychological insight and logical acumen enough to see that sensations and feelings were here wholly irrelevant. It was a matter of reason, and when reason had once awaked, as it did in him, no amount of sophistication could hide the real truth.

C

This is then, I hold, the real character of the argument from values, and only so understood has it either point or cogency. The same general type of argument is, however, often put in another form which may be described as the argument from meaning. Before proceeding to an evaluation of the argument as a whole it will be useful to examine it in this second form— more especially for the reason that, thus formulated, it brings out even more clearly the relation of the argument from value to the historic theistic arguments which argue 'empirically' from the world or cosmos to God. The argument is often put in the following form: 'If the world has a meaning, God, the Supreme Spirit, must be its origin, ground and goal. But the world has a meaning indubitably. Therefore there must be a ground or goal of the nature described by religion as God.'

We have already seen in a general way the relation of the argument from meaning to the argument from value. It may be made more specific by asking ourselves what the phrase 'has meaning' here signifies. If we take it in the sense it plainly bears in this context, it is values and their realization that give life, and the world in which our life is lived, whatever meaning they may be said to have.

Of any action or activity we say that it is intelligible or has meaning—for the two are really identical—when it is rational in the sense that it is directed to the realization of value. Suppose a man deaf from birth saw an orchestra playing for the first time and had never had explained to him what music is; all this activity of men playing through brass tubes and scraping strings of catgut would seem wholly irrational energy, a great volume of effort for apparently no purpose at all. For the person who hears the music the meaning of the activity is the value of the beauty realized by him. Similarly the men from Mars on

Armistice Day would find the sudden cessation of all activity meaningless unless they knew the values realized through the stoppage. This then is what the phrase 'has meaning' itself plainly bears and it is clear from these illustrations that if the world has meaning it must be extended far beyond our own individual lives—at least to that portion of the world which we call society and history. The real question is whether we may say of the 'world' or the cosmos as a *whole* that it has meaning.

Certainly the cosmos gives the impression of having some meaning whether we may say what it is or not. As it is difficult to see an orchestra playing, even if one is deaf, or the cessation of activity on Armistice Day, even if one did not know its meaning, so also it is difficult to see all the activities and operations which make up nature and the world as a whole without having 'a tremendous impression of a meaning and of a gain'—and therefore of values in the world the realization of which determine this meaning and this gain. One cannot, for instance, survey the entire story of 'matter, life, mind and value'—from star dust to society—without an overwhelming impression of what we call meaning and purpose in the world. But after all this is merely an impression—and at times we may have another impression; for such a proposition about the world as a whole there is and can be no purely empirical evidence. If there is any argument for the meaning of the whole, it must be of another character, namely, dialectical.

It seems possible, at least at first sight, to say that there is some meaning in the world and still deny meaning to the whole. Yet it is, I think, only seeming. Denial of all meaning to the whole must, I think, ultimately mean denial of genuine meaning to any of the parts. This comes out most clearly, perhaps, in connection with the postulate of 'progress,' with which for the modern man belief in a meaningful world is largely bound up. At first sight it seems possible that there should be genuine progress in a particular field—let us say from stagecoach to steam engine or from the Magna Charta to the British Constitution—but if either were divorced from that wider progress which we call 'moral,' however we conceive it, it would scarcely remain progress. 'Real progress,' says Sir William Ramsay, 'is learning how better to employ energy and better to effect its transformation,' but surely one need not be told how unreal such progress would be if it ended in the destruction of the culture that produced it. Even more clearly is this relation seen if we consider progress from the standpoint of past, present and future. It seems possible to say that there has been progress in the past, although at a certain time in human history regress set in. Yet little reflection is necessary to realize that if this so-called progress should come to a full stop in time, that which we called progress in the past would turn out to have been only apparent and, in any ultimate sense, never to have really been. Genuine meaning of the parts seems, therefore, to presuppose meaning of the whole—and denial of the meaning of the whole, *ipso facto*, to involve denial of all meaning to the parts.

The starting point of the argument—that the world has a meaning—if then not absolutely undubitable, is, nevertheless, of the same degree of certainty as the starting point of the argument from values with which it is closely connected. It is abstractly possible to deny it, of course, but the antecedent probability against such a view would be too great. Granted this assumption, the inference seems to follow. If meaning in this 'plain' sense of the word is inseparable from the notions of ultimate origin and end—for just as ultimate origins and ultimate ends qualify values, so also they condition and determine meaning—then *if* the world has a meaning, in this sense, God, the Supreme Spirit and the Sovereign Good, must be its origin, ground and goal. This is, as I have already suggested, the true inwardness of the so-called *a posteriori* arguments themselves—the cosmological and the anthropological. The greater cannot come from the less; only the higher explains the lower. It is also the reason why, whether we start with the anthropological or the cosmological, both are implicitly present from the beginning and complement one another.

Cogent as this reasoning seems to be, there is, nevertheless, one way in which the entire argument may be challenged, and that is to deny the conception of meaning from which the argument starts. We may admit that we find meaning in the world, but only in the sense that 'science' understands meaning, and from meaning in this sense no such argument to a spiritual ground of meaning is possible.

It is commonly maintained that meaning or intelligibility in science involves no such reference to ends and values. All that it means is that things stand in necessary connections and that the world has a pattern. From the fact that the universe is rational or intelligible in this sense it cannot be inferred with any cogency that the universe is rational in the former sense. It has been the weakness of the traditional theistic proofs, we are told, to suppose that the one does follow from the other.

Now it is true, of course, that science may, for its own special purposes, arbitrarily confine the notions of meaning and intelligibility to these domestic uses, just as for its own purposes it narrows the notion of knowledge to reference to sensuously observable entities. But when it does so it will, if it is at all self-critical, recognize that the limitation *is arbitrary*, and that meaning and intelligibility in this sense fall far short of the notions which reason, in its full character, actually demands. It will recognize that, in Whitehead's terms, 'all ultimate reasons are in terms of aim at value,' and that merely to find a pattern in nature does not of itself make it intelligible.[1]

D

Of the two forms of the axiological argument, the argument from meaning, although ultimately inseparable, from the argument from values, is in a sense the more compelling. For many it seems possible to say we do not find values in the world, we put them there, but it is not so easy to say this of meaning.

I suppose there are few—even atheists—who would not admit that if the world *does* have a meaning in *this* sense, then 'Spirit' must in some sense be the necessary presupposition of that meaning. Only they would deny that it has such meaning. And yet there are few that really believe this. I do not deny that such exist—complete nihilism is always a psychological possibility—but it is a position very difficult to maintain.

It is difficult to maintain logically or dialectically. The denial of meaning in the world is one of those denials that ultimately refute themselves. I have elsewhere made use of an application of this principle of self-refutation by Prince Troubetzkoy, but he uses it in such a vivid and telling way that I shall yield to the temptation of repeating it in the present context.

With characteristic Russian frankness, he admits that human

[1] This self-limitation of science and its significance for the larger philosophical issues will be developed more fully in Chapter x.

life, as it merely unfolds before our eyes, seems to reveal no meaning whatsoever. It is a meaningless circle, a movement from death to death, attended throughout by suffering—and suffering, too, without apparent meaning or aim. The life of man in the modern State does not alter these conditions but rather intensifies them. It repeats them in a more disastrous form and on a more extended scale. Nor does nature, as mere nature, reveal anything different. We receive an overwhelming impression of a reign of nonsense, of no-meaning, an impression which becomes appalling in virtue of the suffering involved. Progress is an illusion, since every advance inevitably returns to the point of departure and ends in death. . . . And yet, that a meaningless world is not the final truth is clearly indicated, he believes, by the fact that we consciously recognize its nonsense and condemn it as evil. The discovery of nonsense in the world would not have been possible to us unless we were aware of a meaning of life which we perceive to be contradicted by the senseless spectacle before us. Were we merely victims of the vicious circle of existence, we would neither recognize it as vicious nor lament our condition as victims. But we recognize its viciousness, we do lament our condition, and this clearly proves the presence of some element in our nature which is above the reign of nonsense and opposed to it. Let us follow up the clue afforded by this attitude of condemnation in which we view the senseless revolutions of the natural world. May it not be that man, 'in becoming the judge of a natural world, declares himself at the same time the prophet of a better?'[1]

For myself, I find the logic of this ancient *argumentum ad hominem* unanswerable. It is not necessary to admit with the complete pessimist that human life and nature, as they unfold before our eyes, reveal no meaning and that they constitute the vicious circle so vividly portrayed. There are reasons to believe that 'the world has a meaning.' The point is that even if this were so, the statement that there is no meaning in the world is still essentially self-refuting. For in order to condemn the world as meaningless, meaning is already present—not merely in the minds of those that condemn, but in the world itself of which our minds are a part. He who says we do not find meaning in the

[1] Prince Eugene Troubetzkoy, 'The Reign of Nonsense in the World, in the State and in Human Life,' *The Hibbert Journal*, Volume XVI, pp. 117 ff.

world but put it there is talking nonsense, for we are in the world and our meanings, and the values which they presuppose, are already a significant part of the world itself. It is for the mind who acknowledges their presence to determine what that actual presence presupposes or implies. Such presupposition is not, as Nietzsche would have, a prejudice—'the typical prejudice of the metaphysicians of all times.' It is rather the fundamental postulate upon which not only metaphysics, but ultimately knowledge of any kind, depends.

The denial of meaning in the world is then difficult to maintain logically or dialectically. It is even more difficult to maintain it in actual belief. An outstanding illustration is the case of Nietzsche. For him intellectually the world was amoral and without meaning. Nevertheless he understood fully that if human life were to have a meaning there must be some meaning in the world in which that life is lived. What then to do? Man must *put meaning into the world*: 'the superman is the meaning of the earth.' But his 'stillest hour' came when he realized that if meaning is not in some sense there, it cannot be put there. The conflict between the meaning of life and the meaninglessness of the world is expressed in the doctrine of the eternal recurrence. For Nietzsche there was, then, no intellectual solution of this 'fundamental contradiction of life,' only a volitional *tour de force* was possible—we must bite off the serpent's head, so Zarathustra tells us. The note of intellectual hysteria, so plainly present in Nietzsche's later writings, arose out of this terrible realization—a note which one finds sounding ever more plainly in the confusions of the modern world.

We began this chapter with a reference to a popular expression of the argument from values. For similar reasons I should like to close the discussion of the argument from meaning with comment on a recent book which, if it does not explicitly accept this argument, nevertheless appreciates fully the problem involved. I refer to Aldous Huxley's *Ends and Means*, especially the chapter entitled "Beliefs."

After discussing the goals of modern society and the roads that lead to these goals, he takes up the question of the beliefs which alone make these goals intelligible and their achievement possible. One of these is the belief that the world has a meaning. 'Does the world,' he asks, 'as a whole possess the value and meaning that we constantly attribute to certain parts of it (such as human beings and their works); and if so what is the nature of that value and meaning? This is a question which, a few years ago, I should not even have posed. For, like so many of my contemporaries, I took it for granted that there was no meaning. This was partly due to the fact that I shared the common belief that the scientific picture of an abstraction from reality was a true picture of reality as a whole; partly also to other non-intellectual reasons. I had motives for not wanting the world to have meaning; consequently assumed that it had none, and was able without any difficulty to find satisfying reasons for this assumption.'[1] Suffice it to say that, like many of his earlier contemporaries, he now comes to the conclusion that the parts of the world do have a meaning, and that if they do the world must have a meaning as a whole. From this his entire argument proceeds.

It is true that his argument leaves much to be desired. He does much less than justice to the historic theistic arguments as ways of stating the necessity of this ground of a meaningful world, seemingly unable to distinguish between their temporally conditioned form and their inmost essence, and failing to see that it is this very essence that he is himself maintaining. It is also true that, having abandoned all 'rational' grounds for believing in a meaningful world, he finds it necessary to fall back upon a kind of mysticism which is neither very convincing nor appealing. But when all is said, two things stand out with reasonable clearness, namely, that the demand for meaning or intelligibility is not a matter of mere desire (one may *desire* a meaningless world as well as a meaningful one—as indeed many of his contemporaries did); and secondly, that the belief in a meaningful world is the primary condition of there being any intelligible talk about 'ends and means' at all, and that it is high time that we stop all this meaningless babble about practical means until we realize this fact. The conversion of Huxley, like that of Shaw, is symptomatic of a significant change in our intellectual climate and it is for this reason that it is of interest in this context.

[1] *Op. cit.*, p. 312.

III

*Evaluation of the Axiological Argument. Direct and
Indirect Proof*

A

We have now attempted to outline the modern axiological
restatement and reinterpretation of the theistic argument in two
of its most common forms, namely, the argument from values
and the argument from meaning, the two being in essence one.
The question now is as to the cogency of the argument.

We are not surprised to find, of course, that to many it is
merely a case of wishful thinking—not of rationality but of
rationalization—and that, in so far as there is any logic in it at
all, bad logic, in that the argument is plainly circular. And,
indeed, if the argument is interpreted falsely, as is constantly
done, both of these criticisms are doubtless justified. With regard
to the first, it seems plain that if belief in God as the ground
of meaning and value is merely the satisfaction of human desire,
however imperious, then indeed is the entire 'argument' a case
not of rationality but of rationalization. Moreover, in so far as
the argument is directed to others, it is not an *argumentum ad rem*,
but an *argumentum ad hominem*.

The charge that the argument is really circular obviously
goes to the heart of the matter. It is quite commonly said that
to argue that if the world has a meaning, that it is rational in
the sense of realizing values, then Spirit must be its origin
ground and its goal, is really an argument in a circle; that what
the argument comes to is this: If the world is such as to satisfy
the demands of the spirit, then it must be such as to satisfy the
demands of the spirit. If the world has a meaning then the
reality behind the phenomena must be God.

This charge of circularity, it is well to realize, applies not
merely to the theistic argument as above conceived, but to all
arguments to presuppositions of whatever kind—that is from
experience to the presuppositions which make that experience
possible and intelligible. It applies not only to proofs for the
'existence' of God, but for the soul, freedom of the will—in
short for any 'object' that transcends experience in the sense of

sensationalistic empiricism. It applies also to all arguments to the presuppositions which make knowledge itself possible or intelligible. Arguments of this type have been called 'a peculiar kind of proof' for they are neither deductive nor inductive in the sense of 'ordinary logic' but transcendental in the sense of being an argument from the possibility of experience to the necessary conditions of such possibility—in short, what is called 'an argument to presuppositions.' Obviously our first task is a closer examination of this kind of argument.

The essential character of 'ordinary' logic is that it is always progressive, whether deductive or inductive—from experienced facts to some other hypothetical fact formulated to explain the facts. The essential character of the argument from possibility is that it is regressive—from what is experienced to that which is presupposed by the experience. This 'argument to presuppositions,' by which the necessary postulates of both morality and knowledge are established, constitutes an indirect proof of the possibility and validity of the experience in question. These presuppositions have 'the peculiar property that they make possible the very experience which is their ground and support.' A presupposition may be defined as an assumption or postulate the denial of which refutes itself, for it involves the denial of the very experience from which it proceeds.[1]

It is this character of the indirect form of argument which leads its critics to call it an argument in a circle, and it must be admitted that, as Professor H. J. Paton has said, 'it is always possible to raise the question whether such proof does not involve a circle.' He thinks it does not; and I agree with him that this charge can be made only when the nature of the argument is misconceived. It is assumed that the presuppositions or postulates to which the argument leads are of the nature of hypotheses—in other words the argument is from facts to other facts, whereas in reality it is an argument not from the facts of experience but from the possibility of experience.

This distinction, although of crucial importance, is often overlooked. Arguments from the 'facts' of experience can lead

---

[1] This type of proof is discussed by H. J. Paton in Volume II of *Kant's Metaphysic of Experience*, pp. 103–7. He makes it quite clear that, whether right or wrong, the argument is not of the type assumed by the critics of the argument. The indirect proof from the possibility of experience is different from the proof of the facts of experience.

only to other facts, either actual or hypothetical. Arguments from the possibility (or intelligibility) of experience lead to something quite different, namely, to the conditions or pre-suppositions which make such experience intelligible, for in this context possibility and intelligibility mean the same thing. It is this crucial distinction which makes it awkward, if not actually naïve, to speak of the existence of God, of the soul or of freedom, as hypotheses with degrees of probability.

As opposed to this conception of proof, one hears it said that logical analysis 'makes it clear that since all proof rests upon assumption it is vain for any philosophy to pretend to prove all material propositions. It must make indemonstrable assumptions in regard to existence, value, duty. This is particularly cogent against Kant's transcendental method, i.e., the attempt to prove certain propositions true because they explain how experience is possible. We cannot explain experience or anything else without assuming something and it is downright logical fallacy to assert that because our assumptions explain something they are therefore demonstrably true. Obviously Kant does not and cannot offer any cogent proof that there may not be some other set of assumptions that will also explain the facts of experience.'[1]

Now I should not for a moment wish to deny what is here said about material propositions in the sense understood. But when applied to the type of argument with which we are here concerned it is quite irrelevant. The propositions with which Kant was concerned are not propositions about matter of fact at all but about the possibility or validity of all factual propositions. Nor should I deny that all proof must ultimately rest upon indemonstrable assumptions and that it is therefore vain for philosophy to seek to prove all assumptions. But Kant never attempted such an impossible task. Actually he never sought to prove the truth of the factual propositions of science; he assumed it and from this argued to the presuppositions which made them possible. He never attempted to 'prove' the reality of our moral values and of the obligation which springs from their acknowledgment; he assumed it and argued therefrom to the postulates or presuppositions which made them possible. Freedom is for Kant both presupposition and postulate. But we are not

---

[1] Thus Morris R. Cohen, *Contemporary American Philosophy*, Volume I, p. 227.

concerned with Kant as Kant, but rather with the general type of argument which, although connected with his name, is really as old as philosophy itself. More particularly we are concerned with this type of argument as applied to the theistic proof as here interpreted and understood. It too starts with undemonstrable assumptions. Here too the argument is also to presuppositions and not to material fact. It assumes the more than empirical worth of honour, beauty and intelligence—an assumption that can only be acknowledged—and then asks, how are they possible? It is not at all obvious that another set of assumptions than the theistic will 'explain' these values if we understand what explain here means. On the contrary, if they are fully understood any other assumption or presupposition makes them impossible.

I think, then, that the charge of circularity from which this analysis started is possible only when the nature of the argument is itself misunderstood. The argument for God as the necessary presupposition of the possibility of our values makes this pre-eminently clear. The argument does not say that if the world is to satisfy the demands of the spirit it must be such as to satisfy the demands of the spirit and that, therefore, God must be its ground and goal. What it really says is something quite different. Granted the acknowledgment of values—and without this initial acknowledgment there is no argument, for there is no meaning to the idea of God itself—granted this, then one must acknowledge that which the values presuppose and must deny any presupposition which makes them impossible. Surely there is no circle here.

But if the argument is not circular, surely when thus interpreted it becomes all the clearer that it is essentially and in the last analysis, an *argumentum ad hominem*. Now I shall not deny that in a certain sense it is, but my point is that in matters such as this it is also an *argumentum ad rem*. If the initial datum of the argument is the acknowledgment of values surely this must in the nature of the case include an appeal to man, for he alone in the entire realm of nature is the conscious bearer of values and alone can acknowledge them. It is an *ad hominem* argument also in the sense that it asserts that denial of this necessary presupposition involves self-refutation, and constitutes an appeal to the opponent of the argument to avoid the self-referential incon-sistency involved. But while it is an argument *ad hominem*, and involves the irony which one charged with it so dislikes, it is only in appearance that it is directed to the opponent, whereas in reality it is directed against his thesis. With regard to ultimate issues it is always an argument *ad rem*. It is so because the man to whom the appeal is made, and the presupposition the denial of which leads to self-refutation, is part of the material of the argument itself.[1]

B

Most criticisms of the axiological argument really go back to the false conception of its nature with which we started. This is equally true whether the criticism is from the traditional or more modernistic and naturalistic standpoints. I am particularly interested in the former for it is, I believe, on the basis of this false interpretation that criticism by the modern Thomists largely proceeds. This is admirably illustrated in Chapter vi of Hubert S. Box's *God and the Modern Mind*, entitled 'The Philosophy of Value,' and it is from this that we shall take our start.

[1] I should like in this connection to call attention to a penetrating and illuminating article by my colleague, Professor Frederic B. Fitch, entitled 'Self-Reference in Philosophy' which appeared in *Mind*, Volume LV, N.S. No. 217, January 1946.

Professor Fitch discusses the *argumentum ad hominem* from the standpoint of a mathematical logician. In contrast to the general notion as to its unsoundness, he 'regards it as a very important sort of argument and one that is perfectly valid against certain types of theories.' In fact 'its use in philosophy distinguishes the latter from the empirical sciences.' He notes that 'W. M. Urban in his book, *The Intelligible World*, makes repeated use of the *ad hominem* argument. On page 45 he quotes Lowes Dickinson as holding that in ultimate matters the *argumentum ad hominem* is 'the only argument possible and, indeed, the only one in which any one much believes.'

What then is the basis for this logician's defence of the *argumentum ad hominem* which he also recognizes, rightly, as involving the '*argument to presuppositions*'? It consists in what I believe to be a very important distinction between two types of theories, namely, between those concerned with a particular subject matter as in physics and biology (material propositions in the sense above defined) and those of philosophy which deal with the general nature of theories. In philosophy extreme comprehensiveness is sought and here we encounter a situation in which theory is part of its own subject matter. If a theory is included in its own subject matter it is called a self-referential theory. Here the only way of refuting a theory is to show that it is self-referentially inconsistent. It is at this point that the *ad hominem* argument enters in, for its essence is that the critic accuses his opponent of self-referential inconsistency. It is, as Professor Fitch says, a 'very ancient type of argument' and he proceeds to show how it has been constantly used, and alone can be used in ultimate matters. The interesting thing is that he also finds it a very modern type of argument and shows how it is used in modern mathematics and mathematical logic. The point here, however, is that when a theory is a part of its own subject matter an *argumentum ad hominem* is also an *argumentum ad rem*.

Dr. Box recognizes that one of the main characteristics of modern philosophical discussion is the prominent place given to the concept of value. He recognizes further that, since Kant, all progressive theologians have shifted the emphasis away from 'abstract philosophical argument to arguments from value.' It is against this movement, as against other typical developments of modern theological thought, that he protests, and this protest rests, in the last analysis, upon two grounds with both of which we are already familiar, namely, first, upon the assumption that values as here conceived in these arguments are subjective; and secondly, that the notion of value is substituted for the notion of being which has always been primary in traditional philosophy.

The first of these assumptions is demonstrably untrue, and the fact that it is tacitly assumed is sufficient to indicate how seriously the argument is misunderstood. No representative of the axiological interpretation of the theistic argument with whom I am acquainted holds this view and there is none who does not definitely deny the subjective view of value and the disjunction between fact and value that it implies. It is true that at the beginning of the value movement in theology—as at the beginning of the modern value movement in general philosophy—value conceptions had a definitely subjective cast. The contrast between fact and value, characteristic of the Ritschlian movement, led men to put religion on the value or emotional side and science on the factual side, supposing that therewith the opposition between religion and science could be reconciled. But the impossibility of founding a theology or philosophy of religion on a subjective theory of value soon showed itself, and value theology, as now understood, is wholly objective. Even the philosophers specifically cited by Dr. Box, namely, Sorley and Pringle-Pattison, are wholly definite on this point.[1]

Equally untenable is the assumption underlying the second part of the criticism, namely, that the notion of value is *substituted* for that of being, the latter being primary in traditional philosophy. Such a contrast and conflict Dr. Box assumes in

[1] This is particularly true of W. R. Sorley who in his Gifford Lectures, *Moral Values and The Idea of God*, starts specifically with the objectivity of values and their inseparability from existence or being. In fact he accepts specifically the formulations of the present writer. See Chapter iii, entitled 'The Meaning of Value,' especially pp. 77–84.

Chapter vii, entitled 'The Philosophy of Being,' and argues
for the latter as against a philosophy of value. But two important
facts are here overlooked. In the first place, no important
representative of the axiological position substitutes value for
being. It is precisely their position that such substitution is
impossible, for while the two notions are perhaps not identical
they are at least inseparable. If in the development of the
argument the primacy is in any sense given to value, it is only
in the sense that value is the initial datum of the argument—in
the sense, as has been pointed out, that unless we start with the
acknowledgment of value there is no meaning to the idea of
God at all. On the other hand, it is equally untrue to say that
being is the primary category in the Thomistic philosophy in
any exclusive sense, in the sense, namely, that would deny a
similar primacy to the Good or Value.

For St. Thomas *Omne ens est bonum; bonum cum ente convertitur.*
These theses not only summarize the essence of the Thomistic
philosophy but equally, I believe, as I sought to show in
Chapter iv, the basis of all Christian theology. It is true that in
some contexts being is apparently given an exclusive primacy.
In the *ordo cognoscendi*, as St. Thomas calls it, the succession is
being, truth and then goodness, although as St. Thomas says,
'the good is in all things.' Yet this succession in no way detracts
from the value-centric character of the theistic argument. For
side by side with this assertion of the priority in knowledge
(although not in being) of being over truth and goodness, St.
Thomas also recognizes a certain priority of goodness which
shows that he regarded the inspiration of the Good as the motive
of the intellect: 'The intellect understands the will and the will
wills the intellect to understand.' Again good is in a certain
sense prior to being, since goodness implies the idea of a final
cause which for him is the first, among causes, for Good is the
first in the order of causality.[1]

The issue here involved is much more fundamental for
theology, dogmatic and natural alike, than is ordinarily understood. Hegel argued—and it is the key to all his thinking—that
pure being, if *really* pure, is wholly indeterminate and therefore
not-being. *Das reine Sein und das reine Nichts sind also dasselbe.*[2] This

[1] *Summa Theol.* I qu. VI, art. 3; also I, qu. XVI, art. 4.
[2] *Wissenschaft der Logik*, Bd. III, s. 78.

argument, it is maintained by some Thomists, is unsound. Indetermination, they tell us, is indeed the negation of all generic and individual determination but not a denial of being itself. This is doubtless true, but it is also true that the being which is not negated is also inexpressible. For it is only in categories that are generic, specific and individual, that any expression of reality is possible. In any case, and this is the point I wish to make, if *ens* and *bonum* are really convertible, then if being is abstracted from value and given exclusive primacy, it is no longer being in its fullness. In so far as it approaches purity it also approaches nothingness, as indeed all the extreme negative mystics have seen—for whom, as for Meister Eckhart, God is not merely that which is beyond the Good, but also beyond existence.

I have never been able to understand—and I admit it may be a defect in my understanding—how a Thomist, of all men, should take the lines of argument and criticism which we have been examining. Should he not realize that the angelic doctor never for one moment allowed the wholly modern disjunction between value and being, least of all the subjective view of value which makes possible this disjunction? For him 'whatever is, in so far as it is or has being, is at the same time, and for this very reason also, true, good and beautiful.' As Gilson beautifully expresses it, 'the humblest form of existence exhibits the inseparable privileges of being which are truth, goodness and beauty.' Could anything be clearer? How, in the light of such a doctrine as that of the transcendentals, one can speak of the exclusive primacy of being it is difficult to see; and even more difficult to understand how those who maintain the primacy of value should be accused of setting value over against being.[1]

C

The ordinary criticisms of the axiological argument may be recognized then as resting upon these patent misunderstandings. Yet, it may be maintained, there remains a fatal weakness in the argument. For behind both these criticisms there is a still more fundamental one, namely, that the theistic argument, so interpreted, substitutes an anthropological for a cosmological

[1] See on the question of the 'transcendentals,' Fulton J. Sheen, *The Philosophy of Science*, p. 137 ff.

approach, and that, after all, it is only nature and logic that can ultimately bear significant witness to God. Such criticism rests, it is true, mainly upon the merely subjective view of value already examined, but it implies something further, namely, that the argument is purely anthropological and constitutes therefore an argument for a God of humanity, but not for a God of the cosmos also.

This issue was raised, and in principle met, I believe, in the preceding chapter, but some additional comment may make the point clearer. There we found that the anthropological is the primary approach, for the very meaning of the question, Is Divine existence credible? depends upon the question, Is human existence, as we understand it, credible? and, still more, Is human reason *capabilis*? But if without the anthropological we should never start, it is also true that without the cosmological we should not arrive. The point I wish to make here is that the axiological argument as here developed includes the cosmological also. The initial *datum* of the argument is not merely the values of honour and beauty but of intelligence also, and therefore it argues, if not directly, at least indirectly from the concept of nature which our human intelligence by its method called science builds up. To deny that which is presupposed by intelligence is to deny also the significance of the structure which intelligence builds up. In other words science, then, to quote the words of Balfour, 'cuts off the limb upon which it sits.'

I do not mean that, as many have thought, we may proceed directly from the nature as science conceives it to God as its Ground and First Cause. This I believe to be a mistake as a later examination of the 'scientific conception of nature' will, I think, make clear. For, as we shall see, the concept of nature built up by scientific method proceeds by excluding *ab initio* the values which constitute the initial datum of the theistic argument.[1] But this does not mean that the values are not there and, as Whitehead tells us, are not the key to any metaphysical interpretation, even of nature itself. It is from nature only as including man and his values that any argument to God is possible. For these reasons we have quite properly, I think, described this chapter as a continuation of our discussion of the natural and logical witnesses for God. For an appeal to nature

[1] Chapter X, pp. 369 ff.

and logic has no meaning except as an appeal to nature which has not yet been denatured, and to a logic which, however mechanized and technical it may for certain purposes be made, is still an expression of the reason or *logos* and therefore oriented towards the Good. Nature and logic in this primal sense will always witness to the Divine.

A violent paradox of Karl Barth, while essentially untrue and profoundly destructive, may yet serve to illustrate the point we have been attempting to make. 'It is,' he writes, 'sentimental liberal self-deception to suppose that there is any *direct* way [italics mine] leading from Nature and History, from Art from Morals and from Science, from Religion itself, to God's impossible possibility.' Tertullian could not have said anything more violent! But leaving this out of account, there is a point of real significance in this outburst. There is, indeed, no direct way leading from nature, whether physical or human, to God— certainly none by the way called scientific method, if the true character, and consequently the inevitable limitations of this method, are properly understood. Of course God cannot be demonstrated by a syllogism, nor by an induction. But that there is an indirect way from both to God the whole story of human thought shows beyond doubt, and it is this indirect way that our interpretation of the theistic argument has sought to make clear.

IV

Further Comments on the Theistic Argument.
Certitude and Evidence

A

There is, then, I hold, a rational theology and a demonstration to the rational mind of the existence of God as the necessary presupposition of a meaningful world and as the origin, ground and goal of values. But it must of course be kept in mind that when we use the terms rational and demonstration we are using them in that broader and more fundamental sense in which, as we have seen, they were understood by those who formulated the arguments. On the validity of our presentation of the argument the reader must be left to form his own judgment, but there are certain further comments which will, perhaps, make the position clearer and serve to remove certain difficulties.

The first of these comments has to do with a quite common attitude with regard to the historic arguments for the existence of God. It is frequently said that 'it is highly improbable that any one who had no belief in God was ever led to believe in Him by any of the standard proofs of God's existence, the ontological, cosmological and teleological proofs. They are thought of by men who already believed in God as considerations harmonizing their belief, for themselves and others, with a general view of the universe.' This, like so many similar *dicta*, has an element both of truth and of falsity. It is true in the sense that in most cases these proofs do constitute a confirmation of beliefs already existing, but false in the sense that men who have lost this belief have not been led to God by such arguments alone. However improbable it does occur. But even if it had not this fact would signify merely that, unless there be some antecedent acknowledgment of the meaning in the world from which the argument proceeds, the notion of God itself, to which the argument is supposed to lead, would itself have no meaning and consequently all cogency would be lacking. Cardinal Newman tells us in his *Essay in Aid of a Grammar of Assent* that he expects little from purely logical argument, the traditional proofs for the existence of God. If it were not, he adds, for the voice that speaks so clearly in his conscience and in his heart he would be an atheist or a pantheist or a polytheist in his view of this world. The fact is that the argument for the existence of God takes place in a universe of discourse in which certain presuppositions are already acknowledged. Outside this universe it has no meaning. To the hypothetical visitor from Mars the arguments would indeed be meaningless, but so would the problem of the existence of God also.

Closely related to this first position is a second which constantly finds expression. It is quite commonly said that what actually causes men to believe in God is not any reasoning or argument, but primarily the direct perception of something in the visible things from which the invisible are argued, in other words, a direct perception of the Divine. Now the element of truth in this position has already been admitted. Unless there

were in the visible things, both in nature and in man, a quality
which points us to the invisible, we should never be led by
reason alone to Him of whom they are revelatory. But this does
not exclude the element of reason which is a necessary part of
any approach to God. An element of immediacy, of an 'intuition of the Divine,' is doubtless a necessary part of any
adequate theory of religious knowledge, but no less necessary
is an element of demonstration.

B

The natural and logical witnesses for God are not then, as we
have already said, superfluous. But are these witnesses convincing, are the arguments cogent? It is, as we have seen, a dogma of
Catholic theology that the existence of God can be demonstrated by rational inference, and we have maintained that this
is in principle sound. But surely, it will be said, you do not take
this to mean—and no thoughtful theologian would take it to
mean—that God's existence can be demonstrated by arguments
that are sure to be recognized by all men of normal understanding as cogent. For the plain fact is that there are many
men, not only of normal but of high intelligence, who do not
recognize them as cogent. At most it must be meant that these
arguments ought to be recognized as cogent and that they would
be so recognized if people were 'perfectly rational,' or, perhaps
better, understood what rationality in this context actually is
and involves.

Now we must, I think, admit the element of truth in this
statement of the situation. It is surely the plain fact that many
men of normal understanding do not recognize their cogency.
It is equally a fact that many men of very much more than
normal understanding find themselves unconvinced also. But
it does not at all follow that, because one is of normal, or even of
exceptional intelligence in specific fields, the significance of an
argument in any particular field of thought will be fully appreciated. This is true even in science, for often the real
significance of evidence in one field is not fully appreciated by
those whose *criteria* of evidence have been formed in others, and
there is no reason to believe that this is not true in the present
situation also. Who has not known scientists of distinction who,
while highly skilled in the weighing of evidence in the world of

their own techniques, seem wholly to have lost their skill when they enter the world of human relations, social and political? The recognition of the cogency of an argument depends, doubtless, partly on technical training, but still more, I believe, upon that much more fundamental culture of the mind by which we learn what arguments are really all about.

It is frequently said that we ought not to believe in God for there is 'no whit of evidence for such a belief.' One wonders what curious notion of evidence could possibly have given rise to such naïve dogmatism. It would appear that the only notion of evidence such an one could possibly have is similar to that of the anatomist who, having dissected the entire brain, maintained that he had not found a soul anywhere, and that therefore there was none; or of the physiologist who, when asked if there is a God, replied, 'If there is a great big brain up there!' Of such it would surely be said that they were looking for evidence in the wrong place. Not only is it inconceivable that such evidence should be found, but if it appeared that it were found it would obviously be not for the existence of a soul or God but for something else. Now I am loth to believe that such crude notions of evidence are at all common in these latter days of self-critical science. At the same time they do exist and are always possible, and for this reason the entire question of evidence should, perhaps, be presented in a different way. There are indeed some who would go so far as to say that 'the problem (of theism) should not be put in the form, Does God exist? but rather in the form, How is the universe to be interpreted?'[1] I should not want to go this far. The question, Does God exist? is the form in which the problem is alone understandable by the plain man, and, fortunately for him, he finds no difficulty in this form of statement, but there are those who do find difficulties and to whom the argument is more convincing when put in this more general form. Perhaps we may follow the wise injunction of Bishop Berkeley when, in connection with another such issue, he tells us to 'speak with the vulgar, but think with the learned.'

All things considered, then, we should rather say that the theistic argument, while not actually recognized as cogent by all normal minds, ought to be so recognized, and would be if

[1] W. R. Sorley, *op. cit.*, p. 309.

the nature of the problem and the character of the evidence relevant in connection with it were fully and properly understood. When I use the word 'ought' I do not mean merely a moral ought—although as we have seen moral motives are not wholly absent from belief in a meaningful world, and consequently belief in a godless one—but rather an intellectual ought, an obligation to be intelligent in the sense of understanding the nature of the problem and of the evidence relevant to its solution. This involves, to be sure, the fundamental issue about which all rational theology revolves, namely, the meaning of rationality or intelligibility. That there are two quite different senses attached to these notions we have seen. One is almost tempted to say that every child born into this world is predetermined to one or the other, or, as the man in the street would say, is either a little idealist or a little realist. One would doubtless be ill-advised to suppose that minds can be wholly made over, but one can at least cherish the hope that precisely in respect to this question of rationality and evidence one can be made to see what these terms in the larger text of religion and philosophy must inevitably mean. One may cherish the hope that he may be led to see the limits of the scientific concept of intelligibility and that even this scientific concept presupposes a more ultimate notion which alone gives it meaning.[1]

C

Those who have convinced themselves that there is no proof for the existence of God, whether direct or indirect, frequently console themselves and others with the assertion that 'there are some things better than proof,' namely, the certitude that belongs to faith. Now that in the wide range of things that are good for men there may be many things that are better than argument and proof I should certainly be the last to deny. But I should want to ask, better for what? Certainly in some contexts there is no substitute for proof. Faith, it was said of old, has the greater certitude, but reason the greater evidence—and it is a wise saying, but in some contexts certitude can never be a substitute for evidence. Faith may indeed in a certain fashion be the evidence of things unseen, but only when the faith is a rational belief.

[1] Chapter x, pp. 320 ff.

None the less, certitude and evidence are not the same thing. The traditional hierarchy of the modes of cognition has always been for Christian thinkers, faith, reason or understanding, and insight or the vision of God face to face. The place of reason in this hierarchy is the problem of religious knowledge and with it also the relation of evidence to these initial and final certitudes. This is, however, the problem of a later chapter.

Chapter VII

The Literal and the Symbolic in Religion: Symbolism as a
Theological Principle

I — A

IF THE argument of the preceding chapter is valid—if we
know by the natural light of our reason, properly understood, that both nature and logic witness to the reality of
that to which men have given the name of God—then, by the
same token, we know something of what God is; for the
ways that lead us to God are also ways of the knowledge of
God.

What men have known of God has from time immemorial
been said in bodily form, but the same light of reason that leads
us to Him tells us also that what is thus said is not always to be
understood literally, but often allegorically or symbolically. It
is true that something must be sayable of Him literally—otherwise we should know neither what is to be understood symbolically or of what it is the symbol—but just what the literal is
becomes one of the fundamental, as it is also one of the most
difficult, of problems.

The recognition of symbolism in religion in some sense and
in some degree is thus inevitable on the higher levels of religion.
Effectual symbols, as they are sometimes called, the signs and
symbols which develop in any cult, are gradually seen to be not
the reality itself but 'outward and visible signs' of an inward
and spiritual grace. With the development of the distinction
between myth and religion, and the gradual recognition of
mythical language as a symbolic and not a literal representation
of reality, the problem of symbolism is forced into the foreground and some theory of interpretation becomes a necessary
part of any philosophical theology. Finally the problem becomes central wherever mysticism enters into religion and where-
ever a 'mystical theology' is developed. When this element
enters in—and there is no form of religion and religious
experience which does not at some point at least 'trench on the
mystical'—then much in religion which seems literal also
becomes 'types and shadows.' Whether these types and shadows

are 'done away' in the full light of revelation in this world, or whether it is only in a world to come that we shall know even as we are known, is precisely one of the issues of mystical theology itself. Recognition of the symbolic element in the language of religion and theology, and the consequent need of interpretation, is what I understand by symbolism as a theological principle. The principle itself is recognized in all types of theology, the only issue is how far the principle extends.

B

Theology is discourse about God. Whatever immediate experience of Deity there may be it is not until it is mediated by language that it enters into the sphere of discourse or knowledge. Since there is no language which does not contain metaphorical and symbolic elements, the language of religion, whether devotional or theological, contains these elements. Symbolism as a theological principle involves therefore a broader notion of the symbol than that ordinarily employed in common speech. The traditional notion, as expressed in the definitions of the dictionaries, is that it is a 'representation of any moral or spiritual thing by the images or properties of natural things'; the lion is the symbol of courage, the lamb the symbol of meekness and patience. But it is not merely the images and properties of natural things which are symbolic, but the moral or spiritual attributes of which these are symbolic may in turn be symbolic also when applied to Divine things. The lamb is the symbol of meekness and patience, but meekness and patience—in so far at least as they are conditioned by the way in which they appear in us creatures—may, in turn, contain a symbolic element when applied to the Divine.

Even in natural theology an element of symbolism is scarcely to be denied. It is doubtless inevitable that my mind should find itself compelled to pass from secondary motions in this world of space and time to a prime mover; but if I thus think of God I must abstract from all spatial and temporal elements involved in the notion of motion, and if I apply it to a supersensible being called God I cannot apply it literally. It is inevitable that if I pass from secondary causes to a first cause the same processes of abstraction are necessary. 'God's causality' is not our causality, as God's motion is not our motion. In like manner it is inevitable that my mind should pass from finite purposes and ends to the eternal purpose which God purposes, from the perishable human goals to that which is imperishable and which alone gives them ultimate significance. But here again I must abstract from all spatial and temporal elements and in so doing I have ceased to apply these notions literally, for all purposes which we creatures know, in order to be purposes, must be realizable in time; and an imperishable goal is not a goal, for all our goals perish. In sum, no category is applicable to God in precisely the same mode as it is applicable to the created world. It is partly for these reasons that Récéjac has described theology as 'the dialectical development of symbols.' Our examination of theology, both dogmatic and rational has shown us, I think, that theology is more than this, but it has shown us also that a symbolic element is present in all theological discourse.

C

Symbolism as a theological principle is thus a necessary element in any religion which has reached the stage of a theology at all. It is, however, with this principle as developed in our western culture that we are chiefly concerned. Both the principle itself and the method of interpretation had their roots in Hellenic thought—this stage of development having been reached, as we have seen, in both Greek and Hebrew religion—[1] and may therefore be properly characterized as representative of developed religion in general. There is, accordingly, a continuous tradition of symbolic interpretation from Plato and Philo, through Origen and Clement, Augustine and Neoplatonism to the present day.

This tradition reached its culmination and systematization in the Fourfold Method of Interpretation of medieval times. According to this principle, religious assertions are, to use a modern term, 'symbol sentences' which must be expanded or interpreted. There are four stages in this interpretation, or four meanings of the symbol, all of which have their 'truth,' the literal, the allegorical, the tropical or tropological, and the anagogical; and the development of these meanings constitutes a progressive interpretation. This notion was applied primarily

[1] Chapter iii, p. 113.

to the statements of scripture, more particularly the parables and miracles, but it had a universal significance.[1]

It became an established principle that every fact or event, in the realm of nature or of scriptural record, might be conceived as conveying, besides its *literal* meaning, these three symbolic interpretations. The interpretation called allegorical, as the term suggests, had reference primarily to truths of humanity as a whole; the story is an allegory of human life. The interpretation called tropological applied specifically to the moral lesson which might be learned from an event; the assumption of purpose of teleological meaning in nature and history being an underlying postulate of all symbolism. The final truth was that of the *anagoge*—ultimate truth belonging neither to time nor space—such knowledge as had been the norm of all knowledge since the formulation of Plato's doctrine of absolute ideas. Anagogical meaning was essentially metaphysical in character, and ultimately religious and metaphysical truth coincide.

The significance of this fourfold method is that it is the theory of interpretation that was developed *within religion by the religious consciousness itself*—not merely the Christian doctrine, but that of all western religion. We shall turn presently to the specifically Christian formulation; for the moment we are concerned with its more general aspects. Two aspects are of special importance for the understanding of the principle, as well as for the purpose of contrasting it with certain theories of religious symbolism which have been developed in these latter times.[2]

The first of these is that the *literal* rendering of a religious assertion or proposition is not its inner or essential truth. The religious consciousness, phenomenologically speaking, is not

---

[1] For the history of the development of this method and an account of its application in detail see H. Flanders Dunbar, *Symbolism in Mediaeval Thought*, especially Chapters iv and v.

[2] This method, like so many of the medieval instruments of thought, became itself over-elaborated, mechanized and literalized. It led not only to complexities and obscurities, but also to serious falsifications. Applied to nature, it begot many medieval works of pseudo-science, such as the lapidaries and bestiaries. Applied to scripture, it begot absurdities of interpretation which have become the sport of sceptics and rationalists. But in its highest form it was the source of the richest fruits of medieval thought and culture, Dante's *Divine Comedy* being in a sense its epitome.

223

achieved until its symbolic character is realized.[1] But—and
this is an extremely important part of the entire conception and
method—the literal, though transcended, is not negated. The
primary conception of truth, as of language, is the 'copy' notion
and it cannot be completely abandoned without destroying the
notion of truth itself. All intuition involves expression and
the notion of expression cannot be formed without including
the notion of re-presentation in some form. In this sense the
religious consciousness is incurably literal, and the problem of
the meaning of literal in theology becomes of central importance.

The second aspect of importance is the nature and significance of the last two stages of interpretation, the tropic and
the anagogic. The tropological interpretation of the symbol was
always an important aspect of both practice and theory. The
moral significance of the symbol—its meaning for life, both
individual and social—has always been stressed. This practical
element in interpretation has in modern times led to a wholly
moral interpretation of the religious symbol and a purely
humanistic theory of the nature of symbolic knowledge in
religion. But for the classical theory the ultimate stage is the
anagogic, which is not only beyond the phenomenal but
beyond the moral in the narrow human sense. Literally, it
means 'a leading up to,' an elevation of mind to things 'above.'
The things above for this classical theory are, of course, the
denizens of the 'intelligible world,' perfect truth, perfect
beauty and perfect goodness, which, for Christian theology,
constitute the essential nature of Deity Himself. Thus for
Dante, 'the bread of angels,' on which the soul feeds, is both the
Eucharist and the knowledge or wisdom of theology and
philosophy.[2]

The continuity of this tradition of symbolic interpretation
has been pointed out in preceding chapters.[3] It is often spoken
of as the Platonic tradition but it is rather the Greek tradition
as a whole. For, in so far as the basal premise of the method is
concerned, the identification of God with the 'principle of
perfection,' Platonism, Aristoteleanism and Neoplatonism are
all one. There are important differences in these different

---

[1] Chapter iii, pp. 114 f. [2] See on this point Dunbar, *op. cit.*, p. 314.
[3] Chapter iii, pp. 109 f.

types of metaphysics—and these differences have affected in important ways men's views on 'the ways to the knowledge of God'—but the partly symbolic character of that knowledge and the consequent necessity of interpretation of what is said about God is common to them all.

II

The Principle of Symbolism in Classical Christian Theology.
Symbolism and the Principle of Analogy.

A

There is no type of theology which does not, in some sense and to some degree, recognize the symbolic character of its language and make use of symbolism as a theological principle. The most extreme 'revelationist' realizes that statements about God are, and must be, expressed in language drawn from the finite world of things and that no doctrine of revelation, how-ever absolute, supposes these statements to be perfectly literal. All human language requires to be read with certain tacit qualifications before it can be applied to God. On no theory of revelation is the function of theological language to copy the Divine, but rather to symbolize it. This is true whether the theology in question is positive or negative, but the difference in these two types brings with it an important difference in this conception of the nature and extent of symbolism.

The essential of negative theology is that God really cannot be named at all. The infinitely Holy spurns alike all categories—whether physical or moral, or even of being itself. For Meister Eckhart, who represents the extreme of this tendency, He is the 'One who is beyond existence.' With this theory is naturally associated the negative mysticism which seeks oneness with God without any mediation of symbols. But even the negative theology asserts, by implication at least, the anagogic theory of the religious symbol, for even if, so to speak, our symbols are merely a ladder to the infinite, even if in the blinding light of direct vision, they are to be kicked away as false, they are still a ladder without which approach to the absolute is impossible. Positive theology, on the other hand, believes that they are not false, that God can be named, and that from the human names we give to God we may pass anagogically to his 'proper' or true names. Not only do we approach God by symbolic means, but through the symbol itself we may apprehend, in some degree at least, that which is beyond all symbol.

B

The most important source for the understanding of symbolism as a theological principle as it functions in positive theology is to be found in St. Thomas's treatise on 'The Names of God,' which follows in the *Summa Theologica* immediately after the discussion of 'How God is Known By Us'. It is the classical form of 'religious realism' in the sense of maintaining the reality of both substance and attributes.

The attributes of God are divided into absolute and relative, the former pertaining to God as he is in himself, the latter to the operations of God. The former, such as omnipotence, omniscience, and all good, arise from the nature of God as fullness of being, as *ens realissimum* and *ens perfectissimum*; the latter are determined empirically from the perfections in the universe or created things, and therefore on the basis of the analogy of being.

Distinction is also made between the various forms which analogy may take. There is analogy of attribution, as when we say 'the air is healthy,' and there is analogy of proportion. Analogy of proportion may be proper analogy and analogy of metaphor. Metaphorically we say that the lion is the king of beasts. So, too, metaphorically we say of God that he is angry. But since anger is a passion of the sensible order, we see quite well that it cannot properly belong to God. The analogy of proper proportionality, on the other hand, enables us to arrive at attributes which are no longer attributable metaphorically to the Divine, but literally (in the sense of properly), for in this case the analogy is really found in the strict sense, in each of the analogues, and is based on a fundamental relation between the Creator and the created called 'analogy of being.'

The process by which we arrive at a conception of what God is, is, then, to quote a modern scholastic, threefold. 'The first is a process of attribution. We attribute to God all the perfections we find in the universe. . . . Our second process is one of negation or elimination. In the universe there are many perfections which, while good and necessary for the beings that possess them, imply in their very concept limitations. We call them mixed or relative perfections. We do not attribute them to God because . . . the infinitely perfect cannot possess any but unmixed or simple and absolute perfections. The final process is one of ontological sublimation. We ascribe the simple and absolute perfections in the universe to God, not in the sense in which creatures possess them. His manner of possessing them is supereminent and sublime because his is an absolute and necessary . . . possession.'[1]

The treatise on 'The Names of God' takes up and answers twelve questions, the third of which is of special importance in connection with our present study. It is whether any name can be applied to God in its literal sense. St. Thomas answers this question in the affirmative, but in answering it he makes a distinction of the utmost importance, namely, between the perfections themselves and their 'mode of signification.' What is signified by the names, good, wise, etc., belongs literally to God, who is the sum of all perfections, but their mode of signification—e.g., goodness, beauty, wisdom, as they appear in creatures—does not belong properly and strictly to God in whom these perfections are infinite.[2]

This marks the point at which the principle of symbolism becomes an essential part of the Thomistic theology, and it is of the utmost importance for all that follows that this point should be made wholly clear. The mode of signification of these perfections, as they appear in creatures, does not apply literally to God; if it applies at all, it must be symbolic. But does it apply at all? Certainly it is constantly applied, for it is only as they are conditioned by the way in which they appear in creatures that these attributes are emotively significant in ordinary prayer and praise. Now if they are not strictly or

---

[1] See Charles Baschab, *Manual of Neo-Scholastic Philosophy*, pp. 419 ff.

[2] For further details on this question see the *Summa Theologica* of St. Thomas Aquinas. Literally translated by the Fathers of the English Dominican Province. Second and revised edition. Also Rev. R. Garrigou-Lagrange, *God: His Existence and His Nature*. Translated by Dom Bede Rose, O.S.B. St. Louis, 1934. Charles Baschab, *Manual of Neo-Scholastic Philosophy*, St. Louis, 1929; Etienne Gilson, *The Philosophy of St. Thomas Aquinas*, translated by Bullough and Elrington, Cambridge, 1929.

properly applicable, but still are truly applicable—otherwise
prayer and praise are stultified—then they are symbolic and we
may properly speak of 'symbolic truth.'

A further distinction is here of importance, for it will also
bulk large in later discussions, namely, that between the absolute and relative attributes of Deity, the former portraying God
as He is in Himself, the latter the 'operations' of God. The
attributes of omnipotence, omniscience and all-good are
derived from the nature of God as fullness of being and are
therefore absolute, the latter are determined empirically from
the perfections of created things and are therefore relative. The
operations of God include the acts of God—before all time and
in time itself, the latter including the historical and cosmological
pronouncements of religion. It follows from this distinction that
whatever literal truth may be contained in these pronouncements, the form in which they are made inevitably contains a
symbolic element.

C

It is, of course, true that many Catholic theologians distinguish carefully the theory of analogy from the theory of
symbolism. The former is sound doctrine, the latter is error. It
must, however, be noted that when the symbolist view is
denounced it is the humanist theory of symbolism that the
critics have in mind. The terms by which God is represented—
wise, loving, just—are adopted by the 'symbolic' view, so
these critics tell us, simply to satisfy certain human cravings, as
useful fictions, helping to produce desirable modes of conduct
or sentiment. This is, at least, how the Dominican philosopher,
Father Sertillanges, describes what he calls the symbolic view.
Now if symbolism means this we can well understand that no
form of Catholic theology could accept symbolism as a theological principle, but surely that is not what it has meant either
historically or, indeed, among many Catholic theologians
today.

The entire issue turns, of course, upon the degree of agreement between an attribute ascribed to God and that which the
same word connotes when applied to man. If the agreement
were complete we should have literal knowledge; if it is not our
knowledge must be, in some degree, symbolic. On this point
Thomists seem to differ, and we are therefore not surprised that

they differ also on the relation of analogy to symbolism. In so far as St. Thomas himself is concerned, it seems to me that for him symbolism is a theological principle. In so far as the 'mode of signification' as it appears in creatures cannot be applied literally to God, as he himself insists, it would seem to follow that, if it can be applied at all, and St. Thomas seems also to hold that it can, it must be applied symbolically, the notion of symbol being rightly understood; for that which is not literal representation must be symbolic in some sense.

It is scarcely necessary to pursue this controversy further. Our main interest is in the notion of symbol in the broad sense of modern philosophy and epistemology, for the only way in which, as we shall see, science can be brought into any fruitful and significant relation to religion is by the understanding of the relation of the symbols of religion to those of science—of religion as symbolic form to the symbolic form known as science. The main point here is that if symbolism as a theological principle is, as we maintain, an essential part of Thomistic doctrine, it is only in the sense that it is implied in the doctrine of analogy itself. This fact makes it quite clear that the doctrine of analogy is the more ultimate notion upon which that of the symbolic depends. Unless we hold to this doctrine, to the anagogic theory of the symbol—and have rational grounds for so holding—we have, as we shall presently see, no basis for a theory of symbolic truth.

III

Modern Theories of Religious Symbolism. Symbolo-fideism

A

The notion of symbolism which many theologians would distinguish so completely from that of analogy, is, as we have seen, the merely moral and humanistic theories of symbolism which have appeared in modern times in so many forms. There is, first of all, the purely moral theory which holds that while the religious symbol has a transcendent reference, it is primarily moral in import. There is secondly the theory of humanism, to be distinguished from the former, which, starting from purely naturalistic premises, holds, as its critics rightly maintain, that religious notions are useful fictions, helping to produce desirable modes of conduct and sentiment, but which really have no transcendent reference, and refer wholly to the human. Pragmatic theories of the symbol may be of either type, but tend, almost inevitably towards the latter.

The moral theory attaches itself to *one* of the stages of the classical theory. It is, accordingly, even from this point of view, not untrue, but at most inadequate. Its essential character is its denial of the *sensus anagogicus* to the symbol. This theory, as developed in modern times, is naturally connected primarily with Kant for whom, it is ordinarily held, although unjustly I believe, that the religious symbol has only moral meaning and import. However that may be, the moral theory in the Kantian form has given rise to a modern theory of religious symbolism which has become clearly defined and has established itself firmly within the borders of both Catholic modernism and Protestant liberalism. Sabatier, and symbolo-fideism in general are illustrations of this view.

It is unnecessary to criticise at length the moral theory—its inadequacy is already implied in our discussions of the essence of religion.[1] It constitutes, as has been well said, 'a profound misrepresentation of the religious consciousness' and one that 'is possible only because it ignores the postulate of the transcendent life which is of the very essence of religion.' Moreover, as has also been pointed out, the language of morality and the language of religion are in principle different, the numinous character of the latter marking it off uniquely from that of morality. In a sense mere morality has its own language and concepts and, as such, does not demand religious symbols. It requires symbol only when it trenches on the transcendent and metaphysical.

Humanistic theories carry this truncation of the classical theory still further, the outstanding example being that of Feuerbach to whom reference has already been made. The essential character of man as religious is, as he rightly sees, his sense of his own finitude, but this sense of finitude does not imply the infinite but merely 'the stirrings of humanity.' Religious symbols are then symbols of human values, God himself, the great Anthropomorphism, being the symbol of

[1] Chapter ii, pp. 75 ff.

THE LITERAL AND THE SYMBOLIC IN RELIGION

humanity. If the moral theory constitutes a misrepresentation of the religious consciousness, the misrepresentation in this theory is even more profound.

B

Recent naturalistic theories carry this misrepresentation of the religious consciousness even further. In principle they differ in no fundamental respect from the preceding, but they introduce certain novel ideas from anthropological studies such as those of Durkheim and from the psychological studies of the psychoanalysts. In these theories the symbol refers not so much to the stirrings of humanity as of the sub-human, that underworld of the unconscious out of which the fantastic shapes, the baser symbolisms which Hegel deplored, inevitably arise.[1]

Open as these theories are to all the criticisms of the preceding theories, they have the additional defect of misrepresenting the symbolic consciousness itself. They interpret the symbol in terms of that which is not meant by the symbol. Its apparent meaning is its reference to over-individual social values, as in the typical humanistic theories; its real meaning, according to these views, is to be found in the causes, environmental and physical, which have produced the images. The religious symbol becomes thus doubly fictional and doubly illusory. Although apparently referring to the superhuman, it actually refers only to the human; but it is illusory in the second place because, while apparently referring to values, it really refers to physical causes. The symbols of the 'religious imagination' are really fictions, fruitful illusions. The question then is not so much of symbolic truth as of symbolic effectiveness. Such a theory not only stultifies all human discourse—as it most surely does—but in the end, as I believe, reduces itself to absurdity. For to be a symbol at all, it must contain both truth and fiction. If it were wholly a fiction, it would not be a symbol, for it would refer to nothing. If it were wholly true, it would not be a symbol but a literal representation. Any theory that denies either of these conditions refutes itself.

The symbolo-fideism of much of modernism actually eventuates in just this self-stultification. Recognizing, as all sound

[1] For an excellent account of these two theories see Charles A. Bennett, *The Dilemma of Religious Knowledge* (1931), Chapters iii and iv.

analysis must, that the images of faith inevitably contain a symbolic element, it is a short step to the conception that the objects of faith are themselves only symbols, and the theory of symbolism becomes, as its critics maintain, the view that images in which God is represented, have their significance as simply satisfying human cravings and as helping to produce desirable modes of conduct and sentiment. It is here that so-called pragmatic theories of symbolism appear upon the scene. They reflect, as we should expect, the fundamental ambiguity in pragmatism itself. They may lean, on the one hand, to the doctrine of fruitful illusion as represented by Vaihinger's theory, but they may also, on the other hand, lead to theories such as that of LeRoy. Doubtless pragmatic criteria enter into any theory of the truth of the symbol, as LeRoy has shown in his *What is Dogma?* but, as he has also shown, the pragmatic truth itself depends, for its truth, on the anagogic character of the symbol.

IV

The Metaphysical (or Anagogic) Theory of the Religious Symbol.
The Analogia Entis

A

Moral and humanistic theories of the religious symbol are in the main not so much wholly false as inadequate. In the classical theory the allegorical and moral interpretations, to which these theories confine themselves, are all recognized as stages in the process of interpretation, but they culminate in the anagogical and, if valid, presuppose it. The *sensus anagogicus* of early medieval theology develops into the principle of analogy of being and it is therefore, with this concept, as the metaphysical basis of symbolism as a theological principle, that we are now concerned.

The concept of the analogy of being is not without its difficulties and, as Gilson admits, is not wholly clear. And yet it is the key to the Christian solution of the problem of humanity and Deity. It constitutes an attempt to formulate the true relation of God to the world and, on the basis of this relation, to develop a theory of the knowledge of God. The relation of the Creator and the created is unique—the idea of God itself being wholly unique, the relation of God to the world must be unique also. The world is wholly dependent upon God but God is in no way dependent upon the world. The relation is not one of identity, which would imply pantheism; nor is it one of complete difference, for if God were wholly other, with no likeness between Him and created being, there could be no natural knowledge of God and we should be forced to a doctrine of exclusive revelation with its implied agnosticism.

As a theory of our knowledge of God, the principle of analogy appears to be a philosophical translation of the biblical statement that 'the invisible things of Him are known by the things that are made.' 'Our natural knowledge,' St. Thomas writes, 'takes its beginning from sense. Hence our natural knowledge can reach as far as it can be led by the things of sense. But, starting from sensible things, our intellect cannot reach so far as to see the divine essence; because sensible things which are created by God are not equal to the power of God which is their cause. Hence from the knowledge of sensible things the whole power of God cannot be known; from which it follows that His essence cannot be seen. But because they are His effects and dependent upon Him as their cause, we can be led from them so far as to know that God exists, and to know concerning Him, those things which must necessarily pertain to Him in virtue of his being the first cause of all things, exceeding all that He has caused.'[1]

The doctrine of analogy seems, then, according to this passage, to rest wholly on the principle of causality and the causal argument. But if the basis of analogy is God's causality, surely a very different idea of causality is presupposed than that of sensible or natural knowledge alone. For from such a bare principle, as critics of St. Thomas have seen, only a value-free, cosmological idea of God could be inferred, an idea which would offer no satisfactory grounds for an argument to the 'divine perfections.' In order to see that this is actually the case it is only necessary to recall St. Thomas' own description of God's causality. 'Love,' so he writes, 'which works good to all things, pre-existing overflowingly in the Good—moved itself to creation, as befits the superabundance by which all things are generated. . . . The Good, by being, extends its goodness to all

[1] *Summa Theol.* I, qu. XII, art. 12.

233

Waynesburg College Library
Waynesburg, Pa.   15370

things. For, as our sun, not by choosing or taking thought, but by merely being, enlightens all things, so the Good, by its mere existence, sends forth upon all things the beams of its goodness.'[1] Creation, moved by love, and working in the fashion thus described, is not at all the causal notion in the ordinary sense, and the notion of the Creator cannot be adequately expressed but only abstractly symbolized, by such a notion as that of first cause or prime mover. Indeed Dionysius the Areopagite, whose conceptions were not without influence upon those of St. Thomas, speaks of God's causality as 'a living movement, self-moved, which pre-exists in the Good, and bubbles forth from the Good to things existing and which again returns to the Good'—precisely the dramatic language of theology of which we spoke in an earlier chapter. In sum, the metaphysical theory of the religious symbol presupposes the validity of the theistic argument, but of the argument as axiologically interpreted.

B

The principle of the analogy of being has been given two interpretations and has thus given rise to an issue of far-reaching importance in philosophical theology. Either we may hold that the divine perfections are reached solely by empirical reasoning from the finite perfections; or we must assume an intuition of perfection as the driving force of the *via eminentiae*—of the process of 'ontological sublimation,' by which our human attributes are 'moulded' in order to be applicable to the Divine.

The former is the interpretation ordinarily given to the Thomistic principle. The idea we have of a supremely perfect being is, it is held, formed synthetically—that is by apprehending the various perfections in finite beings, excluding from them all limitations and imperfections, and conceiving them as all united in one being. According to this view, the idea of the infinite does not originate in direct intuition but is reached in a negative-positive way. It is not necessary, we are told, to assert that the idea of the infinite is purely negative, as Locke and the empiricists have tended to do, but it is necessary to insist that the positive perfections of creatures which we attribute to God are known only as accompanied by limitations. We arrive at the infinite—this is the important point—only negatively, by

[1] Chapter iv, pp. 126 f.

excluding all limitations which attend the realization of perfections in finite beings and then by thinking all conceivable perfections as united in one Being.

To many theologians, including some scholastics, this position seems difficult if not impossible to maintain, and the present writer shares this view. A purely empirical way of knowing the nature of God is as impossible as a purely empirical proof of his existence. To say that we gain the conception of a perfect being by 'comparing less perfect with more perfect beings is to forget that such a comparison cannot be instituted save by the aid of an already apprehended standard of perfection. How can we say that this is more perfect than that unless we already know what perfection is?' The Thomist speaks here of 'ontological sublimation,' the third process by which 'we ascribe perfections to God in a supereminent and sublime way because His is an absolute and necessary possession'—and it is a telling phrase—but there is sublimation in a psychological sense also, and on what ground can we be sure that this is ontological and not merely psychological? Only, I think, on the basis of some positive intuition of perfection or of the infinite as an initial datum not only of the theistic argument itself but of the entire process of the knowledge of God.

C

The principle of analogy of being, as here interpreted, has, I believe, further implications of great importance for symbolism as a theological principle, and therefore for philosophical theology in general. I shall describe it as an extension of the principle of analogy, an extension which, as I believe, is implied in the original principle itself.

Because there is analogy of being between the Creator and the created world, one may pass from the conditioned perfections of the creature to the unconditioned perfections of the Creator. This is, so to speak, the principle as applicable Godward but it also seems applicable from man to man. The analogy of being between the Creator and creature seems necessarily to imply a similar analogy between all races of men who are the children of God. The 'community of subjective form' which makes it possible for the members of one 'beloved community' to understand one another when they speak of God, seems necessarily to extend *mutatis mutandis* to a further community of ideas between the various beloved communities among the children of God. Because God made man in his own image, the images men form of him must have an analogous relation.

The facts of comparative religion themselves seem to justify such an extension. The images in which 'the Absolute shines out in consciousness' vary greatly at sundry times and in sundry places, but these differences are only one side of the picture. To the discerning eye at least, there are also profound similarities. The variety of imagery, or 'subjective form,' as we shall later call it, in which the basal religious categories of creation and consummation, of incarnation and salvation, etc., are expressed, does not for one moment hide from us the analogies between them, analogies so striking as to have led to the hypothesis of one primeval revelation.

Moreover, when we pass from the lower to the higher levels, from the base to the apex of the pyramid, we find less and less of particular imagery and more and more of the universal, less and less of analogy of subjective form and more and more of identity of essence. Here myth, as myth, is transcended and while the mythical categories are retained, they become the conscious vehicles for the expression of that which is not mythical, the original phenomena of the spiritual life. All of which, if true, implies, as we shall see in the following chapter, that this extension of the principle of analogy is the initial and indispensable condition of the entire enterprise known as the philosophy of religion.

A somewhat similar extension of the principle of analogy is proposed by Jacques Maritain in a recent volume of essays.[1] In an essay entitled, 'Who is My Neighbour?' he attempts to find a basis for what he describes as 'the co-operation of men of different creeds in the temporal order.' This he finds in certain analogical similarities in basal principles and ideas. For such understanding and co-operation, it is not necessary, he holds, that there be identity of doctrine. It is sufficient that the various principles and doctrines have some community and similarity of proportion or, in the technical sense of the word, analogy with regard to the practical end proposed. Such analogies he finds. 'The existence of God, the sanctity of truth, the value and necessity of good will, the dignity of the person, the spirituality

[1] Jacques Maritain, *Ransoming The Time*, 1941.

and immortality of the soul: these and all the other implications bound up with them which I shall not mention here, correspond to spontaneous perceptions of our reason and to primary tendencies of our nature; but they are not understood in an identical and univocal way by believers in the various religions of humanity.'

I am far from wishing to be unduly critical here, but it does seem important to point out that this conception differs in significant respects from the present formulation. Apparently Maritain would confine the application of the principle solely to those 'spontaneous perceptions of our reason,' as he calls them, which find expression in what is called natural theology. In my view it applies also to the symbolic forms in which the intuitions of faith are themselves expressed. In other words, the complete disjunction between revealed and natural religion here proposed cannot be carried out, co-operation in the temporal order cannot be divorced completely from the understanding and expression of that which transcends the temporal order. The important point here is that, whatever view we may hold regarding the range of the extension of the principle of analogy here proposed, the extension of the principle is implied in the theory of analogy of being itself.

V

Religious Symbolism and The Problem of the 'Literal.'
The Truth of Symbol

A

Any talk of symbolism in religion is bound to meet with very definite resistance on the part of the ordinary religious consciousness—still more any talk of symbolism as a theological principle. As the plain man will not hear of religion as poetry or of religion as myth, whether transitory or permanent, so he will not hear of mere symbolism in religion. He feels and rightly —that there must be non-symbolic truth somewhere, and it is this literal or 'blunt' truth that he wants, or thinks he wants.

He wants it, first of all, for practical or pragmatic reasons.

All action seems to require the belief that we have literal knowledge of that towards which our behaviour is directed and this seems to be pre-eminently so in religion. If God is our Father, and if we are to act towards him as such, it seems to be of the utmost importance that we should not act towards him *as if* he were such, but as our Father in reality. We must avoid the moral and intellectual stultification which is the penalty of all *as if* philosophies and it is for this reason, in the last analysis, that the attempt is made to distinguish completely between analogy and symbol, and to the condemnation of symbolism.

That there is some literal knowledge of God, that there are some attributes that may be properly applied to him, must therefore be a fundamental thesis. Quite apart from the more general truth that the very notions of symbol and of symbolic knowledge are meaningless unless non-symbolic knowledge is at some point presupposed, there is also the specific requirement of the religious consciousness itself, that without some literal knowledge of divine things symbolic knowledge is an illusion. In the classical theory of the fourfold method of interpretation while the literal mode of interpretation of nature and of sacred scripture is transcended, this mode is not annulled but always retained. This is true of all doctrines of interpretation, including the Thomistic and thus the problem of the nature and locus of the literal becomes a fundamental problem of all theology.

B

The solution of this problem is one of extraordinary difficulty. It is made difficult, in the first place, by the ambiguities in the notion of the literal itself. The primary meaning is, of course, 'according to the letter' and, strictly speaking, literal has no significance except as applied to language. But even this expression is not unambiguous. In connection with language the notion has at least two meanings, both of which are used more or less indiscriminately in discussion of the literal and the symbolic.

It may mean, in the first place, the original or primary meaning of words. In this sense, to interpret language literally consists in going back to the primary 'undefaced images' implied by the words. It may mean, in the second place, however, merely the opposite of figurative, and the interpretation of religious language consists in passing from imagery to abstract notions, the ontological sublimation of our predicates of which we have spoken.

This ambiguity in the notion of the literal may be illustrated in spheres other than the religious. In his discussion of symbolism Kant speaks of two symbolic representations of the State —the notion of the State as a mechanism and of the State as a living body. In calling the notion of the State as a living body a symbol, Kant meant that it is more than a mere figure of speech, for there is a certain real similarity between the two— not a literal one-to-one correspondence, but, as Kant says, 'similarity in the way in which we reflect upon the two things.' Now a literal interpretation of the symbol of the living body might mean two things, namely, going back to the original meaning of the organic or of the living body and interpreting the symbol as though there were a one-to-one correspondence between the notion of the State and the notion of a living body— with the result that we should have all the absurdities into which the organic theory of the State fell during the biological way of thinking of the nineteenth century. We should make the symbol 'go on all fours'—with disastrous results. The State belongs to another universe of discourse than that of the living body and the latter analogy or symbol could be used only if it is translated into terms appropriate to the universe of discourse in which the State and its members subsist. In this case the 'literal,' in the sense of non-symbolic truth, would be the result of this 'translation.' This would constitute literal truth in the second meaning of the term.

The same ambiguity is present in discussions of the religious symbol and the distinctions made above are applicable here also. The image of the Father in Heaven may be conceived as having a one-to-one correspondence with the object of religion, God; in which case it may also be made to run on all fours with disastrous results—an extreme case being that of the Mormons who carry out the image to the extreme degree of ascribing generation to God in a human sense. It is against this sort of thing that Abelard, and indeed all the great figures in theology, have protested—more especially St. Thomas when he speaks of the extravagances of the Anthropomorphite heretics who depicted God with human features.[1] But we may also follow the

[1] *Cont. Gent.* 20 (That God is not a Body). St. Thomas includes in his condemna-

path of classical theology and, recognizing the symbolic element in such notions, translate the symbol into terms appropriate to the universe of discourse in which theological thinking takes place. In this case, the anthropomorphic element, the mode of signification proper to creatures, becomes the symbolic, and literal truth is found in the ideal concepts and relations appropriate to God as the most perfect being.

It will scarcely be questioned that it is this second notion of the literal which St. Thomas has in mind when he equates it with that which can *properly* be applied to God. Such names as goodness, beauty, wisdom, cannot be applied literally to God 'in the mode of signification as they appear in creatures.' But the perfections themselves, for which the predicates stand, or to which they refer, are true literally. Otherwise expressed, the language of religion, like all language, has a symbolic element in it by virtue of its origin in creatures. But the numinous quality which pervades and informs that language has not its origin in creatures, and refers to nothing in the creature world. It refers to the infinite—to the Perfect—which is the necessary co-implicate of our human imperfections and of their expression. This, then, is the locus—and the only possible locus—of the literal and non-symbolic in a theory such as the Thomistic. Literal is here simply the synonym for unconditional truth—for that which alone is strictly and properly applicable to God.

It is of the utmost importance to realize that this is the meaning of the literal as understood in traditional philosophical theology. It is also of the utmost importance to recognize what are the implications for this same theology if we conceive of the literal in the other fashion, namely, as identical with the primitive or original meanings of words.

This is the concept of the literal which has ruled the so-called empirical philosophies ever since Locke, with his theory of language, and which found overt expression in Bentham's 'Theory of Fictions.' It is, of course, the essence of logical positivism. According to this theory, all meaning involves

tion also the Manichees, who affirmed God to be 'an infinite substance composed of light and spread abroad throughout boundless space.' All these errors arise out of the fact that 'in their thoughts about divine things they had recourse to their imagination, which can reflect none but corporeal likenesses. Wherefore it behooves us to put the imagination aside when we meditate on divine things.'

reference to sensuously observable entities and any terms which have not this reference have no 'literal' meaning. Thus, according to A. J. Ayer, it is 'the rules that determine the literal significance of language' that lead him to eliminate all metaphysical and religious propositions or sentences as meaningless. Again, in discussing the question of religious 'knowledge,' we are told that 'there cannot be any transcendent truths of religion. For the sentences which the theist uses to express such truths are not literally significant.'[1]

It seems quite clear that if we hold this theory of the literal, no literal knowledge of God is, in the very nature of the case, possible. Quite apart, however, from the general question of whether this is the conception of the literal held either in theology or science—I believe that it is not—I should wish to point out what is implied in the conception. The implications for science—especially for physics—are no less serious than those for religion. The physicist also produces sentences which fail to conform to this criterion of the literal; he also makes use of concepts and makes statements that refer to a reality transcending the limits of possible sense experience, and these also this doctrine of literal significance rules out. Once we start ruling out all statements as meaningless that do not have 'literal significance'—in this narrow, and I should say perverted, sense—it is hard to find any place at which to stop and we end by ruling out almost all discourse, both in science and religion, which has any cultural significance at all. In denying this conception of the literal—at least by implication—Christian theology not only formulates a basis for its own 'transcendent truths' but also, as we shall see, for the transcendent element in all human knowledge and culture which is necessary if it is to be genuine knowledge and true culture—if indeed, man is to remain human at all.

C

For the philosophical theologian, then, the literal or non-symbolic is to be found, not by returning to the original and undefaced imagery embodied in the word, but rather by pressing forward, from imagery to essence, to the ontological sublimation of our predicates. This is, however, not the whole story

[1] A. J. Ayer, *Language, Truth and Logic*, especially chapter vi. The passages quoted are found on pages 17 and 179.

of symbolism in religion and theology. If it were our problem would be comparatively simple. Unfortunately the fundamental ambiguity in the notion of the literal still persists in the thoughts and practice of Christian theology as, indeed, it does in all religions, and presents serious difficulties for the problem of interpretation.

The so-called 'historical element in religion,' the facts of history, as they are called, with which religion and theology deal, constitute the main issue. Here the 'locutions,' the dramatic language in which the divine activities in time are described, must, it would seem, be taken in their original undefaced imagery; otherwise the whole of religion evaporates into 'ideas' and religion becomes indistinguishable from a theosophy. There are, I suppose, few theologians who would press for a literal interpretation, in this sense, of all the stories in the Bible—some would be recognized as 'mythical'—but many would insist upon a literal interpretation of what they accept as historical. What is said of God in history—the Divine acts or operations of whatever sort, must, so they would hold, be said in bodily form, for history, in order to be history, must be told in the language of space and time, and if we try to tell it in any other idiom it is no longer history, but rather a timeless shadow of things. The 'thing element,' inseparable, as we have seen, from religion, is so precisely because it is inseparable from history.

All this seems true, and must be given full weight, but the religious philosopher is still bound to point out that the difficulties in such conceptions of the literal are very great, if indeed not insuperable. If, as we are told, we can not know God directly in His essence, in all the fullness of His being, but only in terms of attributes inevitably conditioned by the way in which they appear in creatures, surely we have a right to ask how is it possible that we should know the Divine activities, as manifested in time and history, except as also in terms conditioned by the way in which they appear in the experience of the creature. It is difficult to see how any fundamental difference can be made between the Divine attributes and the Divine activities. Actually this view of the Divine activities is really implied in the Thomistic distinction between the absolute and relative attributes of Deity, the latter, including the 'operations' of God, being determined empirically from the perfections of created things. Surely the operations thus spoken of include those manifested in time and history of which we have been speaking. Revelation of the acts of God in time, no less than of His nature, can be made only in the dialect in which man speaks to man, and this language, even as a vehicle of divine revelation, must have a symbolic element also.

The philosophical theologian cannot, then, it would seem, allow any ultimate distinction between God's essence and God's activities in this respect, and accept as final these two uses of the term literal. Yet surely there is a real problem here; the reasons which have led to this situation are so compelling as to demand the most careful consideration.

The motives which have led to this distinction are very strong and must be given due weight. They seem to be two-fold, partly practical and pragmatic and partly such as arise out of the communion of believers and the confirmation of the faith which is part of religious experience and knowledge.

The plain man demands literal truth because of what he believes to be the exigency of all practical attitudes, eminently those of religion. What is said of anything, especially what is said of God, should, if it is to be significant in a practical reference, be literally true in the sense of the original unde-faced imagery of the words. This demand seems understandable, but we may well ask to what extent it is justified. At first sight it seems that practical attitudes and actions are possible only on the assumption of the literal correspondence of our conceptions with the objects towards which they are directed. But this is scarcely the case. In many spheres of practice—pre-eminently that of physical science—practical manipulation of objects seems perfectly compatible with symbolic representation of the same. It is not at all clear that this is not also true in those spheres of practice which we call moral and spiritual. Certainly in many personal and social relations, symbols are not only adequate, but even often more effective for practice than what we call blunt realism. Nor is religion any exception. If anywhere it may be said, it is in religion that we demand truth altogether, but it may also be said that in this very sphere, the symbol is often truer than the terms into which it is translated.

The second motive is even more significant, for it concerns the matter of fundamental sincerity and the conditions of a valid common faith. How far, we may ask, does such communion depend upon the literalness of the language in which such communication takes place—on the yea, yea and nay, nay, of biblical command? How far does our common faith depend upon the assumption that the lives lived and the acts performed by the historical persons of religion were 'real events' in this sense of the literal? Certainly a strong case can be made out for this contention. And yet I am not so sure. An even stronger case can be made out for the opposite contention. There are reasons for believing that it is only when the principle of symbolism is recognized and acknowledged, that the highest forms of understanding and communion between believers are possible. Indeed any sort of communion between the believers of different racial religions seems to be actually conditioned by the mutual interpretation of symbolic forms.[1]

In sum, sincerity is doubtless the indispensable condition both of practical faith and of genuine communion, and obscurantism, in the long run, the death of both. But we must proceed with caution here. Actually there is no obscurantism in symbolic interpretation except for those for whom all but the simplest ideas are in principle obscure. I sympathize fully with Dean Inge when he writes: 'We know that some of our beliefs are symbolic and mythical, but we do not thank either ourselves or our friends for reminding us of it in and out of season.'[2] There is indeed a time for all things—a time for prayer and praise when such reminders are indeed out of season, but also a time for the recognition of the symbolic element in our beliefs, for without such recognition and the interpretation which follows, we shall not know what these beliefs really mean and say. Genuine sincerity in religious life and thought requires, I believe, that we hold fast to both notions, however difficult it may be, and no theory of religious knowledge is tenable, I also believe, that does not make a place for both.

It is evident, I suppose, that this issue is fundamental for the Christian religion which is the historical religion *par excellence*, but the problem of the historical element in

[1] Chapter ix, pp. 316 ff. [2] *God and the Astronomers*, p. 299.

244

religion is in greater or less degree present in all religion. It is not my purpose to discuss this problem *in extenso* in the present context—that belongs to the following chapter—but merely to insist upon one point, namely, that whatever literal character may be ascribed to these 'events' in time, they are for any form of theology whatever, relevatory in time of that which is before all time and before all worlds. The ascension in time, it is felt, symbolizes what Abelard called a *melior ascensus*, so also, perhaps, the sacred birth in time symbolizes a more ultimate event which is itself timeless. It was doubtless wise advice on the part of St. Thomas not to try to go behind the symbol or dogma, but it is advice that man, being what he is, cannot always heed. Faith will always inquire of the intellect why God became man and in so doing it will always find in the historical event of this becoming a meaning which goes beyond the mere event itself. Indeed the reason for going behind the 'symbol' is already given in the divine revelation itself, namely, in the Prologue to the Fourth Gospel.

D

The problem of the literal and the symbolic in religion obviously goes to the very heart of philosophical theology for it involves the question of symbolic truth and, with it, the entire problem of knowledge and truth in religion. It is not our intention to attempt to solve this problem here—such a solution is possible only in the context of a discussion of religious knowledge as a whole—but some preliminary comment seems necessary and may also serve as the basis for fuller discussion in a later chapter.

The question, as it emerged in an earlier context, is this: How can terms and predicates be truly applicable to God when they are not 'properly' applicable? The symbolic modes of signification of God's perfections, as they appear in creatures, are not literally applicable to God. But certainly they are applicable, for only as they are conditioned by the way they appear in creatures are they emotively significant for prayer and praise; and if they are thus applicable they must be truly applicable, otherwise prayer and praise are stultified. Whether there is a mystical experience which transcends completely the symbolic mode is yet to be considered, but if there is, I think it would be true also that the modes of prayer and praise, as normally understood, would be transcended also.[1]

In view of this situation it is natural to say, and it is often said, that the truth of the symbol lies solely in the inner necessity of the symbol-creating consciousness—otherwise expressed, symbolic truth is truth for our type of consciousness. Certainly symbolic truth cannot be found by reference to sensuously observable entities, for it is precisely the character of the symbol that, while it is taken from the more intuitible regions—of sense imagery—its reference is to the non-sensuous. It cannot consist in comparison of the symbol with reality, for, again, it is precisely the character of the reality to which the symbol refers, that it is beyond such comparison, in that its essence cannot be fully known. In so far as the attributes applied to God are conditioned by the way in which they appear in creatures, their symbolic truth can be known only in the experience of creatures, and that truth will inevitably be determined by its adequacy for our creaturely understanding. But this is only 'one side of the shield,' so to speak; there is also the objective reference to that which transcends the creature. Were it not that in the attributes and activities as applied to creatures there is that which makes possible their 'ontological sublimation'—and therefore their adequacy as applied to God—they would not be adequate, and therefore symbolically true, even for our type of consciousness.

In discussing the relation of the principle of symbolism to the doctrine of analogy we saw that everything turns upon the degree of agreement between an attribute ascribed to God and that which the same word connotes when applied to man. If the agreement were complete we should have literal knowledge; if it is not complete our knowledge must be in some degree symbolic. The important point, however, is that there is partial agreement between the two meanings of the word and this is the basis of symbolic truth. It is upon this analogical relation that all symbolism rests and when the relation is ignored the symbol is not only not understood but has in fact ceased to exist as symbol. Symbols are relevant only in so far as they express partial identity at least of some character or characters common to the symbol and that which it symbolizes.

[1] Chapter xiii, pp. 452 f.

On the other hand, it is equally true that symbols are relevant only in so far as this partial identity or agreement between the meanings of the word involves emotive as well as cognitive meaning, the inner necessity of the symbol creating consciousness. Only so is the symbol adequate for religion in its practical reference. In sum, it is only because, in Thomistic terms, the analogy is in both the analogues, both human and Divine, that we can speak of the truth of the symbol. I shall call this the principle of dual adequacy, on which, as we shall see in a later chapter, depends not only the notion of symbolic truth but also any possibility of relating subjective and objective truth in religion.

This conception of symbolic truth enables us to understand a statement frequently made, and one which at first sight is seemingly wholly paradoxical, namely, that there is often more truth in the symbol itself than in its interpretation. In one sense this is undoubtedly true—in the sense namely that 'subjective truth,' as it is sometimes called, is possible only as conditioned by the 'subjective form,' without which our type of consciousness is not possible. On the other hand, and in another sense, it cannot be true. Genuine understanding of the pronouncements of religion is possible only through interpretation—after we have determined what 'they really say.' In this universe of discourse, that of theology, the interpretation must be truer than the symbol. No significant philosophy of religion is possible which does not include this concept of dual adequacy and with it the concept of a twofold truth.[1]

E

The instinct to resent the dissolving of religion into mere symbolism or fictions is profoundly sound. The difficulty is that the instinct does not always function properly. That which makes the so-called 'literalist' in religion the unmitigated nuisance he often is, is not that he insists upon literal truth—in this he is eternally right—but rather that he persists in finding the literal in the wrong place. This fallacy of misplaced literalism, as we may call it, is, of course, not confined to religion, but has its corresponding form in science as well, and is no less unfortunate there. Indeed it is the conflict of

[1] Chapter ix, pp. 324 ff.

these two 'fundamentalisms' which has led to the so-called conflict of science and religion, as we shall presently see.[1]

The fallacy, as it appears in religion, consists in taking the idea of God—of his nature and his acts—as these ideas are necessarily conditioned by the way in which they appear in creatures, as though they were literally true of God. How serious this fallacy really is, is not realized on the levels of practice and devotion, although even here the consequences may be disastrous for the spiritual life of man. It is rather on the level of thought and intellect that the full consequences are seen. The 'fundamentalism' which is guilty of this fallacy not only jeopardizes the very life of reason in religion, but makes religion appear to say what it never really said, with the inevitable conflict between science and religion. When science takes the sensible and pseudo-sensible symbols of physics as literally true, it is guilty of the same fallacy and a corresponding 'fundamentalism' in science results, no less disastrous to critical thought. When these two fundamentalisms come into conflict nothing but the profoundest self-criticism, on the part of both, can avail.

But we are concerned now with this fallacy within the life of religion itself. Its serious character is, as we have already said, not so obvious on the levels of practice and devotion, although even here the consequences may be disastrous for the spiritual life of man. St. John of the Cross saw this clearly when he wrote, 'He that will rely on the letter of the Divine locution, on the intellectual form of the vision, will necessarily fall into delusion. "The letter killeth; the spirit quickeneth; we must therefore reject the literal sense and abide in the obscurity of the faith." '[2] This is the mystic speaking. But it is not only the mystic who thus speaks out of the fullness of his experience; the true philosopher, out of the fullness of his critical thought, must say the same thing also.

[1] Chapter x, pp. 330 f.
[2] *Ascent of Mount Carmel*, tr. Lewis, 1891. Quoted from von Hügel.

VI

The Paradox of Symbolism and the Dilemma of Religion.
Symbol and Reality

A

That religious knowledge must be in part symbolic we can now see. But what we want, we are told, is the 'blunt truth'—not truth seen through a glass darkly. But literal or blunt truth has, alas, because of the fallacy of misplaced literalism, the unhappy fashion of becoming the most fatal untruth. This is the dilemma which has always faced the religious consciousness and, in one form or another, always will. I shall call it the paradox of symbolism. This paradox consists in the fact that, while symbols, by their very nature as symbols, seem to demand interpretation in non-symbolic terms, this interpretation or 'expansion' of the symbol tends to defeat the very ends of symbolic expression. In one sense the symbol is truer than its interpretation; yet this very interpretation is inevitable if we are to seek the truth. Some resolution of this paradox is inevitable if we are rightly to evaluate symbolism as a theological principle.

Let us note, first of all, that it is but one aspect of the general dilemma of religion out of which all philosophical theology and philosophy of religion have developed. In its most general form, the dilemma is this: Religion cannot do without the supernatural, yet it cannot do with it, for the supernatural refuses to be completely rationalized. It cannot do without it, for if it attempts to do so, it is no longer religion, as the various humanisms make abundantly clear. If it retains the supernatural, it is never wholly happy, for it must then speak in parable and symbol and the symbol constantly demands interpretation which, just as constantly, the religious consciousness finds it difficult to accept. There is a real dilemma of religion and at no point is it clearer, and perhaps more serious, than in this paradox of symbolism.

There are, in the main, two typical ways in which the modern mind seeks to meet this dilemma and to solve this paradox, and modern philosophers have in the main followed

249

these two ways. Both involve dissolving religion into something else.

The first of these is the familiar way of dissolving it into poetry. On the assumption that if assertions do not have literal significance, in the sense of modern positivism, they have no significance at all, religious symbols are *mere* symbolisms, without reference; the language of religion is wholly emotive and it really says nothing at all. It is not surprising that this solution has attracted many minds who seek short cuts to the solution of difficult problems and are not particularly conscientious as to the facts they trample down in taking the short cut. The trouble is, of course, that it is far too simple. It assumes that because the *vis poetica* is necessarily present in all genuine religious language, religion is only poetry; and, secondly, because it is poetic, it does not give us truth, both assumptions being essentially false. It is a question which is the greater stultification of human experience, the inhuman positivism which says that the assertions of religion are pseudo-sentences and meaningless, or the sentimental humanism which seeks to retain religious meanings after their truth value is denied.

The second way of meeting the dilemma is to dissolve religion wholly into philosophy or metaphysics, a solution advocated by certain forms of metaphysical idealism. 'Religion must,' in the words of Croce, 'allow itself to be dissolved into philosophy.' Religion is in principle mythology, in the broad sense of the term, and, as such, its fate is to be the vestibule of metaphysics. It is true that Croce recognizes in religion a puzzling something which is more than philosophy, namely, worship. Nevertheless its fortune, whether good or bad, is to be thus dissolved. This solution obviously does greater justice to the facts of religion than the former. Translation of the language of religion into the language of metaphysics is indeed the condition of there being any theology at all—but that is a far call from the dissolving of religion into philosophy as here proposed. This solution is also far too simple. It assumes that when it is thus dissolved, when the *vis poetica* is eliminated, religion still remains. To eliminate the historical element from religion—and the dramatic language in which that element can alone be expressed—is to degrade religion into a mere theosophy. To dissolve religion into philosophy is to denature it just as surely as to dissolve it into poetry.

Neither of these solutions is, I believe, possible, and, as I also believe, neither is necessary. Neither is possible for neither is a genuine solution, since both dissolve religion into something it is not; it is no solution of a problem to explain by explaining it away. On the other hand, neither is necessary, for there is, as I believe, a middle ground. A dilemma always arises out of the assumption of mutually exclusive alternatives and the dilemma is solved if they are shown not to be exclusive. The assumption underlying both solutions is that religion must speak either the dramatic language of poetry or the wholly abstract language of philosophy. Religion speaks both languages, and it is precisely its distinction, as it is also its glory, that it does and must indeed do so. Of this all developed religions are fully aware; the basal problem for them all is how this is possible.

It was for the solution of just this dilemma that the doctrine of the analogy of being, with its implied principle of symbolism was partly developed. As ordinarily stated, the doctrine of analogy avoids the alternative of anthropomorphism or agnosticism. It does indeed solve this dilemma but it does so because it includes in its solution the no less fundamental dilemma which we have been describing. For it shows us the way in which the poetic language of religion and the metaphysical language of theology can both be retained. It avoids anthropomorphism for it shows us that our language, although conditioned by the way in which it appears in creatures, may also refer to and symbolize that which is not thus conditioned. It avoids agnosticism because it shows us that our language, while unfitted to express completely the inexhaustible riches of God, can yet find names for Deity which, while human in their origin, yet are, when rightly understood, properly applicable to God. Thus is solved the problem of Humanity and Deity in its most difficult because most fundamental form.

It is true that this solution is never completely satisfactory from a practical point of view. Every movement to symbolism is followed by 'fits of literalism,' and every movement to literalism and fundamentalism by violent reactions to liberalism and rationalism. The ordinary religious consciousness thus

presents a disconcerting picture of a precarious sailing between
Scylla and Charibdis. But this is not so sorry a picture as at first
appears. It simply means that, in the nature of the case, religion
is so great a thing that in order to be thus great it must include
both conceptions and speak both languages.

Religion is thus great because, as von Hügel so eloquently
pointed out, it contains two elements that, in the nature of the
case, can never be intellectually completely fused. It is also
the great thing it is because it contains a third element, the
mystical, in which this fusion is achieved. All religion inevitably
'trenches on the mystical,' for only in the mystical experience
is it, as we shall maintain, possible to make this synthesis of
the 'two Gods' which the religious consciousness, in both its
practical and moral character and in its purely intellectual
aspect, cannot wholly achieve. But this is not the point to be
emphasized here. If this solution of the dilemma of religion,
although never completely satisfactory, is yet in principle
sound, the way is now open for an interpretation of the pronouncements of religion on nature and on man which, as we
have seen in the introductory chapter, is an essential part of
any philosophical theology or philosophy of religion. In the
present chapter we have developed some of the main principles
of interpretation; it is to the specific application of these
principles that we must now turn.

Chapter VIII

The Pronouncements of Religion: What Religion Really Says.
The Philosophy of Creed

I — A

Pope Pius XI is reported to have said: 'Those who speak of the incompatibility of science and religion either make science say what it never said or make religion say what it never taught.' I believe this to be in principle true, but for such a statement even to have meaning, still less to be true, clearly some interpretation both of religion and science must be presupposed. Such interpretation is the philosophy of religion and of science respectively.

It will scarcely be questioned that if we are to determine the 'truth of religion,' and still more the relation of religion to science, we must know what these pronouncements are and what they really say. Both of these requirements may, however, be difficult to meet and the problem of interpretation remain ultimately insoluble.

In the first place, it may be said with a show of reason that there is no such thing as religion as such, but only particular religions: the manifestations of religion are so varied that the the word religion is little more than a collective name. When the Pope speaks of religion and of its relation to science, it is of the Christian religion that he is speaking, and this is inevitable, as indeed it is for any one in our western world who speaks significantly of religion at all. If then it is impossible to say, except arbitrarily and dogmatically, what religion as such is, still more is it impossible to say, except thus arbitrarily, what it is that religion 'really says.'

We faced this difficulty, inherent in any attempt at a philosophy of religion, in an earlier context, and formulated a principle which, I believe, requires only to be expanded in order to meet the present situation. On the 'lower levels' of religion what religion says is, indeed, not only varied but often contradictory, but as we pass to the higher levels there appears a fundamental unity in its basal concepts which enables the philosopher to say what the essence of religion is. The same

253

principle holds for the pronouncements of religion—on man and
his relation to the ground of things. However varied in form,
they are reducible, in the major religions at least, to pronouncements concerning the relation of value to existence: on God as
the *valor valorum* and the self diffusing Good; on grace as the
power, not ourselves, that makes for the enhancement of human
good; and on life eternal as the conservation of the values of our
life in time. The difficulties in the way of the application of this
principle are not to be denied, but I do not think that they are
insuperable. The extension of the principle of analogy between
man and man, implied in the principle of analogy of being itself,
justifies an interpretation of religion which proceeds from the
God-ideas of one's own particular religion. Significant parallels
in the various positive religions make it possible to say that their
various pronouncements are analogous expressions—in different
languages and varied symbolic terms—of the same 'original
phenomena of the spiritual life.'[1]

This first principle of interpretation, as we may perhaps call
it, meets, in a general way at least, the initial problem raised by
the phrase, What *religion* really says; there is still the question
involved in the determination of the meaning of the expression,
what it really says.

Here again it may be said, also with a show of reason, that
the pronouncements of religion *mean* so many different things to
different men, even within a given positive religion, that it is
not possible to say, except arbitrarily and dogmatically, what
they really mean. This, too, is a genuine difficulty, but not, as I
believe, insuperable. The answer to it is found in what I shall
call the second principle of interpretation, namely, symbolism
as a theological principle; and it was for this purpose, partly,
that the principle was developed in the preceding chapter. In all
positive religions the same general principles of symbolic interpretation have been developed, and symbolism as a theological
principle formulated. Christianity did not invent its principles
of interpretation but found them already formulated in the
major existing religions.[2] The unanimity of spiritual insight on
the higher levels of religion which makes it possible for religious
saints and geniuses to understand one another is acknowledged,
but it is not sufficiently understood that that which chiefly makes

[1] Chapter iii, pp. 92 f.   [2] Chapter iii, pp. 113 f.

this fact possible is that they share common principles of interpretation. The fourfold method of interpretation is the product
of the Greco-Christian tradition but it has its analogues in all
forms of developed religion.

B

There is then justification for an interpretation of the pronouncements of religion which proceeds from the God-ideas of a
particular religion. But it would be the height of simplicity to
suppose that these principles enable us to say without qualifi-
cation what religion as such really says. Even if the principles
themselves are accepted, their employment leads to a variety of
interpretation. Within the Christian religion such variation is
the rule, as the multiplication of sects attests. Similar varieties
within the other major religions have led to similar multiplication of sects as any one familiar with Hinduism, Buddhism
or Mohammedanism knows full well. Still more simple is it to
suppose that by such principles we can fully bridge the gulf
between the great positive religions themselves, especially those
of occident and orient. Not only are their languages, both the
lyrical language of devotion and the dramatic language of their
'stories,' so different as to make mutual understanding on this
level difficult, but the ways of life they propose and the philosophies they embody manifest differences which, while doubtless
often exaggerated, are not to be minimized without super-
ficiality and misrepresentation. Yet even there there are those
more fundamental analogies of which Maritain speaks: 'the
existence of God, the sanctity of truth, the value and necessity
of good will among men, the dignity of the person, the spirituality and immortality of the soul, which while not understood
in any identical way by the believers in the various religions of
humanity, do correspond to spontaneous perceptions of reason
and to primary tendencies of our common human nature.'
Surely these in themselves constitute in a very important respect
what religion really says. In contrast to non-religious and wholly
naturalistic pronouncements upon man and his relation to the
ground of things, the pronouncements of all religions are immediately recognized as having common elements which, however varied the symbolic form in which they are expressed,
enable us to say with a degree of confidence what the essence

of religion is and what, when properly understood, religion really says.

All this, it will be said, may be true enough, but, after all, it does not meet the fundamental difficulty. If, as we have seen, it is misleading to find the essence of religion even on the highest levels of all religions, still more questionable must it apparently be to find it in the pronouncements of a particular religion, however high that level may be thought to be—especially, as Otto warns us, to seek it in 'those rational attributions essential to the theistic conceptions of God and especially that of Christianity.' There is, I suppose, no way in which this difficulty may be fully met. One might, it is true, accept the postulate of Christianity as the absolute religion, but whatever grounds one might have for so doing, surely it would be both unwise and unnecessary to make it the premise of our present argument. Not only the notion of Christianity as the final religion, but even that of the evolution of religion itself, would be challenged as egregious begging of the question. However that may be, there are, I believe, sufficient reasons to justify our present procedure without resorting to these postulates. It is not only inevitable that, for the western world, religion should in the main mean Christianity, but also that any interpretation of religion that should be significant should start with the pronouncements of the Christian religion.

That which above all justifies, if it does not absolutely require this procedure, is that the pronouncements of the Christian religion are expressed in the same language that the culture and science of the western world in the main still speaks, namely the idiom of Greek philosophy. Granted that both our culture and our science have in a sense emerged from the tutelage of this philosophy and become in a sense autonomous, it is still true that in so far as their fundamental concepts are concerned they still speak the same language. This is pre-eminently true of science. Doubtless there is a sense in which science is universal, transcending all racial boundaries, but there is a sense also in which this is not wholly true. It is difficult to imagine any fruitful discussion of the relation of science to religion in the context of any oriental philosophy. As the oriental mind assimilates western science it is more than probable that it will contribute to that science itself significant insights—in this respect also East and West will doubtless be found complementary—but it is scarcely conceivable that the basal categories and concepts of modern science will be completely changed.

This in itself is sufficient justification for our procedure, but there is a still more fundamental reason. It is that the basal metaphysical categories in which the Christian religion speaks are really the same for the developed religions of all peoples. In discussing the obvious differences between occidental and oriental thought, Hocking makes it quite clear that these differences are largely matters of emphasis: 'The basic categories of both being and value are the same everywhere.' Were it not so, the genuine communication which actually exists would, as he further points out, be impossible.[1] Of this there can be little doubt. Not only, as we have seen in an earlier context, are these basic categories the same everywhere, but precisely the problem of the relation of value to being is the essence of all religion.[2] If, however, this is true, then in so far as we are concerned with what religion really says, the categories of one religion will correspond, at least analogically, with those of another. At the same time, it is these categories as formulated in the Greek tradition and finally fixed in the idiom of Christian thought that western philosophy still employs, and it is consequently in this idiom alone that, as we have already seen, theology both dogmatic and rational can speak meaningfully to us.

II

The Pronouncements of Religion and the Christian Creeds

A

All religions have something to say on human life and its relation to the ground of things. For our western culture, however, it is, generally speaking, the Christian religion which

---

[1] W. E. Hocking, 'The Value of the Comparative Study of Philosophy,' being the introductory chapter to *Philosophy—East and West*, edited by Charles A. Moore. The quotation is to be found on p. 3.

[2] Chapter ii, pp. 70 ff.

alone can be 'lived,' and it is consequently the pronouncements of this religion which, in the first instance at least, must
be the material of interpretation for any philosophy of religion
of the western world.

In the Christian religion, then, which the Pope had primarily in mind, we are told that God created the heavens and
the earth, that he created man in his own image, that man is a
son of God, by redemption and adoption—all of which are
pronouncements of transcendent importance for life and
practice. It goes without saying that what religion says about
man—about his creation, his fall and his redemption, in short
what we call the historical drama of salvation—constitute
the pronouncements which, in the first instance at least, are
the most significant, in a practical reference. But behind these
are cosmological and ontological pronouncements which form,
so to speak, the stage on which the drama of salvation unrolls.
Without these they lose all ultimate significance, and detachment of religion from cosmology, no less than from history,
turns religion into mere poetry or, at best, a mere ideology.

These three types of pronouncements are found in all positive religions, nature and historical myths forming the original
source of the symbolic forms in which they are expressed.
Behind these forms, religion comes to see, are concealed 'the
greatest realities.' But they *are* concealed, and there is no form
of theology which does not recognize the 'obscurity of the
faith,' in this sense, and does not seek to bring these realities
to light. Following this line of thought, we may make a distinction which will be of considerable importance in the discussions to come—between what religion says explicitly and
what it says implicity. The explicit pronouncements of religion
are always in terms of the dramatic language, and the symbolic
form inseparable from a particular religion; what it says
implicitly is, on the other hand, always in terms of a higher
generality, in terms of the basal categories of value and being,
in short in what I have called an axiological idiom which, as
we have seen, theology must speak if it is to speak intelligibly
and reason cogently. This distinction is, moreover, necessary
if a philosophy of religion is to fulfil the task of the evaluation
of the pronouncements of religion in the larger context of
human experience and knowledge. On the level of their

explicit pronouncements those of religion and science are apparently in conflict; it is only on the philosophical level of interpretation of both science and religion that the conflict can conceivably be resolved.

One may be loath to subscribe to this apparently ' undemocratic ' way of thinking, but that does not alter the fact that in the very nature of the case distinctions of this sort must be made. There has always been the distinction between the *fides simplex parvulorum* and the *serena intelligentia veritatis*, and this deeper understanding of the truth has been an essential part of Christianity from the beginning. The wayfaring man, though a fool, need not err in the way of faith and practice on which he is faring, but he may err greatly when he seeks to follow the more difficult roads of theology and philosophy. It is a truism that literalism and over-simplification, inseparable from popular science, inevitably make science say what it really does not say. Is it any the less likely that this should be true in relation to 'divine things'? In any case 'religious obscurity' has always been recognized as an inevitable character of the language of religion, the only question being whether interpretation is the function of individual reason or of the absolute reason embodied in the Church.

B

The explicit pronouncements of any religion may be described as its dogmas although it is primarily in connection with Christian theology and philosophy that the notion of dogma has been developed and defined. Dogma, we are told by Sabatier, 'is the language spoken by faith. In it there are two elements: a mystical and practical element, the properly religious element—this is the living and fruitful principle of dogma; then there is an intellectual and theoretical element, a judgment of the mind, a philosophical proposition, serving at once as an envelope and an expression of religion.' [1] The general truth of the first part of this statement the studies of Chapter iv have made clear. Dogmas are the intuitions of faith and as such are expressible, in the first instance at least, only in the language of faith, which, being in its very essence lyrical and dramatic, is also primarily practical and mystical.

[1] A. Sabatier, *Outlines of a Philosophy of Religion*, p. 264.

But behind what it says explicitly is that which is said implicitly and this can be expressed only in 'intellectual terms.' The Christ of devotion becomes the *Deus Homo* of dogmatic theology, and what the latter says about the God-man contains a great deal more implicitly than what is said in the language of faith. The Christology of the Christian religion presupposes a cosmology—and ultimately an ontology, and this general principle is true of the explicit pronouncements of any positive religion.

In religion, then, we find three main types of pronouncements or propositions. These, following a generally accepted classification, we may describe as: (a) the historical; (b) the cosmological; (c) the ontological or metaphysical. Otherwise stated, they are: (a) propositions about the being of God or the divine (metaphysical); (b) propositions about the relation of God to the world (cosmological); and (c) propositions about divine transactions or acts in time (historical). Every religion contains all three types of pronouncements and every credal statement of belief embodies them in the form of doctrine. If we examine the Christian creeds—let us say the Nicene—the 'articles' of the creed clearly fall under these three heads.

There is no form of Christian theology for which the historic creeds have not in some sense been symbols of the faith. The credal pronouncements are based upon the recorded events of sacred scripture. The latter, according to classical principles of interpretation, have indeed their literal meaning, but their full meaning, and their ultimate truth, can be known only when we pass to the higher stages of interpretation, and ultimately to the anagogical or metaphysical. It would seem inevitable, therefore, that the creeds themselves, known as the symbols of the faith, should have their anagogical as well as literal meaning. It is true that while creeds are thus recognized as symbols, the attempt 'to go behind the symbol' is frequently deprecated—the symbol, it being said, is in a sense truer than the translation. Understandable as this is in a practical reference, and while attempts to 'rationalize dogma' invariably leave much to be desired, this translation is inevitable. In any case, this is what theology in the main has done, and, indeed, must do, if it is to evaluate the pronouncements of religion in the larger context of human knowledge as a whole.

The necessity of higher levels of interpretation has always been recognized, but also the necessity of the retention of the literal as vital to practical religion, and it is this that creates the difficulty, at least when understood in the sense of the 'original undefaced imagery of the words.' Present in connection with all the articles of the creed, it is in connection with the historical pronouncements that the problem becomes crucial for theology. It was natural, and in a sense justifiable, for Gnosticism to find the true inwardness of religion not in the historical but in the ontological or metaphysical propositions which they presuppose. But it was just as necessary and justifiable for the religious consciousness to set itself in opposition to Gnosticism. This is merely a special form in which the general dilemma of religion expresses itself, and it is precisely the character of the religious consciousness that it refuses to accept either horn of the dilemma. It is a complete stultification of the religious consciousness to resolve these propositions into poetry and myth, but it is no less a stultification to resolve them wholly into metaphysics.

III

The Historical Element in Religion: The Drama of Salvation. *What Religion Says About Man*

A

Our first consideration must, then, be given to what is called the historical element in religion. This is necessary for two reasons: in the first place, because it is in connection with the historical propositions that the pronouncements of religion on man are most immediately and obviously bound up; and, secondly, because it is in connection with these propositions that problems of truth and falsity (and of evidence generally) are most acute. It is these pronouncements, both as matters of history and as involving conceptions of man, which, it is believed, come most seriously into conflict with the factual statements of science.

The Christian doctrine of man, or what is known as Christian anthropology, is given primarily in connection with its historical pronouncements. While primarily revelatory of God, and of his acts in time, they are also secondarily, and perhaps equally, revelatory of the nature of man. They tell of a God, 'who for us men and for our salvation came down from Heaven and was made man.' The Incarnation is the centre of history for the Christian, and this is itself of tremendous import, but in the very fact that God took upon himself the nature of man, something of equal import has been said about man. It tells us, implicitly, to be sure, that man, while a part of nature, transcends nature. It is important from this point of view to remember that the original purpose of all the statements made in the creeds about the earthly life of Jesus was to insist upon the reality of His humanity. They are directed against Docetism, not against humanism, which was not a theory of the creed-making ages. That Jesus is very God is the *sine qua non* of Christian worship; that he is also very man is the condition of man's salvation and, indirectly, also of man's humanity to man. If, as we may perhaps be permitted to believe, Christianity has really made man more humane, it is largely for this reason.

For the Christian religion the problem of the historical element in religion centres about what the theologians call Christology. The historical articles of the creed tell us of a Person—of a human life lived in space and time, of certain events—of his birth, his labours, sufferings, death, resurrection and ascension—all of which have a quality which can be expressed only in a language which may be characterized as numinous and in categories described as 'miraculous.' There is no question as to what they say explicitly. They tell us of events in space and time, but of events so 'distorted' (in the technical sense already employed) as to be unlike any other spatio-temporal happenings. The question is then what, by this very distortion, they say implicitly, or in our phraseology *really* say.

In actual interpretation men have consistently looked behind the explicit pronouncements to what they really say. For many, as for Abelard, there is a *melior ascensus* which the actual physical ascension *really* means, but they have sought also to retain the latter. This has presented such difficulties for belief that theologians have felt themselves driven to make distinctions among the historical articles of the creed. Like Bishop

Gore, many are disposed to allow a 'generous latitude of interpretation' with respect to this article, but no latitude at all with respect to the article, 'Born of the Virgin Mary.'[1] One can understand the motives which lead to this distinction, but one also feels that it is very difficult to maintain. Not only are the historical elements of the creed all of one piece—and it is disastrous for faith and logic alike to take them piecemeal— but even more important is it to realize that they are also of one piece from the standpoint of the philosophy of language. If there is one thing which any adequate understanding of language makes clear, it is that it is impossible to describe any real event in time in language that is wholly non-symbolic. Here as elsewhere it remains true that the function of language is not to copy reality but to symbolize it.[2]

This is the crux of the matter. The historical pronouncements cannot escape the symbolic character of the language in which they are enunciated. But the fact that it is impossible to describe any event, whether human or divine, in wholly non-symbolic language does not at all exclude another important truth, namely that real events do take place in time, which have the numinous quality of deity, and that these constitute the historical element in religion. In rendering these real events and their unique quality in words, only a space-time language can be used, and with that use comes inevitably that form of space-time distortion which we call the miraculous. This does not mean, however, that the full meaning of these events—what they really and ultimately say—is adequately expressed in this symbolic form. This no type of theology has ever maintained. For these historical pronouncements presuppose cosmological and the latter ontological, and these alone give them their full meaning. If men persist in going behind the event to its meaning, as they constantly do, it is because they realize that this meaning lies outside space and time.

Christianity is the historical religion *par excellence*, and it is because of what its historical pronouncements thus really say

---

[1] C. Gore, *Can We Then Believe?* 1929.

[2] The issue here raised is discussed with admirable clearness and candour by A. E. Taylor, *op. cit.* Volume II, pp. 141 ff. For him the historical element in religion is an essential part of its nature, but he also rightly insists that no hard and fast line between the symbolical and the historical can be drawn.

that they are of such transcendent significance. Its attachment
to the life and person of its Founder is absolutely necessary,
but necessary only because His real being also lies beyond all
history and beyond all time. If this is not what Christianity
really says—if these events, thus described in the dramatic
language of incarnation, sacrifice, death, resurrection and
ascension, were not thus revelatory of the ultimate relations
of Good to Being, which lie beyond all history—then precisely
these events would themselves be what history, as mere events
in time, always is, sound and fury signifying nothing. If, wrote
St. Paul, Christ be not risen from the dead, then are we, of all
men, most miserable. But it should be equally clear that we
should be no less miserable, even if He did rise from the dead,
if His resurrection did not mean something which transcends all history and is before all worlds. The mere 'fact' by
itself is as meaningless as any other mere fact and, apart from
the truth which it symbolizes, has the additional meaninglessness which always inheres in all mere wonders.

This, it seems to me, is the only tenable theory of the historical element in religion. It permits us to take the historical
as a whole and makes unnecessary those arbitrary distinctions
among events which have always created insuperable difficulties. It enables us to determine what these pronouncements
really say in the sense of our definition. And, finally, as we shall
see, it enables us to relate these pronouncements, when thus
interpreted, to the pronouncements of secular history and to
formulate the supernatural element in history in a way that
does not do violence to secular history and its naturalistic
principles of evidence.

B

What then, according to these principles of interpretation do
these historical pronouncements really say? What is the ultimate
'reality' which, while they do not copy, they yet express
symbolically? I think it is fairly clear what they thus say
implicitly, and has been constantly explicated by the theologians
themselves. They tell us, first of all, that the numinous quality
of certain events in space and time is revelatory—and uniquely
revelatory—of God as goodness and love and still more
ultimately of the identity of value and being. They tell us, moreover, also by implication, that our human life, both the life of the

individual man and the life of humanity we know as history, has a meaning; that both the source and fulfilment of that meaning lie beyond our temporal life and history; and that it is only because of this ground and goal that they have any meaning at all. This is what they *really* say and when a man believes these tremendous pronouncements this is what in his heart he really and ultimately believes.

The historical pronouncements of religion—the drama of salvation which they embody and show forth—are at once an expression of Christian anthropology and of a Christian philosophy of history. *Deus homo* is the heart of theology, but it is at the same time for a religious philosophy the essence of any valid anthropology. For it tells us, not only how to think of God, but how to think of man, the two being inextricably bound up together. It is not my intention to discuss further this Christian anthropology, which can be more adequately treated in later contexts,[1] but some comment on the Christian philosophy of history may serve to emphasize the main point of this discussion.

Christianity tells us that our human life in time has a meaning and that the story of that life which we call history has a meaning also. This meaning, as we saw in an earlier context, can signify only enhancement and conservation of our values in time. Moreover, as we also saw, the meaning of any of the parts cannot be separated from the meaning of the whole, and that therefore meaning of the individual life cannot be ultimately separated from the life of the whole.[2] If then history has meaning, such meaning must include the notions both of 'one increasing purpose' running through the ages and of an 'imperishable goal' which gives meaning to the increasing purpose. These two elements are, however, the essentials of any intelligible concept of progress. I agree then with Croce that the notion of progress has always been implicit in the Christian philosophy of history. The realization of the kingdom of God on earth, to use religious language, is the meaning of history, but such realization is no realization if the values are achieved only to pass away and if the goal towards which the increasing purpose is directed is not an imperishable goal.

Dean Inge calls progress a purely secular eschatology, and that in many of its modern forms it cannot be denied. But it seems to me equally certain that it is also a necessary part of a religious eschatology. The difference between the secular and religious forms is patent and as significant as patent. Both tell us that the time process called history has a meaning, but the religious conception tells us that the source and fulfilment of that meaning lies beyond time and history. It tells us that there is a Divinity that shapes our ends, social as well as individual, rough hew them how we may. It is doubtless true that, as both Tolstoy and Guyau have said, the belief in secular progress is the modern man's substitute for providence; and in so far as it is a substitute it falls far short of the religious conception, although even then it retains something of its former meaning. The historical element in religion presupposes, as we shall see, both a cosmology and an ontology, and it is these pronouncements about the world and about that which is before all worlds which alone give meaning to the historical pronouncements and make pronouncements about that process, including the notion of progress, intelligible. Separated from its cosmological and ontological presuppositions progress itself becomes wholly illusory, especially those concepts which envisage an automatic progress or make of progress itself, *in infinitum*, its own goal. Progress can then not be a substitute for providence for without pronouncements about first and last things, about that which transcends space and time, processes in space and time can have no meaning.

Nevertheless, the notion of progress itself can scarcely be wholly a product of modern liberal self-deception, as some maintain, unless the notion of history itself is also a part of this self-deception, for without these two notions of enhancement and conservation we have no longer history but mere chronology. It may be, of course, that there is no meaningful story of man at all, but merely an eternal recurrence of the same things, but that is certainly not the Christian conception and I doubt whether it is true of any philosophy which remains religious. In any case, not only is the notion of progress, rightly understood, implicit in the Christian philosophy of history, but in telling us that history has a meaning it also tells us not only of things above but of things below, and the only concepts which give meaning to the things of time are those of increasing purpose and imperishable goal.

C

If this is what the historical pronouncements of religion really say, if these pronouncements get their significance by reference to that which transcends nature and history, then obviously their truth and falsity cannot be determined by criteria developed solely for nature and history. Some apologists for the Christian faith need to understand more fully the problem of evidence. That the Word was made flesh and made flesh in a specific person, Jesus, is a proposition which admits of no establishment by any empirical appeal to certified fact. For surely it must be clear that the historical events in religion, so necessary if it is to remain religion, are not the same as historical events as understood in secular history or historical 'science.' For both religion and history the event is factual, but for science, *ex hypothesi*, the event has no numinous quality while for religion it has. The secular historian is, therefore, quite within his rights in maintaining that there is no empirical evidence, in his sense, for such propositions. Secular history which, as secular, eliminates the supernatural *a priori*, quite rightly proceeds on purely naturalistic presuppositions. The secular historian does not so much deny that an historical event has a numinous quality, as hold that, from his standpoint, such a quality has no meaning. He abstracts from it *ab initio*, and, like Laplace, in the related field of cosmology, simply refuses to bring God into the story, maintaining that he has no need of that hypothesis. No one can cavil at such procedure provided the secular historian fully understands what he is doing. For if he is really critical he will recognize that he has excluded God *a priori*—as required by his method—and therefore all evidence that would justify a religious philosophy of history. He should realize also that, with this exclusion, he has perhaps excluded all possibility of finding the historical process ultimately meaningful at all, and should, therefore, if consistent, exclude philosophy of history in any form. For the postulate of progress by means of which secular history seeks to bring meaning into the historical process is as little verifiable empirically, when applied to the process as a whole, as the postulate of providence. Herbert Spencer called progress 'the most certain of all facts,' but actually it cannot be demonstrated as a fact at all, but

merely as a reasonable belief. However this may be, the point
here is that such an interpretation of the historical pronouncements of religion as here proposed, in no way does violence to
the purely empirical principles of evidence which secular
history has developed for its own purposes. Such history does
not of course bring God into the story, but neither does it, if it
knows its own business, dogmatically shut Him out. To do
either would be, as we shall see, to stultify its own postulates
regarding the nature of science and scientific method.[1]

D

The view of the historical element in religion here presented
differs, accordingly, fundamentally from that which would
make it a form of myth, in contrast to the 'fact' of history.
According to this view, 'Christian history is irreparably ruined
but Christian myth remains the most compelling expression of
man's timeless spiritual experience evolved by any religion.'
'The identification of this myth with history was fatal,' we are
told; 'it is only by being completely severed from history that it
now becomes capable of conveying its full freight of metaphysical truth.'[2] Only by severing religion completely from
history can we determine what religion really says.

'Here indeed,' writes one philosopher,'is something new in
Christian theology!' Although not completely new—it is really
a new form of a very old way of thinking—it is yet new enough,
in its details at least, to be of considerable influence in the present
crisis of religion. It is for this reason also that it is important to
distinguish it from the view here developed. That there is a
mythical element in the language in which these pronouncements are made is unquestioned. If this language and the
mythical categories involved were not used, the unique character of the historical events could not itself be expressed. The
mythical categories are indeed indispensable, but it does not at
all follow that myth and history are identical in religion. In so
far as Christian theology is concerned, Christian myth does not
have to be severed from history for the very good reason that

[1] Chapter x, pp. 331 ff.
[2] P. Tillich, 'Mythus und Mythologie' in *Religion in Geschichte und Gegenwart*
2nd Ed. Tubingen, 1930. Also Reinhold Niebuhr, *Beyond Tragedy*, New York,
1937.

the two have never been completely identified. In so far as this theology is concerned, its very existence depends upon the translation of the dramatic language of religion into the axiological idiom of philosophy, and this is what the Christian philosophy of history has done.

IV

The Cosmological Pronouncements of Religion. The Origin and End of all Things

A

The historical propositions of religion are, then, an essential part of its nature. Attempts to divest religion completely of attachments to historical persons and events can end only in denaturing it. Still less is it possible to divest religion of its attachments to cosmology. 'The theme of cosmology,' writes Whitehead, 'is the basis of all religions.' It is, as he further writes, 'the story of the dynamic effort of the world, passing into everlasting unity, and of the static majesty of God's vision accomplishing its purpose of completion by absorption of the world's multiplicity of effort.'[1] Whether the words here chosen best tell the story or not we may leave undetermined—to me they seem singularly unfitted for that august task—the fact remains that cosmology is a 'story' and that with this story is bound up the meaning and the fate of religion.

This 'theme of all religions' has always contained propositions of two types—assertions about the beginning or creation of the world and about its end or destiny. The cosmic myths from which religion gets its language and its symbolism are fundamental elements in every positive religion and cosmological propositions basal in every religious view of the world. The attempt is constantly made to deny this. Indeed there are many who assert that the essence of religion can be retained only by detaching it, not merely from history but from all cosmology. If Christian history is irreparably ruined, still more is any religious cosmology. This is the burden of all naturalistic humanisms, but I think it may fairly be said that that position

[1] A. N. Whitehead, *Process and Reality*, p. 529.

has shown itself to be but a temporary halting place on the road either to a downright atheism or to some restatement of theism; for the theme of cosmology still remains the basis of all religion.

B

When it is said that 'God is the Maker of heaven and earth, and of all things visible and invisible,' something of tremendous import has been expressed. What then does this pronouncement really say?

The language in which this explicit statement is made is clearly symbolic in form. The category of creation itself is not mythical, but the imagery in which it is expressed is mythical in origin. God, if there be a God, is clearly not a 'maker' in any literal sense. Maker is a purely phenomenal notion and, like the notion of the prime mover of which Kant wrote, is inseparable from spatial and temporal elements, and therefore cannot be applied in an empirical or literal sense. It is only when thought passes from its literal to its anagogic sense—to what is said implicitly—that its true significance is understood. Now I think there is little doubt as to what the dogma of creation really says. It tells us, implicitly to be sure, something of crucial significance for the life and spirit of man. It tells us that the meaning and value of things cannot be separated from their origins; that the ground of things determines their ultimate nature and their ultimate end. Yet it is precisely the contention of much of modern thought that this separation is possible or intelligible. It must be admitted that there is something to be said for this position. If there is one thing that the modern man has learned it is that it is a fatal fallacy to interpret the meaning and value of a thing in terms of its temporal origins, biological or historical. This 'genetic fallacy,' as it is called, has been so constantly exposed in various fields of thought and knowledge that conscious avoidance of it has become an essential part of modern critical method. But if our thought is to be really critical a further distinction must be made at this point, namely, between historical and ultimate origins. Origins in the former sense do not, of course, determine values, but in the latter sense they 'notoriously do,' as Balfour has pointed out.[1]

This, I am sure, is not merely a matter of feeling but of the

[1] *Theism and Humanism*, p. 61.

deepest reason also. It is inconceivable that if our values come from nothing they should not ultimately be thought to be of the same nothingness from which they come. I am well aware that this is constantly denied, but to sensitive intellectual ears such denial always has a note of intellectual hysteria, such, in fact, as that which one feels in Nietzsche's amoral cosmology. We cannot really put values into the world unless they are in principle already there. There are theories of the cosmos which make our values impossible. This is not merely what the Christian dogma actually says, as translated and explicated by theologian and philosopher; it is rather what in the nature of things it must say, and what every concept of creation must say, implicitly.[1] It is for this reason that despite the recognition of the mythical origin of its imagery it is constantly reaffirmed, even after the symbolic character of the mythical embodiment is fully realized; it is for this reason also that if one formulation of the conception is refuted it will immediately take another. The true inwardness of the dogma of creation is expressed in the axiom *ex minimo maximum non fit*, the greater does not arise from the less; only the higher explains the lower, that principle of the general proof which condenses in a single formula the principles upon which the five typical proofs rest.[2]

Religion then, to be a religion, must have a cosmology. But to be a cosmology it must also include an eschatology. The latter is an essential part of the former. As has been truly said, causality and finality are really the same thing seen from two ends. Religion can no more avoid pronouncement upon the end than upon the origination of all things. This Kant saw clearly when he said of the dogma of the last judgment, and of the conception of 'last things' which it presupposes, that it is a part of the very texture of human thought. This is obviously true in the emotional life of man. If all our values end in nothing, it

---

[1] This is, I think, the true inwardness of the Christian opposition to the Averroists who, following Aristotle on this point, denied that the material world had a beginning and an end. For this doctrine is in many ways the ancestral form of modern naturalism and mechanism. Such a doctrine seemed not only inconsistent with theism but with any really religious conception of the world. It was, however, Leibniz who saw most clearly the real issue when he insisted that the question of ultimate origination is logically independent of the space-time form. It is rather the validity of our values that is in question, and this conception cannot be separated, from some notion of intelligible causation. Chapter iv, pp. 129 f.

[2] Chapter v, pp. 178 f.

is impossible not to feel that they are ultimately of the same nothingness into which they go. But it is, I believe, true for man's reason also. Historical ends, no more than historical origins, determine values, but ultimate destiny no less than ultimate origination inevitably does. The world bank is the one bank of which it may be said that if it is ultimately insolvent, it has always been so.

It is inevitable, of course, that the form in which this great truth is expressed should also be in part symbolic, the imagery describing last no less than first things being taken from the world of finite things. The 'eternal purpose' which God purposes is as inseparable from spatio-temporal imagery as are the notions of 'maker' and prime mover. The poet speaks of the 'one far-off divine event towards which the whole creation moves,' and in so doing he speaks necessarily in poetic imagery, but that does not prevent what he says from having truth that is more than poetic. When he 'doubts not through the ages one increasing purpose runs,' the purpose which he envisages cannot escape being partly 'human' and therefore symbolic. We may even go further in our admissions and recognize the dialectical difficulties involved in these notions. An eternal purpose, it may be said, is not a purpose, for all purposes known to us must be such as to be realizable in time. An imperishable goal is not a goal for in human experience all our goals perish. But neither the symbolic character of the concepts, nor the inevitable contradictions which are engendered when these images are taken literally, affect the truth of what is thus symbolically expressed. The notion of an ultimate end or last judgment is as necessary a part of the implicit content of religion as that of ultimate origination or ground, and the former as much a necessary part of the entire texture of human thought or reason as is the latter.

C

These pronouncements—on first and last things—precisely because they embody a fundamental principle of reason or intelligibility, have far-reaching implications for the practical and spiritual life of man. These dogmas regarding creation and consummation tell us not only, as LeRoy says, how not to think of God, but how not to think of man. It is not an accident that when men transfer their spiritual allegiance from eastern to western ways of religious thought, they invariably find the greatest significance at these two points. It involves in many respects a complete revaluation of man.

The dogma of creation has special import in this respect. To be a creature of God, we are told, is one thing; to be a part of God or identical with Him is quite another. In the former one feels an extraordinary lightening of the burden, whether of obligation or fatalism, for while obligation still remains it is, after all, only that of a creature, and the will of the Creator is accepted not as fate but joyfully, as that in which the free creature finds his peace. Like the dogma of creation, so that of the last judgment has a profound practical and moral significance. It makes a great difference whether a religious eschatology contemplates realization of purpose or merely an eternal recurrence, a genuine conclusion to our finite life or an endless reincarnation. Here, too, it is not an accident that at this point also those who have transferred their spiritual allegiance from eastern to western ways of religious thought find the greatest moral significance. To be a creature of God, to be judged for the deeds done in the body, is one thing; to be subject to the endless wheel of reincarnation is quite another. If an infinite regress in the direction of origins is 'unthinkable,' still more is infinite progress in the future. It is felt that ' time must have a stop ' and the opposite is felt to be not only unthinkable but intolerable, despite what Nietzsche may say. The notion of ultimate consummation, no less than that of ultimate origination is, I think Leibniz would say, independent of the space-time form.

It is at these points, doubtless, that the really significant difference between the religions of East and West, speaking very broadly of course, chiefly appear, and they are not to be minimized. But even so, they may also be exaggerated. These differences may still be conceived, I think, as variations on one fundamental theme, namely, that of God, grace and the eternal life. The notions of ultimate origination and of ultimate consummation are present in all of them and bring with them inevitably some notion of God, even if men have ceased to use the word, and some conception of eternal life even if they have abandoned all images and symbols in terms of which that life may be envisaged. Whatever the mythical form in which these

273

notions have been originally embodied, and however critical developed religion and philosophy may become of this form, the fundamental notions themselves remain.

D

The symbolic form in which any religious cosmology is inevitably expressed often leads to an interpretation, even within Christian philosophy itself, which tends to divest religion of its attachments to cosmology, no less than to history, and to dissolve it wholly into ontology. In his very suggestive book, *God and the Astronomers*, Dean Inge seems at least to follow more or less this path. It appears especially in what may be called his eschatology.[1]

Assuming, as he does, that the dissipation of energy and the running down of the universe is what 'science says' about the end of all things, his problem is to relate this to what religion says about the destiny of finite things, and concludes that what science says, or seems to say, makes no difference to religion, for religion deals with 'things above' in the sense of Platonism— with the timeless world of eternal ideas and values. Now with the questions, whether science really says this, and whether, if it did, it would affect the essence of religious belief is one which we shall consider in a later context.[2] I may say, however, that it seems extremely doubtful whether science really says these things, and still more doubtful whether, if it did, what it says would have the significance for religion it is supposed to have. This is, however, not the question here but rather whether the interpretation of the eschatological pronouncements of religion, as given by Dean Inge, is satisfactory. I do not think that it is. It is true that religion deals with things above, but it also, if it is to be significant, must deal with things below, with the time process and all that it includes and implies. If progress is a purely secular eschatology, so any philosophy which gives significance to the time process must be a secular cosmology

[1] W. R. Inge, *God and the Astronomers*. This is one of the most suggestive of recent books on the problems of religion and science. He takes issue, to be sure, with the views of the present writer on both history and cosmology as developed in *The Intelligible World*, especially with regard to the notion of progress as essential to an intelligible concept of history, but on the more fundamental issues, of the relation of value to being, we are in essential agreement.

[2] Chapter x, pp. 359 f.

also. Such a view does scant justice to the historical element in religion but just as little does it do justice to the cosmological. As history, so conceived, tends, as history, to be sound and fury signifying nothing, so the cosmic process as a whole seems to be not only a wasteful but a ghastly process—in Schopenhauer's figure a magic lantern in which the eternal values are eternally shown forth. So conceived, it is likely to become, as it did for Nietzsche, merely a play and solely of aesthetic significance. I do not, of course, say that this is what the cosmic process is for Dean Inge, but ways of thinking similar to his have often led to this result.

E

If purely empirical criteria of evidence are inapplicable in the case of the historical pronouncements of religion, it is obvious, I suppose, that they are *a fortiori* inapplicable to the cosmological. If the proposition that God entered into the historical process by becoming man admits of no establishment by an appeal to what science calls certified fact, it is scarcely likely that the still more ultimate pronouncements—that God created all things visible and invisible and that he will come again to judge the quick and the dead—can be established by such an appeal. Here also apologists need to reflect more deeply on the nature of evidence. For the cosmological pronouncements of religion there is, of course, no 'scientific' evidence. God's causality and God's teleology are not ours and cannot be verified by criteria developed for the determination of finite causes and ends in nature. But the critical scientist will also realize that cosmological pronouncements of science about the beginning and end of things—if indeed science makes such—are equally unverifiable empirically, for they are statements about the whole and no statement about the totality of things can in the nature of the case be thus verified. They too can give grounds only for reasonable belief. It is often assumed that religion and science differ in this respect, but examination of the cosmological pronouncements will show, I think, that this is not so.[1]

There is a much quoted saying of Clutton-Brock to the effect that religion is forced to tell many little lies in the interest of a great truth, while science is inclined to tell many little truths in the interest of a great lie. The element of truth in this dictum is

[1] Chapter x, pp. 342 ff.

undoubted but, as it seems to me, expressed in an unfortunate way. If science did tell us that the historical and cosmic processes are self-originating and self-controlled, it would deny the great truths of religion as expressed in its pronouncements on first and last things, and would indeed tell a monstrous lie in comparison with which all its little truths would be as nothing. But I do not believe that science tells this lie. Indeed it will be one of our main tasks to show that science, properly understood, does not really say this. On the other hand, it is no less unfortunate to speak of the explicit pronouncements of religion as little lies, even if told in the interest of a great truth. For they are not lies unless we are guilty of the fallacy of misplaced literalism which begets lies in every sphere of human knowledge and discourse, even in science itself. What these pronouncements really say, when properly interpreted, far from being little lies, are themselves true, for they present in symbolic form, the only form possible, the greatest of all truths.

V

The Ontological Pronouncements of Religion :
Religion and Metaphysics

A

As the historical element is an indispensable part of religion, as the theme of cosmology remains the basis of all religions, so the ontological pronouncements constitute the ultimate essence of all religious belief. This is pre-eminently the character of the pronouncements of religion as we find them in Christian theology. The historical presuppose the cosmological and the cosmological the ontological or metaphysical.

'The Incarnation,' so Father Thornton tells us, 'presupposes' a cosmology. It asserts that 'He who entered into the historical process by becoming man for our salvation is also the Creator and Lord of the physical universe, the source and sustainer of its existence and of all its processes.'[1] But by the same token it also presupposes an ontology. This cosmology tells us indeed that God is the Maker of heaven and earth and of all things

[1] L. S. Thornton, *The Incarnate Lord*, p. 27.

visible and invisible, but in so doing it also tells us, by implication, that this created world is revelatory of the absolute Good, that the invisible things of Him are known by the things that are made and that thus we may pass from the knowledge of the creature to the knowledge of God. Thus this cosmology presupposes a fundamental metaphysics—that there is one transcendant and supremely given reality, God (before all worlds), and that this being is identical with the Good, which, by merely being, extends its goodness to all things. This is the supreme ontological pronouncement and without this all the other pronouncements, historical and cosmological, crumble into dust. The attempt is constantly made to divorce religion not only from history and cosmology but from metaphysics also. One wonders what is left. Even more than cosmology is ontology the basis of all religion.

B

Credo in unum Deum is the first article of the Nicene Creed, and it is this credo, with all that it implies, that determines all the other articles. The interpretation of this article has been a large part of the task of both dogmatic and rational theology. Indeed a philosophical theology cannot avoid the problem of what this dogma really says. Here too, it is clear, we must distinguish between what it says explicitly and what implicitly, for theological discourse and argument cannot proceed until the dramatic language of religion is translated into the idiom of metaphysics. What then does this pronouncement really say?

No question of the being or existence of God can be significantly raised unless in some way and some degree, even if only confusedly, we know what God is—the 'that' cannot be separated from the 'what.' Some 'formal principle of Deity' at least must be acknowledged before the question of existence can be even raised. Thus at the end of each of the arguments for God's existence St. Thomas says, 'and this is what men mean by God' (or equivalent words) which presupposes, as we have seen, that men know, however confusedly, something of what God is.

The pronouncements in which this knowledge of God is embodied are of two kinds, those which we predicate of Him analogically and therefore partly symbolically, and the 'metaphysical attributes of Deity' deduced from the formal principle of perfection. The former He possesses only eminently for they are relative, the latter with an absolute possession. It is the latter which constitute the central principle of Deity for, as we have seen in the preceding chapter, it is only on the basis of such knowledge that the ontological sublimation of the relative predicates is either possible or intelligible. The relative attributes are embodied in the historical and cosmological pronouncements; it is with the absolute attributes that we are here concerned.

The Being called God is one, transcendent, and identical with the Good. The transcendental predicates, *unum, verum, bonum*, are not attributes which Deity might or might not have and remain Deity. He possesses them, to be sure, but with an absolute possession which is the same thing as saying he does not *have* them, but *is* them. Thus it is that the terms substance and attribute, having and possessing, taken as they are from the world of finite things, also contain a symbolic element which must be interpreted. Thinghood itself, from which the categories of substance and attribute primarily derive, is obviously a term which cannot be applied to God in the original and undefaced meaning of the word, nor can the terms substance and attribute themselves. It is, however, pre-eminently the meaning of 'existence' which is at issue here—of this Being Who *is* before all worlds.

What then does religion say implicitly when it asserts explicitly that God 'exists'? One thing we may be sure it has never said, namely, that God exists in the sense of the 'blessed isles' of Gaunilo, or of the 'dollar in the pocket' of Kant's illustration. He exists in the sense that a Being such as God alone could exist—in the sense that his very essence implies His existence. I contend, therefore, that religion, unless it is made to say what it really does not say, never has, never will, and indeed never can say that He exists in any other way. Of that substance which is God subsistence alone can be predicated.[1]

Religion tells us, to be sure, that if we 'take the wings of the

---

[1] The anathema at the end of the Athanasian Creed says: 'But those who say, "There was a time when He was not," or profess that the Son of God is of a different substance *or subsistence* or that he is created or changeable or variable, let him be anathema.' (Italics mine.)

morning and fly to the uttermost parts of the earth, behold He is there', that even though we make our bed in Hell he is there also; and we know that this is true, but we know also that this is the dramatic language of poetry and that it must be translated in order to be really understood. The schoolmen attempted, it is true, to express this existence of God, this *ubeity* which they called omnipresence, as 'repletive,' distinguishing it from other kinds of whereness, 'circumscriptive' and 'definitive,' the first being applied to bodies, the second to souls. Leibniz remarks that he does not know 'whether or not this doctrine deserves to be turned into ridicule as some people endeavour to do' and therein he manifests his characteristic wisdom and intellectual magnanimity—but while it should not be turned into ridicule, it should be recognized as an attempt to express, in spatio-temporal form, relations which are not spatial and temporal. The *ubeity* of God, real though it is, cannot be expressed in any but symbolic form.

This is the crux of the matter. But precisely this fact—that even existence when applied to *Him Who Is* contains a symbolic element—raises of course one of the most difficult of all theological problems. Meister Eckhart spoke of God not only as 'the One beyond the Good' but also as 'the One who is beyond existence,' and in this he but carried to the last stage a motive present in all western thought since Plotinus—the inevitable last stage of a negative theology. Theology itself is then but a 'dialectic of symbols', and the outcome of the dialectic is the abandonment of all symbols for pure mysticism. If God is beyond all existence we have indeed come to the abyss of unknowing before which true believers and true worshippers have always drawn back aghast.[1] To this it would seem there can be only one answer. God is not beyond existence—that is not only absurd but even blasphemous, for 'He Who is' is God's name—but he is beyond the category of existence which we use when we speak of Him in 'bodily form.' The word God involves, as we have seen, a double meaning. It connotes, and indeed must connote, an object endowed with qualities and actions—otherwise it could not be an object of prayer and praise; but it also connotes the unconditioned transcendent. The former must

[1] Of this 'fanatical element' in some forms of mysticism I shall speak more fully later in Chapter xiii, pp. 435 f.

in the nature of the case contain a symbolic element and this applies also to the categories of existence in terms of which we speak of Him; the latter is, in the strictest sense of the word, precisely what it is said to be. It is this metaphysical truth that the so-called ontological argument embodies, and while it is not an argument for the 'existence' of anything in the sense of Meister Eckhart—and indeed in the nature of the case could not be—it nevertheless embodies an intuition which makes it the initial datum of all the other arguments. In this 'argument' human truth comes nearest, it would seem, to that *veritas ontologica* which is truth as God sees it.

C

For the ontological pronouncements of religion, both as to the being and nature of God, there is, therefore, no purely empirical evidence, as indeed there is none for *any* metaphysical propositions. What is true in this respect of the historical and cosmological pronouncements is *a fortiori* true of the ontological. If then God is *ens perfectissimum*—as He must be to be God—there can in the nature of the case be no purely empirical verification of His existence, for being verified in this way He would not be God at all but 'something else.' This is the true inwardness of Kant's criticism of the traditional empirical arguments.

It is sometimes thought, however, that this situation may be escaped by denying that God is infinite perfection and insisting that there is empirical evidence for a 'finite god.' With the motives that have led to that doctrine in modern times I am not here concerned, but merely with its status with respect to the problem of verification.[1] It is sometimes supposed that while an infinite or absolute God cannot be empirically verified, a finite god might be. That is, however, I am sure, pure delusion. Finite though such a God might be, if he is a God at all, He is still transcendent and could not be verified in a purely empirical fashion. The cosmological and teleological arguments could at best demonstrate the existence of a finite god, but it does not at all follow that they can demonstrate the existence even of such

[1] The motives which have led to this idea of God will be discussed in Chapter xii, *Theism and Humanism*. These motives are partly the logical and empirical here described but they are largely humanistic in nature, among other things, of course, those generated by the problem of evil.

a God. Even a finite God, in so far as he is superhuman must, as, we shall later see, be also supernatural.[1] For such a being the *criteria* of evidence devised for natural entities would not apply.

Here, too, certain modern apologists for theism need to reflect more deeply on the question of empirical verification to which they fondly suppose that they may appeal. The notion that the unique being called God can be demonstrated either deductively or inductively and that the theistic argument in any form is thus an extension of the scientific method involves an illusion as fatal to science as it is to religion. Evidence here involves the 'peculiar kind of proof' which we described in an earlier chapter. But if the theologian should reflect more deeply on the nature of empirical evidence, no less should many protagonists of science. They are likely to think that while the metaphysical beliefs of religion are not empirically verifiable, their own metaphysical beliefs are in a different case. If so, they too are greatly deceived. It may be said of course that there is no issue here for true science makes no such pronouncements; science is method, not a philosophy. We may take this view, but it should be evident that science then has nothing to say regarding the pronouncements of religion, for on this assumption they are irrelevant and meaningless. With this I should concur up to a point, as we shall see in a later chapter. But if so it does not at all follow that because they are without interest and meaning for science they are such *per se*. Science so conceived is merely not interested. If, on the other hand, science and scientific method really have metaphysical implications then the criteria of evidence for such propositions can be only those for metaphysical propositions of whatever type. In either case the relation of science to religion is not that which it is often supposed to be. On the former view, they do not touch at all, for they are not talking about the same things. If we take the latter view it is clear that the two cannot be related on the level of either science or religion alone, but only on the more ultimate level of philosophy and philosophical method.

VI

Evaluation of the Pronouncements of Religion :
Their Meaning and Their Truth

A

The primary task of this chapter is that of interpretation—of determining what the pronouncements of religion really say. But closely connected with this problem is that of evaluation of these pronouncements, the two problems of the philosophy of religion, of interpretation and evaluation, being, as we have seen in an earlier chapter, ultimately inseparable. The first part of this double task has now been attempted, but before we proceed to the second there is a question which will inevitably be raised, namely, as to the validity of the foregoing interpretation.

It may be maintained—and indeed often has been—that these things are not what religion really says. To say that the historical element in religion means essentially that history is a revelation in space and time of non-temporal values; that cosmological propositions of religion mean that values have cosmic significance and are conserved; that the metaphysical propositions mean that the Good or value and being are inseparable—that the *ens perfectissimum* and the *ens realissumum* are identical—to say such things is to emasculate religion and to reduce it to a mere theosophy.

There is something to be said for this attitude. If this were *all* that religion said, such an interpretation, if not wholly false, would be inadequate, to say the least. It is true that, as Renan observed, 'if we tell the simple to live by aspiration after truth and beauty, these terms would have no meaning to them. Tell them to love God, not to offend God, and they will understand you perfectly. God, Providence, Soul—good old words, rather heavy, but expressive and respectable, which science will perhaps explain, but never will replace with advantage.' Certainly, they can never be replaced—and no philosophy of religion that understands its real business would for a moment think of replacing them—but they can be interpreted. They can, in a sense, be 'translated' and a translation is possible which retains all the *vis religiosa* of the original language. Such translation is not only possible but necessary, for without it all theology is impossible. It is, however, *toto genere* different from explaining them scientifically, for translation into the language of science is, as we shall see, impossible. A philosophical theology becomes then an *apologia* for simple faith, but no less for that fuller understanding of the truth of Divine things which is possible only to the learned.

Such an *apologia*, it will doubtless be urged, is an apology for ambiguity—and in a sense it is—but it is an ambiguity arising out of the very uniqueness and greatness of religion itself. The tension between the temporal and the eternal which is of the very essence of religion, involves necessarily not only that every event shall be seen in two ways but that the categories in which our meanings are expressed shall have this dual character. Impatience with such ambiguity is natural. When Jesus said to his disciples, 'a little while ye shall see me and a little while ye shall not see me,' it was only natural that they should murmur among themselves: 'A little while, a little while; we cannot tell what he saith.' That which the founder of the Christian religion Himself could not avoid it is hardly likely that the exponents and interpreters of His religion will be able to escape. It is but part of what St. John of the Cross called the 'obscurity of the faith'—a very different thing from obscurantism. In any case, it is only when these two equally necessary aspects of religion are rightly understood that any adequate evaluation of its pronouncements is possible.

B

As the meaning of the pronouncements themselves is ambiguous in the sense defined, so also is the meaning of the expression, their evaluation. They might conceivably have value in a practical reference, even if the question of their truth or falsity is not raised, just as it is often maintained that poetry, with which religion is closely connected, belongs to a sphere of meanings in which questions of truth and falsity are irrelevant. Or it may be said that religious ideas have value as temporary symbolisms or surrogates for truths about human relations which will ultimately be understood and expressed directly. Nevertheless, it seems clear that when all is said, neither of these things can be true. It is conceivable that the poet may think of his images and symbols as merely means of evoking feelings and merely to be enjoyed, although actually, as we shall see, he rarely does. It is even conceivable that a scientist might take a wholly operational view of his concepts, as mere symbolism, merely shorthand language for the control of phenomena, although few scientists would admit that this is all there is to science. In any case it is not possible for the genuinely religious man to think in this way. The attempt is indeed often made, but when it is the believer either loses his faith or, in moments of worship or action, abandons his sophisticated attitude. In such moments, however it may be elsewhere, pronouncements to be of value must be true, and to be true at all, he is likely to feel, must be 'true altogether.'

The problem of the truth of religion has, accordingly, become more and more insistent as we have proceeded, and has finally come to a head in connection with the issues presented by the problem of interpretation. No final answer can be given until we have examined the entire problem of religious knowledge and the relation of that knowledge, if there be such, to other forms, pre-eminently the scientific, but the main issues have already become clear.

In the first place, no theory of religious knowledge is possible which does not take into account the dual character of the pronouncements of religion and starts with this as its initial fact. These pronouncements are expressed, in the first instance at least, in the language of faith. As such they contain practical and mystical elements which are intuitive in character. But these same pronouncements contain an intellectual element, and it is therefore only when these intuitions of faith are translated or interpreted in terms of theology that rational justification of belief is possible. Any theory of religious knowledge must include both elements, the intuitions of faith and demonstration, and it is the nature of these two elements and their relations to each other that constitute the primary problems of religious knowledge.

Closely related to this problem—and indeed a part of it—is the question of the evidence for the pronouncements of religion. The historical, the cosmological, and the ontological propositions —the translations of the intuitions of faith—are all propositions about that which transcends experience. For none of them, we have seen, is there any purely empirical evidence—in the sense of the empirical criterion. But it does not follow that there is no religious experience with its inward witness, nor that there are no rational grounds in logic and nature for a reasonable belief. Actually the pronouncements of religion when translated into intellectual terms are seen to be identical with those propositions which the traditional theistic arguments were designed to 'demonstrate.' The nature of this demonstrative knowledge and its relation to the intuitive—of subjective and objective truth—constitute the fundamental problems of religious knowledge.

Finally, as we have seen, the pronouncements of religion constitute a total world view, the elements of which cannot be taken separately—the historical presuppose the cosmological and the cosmological the ontological. When the significance of this fact is realized it is seen that these theistic proofs constitute a cumulative process with a corresponding consilience of proof. It is, we saw, a fundamental blunder to take these intellectual propositions separately, abstracted from the total world view of which they are a part. By the same token it is a similar blunder to consider the explicit pronouncements of religion, the articles of the creed, separately, abstracted from the total world view of which they are parts. This leads to what I shall describe as the philosophy of creed.

VII

Interpretation of Religion and the Philosophy of Creed.
The Problem of 'New Creeds for Old'

A

A philosophy of religion involves also a philosophy of creed. Evaluation of the pronouncements of religion involves also inevitably an evaluation of the credal forms in which they are normally, if not universally, expressed. The explicit pronouncements of any positive religion constitute its dogmas; the relating of these dogmas constitutes its creed.

Such a philosophy of creed is concerned with the problems already raised in our study of the *Critique of Dogmatic Theology,* for the articles of the creed, taken separately and analytically, are precisely the dogmas which for this critique either refer to nothing or are logically contradictory. But a philosophy of creed involves more than this. These pronouncements, when interpreted, are seen to constitute a unity, to represent a total world view which can be evaluated only as a whole and, in so far as it is brought into relations with science, can be evaluated only in relation to the total world view which we call scientific.

The main issue here, as it was in the former context, is the relation of the language of theology to the language of religion. The 'defense' of dogmatic theology against its critics, both within and without religion, consisted in the maintenance of the thesis that the language of theology is a translation of the language of religion into an idiom which retains the *vis religiosa*. The issue now, in so far as it concerns the creeds and their interpretation, is in principle the same, namely, whether the explicit statements of the creeds and the explication of what they say implicitly is also one and the same. This is the contention of the present discussion and from it follows the further inference that it is the total world view embodied in the creed that must be understood and evaluated.

The supreme question, then, is whether one accepts the total world view, on nature and on man—which the creeds embody —the eternal values which they enshrine and guard. Religious faith is by its very nature integral and not analytical. There is not a single article of the Nicene Creed which, if taken from its context and set down in a purely naturalistic world order, is not ridiculous. The fatherhood of God, the sonship of Christ, the Holy Spirit, the Lord and giver of life, the entire notion of the Incarnate Word—these, we may just as well recognize, cannot be translated into the language of 'science'; cannot be rationalized in the sense of Tolstoy and men of like mind. But it is just as true—and this should be recognized—that the Christian life itself—the Christian morals and values—are just as ridiculous in such a world. In the world of modern evolutionary naturalism 'the sermon on the mount is as much an accident as the ninth symphony.'

B

Despite these indubitable facts—indubitable at least to one who has grasped the essence of religion and the language or

286

symbolic form in which this essence must inevitably be expressed—men continue to speak of a creedless religion, or at least of new creeds for old.

It is true that few who understand the nature of religion really argue for a completely creedless religion. To the modern mind the idea of 'belief unbound' has indeed its initial appeal, but one soon learns not only that such uncharted freedom tires but that belief, if it disdains one set of bonds, does so only to embrace another. One learns, moreover, that a religion without any creed is a contradiction in terms. A really creedless religion would be no more than an amorphous feeling—a vague awareness of the numinous, perhaps; but the moment it found expression in language we should have some pronouncements on man and on his relation to the ground of things, and thus the beginning of a creed. It is, then, not so much a creedless religion as 'new creeds for old' that the modern demands.

We can no longer, we are told for example, 'accept the Creed (the Nicene Creed) *ex animo* because it represents not our mind but that of a generation which, however great, was mistaken in its views of the scriptures, of cosmology and of metaphysics.' It is assumed, not only that creeds are wholly man-made and can therefore be remade, but also that, when thus remade, they must reflect, in both thought and language—for the two are inseparable—the scientific consciousness of the time. This view is sometimes carried to ridiculous extremes as when it is argued that the old terms of the Good Shepherd, Lord and King, the product of agricultural and feudal forms of life, should be abandoned as meaningless, if not worse, in our industrial and democratic age. If we are to envisage God at all we should rather think of Him as a great dynamo, as some have, in fact, suggested. In Eugene O'Neil's play of that name a very modern young man did precisely that; and it is a tribute to the playwright's insight, that he made the young man go mad! Mad also are those who were blasphemous enough to call the great bombers which lay waste cities and cathedrals God's angels.

One need not take these extravagances too seriously for the argument is equally fallacious even in the more moderate form of the so-called liberal theologian. For this assumption, that creeds must conform to fashions in cosmology and metaphysics, fashions determined by changes in scientific concepts, is of the

Waynesburg College Library
Waynesburg, Pa. 15370

same character and is grievously to misunderstand both religion and science. He who understands what science really is and the language which it necessarily speaks, could not possibly make so egregious a blunder. The language of science is a physico-mathematical language and in the nature of the case can say nothing meaningful which is not expressible in that idiom—certainly nothing meaningful about the first and last things with which religion is concerned. He will understand also that the language of religion, like that of poetry with which it is closely related, alone can speak significantly of these things.

'I have written entirely in vain,' so Paul Elmer More tells us, 'if I have concealed my conviction that the Apostles' Creed at least is magnificently contrived to the use of common prayer and praise. It might be called the lyric or rather the brief epic of Christianity—poetry in the sense that it clothes the fundamental articles of belief in symbols of exquisite beauty and enduring appeal, faith in the sense that behind the symbols, vivifying and justifying them, lie truths of the eternal spiritual life as revealed in the divine economy of the Incarnation.'[1] I should be concealing my own inner conviction also if I did not in principle subscribe to these words. I should want merely to add certain comments of my own. To me the Nicene Creed appears even greater in these respects, for behind the symbols of that creed lie even more clearly and deeply 'the truths of the eternal spiritual life,' and precisely because of their profounder ontological significance have a still more enduring appeal. Moreover, while the credal form is indeed 'poetry' in the highest and transcendent sense, it is poetry so transposed to another key or scale that the word no longer suffices to express its inmost character. The truths of the eternal spiritual life are neither truths of poetry nor truths of science, but that more ultimate truth of which both of these are but broken lights, and to which both, if they are properly understood, in their several ways attest.

[1] *The Catholic Faith*, p. 117, in the chapter on the Creeds.

Chapter IX

The Problem of Religious Knowledge: Intuition and Demonstration, Certitude and Evidence

I — A

THAT THERE is religious knowledge in some sense is affirmed by most philosophies of religion, but the notion of knowledge in the religious context often seems to mean something significantly different from that in science and philosophy. In religion men speak of the certitudes of faith rather than of the evidence of knowledge—and often think of certitude as better than evidence. Yet in religion, as elsewhere, it is idle to speak of knowledge without its correlative truth and equally idle to speak of truth without some conception of evidence or verification. Knowledge is knowledge, and whatever distinctive characters, if any, so-called religious knowledge may have, it must fall under the general notion.

All men are agreed that knowledge is apprehension of the real and that knowledge and truth are correlative conceptions, but beyond that point their agreement seems to end, and different meanings of knowledge begin to appear. For our purposes one difference may be singled out as of paramount importance—namely, between what we may call the narrower view and one that is broader and more humane. For the former knowledge is confined exclusively to reference to sensuously observable entities. The latter, the classical view of knowledge, includes not only the 'moral' truths of the humanities but those of religion and speaks of the 'science of God and of the blessed.' One need not quarrel with the narrow notion of knowledge developed by modern science—it has, as we shall see, its purpose and its value[1]—but merely challenge it as the norm of all knowledge. Its exclusive dogmatism is possible only to one who cuts himself off deliberately from a large part of human discourse of which the broader view of knowledge has always been the necessary presupposition.

Whether we take the broader or narrower view, it is in general held that there are two main sources of knowledge,

---

[1] Chapter x, pp. 334 f.

namely, intuition and demonstration. It is true that the meanings we give to these terms will to a degree be determined by our initial view of knowledge. If we take the narrower view, intuition will mean merely sense intuition and demonstration merely the development of the formal relations of concepts or indirect inference from sense data. If, on the other hand, we take the broader view, intuition will mean something more than mere sense intuition and demonstration not merely deductive and inductive inference but rather the 'showing forth' to the mind that acknowledges certain experiences the necessary implications or presuppositions of these experiences. For those who speak of the intuitive and demonstrative knowledge of God these terms have always had these broader meanings, whether they have known it or not, as we have seen in Chapter v. In any case, when men speak of religious knowledge they have always had these two sources of such knowledge in mind.

There are, and always have been, as the former member of the Oratory, Alph. Gratry, tells us, 'two natural ways of knowing God, the way of logical argument and another way which, on the basis of an original sense of the Divine, proceeds by way of intuition.'[1] It is both instructive and impressive to see how he finds these two elements in St. Anselm, St. Thomas, Descartes, Pascal, Malebranche, Fenelon, Bossuet and Leibniz, and analyses out these two factors as they appear in the different philosophers. It is here that a basal problem appears which is present throughout western theology and philosophy. So runs the alternative: proof of God or experience of God—intuition or discursive thought—or perhaps both. The answer to this alternative, implied in all our preceding discussions, is, as must now be abundantly clear, that both of these 'natural ways' are necessary to an adequate theory of religious knowledge—knowledge not only of God, that he exists, but also of His nature. The thesis of the present chapter is precisely this dual character of religious knowledge, and the task of the chapter is to determine their relations.

[1] Alph. Gratry, *La Philosophie du Credo*.

II

Intuition of the Divine: The Problem of 'Religious Realism'

A

The notion of an original intuition of the Divine, whatever form it may take, constitutes a doctrine of religious intuition, and, corresponding to it, there is always some theory of religious realism. It is accordingly with this problem that we are first concerned and it is for this reason that it appears as the subtitle of this section.

Realism in religion, as elsewhere, has two meanings. In the first place, there is the opposition of realism and nominalism which determined in so many ways the direction of scholastic theology and philosophy. Religious realism in this sense holds that the 'names of God'—and the 'Name of names' itself—have real referents and are not mere expressions of emotion. Realism in this sense is, of course, the necessary basis of all theology. But religious realism may also mean something further, the opposite of idealism. Indeed religious realism in the modern sense is a reaction against the idealistic religious philosophy of the nineteenth century. It involves a doctrine of immediate intuition—of Deity or a 'quality of deity' as a part or aspect of an external world of things or entities. It asserts, not only that religious ideas have reference, but that this reference, like that involved in the knowledge of a physical object, is to something which wholly transcends our subjective experience. Both forms of religious realism have played significant roles in the philosophy of religion and an examination of both is a necessary prolegomenon to an adequate theory of religious knowledge.

The classical theory of religious knowledge is realistic in this first sense. For it the 'names of God,' the predicates or attributes applied to Him have objective referents. Humanistic and pragmatic theories of modern times are, on the other hand, all nominalistic in that for them these attributes have no such objective reference. They have referents, indeed, but they are wholly human and social values; the object God has none. The name of God stands for no object but still has pragmatic meaning. This is the essence of religious nominalism.

Religious nominalism has received repeated statement throughout our modern era. I choose as my illustration a presentation taken from Ludwig Feuerbach's *The Essence of Christianity*. 'If,' he writes, 'the predicates of God are an anthropomorphism, if love, goodness, personality are human attributes, so also is the subject which you suppose here, the existence of God, the belief that there is a God, an anthropomorphism, a pre-supposition purely human. Yet he alone is the true atheist to whom the predicates of the divine being, e.g., love, wisdom, justice are nothing, not he to whom the subject of these predicates is nothing. And in no wise is the negation of the subject necessarily also the negation of the predicates considered in themselves. These have an intrinsic, independent reality; they force their recognition upon man by their very nature. The idea of God is dependent on the idea of justice, of goodness, of wisdom . . . but the converse does not hold. Religion, however, knows nothing of anthropomorphism; to it they are not anthropomorphisms . . . they are pronounced to be images only by the understanding which reflects on religion.'[1]

The essential of all forms of religious nominalism is expressed in this passage. It is that the existence of God, the belief that there is a God, is itself an anthropomorphism, a supposition purely human. It is an attempt to retain the religious symbols and their values without the object which alone gives them significance as values. Religious nominalism is *empty* symbolism. Being thus empty, it tends to the stultification of all religion. The only alternative to such stultification is the thorough-going atheism as represented in the next stage of development of Feuerbach himself, and as expressed in his completely naturalistic and cynical *Lectures on the Essence of Religion* (1851). In the earlier stage there is still conviction of the reality of the divine predicates, but with the denial of the bearer of the predicates the values which they embody disappear also.

The point at issue here is epitomized in the statement: 'The idea of God is dependent on the ideas of justice, goodness, wisdom, etc., but the converse does not hold.' In other words, the essence of religion—its moral essence—remains when the idea of God itself is seen to be merely an 'anthropomorphism.' The question is whether this is true. That the idea of God itself

[1] *Op. cit.* (1841), pp. 17 ff.

is dependent on these 'ideas' is undoubtedly true—the initial datum of all significant argument for God's existence is their acknowledgment. But the converse is also true, as the entire argument of Chapter vi has, I hope, made clear. I shall not pursue that argument at this point, but content myself here with a reference to Nietzsche which brings out the point admirably. Nietzsche remarks that 'the disappearance of the idea of God deprives the ideas of equality and justice of all justification.' What he means by this is that if God is a presupposition of these ideas—and he holds that He is—then He is a presupposition more than human. These very ideas (ideals or norms) presuppose that the world is not merely an order of nature. Nature, as such, at least as science conceives it, knows nothing of equality or justice. If there is no moral order, a super-nature transcending the order of nature, there is no logical justification for these ideas whatsoever. Nietzsche believed that 'God was dying,' if not already dead. What he wanted above all was to hasten that death, for he wished to deprive these ideas of equality and justice of all justification and to erect new tables which would give a romantic warrant for the ethics of force. These he saw were inevitably bound up with an atheistic view of the universe. Here, as at so many points, Nietzsche saw more clearly than many of his contemporaries. A position such as that of Feuerbach seemed to him as sentimental as it was muddle-headed.

B

Religion is then always 'realistic' in this first sense and is always opposed to nominalism which is 'the greatest of all heresies.' It insists that assertions about God, his existence and his nature, are genuine, not pseudo propositions, and that theological descriptions are not 'descriptions that describe nothing.' But there is, as we have seen, a second meaning to the term, namely, a doctrine of intuition which insists that there is an immediate, non-symbolic knowledge of the Divine, a form of knowledge distinct from other kinds of knowledge.

There are certain forms of modern 'religious realism' which, associating themselves with ordinary empiricism, liken the awareness of God to the perception of physical objects. Accepting as the norm of all knowledge the perception of the physical object, they attempt to construct analogously, on this primary model, some theory of perception of the Divine. This theory of religious realism has various representatives, but we shall examine it in the forms most familiar to Anglo-American thought. Two names are especially associated with it in the religious philosophy of America, namely, those of D. C. Macintosh and H. N. Wieman, both of whom may be considered as, in a sense, continuing the tradition of religious empiricism inaugurated by William James.

According to Professor Macintosh, in the case of religious knowledge we proceed, as in the knowledge of any other object, from direct perception. In awareness of God we have the same 'perception in a complex' as in the awareness of physical objects, only the data are not sensuous. This difference is, however, all important, for we have a perception which is not sensuous and the response of the individual is a response not of sense organs but of volition. Professor Macintosh believes that the hypotheses based on these data are as verifiable as those of science and in the same way—that, in other words, theology can be made an empirical science. The difference in the data of religious experience need, he holds, mean no lessening of the rigour of scientific procedure, but merely an extension of its application.[1]

I may not understand this view aright, but it has always been difficult for me to see how there can be perception of God—in any intelligible sense of the word perception—which is not based on sensuous data. It is even more difficult to see how, on this view, it can be held that verification in this field is identical with that in science and merely an extension of its methods. It is entirely understandable, then, that in pursuance of this 'scientific' ideal, Professor Wieman should take the further step of asserting that the data of religion are *sensuous*—as sensuous as those of science. 'Either God is an object of sensuous experience, or else he is purely a system of concepts and nothing more.'[2] But if Professor Macintosh's version of empiricism in religion is hard to understand, this version is still harder. Associating himself with the immediate empiricism of Dewey, he speaks of God as process and as pattern in nature, the only difference between God and other processes and patterns is its distinctive character

[1] D. C. Macintosh, *Theology as an Empirical Science*.
[2] H. N. Wieman, *Religious Experience and Scientific Method*.

which he describes as mutuality. The outcome is what Professor Macintosh speaks of as a "behaviouristic theology".[1] I agree wholly with Macintosh's criticisms of this position, but I cannot find it as interesting as he does. It seems to me as uninviting as it is untenable. But it has the merit at least of seeing that an empiricism based on scientific method can proceed only from data that are sensuous.

This doctrine of religious realism, in either form, plays directly into the hands of the positivist and humanist. An object, to be experienced in the sense of empiricism, must be a sensuously observable entity, and God, to be thus experienced, must be such an entity. Religious words, 'the names of the gods,' we are told, did have such empirical reference for they referred, although falsely, to observable entities such as light, thunder, fire, etc. But they no longer have meaning for they no longer refer to anything observable. It is for this reason that, for the positivists, religious sentences have no literal significance and, since for them only literal sentences are significant, religious assertions refer to nothing and constitute descriptions that describe nothing.

Somewhat more plausible is a third form of religious realism, one which speaks not of an entity which is the object of perception, not *the* Deity, but a 'quality of deity,' or in some cases of a quality of infinity. For S. Alexander deity is an empirical quality, like life and mind which he also calls qualities; it is the next higher quality to mind which the universe is engaged in bringing forth. Deity is thus an emergent quality—the next level in a developmental series and, as such, is subject to the same law as other empirical qualities. Deity, like everything else in the 'world,' is 'in the making,' or, in the words of Whitehead, who in principle shares this same point of view, God, as well as the world, 'is in the grip of the ultimate metaphysical ground, the creative advance into novelty.'

This is to many an attractive and fascinating conception, for it seems to them to afford an equivalent, in the idiom of English empiricism, for the notion of the numinous which, as we have seen, is an inevitable development in the phenomenology of

[1] See in this connection 'A Conversation About God' in the *Christian Century*, January–June 1932, in which two of the participants are D. C. Macintosh and H. N. Wieman.

religion. It has the further advantage of seemingly inserting this unique *quale* into a purely empirical scheme of nature and thus retaining religion without the supernatural, to the modern mind a *desideratum* devoutly to be desired. But it has its own difficulties, in many respects even greater than those of other forms of religious realism. For, after all, the 'quality of deity' is at best a metaphor which, while suggestive, can scarcely be taken literally. Strictly speaking, there is no organ by which such a quality could be intuited and, on a strictly empirical basis, a quality without corresponding sense organs is an *Unding*. Moreover, the notion of Deity as an emergent quality is one hard to make intelligible to the religious consciousness, for the attitudes integral to such consciousness, namely, prayer and praise, become stultified, if not wholly ludicrous, when directed to an emergent quality. Certainly it corresponds to no idea of God as that idea functions in the great positive religions.

There is, to be sure, a sense in which we may speak of a divine quality in things and in men and call it the quality of deity. The element of truth in this conception has been beautifully expressed by G. K. Chesterton in the last chapter of his *Autobiography*, entitled 'The God with the Golden Key.' Even the common dandelion has a quality—a 'glory'—which, when we really see it, takes us beyond nature. Gratitude for that quality is possible only when it is related to God of whom it is revelatory. 'What nonsense,' he writes, 'all this is; do you mean that a poet cannot be thankful for grass and wild flowers without connecting it with theology, let alone your theology? To which I answer, Yes; I mean he cannot do it without connecting it with theology, unless he can do it without connecting it with thought. If he can manage to be thankful when there is nobody to be thankful to . . . then he is simply taking refuge in being thoughtless in order to avoid being thankless.'[1] The simple dandelion has indeed a quality which leads us to God and this quality we may, perhaps without sacrilege, call the quality of deity. For such glory, whether it be the greater glory of the sun and moon or the lesser glory of grass and wild flowers, is revelatory of the goodness of God, for, as the canticle says, Heaven and earth are full of His glory. They are 'particles of perfection,' as has been beautifully said, and are revelatory of

[1] *Op. cit.*, p. 348.

296

that Perfection which is without parts or passions. They are revelatory of God but are not God. The latter is not only pantheism, but also an absurdity which would compel us to be thankful when there is no one to be thankful to.

C

None of these modern forms of religious realism is, it would appear, tenable. Surely the 'resort to religious realism has raised as many problems as it has solved.'[1] Nevertheless it remains true that no theory of religious knowledge is possible which does not include some doctrine of religious intuition and the 'realism' which it presupposes. Some conception of an intuitive element in our knowledge of God has always been, as we have seen, a constant element not only in theology but in philosophy also.

The notion of intuition has various meanings, but despite its ambiguity there is always a common element, namely, that of immediacy or givenness. The problem of intuitive knowledge, including that of an intuition of the Divine, has always involved two fundamental questions, namely, *what* is given and *how* it is given. Let us consider them in reverse order.

It is ordinarily assumed that to be immediately given to intuition such immediacy must exclude all mediation, and that what is given is given directly to consciousness. Actually, there is no intuition, sensuous or non-sensuous, which is not mediated by the language in which it is expressed. Intuition and expression are inseparable, the language being an essential part of the intuition.

It is often supposed that the mere sense datum without any element of 'description' constitutes knowledge, knowledge, as it is said, of 'simple acquaintance.' 'Suppose,' writes Bergson, 'language fallen into disuse, society and communication dissolved . . . the dampness of the ground will subsist none the less, capable of inscribing itself automatically in sensation and of sending a vague idea to the deadened intellect. The intellect will still affirm in implicit terms. . . .' And, consequently, he adds, 'neither distinct concepts, nor words . . . nor the desire of

[1] See on this point Professor Seelye Bixler in his thoughtful article 'Can Religion Become Empirical?' in the volume *The Nature of Religious Experience*, essays in honour of Douglas Clyde Macintosh, 1937.

spreading the truth . . . are of the essence of affirmation.'[1] This I believe to be sheer illusion. We should indeed *have* sensation, but we should not *know* anything. We should have merely the vague feeling that *something* is, but the moment it became something more—even the dampness of which Bergson speaks—the immediacy would have to be mediated by language and its categories, for they are present in the intuition itself.[2]

These reflections are applicable, *mutatis mutandis*, to any intuitive knowledge of the Divine. Here, above all, there is no knowledge of 'simple acquaintance.' Such knowledge is always mediated by the way in which it is conditioned by our creaturely existence. It is, of course, possible—and this must be constantly kept in mind—that there is an element in religious knowledge which is in this respect unique, that it includes mystical experiences of pure immediacy. I think it can be shown, however, that even these experiences, while constituting perhaps the nearest approach to such immediacy, are nevertheless always mediated by the language and categories of the religion in which the mystic lives.[3] An intuition of the Divine, if there be such, is always thus mediated.

What then is this intuition and how is it mediated? On neither of these questions have the classical representatives of intuitionism, St. Anselm and Descartes, been in any doubt. Let us see, then, what in their view is given and how it is given.

As Anselm sees it, the fool who has said in his heart there is no God already knows the God whose existence he denies; otherwise he could not deny it. What is it then that he knows and how is it that he knows it? On neither of these points is Anselm in any doubt. The God whom even the fool in his heart knows is the God of religion, but when translated into a language of theology, in which alone the problem of the knowledge of God can be significantly discussed, becomes that most perfect and holy Being which for the philosopher alone can be God. But how does the fool know this unique being and how does he have this unique idea in his heart or mind? He certainly does not have this knowledge wholly unmediated—as such it could neither be apprehended nor endured. The God whom the fool

---

[1] H. Bergson, *Creative Evolution* (English translation), p. 292.
[2] *Language and Reality*, pp. 341 ff.
[3] Chapter xiii, pp. 446 f.

denies actually comes to him in all sorts of imagery—often in
the childish pictures of a vulgar background—and it is usually
the images, not the intuition, which are denied. This is, however,
precisely what makes him the fool he is, the wise man knowing
always that the image is not identical with the intuition. The
idea does not come unmediated, nor does it come directly—
there are no phenomena or images in which such a transcendent
idea could be directly manifested. What is given directly is the
sense of his creaturely existence, of his own finitude, which even
the fool cannot only feel but, in his own degree, understand. But
the finitude of his own existence could itself not be known were
it not for the consciousness of infinitude, of infinite perfection,
which is its necessary coimplicate.

Even more than St. Anselm, Descartes realized the nature
and conditions of such religious intuition and the argument in
the third mediation, by which it is shown forth goes much
deeper than that of Anselm, for it plunges even more dramatic-
ally into the depths of the soul. 'I will now close my eyes. I
will stop my ears. . . . I will even efface from my consciousness all the images of corporeal things . . . and thus holding
converse with myself . . . endeavour to obtain by degrees a
more intimate and familiar knowledge of myself.' The sum of
that knowledge is that the more intimate the knowledge of
the self the more certain the knowledge of that which transcends the self, for the knowledge of the finite self and of the
infinitude which it presupposes are inseparably linked, so
intimately related to each other that to deny the one is to deny
the other.

This fact of finitude presupposes its opposite, that of infinitude. 'For were I independent of other existence and the author
of my own being, I should doubt of nothing, I should desire
nothing and, in fine, no perfection should be lacking to me. I
should not know of perfection and imperfection. And I must not
imagine,' continues Descartes, 'that I do not apprehend the
infinite by a true idea, but only by the negation of the finite in
the same way that I apprehend repose and darkness, by the
negation of motion and light: since, on the contrary, I clearly
perceive that there is more reality in the infinite substance than
in the finite, and therefore that in some way I possess the perception (notion) of God before that of myself, for how could I

know that I doubt, desire, or that something is wanting to me and that I am not wholly perfect, if I possessed no idea of a being more perfect than myself, by comparison with which I knew the deficiencies of my nature?'

The idea of God—this idea of perfect being—must then, Descartes concludes, have been 'born in me ... And in truth it is not to be wondered at that God, at my creation, implanted this idea in me that it might, as it were, form the mark of the workman impressed on his work . . . considering that God is my creator, it is highly probable that He in some way fashioned me after His own image and likeness and that I perceive this likeness, in which is contained the idea of God by the same faculty by which I apprehend myself.' In other words, 'when I make myself the object of reflection, I not only find that I am an imperfect and dependent being, and one who increasingly aspires after something better and greater than he is, but at the same time I am assured that he upon whom I am dependent possesses in himself all the goods after which I aspire . . . and that not merely indefinitely and potentially, but infinitely and actually, and that he is thus God.'

Austin Farrer in his *Finite and Infinite* uses this third mediation in a similar way, but when he speaks of it as 'a pleasant and naïve expression of theistic thinking,' I cannot agree. We may indeed express the same great truths in more sophisticated phrases—and they doubtless have their use—but when we do so we shall probably lose the dramatic drive of the argument. No really philosophical reader will, as he suggests, 'smile over these venerable phrases,' for if he is philosophical he will know that the phrases are venerable just because truth itself is venerable. The only naïve element in this account is the idea of innateness, but that too, if we are really philosophers, will scarcely elicit our smiles, for we shall know also that this was but a temporal form of stating a truth which is itself timeless.

D

To the question, then, Can religion become empirical? the answer must, I believe, be, Not wholly so; certainly not if empirical is understood in the sense of modern sensationalism. 'The empirical principle in philosophy' does indeed demand, as Whitehead tells us, that 'nothing shall be admitted into the philosophical scheme which is not discoverable in subjective experience,[1] but it certainly does not demand that anything to be admitted must be discoverable by the senses alone. Still less does it demand that from this experience shall be excluded all reference to that which is beyond itself. The presuppositions of experience are as much a part of it as the immediately sensed or felt 'phenomena' themselves—this Kant showed once for all. In the case of religious experience, the presupposition of the infinite is part of the subjective experience of finitude itself—the presupposition of the *ens perfectissimum* as much a part of our experience of values as that experience itself.

This, then, is the main contention of this part of our analysis. But it may be asked, in the terms of Martin Heidegger—one of the more recent critics of this notion—what intelligible meaning can be given to this conception of the presupposition of infinitude? He rightly asks, 'Can the fact of the finitude of existence even be raised as a problem without the presupposition of the infinite?' But he then further asks, 'What does this presupposed infinite mean? What is the character of such presupposition?'[2] This is a question which is inevitably raised and one to which, just as inevitably, some answer must be given.

One answer quite commonly given is to place this presupposition in the 'unconscious.' When not only the fool but the wise man insists that he has no such intuition or idea in his mind, it is often replied, not 'at the top of his mind, but in the depths of the unconscious.' Not only the simple but the learned have lent themselves to this unfortunate way of expression. It is true that, as we have seen, the primordial infinite of the mythopoeic imagination may be said to be in the unconscious, but we know well enough what kind of gods we get if we start digging there— the revived polytheism of William James scarcely encouraging us to look for God in that direction. It is not at the bottom but rather at the top of his mind when the soul is at its fullest stretch, that man should be told to look for God. Actually, of course, the infinite is present neither at the top nor the bottom of the mind —that is pure metaphor, and a rather unfortunate one at that.

[1] A. N. Whitehead, *Process and Reality*, p. 253.
[2] Martin Heidegger, *Kant und das Problem der Metaphysik*, p. 236. 'Lässt sich aber die Endlichkeit im Dasein auch nur als Problem entrücklen ohne eine vorausge-setzte Unendlichkeit? Welcher Art ist uberhaput "dieses voraussetzen" im Dasein? Was bedeutet die so "gesetzte" Unendlichkeit?'

What is actually present directly in consciousness—present as an incorrigible part of all experience, is the *tension* between the finite and the infinite; but the tension is *there* and can never be experienced, still less understood, without reference to the two poles which alone give it meaning.

Can, then, to repeat our question, this notion of the pre-supposition of the infinite be made intelligible? What does such presupposition mean and what sort of 'existence' does it have? It is, as we have seen, a coimplicate of experience the denial of which denies the experience also. It has the same existence as the finitude to which it alone gives meaning. The astonishing thing about man—and it is this which makes him religious—is that he alone of all creatures, so far as we know, is aware of his own finitude. 'Man's sense of imperfection is,' as Emerson said, 'that fine innuendo by means of which he makes his immortal claim.' But he does more than make his immortal claim; by this same fine innuendo he also rises to knowledge of the perfect, however confused that knowledge may be. He who recognizes a limit is already in reflection beyond it. If he follows this reflection to its conclusion he will not only rise to a 'demonstrative' knowledge of God's being but of His nature also. For it is only on the basis of such reflection that we can with any justification extend our human categories to the Divine. Without this presupposition, ontological sublimation is merely psychological sublimation. Perfection is not a predicate of Deity, but the essence of Deity itself.

E

There is, then, to return to the initial problem out of which this entire discussion arose, an original intuition of the Divine, if the notions both of intuition and of the Divine are properly understood. It is commonly held, as Professor Tennant admits, that 'religious experience contains data other than those of rational theology,' and that in this experience 'there is something which renders it unique, *sui generis*.'[1] Of the uniqueness of this experience there seems little question, the real problem is just what it includes.

It is a commonplace of present-day discussion that the so-called 'experience philosophies of religion' tend to include in

[1] Article on 'Theology' in the *Encyclopaedia Britannica*, already referred to.

their data either too little or too much. The major error is, doubtless, to include too little—to make of it a vague emotive experience without any cognitive content. But it is just as serious an error to 'overload' the original intuition, to include the varied imagery and subjective forms in which the original intuition is mediated. It is against this error that Otto warns us, especially against including in the original intuition all the metaphysical attributes of a developed theistic theology, including that of personality itself. Nevertheless, 'person' is the one 'name,' to use St. Thomas's expression, so apparently inevitable when we name the name of God that it seems to be an essential part of the original intuition. The problem of our knowledge of God as person becomes thus a central question of religious epistemology and of the philosophy of religion.

III

Our Knowledge of God as Person. The Literal and the Symbolic in Such Knowledge

A

To know God and to enjoy Him for ever, which the Christian holds is the chief end of man, is to know a Person, the Heavenly Father, and knowledge of persons is in principle different from the perception of a quality as it is also different from the 'intuition of perfection' if there be such. The glory of which heaven and earth are full leads, indeed, to thankfulness and praise, but in order to give thanks there must be, it would seem, some *One* to be thankful to. Do we have, then, an immediate intuitive knowledge of God as person or do we reach that knowledge through thought? The latter seems to be the view of traditional theology, but opposed to it we find a more modern conception which insists that our knowledge of God as person is immediate—not merely a perception of a 'quality of deity,' nor an intuition of perfection, but direct personal 'acquaintance,' analogous to our acquaintance with human persons.

That such an immediate knowledge of a supernatural Person *seems* to be an essential presupposition of religion can scarcely be denied. The lyrical and dramatic language of religion assumes it. We can scarcely be surprised when men insist that there is this direct intuition. Nor should we be surprised to hear them exclaim, with Cook Wilson, 'We don't want merely inferred friends. Could we be satisfied with an inferred God?'[1] A theory, then, to be in conformity with the facts of religious experience must, it is held, include the immediate knowledge of God as a person.

This theory is made possible by a fundamental revision of our conceptions of the nature of our knowledge of human selves. The theory of inference, in both its ancient and its modern form, is based upon the assumption that the only thing we know directly is the physical object, and that all other knowledge, whether of other selves or of God, is inferential. It is now maintained that our knowledge of other selves is not inferential but immediate, and that the main epistemological difficulties in the way of the idea of an immediate intuition of a supernatural person are therefore removed.

B

·I am myself not disposed to question this doctrine of an immediate knowledge of other mind. For many years and in many contexts I have maintained it. Indeed, it seems to me that the arguments for the view that such knowledge is based upon analogical inference are wholly untenable as I have shown at length in a recent book.[2] There is no belief to which may be ascribed greater certainty than that of the existence of other selves—not even the belief in an external world itself—but according to the inferential theory this most certain of all beliefs is based upon the most uncertain of all arguments. It is not, therefore, with this aspect of the argument for immediate knowledge of a supernatural person that I find difficulty, but rather with the extension of the argument from such knowledge of the human person to a similar knowledge of a superhuman Person. The difficulties involved in this extension seem to me insurmountable.

The idea of a direct perception of the human person, whether that perception be thought of as sensuous or emotional, is doubtful enough—knowledge by simple acquaintance in this

[1] Cook Wilson, *Statement and Inference*, Volume II, p. 853.
[2] *Language and Reality*, Chapter vi, especially pp. 251 ff.

sense is difficult to show—but the difficulty becomes insuper-able when it is extended analogously to the Divine Person as our examination of religious realism has shown. This is equally true whether we think of the 'perception in a complex' as taking place in a complex of sense data or data that are emotional and volitional. For such a complex of human feelings, volitions and purposes could of themselves be the organ of apprehension only of a phenomenal and finite object, never of the transcendent object men call God.

There is, I think, only one possible way in which the theory of direct knowledge of a supernatural person can be made in any way intelligible and this must accordingly be examined with great care. It is pointed out that it is primarily in processes of communication that we know other minds—in the first instance through behavioural communication and ultimately through the medium of words. It is therefore natural to argue analogically that when we hear the 'word of God,' God speaks directly to our souls and in thus speaking we know him as a Person. With the premises of this argument I would wholly agree. It is through communication and communication alone that knowledge of other mind is possible, and intelligible com-munication, as distinct from mere behavioural, takes place wholly through language. In such communication we have direct intuition of other persons. But to argue analogically that it is thus also that we come to know a supernatural person is, I think, to overlook one very important thing. The assurance of the existence of other finite selves is, I fully believe, the most certain of all our beliefs, even more certain than the assurance of the external world itself—and this assurance is given us in the very processes of communication themselves—but by the very nature of the divine locution, the assurance of God's reality as person, if there be such, must be of another order. Granted that in some sense 'God speaks to my soul,' it cannot be directly, for it is always mediated in the language of man. It follows—and this is for the philosopher the important con-sideration—certitude of God as person can also be only mediated and indirect. To this extent knowledge of God as person must always contain an anthropomorphic and symbolic element.

It is sometimes said that 'the awareness of God, as *personal will*,' is given immediately in the impact of unconditional value,' that further, 'since morality is essentially a function of personality, we can feel no obligation to an Absolute who is not apprehended as a personal being.' I doubt very much whether this can be maintained. It is true that the sense of obligation has as its coimplicate an intuition of unconditional value, but to insist that such intuition includes necessarily the awareness of personal will seems unnecessarily to overload our intuition of the Divine. Nor can it be said that such an awareness of God as person is given in any other impact of value. In a recent book Helen Wodehouse tells us that she 'uses the name of God for the sum and substance of all Good,' and affirms that 'man is in touch with some aspect of God whenever he is in touch with some goodness, even if it proves to be the gleam of light reflected from a tawdry jewel or an edge of a broken glass, or the technical colour of a poison,' and who would deny her the right to call this 'one kind of religion'?[1] Certainly I should not wish to do so. When a man cries, God, that is beautiful, I do not think that he is taking God's name in vain. Nor is the youthful exuberance which speaks of even trivial things as 'too divine,' as superficial as it seems. There are qualities of deity, 'particles of perfection,' both in nature and in man, which witness to that Absolute Perfection which is God. It is, to be sure, more difficult to follow this way of thinking when religion is held to include, as it does for Miss Wodehouse, worshipful attitudes of prayer and praise. For there remains the element of thankfulness and it is a queer kind of thankfulness when there is no One to be thankful to. Nevertheless, to 'thank whatever gods there be' for one's 'unconquerable soul' is not wholly blasphemous. It is therefore at least conceivable that the essential religious attitudes of both prayer and praise may still be present without the apprehension of God as personal being. In any case, it can scarcely be said that the awareness of God as person is given immediately in the very impact of unconditional Good whether that impact be felt either in the form of transcendent obligation or transcendent beauty.

[1] Helen Wodehouse, *One Kind of Religion*, Cambridge University Press.

C

It seems difficult then to maintain the conception of an immediate perception of God as person in the sense of a naïve religious realism. On the other hand, it seems no less difficult to think of the Divine Person as merely the product of inference. Some intermediate position between these extremes must, it would appear, be possible if we are to do justice to the actualities of religious experience. Such a position the traditional view of the knowledge of the Divine Person, I believe, affords.

'Person,' writes St. Thomas, 'signifies the most perfect thing in nature. . . . And since the dignity of the divine nature exceeds every other dignity, this name of Person is applicable in a supreme degree to God.'[1] Person is, therefore, one of the 'names' strictly and properly applicable to God but, like the other attributes, it is applicable only by virtue of the principle of the *analogia entis*. If it further be true that, as we have sought to show, the doctrine of analogy itself includes a doctrine of symbolic knowledge—and that no absolute distinction between the two is possible, then it must be admitted that our knowledge of God as person is in part symbolic and that, however funda- mental the symbol may be, it is through that symbol that the non-symbolic element is mediated. The name of Person is in- deed applicable in a supreme degree to God, but the Heavenly Father, of justice, mercy and love, whom we invoke in prayer and praise can be intuited only in attributes as they are conditioned by the way in which they appear in creatures and the intuition is, to that extent, symbolic.

I agree then with Dean Inge when he says, 'Personality when attributed to God, is a symbol,' but I cannot wholly follow him when he adds, 'and a very inadequate one.'[2] He points out, truly, of course, that 'we do not know how far we ourselves can call ourselves persons'; that the soul, the wanderer of the spiritual world, is not really quite at home anywhere. Yet he also points out that it is in the life of devotion that the personality of God appeals to us most strongly. '"Speak to Him, thou, for he hears, and spirit with spirit can meet." We know that in prayer we are not merely soliloquizing.' If, however, we are not

[1] *Summa Theol.* I, qu. XXIX, art. 3.
[2] W. R. Inge, *God and the Astronomers*, p. 255.

merely soliloquizing it seems certain that, whatever element of the symbolic there may be in the notion of the Divine Person, the symbol must ultimately refer to that which is non-symbolic. Wherein this adequacy of the symbol consists is a question yet to be answered. It may be noted, however, that precisely this question is an outstanding issue not only between the East and the West as a whole, but also, to a degree, between the two major tendencies in Christianity, exhibited in the theologies of East and West. It is sometimes pointed out that the theory of God as a person is relatively novel in Christian thought; even the Protestant reformers did not assert it. It is, perhaps, as Lossky surmises, the product of Deism and really the denial of the Christian doctrine of the Trinity. For traditional theology God is the unity of three personalities, or, if you will, three hypostases.[1]

IV

Religious Intuition (or Experience) and the Problem of Certitude. Knowledge and Faith

A

While religion cannot be wholly empirical in the sense of modern empiricism, it is nevertheless true that there is religious experience, although just what that experience is and how it witnesses to God is not immediately clear. Certainly, except as maintained by certain naïve forms of religious realism, it is not to be thought of as sense experience. Equally certain is it that if there is to be any verification it cannot be verification in the sense of the 'empirical criterion' as ordinarily understood, and it will greatly simplify our problem if these facts are understood from the beginning. When Job cries, I *know* that my Redeemer liveth, he does know something although just what he knows may require interpretation. But not only does he know it, but that cry has drawn from thousands of hearts and minds an answering response which is in some sense knowledge also.

This 'knowledge' is commonly described as the 'intuitions of faith' and of these intuitions it is also commonly said that they

[1] See on this point, N. O. Lossky, *Value and Existence*, p. 180.

'are called true, not because their necessary correspondence to truth can be demonstrated' (i.e., either by the empirical criterion or by logical argument) 'but because a man, dwelling upon these intuitions, is conscious of a moral transformation, of a certain warmth and energy of life. To the religious man religion is inwardly justified. God has no need of natural or logical witnesses.'[1]

There can be little question that the first part of this statement contains a partial truth. However untrue it may be that there is no need of other witnesses, it is certainly true that without the inward witness, other witnesses would witness in vain. To the religious man religion is inwardly justified, and this 'justification by faith,' if we may so call it, is the Alpha if not the Omega of religious knowledge; it contains in it the beginning if not the whole of verification in the sphere of religion. It is with the nature of this inward justification that we are first concerned.

The intuitions of faith upon which the believer dwells are, in the first instance at least, the dogmas of religion, for 'dogma is the language of faith'—the religious ideas of which Höffding speaks—the ideas of God, grace and the eternal life which, as we have seen, run like a leit motif through all the great positive religions. In the Christian religion they are the 'loving Father in Heaven, the incarnate Son of God,' together with all the secondary dogmas which centre around the primary objects of faith. The central intuition is obviously that of God as person, discussed in the preceding section, for it is chiefly in connection with such a person, however conceived, that faith in this sense is possible, and that the transformation and the warmth and energy of life which witness to the Divine are experienced.

That there are the experiences thus described and that they are the inseparable accompaniments of this inward justification, few would, I suppose, deny; nor that in the enlargement of life the believer rightly finds a sign of the presence of God. All the confessions of religious history, great and small, witness to this fact. But these are not, even to the believer himself, the ultimate grounds of the inward justification. The warmth and energy of life, the renewal of the sense of meaning after the feeling of meaningless of existence, of peace after restlessness—all these

[1] G. Santayana, *Poetry and Religion*, p. 8, also *Reason in Religion*, pp. 14, 98.

subjective accompaniments of experience—are indeed significant, but they may also be illusory, as many have found. Being,
in the first instance at least, phenomena of the physical organism, they may also be 'explained' physiologically and natural-
istically, as they often are, as merely signs of readjustment after
maladjustment, of no more ultimate significance than any other
biological phenomena. Emotional and volitional experiences
cannot, in themselves, justify faith in any sphere of human
experience, least of all in religion, where faith, by its very nature,
goes beyond experience. And yet without these experiences, and
the transformations of life of which they are the signs, there
would be no inward justification, no vital or 'existential' truth
such as is essential to religion. Truth in religion may not be
subjectivity, to use Kierkegaard's terms, but the subjective
aspect of truth must find a place in any tenable theory of
religious knowledge.

Any 'inward justification,' in order to be either inward *or*
justification, must involve emotional and volitional factors. It is
only in that which is highest and deepest in *us* that there can be
any inward witness to the Divine. But what makes these experiences thus high and deep? There is no other conceivable source
than the intuition of perfection or of the infinite which is given
as the coimplicate of our emotional and volitional experiences
themselves. The locus of this inward justification is, then, not
the emotional experiences as such—by themselves they may
deceive us—but solely in that which gives them their religious
quale. It is true that one must needs *love* the holiest when he sees
it, but in order to love it one must first *see* it, even though it be
through a glass darkly. It is this combination of seeing and
feeling which makes of the love of the holiest the witness, not
only of subjective but of objective truth also.

This way of conceiving emotional intuition enables us also to
understand the undoubted element of truth in religious realism
—even in those forms which, in certain respects, we found it
necessary to criticize. Unless with the complex of human feelings, volitions and purposes, were also given, as its coimplicate,
the intuition of perfection, we should not apprehend God but
'something else.' If, on the other hand, this coimplicate, however
mediated, is present in the intuition, apprehension of God becomes possible. Recognition of this element of truth in religious

empiricism does not, however, warrant the identification of this kind of knowledge with scientific knowledge, still less the characterization of theology as an 'extension of the scientific method.' There are fundamental differences here, differences as significant as they are fundamental. Such an identification of the two involves erroneous conceptions of scientific method no less than of religious knowledge, errors so far-reaching as to be wholly disastrous for philosophical theology.[1]

B

The intuitions thus inwardly justified are described as intuitions of faith. This expression seems also, at first sight, to contain two wholly incompatible ideas. Actually the two are inseparable and it is only when this fact is understood that any adequate conception of knowledge, religious or otherwise, is possible.

Even in the sphere of physical knowledge the two notions are far from incompatible. We 'intuit' the object sensuously, but in the very intuition is included an element that can be described only as faith. Few 'realists' would deny this fact; some would

[1] This issue is brought definitely to a head in a recent article by D. C. Macintosh entitled 'Theology and Metaphysics' (in *Twentieth Century Philosophy*, 1943). After discussing verification in science, he writes, on page 213, about religious knowledge, in the following way:

'Similarly, we may apprehend divine processes within the complex of religious experience, the criteria of the divine being subjectively the numinous and objectively the spiritually ideal, the absolute realm of values, the worshipful. On the basis of the religious perception of such divinely valuable causality as is involved, for instance, in spiritual regeneration, we can claim to have discovered the divine revealed directly within the field of experience. This means the possibility and actuality of a limited amount of verified religious knowledge, a certain body of data for an essentially empirical theology.'

This seems plausible but the illustrations given show just how disastrous this idea of a 'scientific theology' really is. For 'spiritual regeneration' happens to be one of those religious idioms which simply cannot be translated into the language of science without denaturing them. For what would verification in the strictly scientific sense here mean? Science could verify the existence of physiological and psychological phenomena (the 'warmth and energy of life') but it could not verify the religious meaning of these phenomena—the 'divinely valuable causality' of which Dr. Macintosh speaks. All this will become of great importance when we turn in the following chapter to the question of 'what science says,' and especially to the results of the application of the scientific method, as it really is, to the phenomena of religion. We shall find that the scientific method, by its very nature, not only cannot verify the objects of religious experience, but when really applied stultifies that experience itself.

indeed call our belief in the independent reality of the physical object merely a matter of 'animal faith.' In any case all would agree with Locke, I think, that 'this assurance probably deserves the name of knowledge,' but only if in the notion of knowledge is included a moment of faith. There are other forms of 'assurance,' however, that also deserve the name of knowledge: our knowledge of other selves, and, if our account of the knowledge of God as person is true, our intuitive knowledge of the Divine Person; but, like the knowledge of the physical object, they have also the character of faith. Intuition and faith are inseparable in all spheres of human experience and knowledge.

The reason this is not always seen is that this intuitive faith is not sufficiently distinguished from intellectual belief in the truth of propositions. It is doubtless true that the two cannot be completely separated in religion any more than in any sphere of experience and knowledge, but a relative distinction must be made. The difference between the practical assurance of an external world and intellectual belief in propositions about it, is recognizable by every one, as is also, I suppose, the difference between practical assurance of other selves and intellectual belief in their reality. This same difference is also recognized in one way or another in all forms of the phenomenology of religion. To the practical and mystical elements—'the properly religious elements' in dogma, according to Sabatier—attaches faith; to the intellectual or theoretical 'envelope,' belief alone is applicable.

This distinction the studies of the preceding chapter have, I hope, served to make clear. There are the intuitions of faith embodied in dogma, for dogma is the language of faith, but there are also the translations of this language into the intellectual propositions of rational theology and these are the objects of reasonable belief. Faith in the above sense has been characterized as acknowledgment—acknowledgment of absolute value, the *valor valorum*, and the commitment of the soul which such acknowledgment entails. This characterization is acceptable if in this primary acknowledgment is included the element of knowledge, for one must know, however confusedly, in order to acknowledge. We must needs acknowledge the holiest when we see it but we must first see it. Thus between the two notions,

THE PROBLEM OF RELIGIOUS KNOWLEDGE

intuition and faith, there is no essential incompatibility and faith has therefore been held to be a mode of knowledge by all forms of Christian theology and philosophy.

For the Christian, the essence of such faith is the acknowledgment of the perfections found in a supereminent degree in the Divine Person—'the fullness of the Godhead bodily in the face of Jesus Christ.' It is true that, for theology, 'no one can call Jesus Lord, except by the Spirit'—and faith in this theological sense is the gift of grace, the Thomistic doctrine of faith being developed along these lines. None the less, supernatural faith can no more be completely divorced from natural faith than supernatural revelation from the natural language in which it is expressed. If we envisage the acknowledgment we call faith as something unrelated to the primary acknowledgments of the moral consciousness of man we end in making it wholly unintelligible also. The Christian by grace presupposes the *Christianus naturaliter*, and all forms of theology have been compelled to acknowledge the existence of the latter.

The certitudes of faith are thus an essential part of religious knowledge as they are of any kind of knowledge. This 'assurance' of which Locke speaks, whether it be of the existence of the physical object, of other selves, or finally of that transcendent reality we call God, surely deserves in every case, the name of knowledge. The traditional heirarchy of the modes of cognition has for Christian thinkers always been faith, understanding, and the vision of God face to face. St. Thomas, with all his emphasis on rational theology, places the reason of the Christian midway between the faith that guides his first footsteps and the full knowledge which the beatific vision will bring hereafter. The principle of justification by faith, doubtless unduly exalted in Protestant theology, has nevertheless its basis in the nature of things. God may indeed require no other witness. He can doubtless, if He will, make Himself known in a certitude so immediate and personal that other witness may seem superfluous. But man, being human, does need other witnesses. Being social he requires confirmation of the faith and such confirmation can come only from the witness of the beloved community. Being rational, and endowed with discursive reason, he requires the still more impersonal witness of the universal reason in man. Reason cannot be excluded from its place between faith and vision, and if men attempt to exclude it, faith inevitably weakens and the vision perishes.[1]

C

The fact that the intuitions of faith—although they contain an element of immediacy—are always mediated and thus symbolic, brings the entire problem of symbolic knowledge to a head. The crux of any theory of religious knowledge is thus the problem of symbolic knowledge and of its correlative, symbolic truth.

The fundamental character of all symbols, whether in art, science or religion, is that they are conditioned, in some aspect at least, by the nature of the symbol maker, whether they are consciously made or spring out of the original symbolism of the race. For this fundamental character we may make use of the terms of Whitehead, namely, that 'they are conditioned by community of subjective form,' and we may add as a consequence, that symbolic truth is conditioned by this same community of subjective form.[2]

Symbolic knowledge is therefore, as we now see, a special case under the general notion of mediated immediacy. The symbolic form of representation is, as Kant rightly saw, not opposed to the intuitive but rather a sub-form under the intuitive.[3] And Récéjac in his study of mysticism, doubtless relying on Kant, finds it a great mistake to contrast the symbolic with the intuitive. For Croce also, 'the symbol is a synonym for intuition.' These views represent, I think the truth, and if so the symbolic as we have described it is the form *par excellence* in which intuition and description are combined.

As a special case under the general notion of mediated immediacy symbolic knowledge has all the characters of religious knowledge already described. Such knowledge, as we saw earlier, cannot consist in comparing the symbol with reality, for it is the very character of the reality for which the symbol stands that it is beyond such comparison. Symbolic truth can therefore be found, in the first instance at least, only within experience, or

---

[1] Even Kant, despite the violence he did to the traditional hierarchy of knowledge, held that the certitudes of faith deserve the name of knowledge. In the *Critique of the Practical Reason* he uses the terms faith and knowledge interchangeably, the term knowledge being used more frequently than the term faith.

[2] A. N. Whitehead, *Adventures of Ideas*, Chapter xvi.

[3] *The Critique of Judgment*, translated by J. H. Bernard, 1914, p. 248.

314

in the 'inner necessity of the symbol creating consciousness.' Being conditioned by community of subjective form, or by the way in which that form appears in creatures, the symbol must inevitably be truth for our type of consciousness. On the other hand, to be adequate, even for our type of consciousness—if the creaturely attitudes of prayer and praise are not to be self-stultifying—it must be adequate in another sense also, in the sense namely that it refers to that which transcends our type of consciousness, namely, the Divine.

This criterion of dual adequacy, developed in an earlier context is, however, possible, we now see, only on the assumption of an original intuition of the Divine mediated by the subjective. Were the symbol not thus subjectively conditioned it would not be true for our type of consciousness. On the other hand, were it merely the product of the symbol-creating consciousness, and its necessity merely inner, it would not have that objective reference which alone makes it adequate. The only conception which makes symbolic truth intelligible is, as we have already found, that of the analogy of being—symbolism presupposes this analogy—but, and this is the important point here—the only conception of the analogy of being which is intelligible is that which includes the doctrine of an original intuition of the Divine.[1] Otherwise sublimation of our human predicates would remain psychological and never become ontological, and the truth of these predicates would inevitably remain subjective. Thus, without an intuition of perfection mediated by the symbol, religious symbolism would remain mere symbolism and religious knowledge evaporate into a pan-symbolism.

All of which finds its supreme exemplification in that most fundamental of all religious symbols, the notion of the Divine Person. When Dean Inge tells us that the notion of person as applied to God is a symbol, 'but a very inadequate one,' he is assuming, quite rightly, that the only terms in which the value or validity of a symbol can be determined are those of adequacy —truth in this context can mean only adequacy—but, obviously, the notion of adequacy is meaningless unless we further specify adequacy *for what*. Its adequacy for prayer and praise is not denied—indeed it is admitted that, with the possible

[1] Chapter vii, pp. 234 f.

exception of certain mystical attitudes, it is not only adequate but indispensable. But to be really adequate here it must symbolize something properly applicable to the Divine. The reason it is properly applicable, and therefore adequate in the more ultimate sense, is that person does actually signify the most perfect thing in nature. It might be asked—and possibly Dean Inge himself might ask the question—how do we know that it signifies this? If the amoeba were consulted 'he' might answer differently and so might angels, so far as we know. But surely neither need be consulted, for it is nature, as man sees and knows it, of which we are speaking, and it is to man and his human reason that any argument of this kind alone can be directed. Symbolic truth is truth conditioned by our form of consciousness, but that human consciousness includes an original intuition of perfection and therefore of the Divine.

D

The notion of symbolic truth as truth conditioned by community of subjective form, raises the entire question of the role of communion and of communication in religious knowledge. There is doubtless a sense in which faith is a matter of a man's own solitude, but it does not follow that that faith needs no other witness. Certainly he has certitude in the sense of being privately convinced, but when it comes to a question of what it is about which he is thus confident, other witness is required. There is no merely solipsistic verification in religion, any more than in any other sphere of human experience; 'subjectivity' cannot alone be truth here, any more than in any other sphere of human knowledge.

It is a significant fact that the notion of confirmation of the faith bulks so large in both the practice and the philosophy of all religious communities. In the Christian community of the New Testament men speak constantly of confirming each other in the faith—a confirmation which takes place through the communication and mutual interpretation of religious experience. This is the significance of the 'experience meetings' of more evangelical types of Christianity. It is the significance also, in part at least, of the more catholic forms of Christianity, for which mediation through the Church confirms the believer in his faith and creates that assurance which deserves the name of knowledge. Both know that their Redeemer liveth and this certitude finds confirmation in the experience of the beloved community.

This is the significant element in certain developments in recent theology of which Ritschl's greatest work, *Justification and Reconciliation* is, perhaps, the outstanding example. For him both justification and reconciliation are mediated through the Church, not, it is true, in the sense of catholic theology, as a divinely authorized institution, but as the *communio sanctorum*, the body of all faithful people. This is also the root notion of Royce's *The Problem of Christianity*. The beloved community is the source of verification in religious experience, as indeed, for him, a community of interpretation is the ultimate source of verification in all realms of knowledge. This aspect of religious knowledge may be over-emphasized, and even in certain respects expressed unfortunately, as perhaps it was in the case of both writers cited, but this does not alter the fact that without the notion of confirmation through communication, no tenable theory of religious knowledge is possible, or as I believe of any type of knowledge.[1]

The role of communication in knowledge is a central conception of traditional European philosophy. 'Knowledge,' said Plato in the *Theataetus*, 'is judgment plus discourse,' and from that time on, communicability has been recognized as a necessary presupposition of knowledge. The scholastics continued this tradition. All science, as they asserted, assumes it. There is hardly a work of St. Thomas in which this doctrine is not in evidence. Every form, in so far as it is a form, is communicable and communicability pertains to its nobility. Community pertains, however, not only to the nobility but to the intelligibility of forms. It is, moreover, this communicability of forms and patterns that alone makes knowledge possible. *Scientia est de universalibus.*[2] For this way of thinking, communicability is also the presupposition of religious knowledge. Here, as elsewhere, knowledge presupposes the universal, a formal

---

[1] This holds true, I believe, even of the mystical experience if it claims the name of knowledge. It is, as we shall see in a later chapter, the identity of the mystical experience despite differences of expression which makes it possible to evaluate it as a part of religious knowledge, but this identity could not be known were it not for its communicability and its confirmation in the experience of others.

[2] For the various places in St. Thomas's writings in which this principle is affirmed, see Fulton J. Sheen, *Philosophy of Science*, pp. 114 ff.

principle of Deity as theology calls it. It is upon this conception of communicability, of the mutual acknowledgment of the principle of perfection, that the argument *de consensu omnium*, which has always been of great significance in the philosophy of religion, is ultimately based.

There are those, to be sure, for whom such conceptions are little less than anathema and who hold that confirmation, while socially significant, is irrelevant to the truth notion itself. In modern science, which they hold to embody most completely the ideal of knowledge, and which is therefore normative for all other knowledge, verification consists solely in reference, direct or indirect, to sensuously observable entities; and it is these entities which do the verifying, confirmation within the scientific community being merely a 'social *addendum*.' It is difficult to see how this position may be maintained. Leaving out of account the dogma of the primacy of scientific method which I should be disposed to challenge, it seems quite clear that this is a false reading of the situation even within science itself. Private sense data, as such, never verify anything. They must first be interpreted and interpretation involves a community of interpreters. More and more in science itself there is a shift of emphasis from verification in this limited sense to 'confirmation', the potentially public character of all genuine knowledge requiring this shift. For science nothing enters into the sphere of knowledge at all except that which is intersubjectively public. For it a fact is not a fact until it is enunciated, and when once enunciated it has entered into the social context and must be socially confirmed. This does not mean that the scientific community *makes* the truth—that is manifestly absurd—but merely that social confirmation is necessary before a proposition can lay claim to human truth. Truth, as *veritas ontologica*, doubtless needs no such witness, but truth as *veritas humana* obviously does.

There is little excuse for the misunderstanding of the role of communication in scientific knowledge, and still less for its misunderstanding as it functions in religious knowledge. No one for a moment supposes that the *communio sanctorum*, or the beloved community, *makes* truth—the *veritas ontologica*—but truth as God sees it and truth as men see it are different things. The variety of subjective forms in which the intuitions of faith are expressed requires that the intersubjectively public shall be one of the

THE PROBLEM OF RELIGIOUS KNOWLEDGE

conditions of verifiable knowledge. It is, however, identity of intuition, despite this variety, which makes this confirmation of the faith possible. The doctrine of an original intuition of the Divine, at once immediate and mediated by the symbols of the empirical faith community, alone makes intelligible that inward justification which is an essential part of religious knowledge. It is this same doctrine, we now see, that alone makes possible that mutual understanding among all truly religious people which, since it confirms them in the faith, is an essential part of religious knowledge also. No more than the faith of the individual, is social confirmation of that faith the whole of religious knowledge. There is still the question of natural and logical witnesses for God. But without the intuition and without this communication and mutual understanding, objective knowledge could never be achieved.

How far this confirmation of our human faith extends—how far truly religious people understand one another despite the variety of subjective forms in which their intuitions of faith are embodied—is a problem of both theoretical and practical import. Surely it extends far beyond the limits of any single beloved community—to the community of all faithful people. Surely the more one comes really to understand the language and symbolic form of his own religion, the more he comes to understand those of other religions, and the ways in which the more ultimate intuitions of faith are expressed analogously in this variety of subjective forms. We are not surprised then that Christian priests and Buddhist monks smile understandingly and salute each other gravely across the street, for in contrast with the purely secular and irreligious, they share a common understanding—and what is more, a common peace which is beyond all understanding.

Of all this the marvellous story of Pentecost, as told in *The Acts of the Apostles*, may perhaps be taken as a symbol. If we may be allowed to use it in the spirit of much of St. Augustine's interpretation of Holy Scripture, it will perhaps express the ideas of this section better than any number of philosophical words that we might employ. 'They marvelled,' we are told, that they did hear them all (Parthians, Medes, Cretes and Arabs) 'speak in their own tongues the wonderful works of God.' Like them of old we too may marvel that we hear them all, the manifold races of man, speak, each in their own tongue, the wonderful works of God. Religion is the great thing it is because, however varied the language it speaks, it really ultimately says the same thing.

V

Intuition and Demonstration. Faith and Reasonable Belief

A

The intuitions of faith do, then, witness to the truth of religion in that which is highest and deepest in man, a witness further confirmed in the communion of all faithful people. But it does not at all follow that this truth needs no further witness. There have always been two ways to the knowledge of God, namely, intuition and logical argument or demonstration. There remains then the problem of the nature of such demonstrative knowledge and of its relation to the intuitive. This was, to be sure, the theme of earlier chapters. We shall not repeat the details of that exposition here; our present task is merely to connect the results with the more general concepts of religious knowledge as now developed.

It is impossible, we saw, to demonstrate God's existence by pure inference alone. God, being a unique existent, must be apprehended in some way, otherwise we should not even know what is meant when we speak of God or what to look for as evidence when the reality of such a being is to be shown. 'Had I not known Thee I should not have sought Thee,' cries St. Augustine, and St. Thomas tells us that unless we already know, however obscurely and confusedly, *what* He is, we cannot know *that* He is. The real problem, then, is not whether we have this apprehension, but what it includes. It is possible, as we have seen, to overload the original intuition and to identify this initial awareness with the varied images or symbols in which it is mediated. That which is immediately given—and it is not necessary to recall how it is given—is the sense of Perfection, of Absolute Good implicit in our sense of relative good; of infinitude implicit is our sense of finitude—that which is our being's heart and home. The images in which this primary intuition is given, and which vary from place to place and from time to time, are not the intuition itself—that which is intuited through the symbol is itself without variableness, neither shadow of turning. It is the latter and this alone which is the initial datum of the ontological and all other argument.

Our understanding of the relation of intuition to demonstration depends then upon a true conception of religious intuition, but it also depends upon a right conception of the meaning of demonstration in this context. Demonstrative knowledge of God consists, as we have seen, in showing forth to one who acknowledges ultimate values—acknowledgment of which alone enables one to understand the meaning of God in human experience—that a principle of perfection is presupposed by them and that the 'existence' of this Sovereign Good is the necessary ground of the validity of our values. In the terms of our present discussion, not only is the idea of God dependent upon the ideas of goodness, justice and wisdom, but the converse also holds true. Not only is God a 'human presupposition,' but to be such He must be a 'presupposition more than human.' To show this is demonstrative knowledge of God. This, as we have seen, is the essence of the axiological interpretation of the theistic argument, an argument which is itself ununderstandable except as so interpreted. It is unnecessary to recall in detail the reasons for this interpretation; it will be sufficient to remember that an examination of the Thomistic argument itself, viewed as a whole, seemed to justify it. Nor is it necessary to recall the character of the argument as thus conceived or the criticisms brought against it—all this may be assumed; it will be sufficient to emphasize one aspect of the previous discussion especially significant in the present context.

B

The argument, as thus interpreted, constitutes what has been called a 'peculiar kind of proof,' and it is peculiar if from the notion of demonstration or proof be excluded all argument except direct inference in either its deductive or inductive forms. The argument to presuppositions is peculiar in this sense, but if so it is an essential part of philosophical logic, one in fact upon which the procedures of ordinary logic are themselves ultimately based. For such proof is the only kind, as we have already seen, which is applicable to first and last things. It is therefore *a fortiori* the only kind applicable to the unique Being men call God. For any direct argument, deductive or inductive, would, as we have also seen, in the very moment that it proved God's 'existence' also prove that the being thus supposedly demonstrated is really not God. There is no wholly direct argument from either man or nature to God. While doubtless not merely modern liberal self-deception so to believe, surely it involves a grave misunderstanding of the nature of the argument.

It may be said that this indirect argument merely develops in reflection that which was implied in the original intuition, and this is in part true. To be conscious of our own finitude is already to be in reflection beyond it, and to be conscious of what is presupposed in our relative values is already to have risen in reflection to the *valor valorum* which they presuppose; the general proof into which the theistic arguments are resolvable, namely, that the higher cannot arise out of the lower, the greater from the less, simply carries out in reflection this initial insight. Nor does this fact make such reflection superfluous, as the so-called experience-philosophies of religion affect to believe. Doubtless intuition has its own certitude, but certitude is not evidence. The intuitions of faith are always mediated in subjective symbolic form and must be translated into terms of higher generality before their truth or falsity can be determined in terms of objective knowledge. Subjective and personal faith must be raised to the level of justifiable belief and here only demonstration is possible. Thus it is that the 'general proof' of which the theistic arguments are the expression is, as has been said, 'actually used unreflectively by the most untrained people' and it has been so used because even for the simplest mind reasons for belief are not superfluous. It was only natural that when men sought to express this general proof in philosophical terms they should have broken it up into separate arguments, but it was equally natural and inevitable that when they came to reflect more deeply upon these proofs they should come to see that 'they are not to be regarded separately,' but that they are cumulative and that the cumulative drive of the entire argument derives from the appeal to the 'moral' reason of man.

But is not, after all, such 'demonstration' merely a rationalization of an antecedent faith? In a sense, yes, but only in the sense that all intuition involves an element of faith. Unless, as

322

we have already seen, there were an antecedent 'animal faith' in an independent external world, no intellectual arguments for such belief would have either meaning or cogency. In like manner, unless there were an antecedent faith in the existence of other selves, as the presupposition of communication itself, all intellectual argument would be in vain. Finally, unless there were this fundamental human faith in a transcendent Good which alone gives meaning and validity to our human values, the rational arguments for the 'existence' of this transcendent Good would also be neither meaningful nor cogent. But in all these cases—and that is my main contention—belief in propositions is a different matter from faith, whether animal or human, and demonstration consists in showing forth the grounds for such reasonable belief.

If one should reply that such demonstration is not cogent in the sense of compulsion, but rather persuasion, I should not object. The question of cogency has already been discussed in the earlier context and our conclusions need not be repeated here. While demonstration as here understood is an appeal to reason, the reason to which the appeal is made is our human reason of which reference to value is a part. Moreover, coercion belongs to reason viewed only as the mechanical or quasi-mechanical processes of logic from which all reference to value has been abstracted, and consequently any proof of this kind would lead only to value-free concepts which could represent the God neither of religion nor philosophy.

It cannot be denied that in some ways certitude is better than evidence—and this is the element of truth in the 'primacy of faith' in the so-called faith-philosophies—but there are also some contexts in which evidence is alone relevant. To be privately convinced is doubtless the Alpha of religion and a mystical oneness with the Divine, which passes all understanding, perhaps, its Omega. But even so, between Alpha and Omega there is an entire alphabet, and between subjective certitude and objective insight there is the inevitable stage of understanding and of reasonable belief. However immediate and personal the initial intuitions of faith, however beatific the vision of the saint and mystic, neither can dispense with this intermediate stage. The principle of necessary stages is a fundamental law of knowledge as it is of life. The simple believer must live the faith, but in order to live it sincerely, he must know that it is true for his reason also. The mystic may achieve the vision of God, but for that vision to be really beatific it must also include the knowledge that the vision is true for his reason also. The former is not secure in his faith until the second mode of knowledge has been achieved; the latter is not secure in his vision unless the vision is the reward for both faith and reason. Truth, to be really true, must be both subjective and objective and it is the relation of these two aspects of truth which has always constituted the final problem of all religious philosophy. How men have sought to solve it is the final theme of this chapter.

VI

Knowledge and Truth. Veritas Humana *and* Veritas Ontologica

A

It would, perhaps, be a blessed thing if we could enjoy God and speak about Him without all this talk of our knowledge of God and without raising the question of the truth of our discourse. If, like Pilate, we could ask what is truth and not stay for an answer. But whether for good or ill, even the plain man, and still more the philosopher, must not only ask the question but stay until it is answered. For we cannot enjoy God unless we know Him, and knowledge and truth are correlative terms. There is thus a continuous discussion of the nature of truth from St. Augustine on, including the *Dialogus de Veritate* of St. Anselm, the *De Veritate* of Robert Grosseteste, and the *De Veritate* of St. Thomas, all of which attempt to answer Pilate's question.

However they may differ on particular issues, all agree on two fundamental points. All recognize implicitly if not explicitly two sources of knowledge of the Divine: intuition and demonstration; and, secondly, two kinds of truth: truth human and truth Divine. It is with the latter that we are now concerned.

To the question, what is truth? the answer is uniformly, God is truth. In the words of Grosseteste, 'Truth says that He is the truth.' God and truth are one. But while truth is one, there are two meanings of truth, divine and human. Truth is the adequation of thing and understanding, but as Grosseteste also says, there are two truths for each thing, as there are two under-standings with which it may be adequated, divine and human. There is indeed a single Truth, which is one in itself, but it is 'multiple and diversified in its applications.'[1] This, in one form or another, is the major premise, explicit or implied of all later discussions.

The argument for the indivisibility of truth is *a priori* in char-acter and was indisputable to the dialectical mind of the middle ages. Not only is truth, like God, one and indivisible, but the very notion of truth itself requires it. Truth, as *adaequatio intel-lectus et rei*, requires, to be truth, perfect adequation of the know-ing mind to the thing known. There can therefore be no ques-tion of more or less about it. Either knowledge is absolutely identical with its object and then it is true; or it is not wholly identical with it and then it is not at all true. There is no middle ground.[2]

This is true of 'Divine truth' but it can scarcely apply to human truth, even in religion, for if it did, man could scarcely have any truth at all—even of revelation, for such truth, con-ditioned as it must be by language as it appears in creatures, cannot be completely identical with its object. For human truth there must be some middle ground—namely, an understanding which is not complete understanding, truth which is true with-out being 'true altogether.' This concept of truth as adequacy, to use the terms of the preceding discussion, and the notion of dual adequacy which it involves is, I think, implied in any tenable conception of religious truth.

It is doubtless true that even in the human context there can be no conception of truth that does not retain, in some form and in some degree, the primary notion of adequation and therefore of correspondence. To this religious truth is not an exception; indeed it may be said that while in other spheres, such as science, pragmatic and operational theories may conceivably work, the 'moment one comes to the world of conscious spirit every theory of truth except the correspondence theory becomes absurd.'[3]

Now while I should venture to doubt the absurdity of these

---

[1] Robert Grosseteste, *On Truth*. See a translation in *Selections from Mediaeval Philosophers*, Modern Student's Library, p. 275.

[2] É. Gilson, *The Unity of Philosophical Experience*, p. 113.

[3] Edwyn Bevan, *Symbolism and Belief*, p. 300.

other theories, whether in religion or elsewhere, I am also sure that they escape it only because they also assume the notion of correspondence in some form and in some degree. In so far as religion is concerned, it is doubtless absurd to say that the intuitions of faith are called true not because of their necessary correspondence to truth but because of a certain warmth and energy of life. It is also absurd, although perhaps less so, to say that these intuitions are called true not because of their correspondence to reality but because they are confirmed in the experience of the beloved community. But it is not absurd to say that both witness to truth in a practical reference and that this witness is true because they presuppose a correspondence which, while partial, is yet adequate for our type of consciousness.

This then is the middle ground which religious no less than any other aspect of truth, in so far as it is human truth, demands. It is a fundamental tenet of philosophical theology that God cannot be known by man in His inmost essence, in all the fullness of His being. The truth of divine things cannot therefore consist in an absolute correspondence of intellect and thing, for it is the very character of the object that such a comparison is not possible. On the other hand, it is an equally fundamental tenet that God can be known in terms conditioned by the way in which they appear in creatures. Between these predicates and their object there is correspondence but it is only partial and these predicates, although only relatively, are still 'properly,' applicable to the Divine. Only such predicates as are *a priori* deducible from the idea of perfection itself are absolutely applicable, all others only partially and relatively. Thus, just as all discussions of truth inevitably recognize two adequations, the one human and the other divine, so also they have assumed explicitly or implicitly, some original intuition of perfection. For only on this assumption is either partial or absolute adequation —and therefore any relation between divine and human truth— intelligible.

B

This then is, in general, the fashion in which the religious philosopher has sought to solve the problem of truth, human and divine. A comparative study of the religious philosophies of all times and all places would, I am inclined to think, show that wherever the level described as 'developed religion' is reached similar problems with essentially similar solutions have been reached. It is, however, with Christian philosophy, as pre-eminently significant for our western culture that we have been concerned, so I shall not pursue this point further.

There is, as we have seen, a fundamental dilemma out of which this philosophy developed and the solution of which has constituted its main task. It may be stated in various forms, but in the last analysis all are resolvable into one, namely the dilemma between anthropomorphism and agnosticism and therefore ultimately between truth as it appears to our human understanding and truth as it must appear to God. It is this dilemma that the doctrine of the two adequations in its various formulations sought to solve. Truth, to be truth for us, must be truth for our type of consciousness, otherwise it would not be living truth. But to be even truth in this sense it must be more than truth for our type of consciousness, otherwise it could not be *veritas ontologica*. The combination of these two adequations in one doctrine Christian philosophy has constantly sought, and it found its final expression in the *analogia entis* with its implications of symbolism as a theological principle. We have indeed no experience of the Absolute except as symbolic representation, but it does not at all follow that because without such representation experience of the Absolute is not possible, that such experience is not true. The criterion of dual adequacy developed in connection with our discussion of symbolic knowledge is a statement of the doctrine of the two adequations.

This dilemma of all religion has, as was only to be expected, appeared in these latter days in a peculiarly drastic, not to say tragic, form. It is the dilemma of 'subjectivity—objectivity' about which so much of so-called neo-Protestantism revolves. 'The objective thinker,' so we are told, 'fails to attain truth wholly separated from himself, and if he attempts to do so he creates a philosophy which he cannot live.' This is doubtless true but, on the other hand, it is equally true that the subjective thinker fails to attain truth which is beyond himself and creates a philosophy which he cannot really hold, for we believe only in that which is independent of our belief. If he does not seek grounds for such belief he stultifies not only himself, but the entire creaturely existence of which he is a part. Truth is indeed subjective, as Kierkegaard and his many followers insist—the intuitions of faith have their own witness, and 'religion is inwardly justified'—but such inward witness can justify faith only because it is at the same time an objective intuition of that which transcends inner experience. It is only in that which is highest and deepest in us that God is known, but He is truly known only because of that which makes them high and deep, an objective intuition of the Divine. Subjective truth—'truth in a practical reference'—must then find its place in any adequate philosophy of religion, and pragmatic criteria of truth a place even in the sphere of dogma. But pragmatism is, in the words of Windelband, merely the vestibule of truth, not its inner shrine. In this inner shrine only the *veritas ontologica* is worshipped. We cannot enter this inner shrine without going through the vestibule but, by the same token, we cannot remain in the vestibule, for were it not for the inner shrine the vestibule would itself be a blind alley, as indeed it is for many modern philosophers.

C

The doctrine of the two adequations and their relation, as here interpreted, is the necessary outcome of the conception of religious knowledge developed in this chapter. For the conception that truth is 'multiple and diversified in its applications' constitutes the broader conception of truth which must necessarily correspond to the conception of knowledge which is broader and more humane. But this conception has further implications which raise some of the most difficult questions of the philosophy of religion. As *divine*, truth is one and indivisible; but as *human* it is multiple and diversified in its applications. The problem is how multiple and how diversified.

Two different applications have always been recognized, namely, 'the truth that the inquiry of reason can attain and the truth of the intelligible things of God which surpasses the whole range of human reason.' This notion of the whole range of human reason raises immediately the further question of what that range is, and of the various forms that human reason may take. There are various employments of the reason, to use Kantian terms. To these correspond multiple and diversified notions of truth. The special problem of the modern world centres in the empirical employment known as science.

Science, having developed an autonomous method, claimed

first an autonomous status in the world of knowledge and truth. This claim to autonomy finally developed into the demand for primacy and, with this demand, came the narrower view of knowledge which identifies it completely with the so-called scientific method as now understood. This situation has given rise to two major tendencies in modern thought. The first, acknowledging the primacy of scientific method, would exclude religion entirely from the sphere of knowledge and ascribe to it a wholly emotive significance. The second, also acknowledging this primacy, attempts to subsume religious knowledge under scientific and to show that theology is but an 'extension of the scientific method.' Both of these positions rest upon serious mis-understandings of the nature of science and scientific method which it will be the task of the following chapter to point out. Be that as it may, it is obvious that, granting this situation, no final solution of the problem of religious knowledge is possible until knowledge in this sphere is related to that given us by science and scientific method. Still more is it evident that the pronouncements of religion on man and his relation to the ground of things can be properly evaluated only after they have been related to corresponding pronouncements, not only of science but of the humanities also. Both tell us certain things about man and about nature. It is only after we have determined what both really say that their pronouncements upon these issues can be related to those of religion. Finally, it is also evident that the pronouncements of religion cannot be properly evaluated until we have examined the mystical element in religion and determined what contribution, if any, mysticism makes to our knowledge of God. These constitute the problems of the following chapters.

Chapter X

*Religion and Science: The Pronouncements of Science on
Nature and on Man*

I — A

THE CONFLICT between science and religion which
reached its zenith about the turn of the last century
was partly due to the fact that religion was made to
say many things which it really never taught. But it is equally
possible to say that in that same period science was made to
say many things which it also never taught. We were constantly
told that 'science says' this and that about nature and about
man and it was forthwith assumed that, science having spoken,
the last word had been said. It was rarely understood that the
pronouncements of science, no less than those of religion, or of
any other form of 'language,' must first be interpreted before
we know what they really say. The absurd literalism of much of
the religion of that epoch was matched by an equally absurd
literalism in science, and the latter was as inimical to understanding as the former.

It should have been obvious that if we take the explicit
statements of both religion and science literally—in the sense of
the fundamentalists of both camps—these statements are not
only incompatible but, in the nature of the case, must be. In the
universe of discourse we call science the pronouncements of
religion are not so much untrue as meaningless. For science
there is, and can be, no meaning to the idea that man is a son of
God for in this universe there is neither God nor man in the
sense of this tremendous assertion. For science there is no ascension into Heaven, for in this universe of discourse there is no up
or down and no Heaven in the religious sense, into which to
ascend. For science there is no creation of the world in six days,
whether we think of the 'days' literally or as aeons; no consummation of all things, for first and last things in the sense of
religion have no meaning. Scientists may still name the name of
God, not as scientists, however, but always as men. In the
limited universe of discourse called science there is, as they have
come to see, no way in which it may significantly be used.

It is, to be sure, in a sense natural that men should have at first tried to 'harmonize' these two different types of pronouncements on the level of literal interpretation and apologetic literature is strown with the pathetic wrecks of an endeavour which now has merely an historic interest. It is natural also that they should have even tried to translate the language of religious experience into the categories of science—the so-called psychology of religion is full of such attempts—with the result that these same translations are neither religious nor scientific, and are properly deprecated, by theologians and scientists alike, as lacking in scientific no less than religious understanding. But because there is incompatibility between the two on the level of the explicit and literal it does not at all follow that they are in ultimate contradiction when we understand what both 'really say'—that is, if we 'go behind the returns' in both cases to their implicit pronouncements on nature and on man. This is the philosophy of religion and the philosophy of science respectively and it is only on this level—of philosophy—that the issues with which we are concerned can be significantly discussed at all. In an earlier chapter we sought to determine what it is that religion really says—in its anthropological, cosmological, and ontological pronouncements; it is now our task to discover, if possible, what science really says on these same issues. In order, however, to know what science really says, it is necessary to know what this thing men call science itself actually is. Our first problem is, then, one of definition, and with this is opened up again the question, discussed in a preliminary way in the introductory chapter, of the relation of science *eo nomine* to knowledge and reason as a whole.

II

What is Science? The Problem of Definition and of the
'Unity of Science'

A

It may seem absurd even to raise the question of what science is. We know well enough what it is—it is just another word for knowledge or *scientia*. In the ancient world science was

331

always synonymous with all knowledge. For the Greek philosopher, and still more for the medieval thinker, theology is a
science just as much as physics. Thus for St. Thomas there are
'two kinds of sciences.' There are some which 'proceed from a
principle known by the natural light of the intelligence such as
arithmetic, geometry and the like. . . . So it is that sacred
doctrine is a science because it proceeds from principles established by the light of a higher science, namely, the science of
God and the blessed.'[1] For the modern man, however, 'science'
is something quite different. There may be knowledge of God,
but if there is one thing that he is sure of it is that such knowledge is not an 'extension of the scientific method.' If it were
he might be permitted to wonder whether it is understood what
the scientific method really is and why, if this is so, there
should be this conflict of science and religion which has raged
ever since the development of modern physical science.

'Science,' we are constantly told, 'consists, broadly speaking,
in framing wider and wider generalizations based on observation and experiment.'[2] This, however, is to speak very broadly
indeed, and the definition must be narrowed significantly if it is
to represent the modern conception of science. More and more,
observation has come to mean sense observation and the verification of the generalizations based upon such observation has
come to mean exclusively reference direct or indirect, to
sensuously observable entities. This so-called 'empirical
criterion' has come to be the criterion of scientific method, and
the 'empirical employment of the reason' becomes, as in Kant's
critical philosophy, the only method to which the term scientific
is applicable. This was implicit in modern science from the
beginning, although it took generations of reflection upon
method, to say nothing of the critical philosophy of Kant, for
scientists finally to recognize the fact.

This is one aspect of the modern notion of science, but there
is another of equal importance which, in contrast with the
former, we may describe as the mathematical-logical ideal.
Instead of giving the primacy to the notion of sense observation,
it stresses that of mathematical exactness and rigour. More and

[1] *Summa Theol.* I, qu. I, art. 2.
[2] This is the definition of Lloyd Morgan in his discussion of *Science and Drama*,
already referred to.

more, from the time of Galileo on, science is conceived in these terms, and increasingly ordinary speech, even the 'physical' language of science itself, gives way to the 'purer notation' of a mathematical symbolism. This also was implicit in the ideals of modern science from the beginning, but it also took generations of reflection, as well as the Kantian critical philosophy, to make it quite clear. This second aspect of modern scientific method does not, of course, exclude the first. However far from the actual world of sense these mathematical symbolisms may lead us, they must in the end bring us back again, often most indirectly, to the world of sense itself, if the term science is to be applicable.

The question, What is Science? can then be answered, in the first instance at least, only in terms of *method*. The condition of there being any science at all, in the modern sense, becomes then 'the requirement that all the concepts which science uses shall be resolvable only within the sensible and the measurable.' All other concepts, formerly conceived as existential, are now reduced to the role of ideal entities or constructions whose function is no longer that of copying objects but merely of correlating phenomena or, as it is sometimes said, of 'sustaining a tissue of mathematical relations and structures.' The ideal of science thus becomes a science of phenomena as such.

With this limitation of the notion of science has, moreover, come a significant clarification of its objectives, for the notion of method has meaning only with reference to purposes and ends. The ancient identification of science with knowledge as such implied the notion that the object of science and of scientific method is the systematic effort to 'explain' nature or the cosmos. The progress of science consists in the gradual acquirement of clearer and more comprehensive views of the truth behind the phenomena in so far as it can be apprehended by rational inference from the phenomena themselves. This idea is, however, as many scientists now inform us, quite false—that is, it does not correspond with what science actually is, whatever we we may think it should be.[1] It actually consists merely in establishing rational relations between phenomena, or, as it has also been said, 'intelligibility in science consists exclusively in

[1] See on this point Professor Herbert Dingle in 'A Current Misconception of Science,' *The Hibbert Journal*, October 1939.

necessary connections. The fact is no longer isolated and is therefore intelligible.'[1]

No one would wish to quarrel with this limitation of scientific method which has accomplished such wonders of accuracy and control, nor with the notion of intelligibility which it presupposes. The only quarrel one could possibly have is with the dogma which identifies all knowledge with this method, and therefore excludes *ab initio* the broader and more humane notion which, from the beginning, has been the necessary presupposition of every form of culture. The challenge of this dogma is, however, justified even by critical science itself. Few scientists would wish to consign to the flames all books not concerned with experimental reasoning concerning matter of fact or abstract reasoning concerning quantity and number, although there are still some who would consign them to the limbo of emotion, which for them is a fate in some respects worse than the flames. The more critical would recognize that to rule out by definition everything from the sphere of knowledge which cannot be said in their language constitutes an *a priori* prejudice to which few would care to confess. More than this— and this is even more important for the argument of this chapter —they would also recognize that if science is thus concerned exclusively with necessary connections it is not in 'science' that the ideal of knowledge is most completely realized—science cannot be identified with *scientia*—nor, having the limited ideal of science, can they in the same breath make pronouncements on the universe as a whole which obviously go beyond all conceivable connections of phenomena. The objectives of modern science being what they are, one could scarcely say that the pronouncements of religion should be based upon the pronouncements of science.

B

The condition of the possibility of our answering the question, what science really is, is that science shall have sufficient unity or self-identity to make it possible to speak of it as a whole. Such unity the modern conception of scientific method seems to justify, and 'the unity of science' has become part of scientific dogma. On the other hand, this dogma is increasingly

[1] L. S. Stebbing, *A Modern Introduction to Logic*, p. 392.

challenged, a further indication of the ambiguities which result when science is identified with knowledge as such.

There has been a significant movement towards what is called the 'decentralization of the sciences,' a recognition, so to speak, of different levels of reality to which correspond different methods. 'Each science,' as we are told, 'represents a distinct level and each level is a natural one in the sense that it possesses its own fundamental intuitive language which is *largely if not completely* independent of that used on the other levels (italics mine), and that the only natural view is 'to regard these levels as having co-ordinate reality.'[1] Thus is, apparently at least, restored that ancient doctrine of the hierarchy of the sciences which was one of the central theses of the Thomistic philosophy of science.

There is, I take it, no question in anybody's mind that there are these different languages and levels. Nor is there any question that for any adequate rendering of the varied characters of reality—more specifically of the qualities of life, mind and value—all are necessary. The only question is whether these varied languages and symbols shall all be called 'science.' This, it may be said, is merely a matter of definition and therefore of postulation, but it is with definition that we are here concerned and with the postulates that lie back of such definitions. There are obviously two possibilities here. We may either identify science with all knowledge and include all languages and symbolisms, or we may define science more narrowly and while, perhaps, including these other forms under knowledge, exclude them from science in the sense of the modern definition. My own view is that the development of scientific method at least favours, if it does not compel, the latter alternative. For it seems clear that to call all these intuitive languages, however fundamental, science, is to forfeit all the advantages which the narrowing of the concept of science has indubitably brought, without any corresponding gain.

There are at least two considerations which seem to support this view. In the first place, I would point out that whatever scientists may say about the decentralization of the sciences, actually they are in the end forced to fall back upon the dogma of unity by the exigencies of scientific method. Verification by

[1] George Birkhoff in an article in the volume entitled *Science and the New World*.

experience is a conception which appears to permit of wide latitude, but actually in practice it is sense experience to which, in the last analysis, appeal is made, and the physical-mathematical method tends to become exclusive. One hears the biologist say that 'while he may suspect that there is more to life than science can say, nevertheless all advances in explanation have been conditioned by exclusion of all non-physical postulates,' and one hears the psychologist say essentially the same thing. In the second place, while the 'higher' level is said to be 'largely independent' of the lower levels it is never 'completely' so. It is independent in so far as there are aspects of the higher levels not exhaustively expressible in the categories of the lower; but it is dependent in the sense that the categories of the higher can never, from the scientific point of view, negate the lower. Whatever more we may say about life or mind than can be said in the categories of physics and chemistry —and this 'more' certainly requires another language than the physico-mathematical—this can never gainsay what has been said in this language. This principle of 'the irreversibility of the categorial scheme,' as it has been called, properly understood, does not tell us, as is sometimes supposed, that the higher categories are reducible to the lower, but it does insist that all knowledge, in science at least, begins with the lower and that this order of procedure cannot be reversed. It tells us that in what we, broadly speaking, call the hierarchy of the sciences— a hierarchy determined by the principle of degrees of abstraction—it is inevitable that the more abstract and universal should dominate for purposes of 'explanation,' however it may be for purposes of 'understanding' and evaluation. For this conception of the 'unity of science' I shall make use of Leibniz's term, 'dominant unity,' employed by him in a somewhat similar context.

If this is true—and I think it is—it follows that physics, in the broad sense of the term, tends to become the basal science and its categories the dominant categories in the categorical scheme. Physics is notably the basal science of the existent and what it has to say, both as to the method of science and as to the ultimate concepts of physical nature, is, in certain respects, determinative for the other positive sciences. Space-time is the matrix of the existent—the all-pervasive form of everything that 'is'; matter and its constitution the ultimate physical notion; physical law the structural notion of everything we call nature. What physics has to say about these things, if it says anything at all, either explicitly or implicitly, cannot but have important consequences for our beliefs about first and last things. Thus it is commonly recognized that it is changes in these fundamental concepts which have led certain physicists to 'some form of idealism,' and with it to an altered attitude towards religion. Two main factors, we are told, are responsible for this tendency. 'There is first, the change in the conception of matter; secondly, the change in the status assigned by many physicists to natural laws.'[1] Whether this is true or not, and if true it has the important consequences for religion and philosophy supposed, is a question for later discussion. My sole point here is that, because of the place of physics in the categorical scheme, the interpretation of his own categories, by the physicist himself, is of fundamental importance. In other words it is the cosmological and metaphysical implications of these changes—if indeed there be such, for that is, of course, one of the points at issue—that are primarily significant for the problem of the relation of science and religion. To find out what science really says on these questions becomes of primary significance, not only for a philosophy of science but for a philosophy of religion.

C

The concept of science and of scientific method developed in the modern world, differs, as we have seen, significantly from the traditional notion which had hitherto dominated western thought. It is only natural that among critics of this conception the upholders of the Thomistic conception of science should have an important place. In any case, their criticisms are especially relevant in the present context and shall therefore chiefly engage our attention.

The chief point of attack is, of course, the principle of the autonomy of science which is an essential part of the modern notion and based upon the conception of the uniqueness and dominant position of so-called scientific method. Critics such as Professor Fulton Sheen are careful to recognize this autonomy in so far as method is concerned, but insist that autonomy of

[1] L. S. Stebbing, *Philosophy and the Physicists*, p. 266.

method does not imply autonomy, still less primacy of value and wax eloquent against that 'scientific lyricism' into which representatives of modern science and scientific naturalism too easily fall. They condemn 'the fallacy of the uniform method of science' and invoke the doctrine of the hierarchy of the sciences based upon the principle of abstraction. They contend that the modern conception of science devalues it by separating it from its metaphysical basis and seek to save modern science from itself.[1]

However one may sympathize with the motive, one may well wonder whether the attack itself is wisely conceived. It seems difficult to recognize autonomy of method without acknowledging the concept or ideal of science which underlies it, for as the notion of method is meaningless unless related to the objective which determines it, so also the objective and therefore the nature of science cannot be separated from its methodology. I am far from maintaining that science is autonomous in any ultimate sense—still less that such autonomy implies primacy in the sphere of knowledge as a whole. All that I am saying—and I think the point is important—is that it is for science itself, in the first instance at least, to say what its objectives are and therefore, what it ultimately 'really says.' Nor am I arguing that science is ultimately unrelated to metaphysics; indeed it seems impossible that it should be so. The very limitation of its method and objective, implies other objectives and other ways of knowing. My only point is that, however science may ultimately be related to the other activities of man, however its narrow conceptions of knowledge may be modified by further reflection, it is from the philosophy of science itself that this reflection must take its start.

[1] Fulton J. Sheen, *Philosophy of Science* (1934), especially chapter x; also *Religion Without God* (1928), chapter viii, 'The Fallacy of the Uniform Method of Science.'

III

The New Scientific Epistemology: Symbolism as a Scientific Principle.
Symbolism and the Principle of Abstraction

A

The philosophy of science may, I think, be adequately defined in the following way. It investigates the scientific way of knowing and evaluates the pronouncements of science upon the cosmos and upon the place of life and mind in the cosmos. It investigates the 'value of science.' in the sense that it seeks to determine the validity of its pronouncements in their relation to other activities of the human spirit.

It requires no argument to demonstrate that these problems are recognized by scientists themselves. In the beginning of the nineteenth century it was assumed without question that the picture science drew of nature constituted a literal representation of a structure actually existing in the world of intuitible facts. As the result of reflection upon their own work, scientists themselves began to question this view and, as we have seen, to form the notion that science is essentially hypothesis and deals, not with intuitible reals, but with formal systems of relations. Finally—and most important of all—is the recognition of the fact that science is based upon a principle of abstraction—a fact long recognized by the philosophers—namely, that science, as method, and as a way of describing reality, proceeds by making far-reaching abstractions for its own purposes, and that these abstractions have value solely from its own point of view and for its own purposes.

As a consequence of these beliefs, there has resulted a re-valuation of science as a way of knowing—what has been called 'the new scientific epistemology.' This new epistemology includes, besides the recognition of the facts presented in the preceding paragraphs, a most important principle which follows necessarily from them—namely, the notion that *science itself is a form of symbolism*—one among other symbolic forms—and that symbolism is as much a necessary principle of science as of religion or any other form of expressing experience. When this is really understood, it is seen that what science really says about reality is significantly different from what it at first sight seems to say, that is when its concepts are taken literally, as copies, corresponding in all their parts to reality. The recognition of this principle affects vitally, not only our interpretation of the pronouncements of science themselves, but also, as we shall see, their relation to pronouncements expressed in other symbolic forms.

In order to understand the principle of symbolism as recognized by science two important developments in modern physics must be fully appreciated. The first of these is the abandonment of the copy or model theory of the scientific concept for the symbolic; the second, which follows from this, a significant change in the conception of the ontological status of the scientific symbol or construct.

B

The first is a commonplace of modern physical science. Over and over again we are told that between what is called Newtonian science and that of the present there is in this respect a great gap. Sir William Thomson's idea of the 'understanding' of a phenomenon of nature is constantly contrasted with the notion of the scientific concept since Hertz. For the former to understand was to construct a mechanical model which should 'represent literally the happening in all its parts.' For the latter, to understand involves no such literal copy, but a relation that is purely symbolic. This contrast of the symbol with the literal or copy theory is a commonplace of present-day scientific epistemology.

It is customary to distinguish between three classes of constructs or symbols in physics, namely, (a) the sensible or *anschaulich*, of which the physical models are examples; (b) the pseudo-sensible which includes atoms and electrons and many similar entities; and (c) a class which is described as 'abstract' which are wholly insensible. Quantum mechanics actually replaces the electron and any other physical system by an abstract construct of this sort.[1]

This third class of constructs, the 'abstract,' is of the utmost

---

[1] For the details of this principle of symbolism in science see my *Language and Reality*, chapter xi, in which may be found a wealth of material taken from modern science impossible to reproduce in the limits of the present discussion.

importance in our general view of physical science. Certainly it is true, as we are told, that if the physicist were to restrict himself exclusively to the sensible and pseudo-sensible constructs, his ideal of an ultimate system of explanation would never be realized. The story of the breakdown of these symbols in special fields of physics is too well known to require retelling here. The main point of interest is that it became possible to work in physics with abstract symbols for which there is no corresponding intuition and for which there is no existential status in the world as known by the senses. The success of this symbolism has led to the notion of which we spoke at the beginning—the mathematical-logical ideal of science. Thus we find Jeans saying: 'Our knowledge of the universe must always consist of numbers and our picture of the universe—the synthesis of our knowledge —must necessarily be in mathematical form. All the concrete details of the picture, the apples, the pears and the bananas, the ether, the atoms, the electrons, are mere clothing with which we drape our mathematical symbols—they do not belong to nature, but to the parables with which we seek to make nature comprehensible.'[1]

These symbolic constructs correspond to the perceptible world, but the correspondence is not a one to one correspondence as in earlier theories; they do not therefore represent their objects literally. A popular figure representing this relation is that of the music and the score. Between a piece of orchestral music as played, and the same piece of music as printed in the score, there is a certain resemblance of structure—a resemblance of the sort that when you know the rules you can infer the music from the score and the score from the music. Granting that this is a valid analogy, it seems clear that the function of the language of science, as of all forms of language, 'is, as Cassirer says, 'not to copy reality but to symbolize it.' With this change in our conception of the function of physical concepts comes also a change in our conception of their truth. Here, as elsewhere, some element of correspondence must be present in any truth notion but for any critical science such correspondence can be only partial.

Of even more importance for the philosophy of science is the

[1] Sir James H. Jeans, *The New World Picture of Modern Physics*, British Association for the Advancement of Science, Aberdeen, 1934. Printed in *Nature*, 1934.

question of the existential or ontological status of these constructs, or as Eddington formulates it, 'the meaning of existence in physics.' On this point there is, of course, considerable variety of views. They vary all the way from the most naïve conception (although this is rarely held) that they exist in the same sense as sensuously observable physical objects, although they cannot be actually observed, to the view of Eddington, that they are merely 'dummies in our mathematical equations.' A more critical view than either of these extremes is, I believe, that the question of their existential status is irrelevant for science which is concerned only with the establishment of functional relations, and that the question of the ontological status of these constructs can be determined only by wider metaphysical considerations which go beyond science itself.[1] If, however, this is so, metaphysical issues, while irrelevant for scientific method, are not hereby excluded as irrelevant for knowledge as such, since precisely such issues are implied by the method itself. If science is symbolic form, there remains, for the philosopher at least, always the question of *what* it is that is expressed in this form.

C

The symbolic character of our physical concepts is, then, quite generally recognized. It represents, as Cassirer tells us, the essentially scientific standpoint today.[2] The proof of this statement could be found in the *ipsissima verba* of all the leading physicists—Jeans and Eddington, Max Planck and Hermann Weil, etc.—for all of whom our concepts of the physical world are constructs or symbols. In the words of Weyl, 'science concedes to idealism that this, its objective world, is not given, but

[1] See on this point, H. Margenau, 'Methodology of Modern Physics,' *Philosophy of Science*, Vol. II, Nos. 1 and 2 (January and April 1935). This is an important study of the philosophical problems set by the developments of modern physics.

[2] Ernst Cassirer, *Die Philosophie der Symbolischen Formen*, Vol. III, p. 545. Making use of an immense array of evidence from present day science, Cassirer concludes that 'physics has finally abandoned the reality of description and representation in order to enter upon a realm of greater abstraction. The schematism of pictures has given place to a symbolism of principles. Physics is concerned no longer with the actual, but is concerned with structure and its formal characters. The tendency to unification has conquered the tendency to intuitive representation. The synthesis which is possible through pure concepts of law and relation has shown itself more valuable than the apprehension in terms of objects and things. Order and relation have then become the basal concepts of physics.'

only propounded (like a problem to be solved) and that it can be constructed only by symbols.'[1]

It is not necessary for the present argument to draw any philosophical conclusions, whether idealistic or realistic—although as we shall see they are not without significance for our present problem—all that is necessary here is to recognize symbolism as a scientific principle. There are, as we shall see, important consequences of this principle, but before turning to these more ultimate issues it is necessary to discuss a specific application of the principle, namely, with respect to the supposed pronouncements of science on the cosmos as a whole. The cosmological pronouncements of religion, which are in a sense the basis of all religion, are, as we have seen, symbolic in form. This is true also of the cosmological pronouncements of science. The recognition of the character changes vitally the problem of the relation of science to religion at this point. For it is chiefly the assumption of the literal truth of these pronouncements which leads men to suppose that religion must be based upon scientific cosmology.

By cosmological propositions in science I understand all those statements about the physical 'universe' which profess to tell us about its character as a whole and about its origin and destiny. It is commonly supposed that pronouncements of this type are of the same general character as the ordinary generalizations about phenomena and their relations within the universe. Quite the contrary is the case, and since it is precisely this difference which is of significance it is of the utmost importance that it should be fully understood.

This difference is emphasized by Sir James Jeans in the address already referred to, in which he discusses the relation of scientific concepts to 'physical wholes,' a discussion which is pre-eminently significant for our purposes, in that he raises the entire question of the relation of the symbolic and the literal in physical science. He points out that literal knowledge in physics is very limited. By literal knowledge he understands the representation of each part of an object in its proper shape and relatively proper size, and illustrates the notion by means of a map or spatial picture. Such literal representation is possible only when the map is of a very small part of the globe, as for

[1] *Mind and Nature*, 1933, p. 38 f.

instance the county of Surrey. The larger the whole, he tells us, the more 'symbolic' the representation. Passing then, to what he calls the 'wholes of physics' such as the physical cosmos, he points out that, in analogous fashion, the Newtonian mechanics, like the map of Surrey, while good as far as it goes, is not adequate for picturing the whole. The inconceivably great and the inconceivably small are both beyond our ken.

The cosmological pronouncements of science are then, not only symbolic, but symbolic in a special way and degree. Being propositions about physical 'wholes,' they differ in significant ways from the ordinary generalizations of science. Such wholes are illimitable and in their very nature metempirical; as such, propositions about them are not empirically verifiable as are propositions about the parts. It is not merely that the larger the whole the more symbolic the representation but the relation of the symbol to that symbolized is in principle different. We are no longer in the world of statistical generalizations such as are applicable to the relations of symbolic constructs to the world of perceptible relations but rather in a world of speculative hypothesis in which one world picture seems to us more 'comprehensible' than another. The inconceivably great and the inconceivably small are indeed both beyond our ken.[1]

All of which, if true, we can readily see, alters significantly the entire problem of the relation of religion to science at this point. Science does not give us literal truth about the cosmos whereas religion gives us symbolic. The scientific propositions are no less symbolic than the religious although the symbols are of a different type and constructed for a different purpose. The problem is then no longer how we can square the symbols

[1] It might be supposed that we can argue by extrapolation from the great to the infinitely great and from the small to the infinitely small, and from the relative wholes of physics to the *omnitudo realitatis*. But surely this is impossible. Extrapolation is doubtless valid in a mathematical series and, within limits, in a phenomenal series, but not, it should be evident, I think, in any inference to wholes not phenomenal. For these reasons, the positivistic scientist, when he is logical, is disposed to exclude from science all such cosmological speculations and even to call them the myths of science. In any case—and this is all of interest in the present argument—it must be evident to one who reflects, that cosmological pronouncements in science, no less than in religion, are, in the nature of the case, not empirically verifiable. For the same reasons the notion of probability when applied to such propositions, is no longer the calculable probability of phenomenal connections but has undergone that significant change described in an earlier context. (Chapter v, p. 183.)

of religion with the truth of science, but rather what, in the larger economy of the human spirit, is the relation of these two different languages and different symbolic forms. No modern discussion of the relation of science to religion is significant which does not state the problem in this form.

D

The recognition of symbolism as a scientific principle has important implications for the entire philosophy of science, one of the most important of which is the meaning of the literal and the relation of the literal to the symbolic in science. Earlier we had occasion to remark that the literalist in science is as much a nuisance as in religion. Not because they both insist upon literal or non-symbolic knowledge, but because they both find the *locus* of the literal in the wrong place.[1] We called this the fallacy of misplaced literalism and it is with this fallacy as it appears in science that we are now concerned.

This fallacy is evident on the slightest inspection and is recognized by all of the more enlightened physicists. It consists in attributing to our symbolic constructions the status of sensuously observable entities. We need not go to the length of calling electrons 'merely dummies in our mathematical equations,' nor of calling them 'clothes with which we drape our mathematical equations'; but we can agree that the question of their ontological status is irrelevant for scientific methodology and is in the last analysis a metaphysical question. In any case, the fallacy of misplaced literalism consists in taking our sensible and pseudo-sensible constructions, to say nothing of the purely abstract constructs—in other words our scientific anthropomorphisms—as though they were literal copies. It is easy to see why this scientific fundamentalism should have wrought such havoc in nineteenth-century thought and why the dogmatic mechanism and materialism which resulted should have been so inimical to religion. Recognition of this fallacy does not, of course, exclude the notion of the literal from science any more than it does from religion. Unfortunately this problem, of the *locus* of the literal, is as difficult for science as it is for religion. Those who stress the observational side of science are likely to think of its 'literal sentences' as those which refer directly to

[1] Chapter vii, p. 247.

345

sense data, while those who stress the mathematical aspects are likely, like Jeans, to find it in the mathematical relations, and to consider all sense imagery as fables with which we deck the mathematical equations. But this issue need not concern us here; it is enough for our present purpose that for none is the literal truth to be found in the constructs, sensible, pseudo-sensible, or abstract, with which we seek to manipulate phenomena or to make comprehensible our mathematical equations. To take these as 'existent,' in the literal sense of existence, is to be guilty of the fallacy of misplaced literalism and evidences a complete misunderstanding of 'the meaning of existence in physics.'[1]

As there is what the theologian calls religious obscurity so also there is that which we may call scientific obscurity, and the philosophical scientist would do well to recognize it. This obscurity arises, moreover, out of much the same sources as the former. It is, indeed, widely recognized that the literalism and over-simplification necessary for the popularization of science result almost inevitably in misrepresentation, but it is not sufficiently recognized that this very misrepresentation arises mainly from the fallacy of misplaced literalism. It is not true that the plain man, though a fool, need not err in science any more than in religion, and what holds of the plain man holds of many scientists also.

E

The problem of the literal and the symbolic in science raises a further question, namely, as to the relation of the modern principle of symbolism to the 'principle of abstraction' in the classical philosophy of science, for it is at this point, apparently, that one of the chief issues between the traditional view and the new scientific epistemology arises.

The 'principle of abstraction,' as it has been technically called, constituted the basis of the philosophy of science from the Greeks on, but found its explicit expression in later scholasticism. It was upon this principle that the hierarchy of the sciences was based, the fundamental sciences of physics and mathematics representing the limits of abstraction. To take these abstractions for concrete entities has for traditional philosophy also always

[1] For a more extended discussion of the problem of the literal and symbolic in science see *Language and Reality*, pp. 542 ff.

been the beginning of fallacy, but there is apparently one difference between the two views important not only for the philosophy of science itself but also ultimately for the problems with which this chapter is concerned. It is the question whether the principle of abstraction involves also a principle of construction, as the modern epistemology of science maintains.

So far as I can see, the methodology of modern science leaves no doubt on this point. The entities of science are not merely given; it is rather, as Weyl says, the problem that is given and it can 'only be constructed by symbols.' If this is true—and I think that there can be little question of its truth—then the symbols thus constructed are, like all symbols, conditioned in some degree by community of subjective form. It is only the new scientific epistemology that has finally made us understand the full significance of Goethe's saying, 'man does not know how anthropomorphic he really is.' Few scientists would contest the notion that physical concepts are man-made, for certain specific purposes of manipulation and control, although they are not always fully aware of the human conditioning of these concepts or that they have validity only for the purposes for which they are constructed. It is just this fact, that scientific conceptions are the products of abstraction, which makes them man-made; and being abstractions they can correspond only partially, and therefore symbolically, to concrete reality.

Be this as it may—and the fuller development of this point is part of the theme of the following section—so far as the present issue is concerned the results of the principle of abstraction and of the principle of symbolism are much the same. It is as much a fallacy to take the abstraction for concrete reality as to take the symbol for that which it symbolizes. The fallacy of misplaced literalism corresponds then to that which in the larger philosophical context is called the fallacy of misplaced concreteness. To take as concrete entities the abstract constructs of science, is recognized as an error the avoidance of which is the *sine qua non* of any valid philosophy. Doubtless there is a possibility of serious misunderstanding here due to the scientific obscurity of which we have spoken. When we are told that the atoms and electrons are conceptual constructs, we may jump to the conclusion that they are 'picturesque ways of saying something that is not true.' But that is a wholly mistaken inference.

347

In order to recognize the symbolic character of physical concepts it is, however, not necessary to deny the existence of something in the objective world to which they refer. It merely signifies that, since the physical concept is a symbol, like all symbols it is conditioned by community of subjective form and cannot therefore represent its object literally. Truth here, as in every field of human knowledge, is human truth and adequation adequacy for our type of consciousness. In any case—and that is the important point here—so far as science itself is concerned, the existential status of these concepts or constructs is irrelevant and can be determined only by wider philosophical considerations which go beyond science itself.

IV

The New Scientific Epistemology and its Implications for Philosophy and Religion. The 'Value of Science'

A

This notion of science as symbolic form has been expressed in various ways. I choose, however, a formulation by Eddington especially relevant to our present discussion. It is found in its fullest form in his *Philosophy of Physical Science*, but for our present purpose its best expression is found in his *Science and the Unseen World*. The notion itself is quite independent of the 'idealism' with which it is bound up, and expresses, when freed from this element, a general epistemological thesis, shared, I believe, by a great many physicists. 'The exploration of the external world by science, leads,' he tells us, 'not to concrete reality, but to a shadow world of symbols beneath which these methods are not adapted to penetrating. Force, energy, dimensions belong to the world of symbols; it is out of such conceptions that we have built the external world of physics.' What other conceptions, he asks, have we? 'After exhausting physical methods we must again return to the inmost recesses of consciousness. It is the very essence of this world that the conception of personality should dominate.'[1] The contrast of these two world views and their relations constitutes the ultimate problem to which all this

[1] *Op. cit.*, p. 82.

analysis leads—and to this we shall devote our attention in the sequel; the important point here is the limitation of the symbolic form of science and the necessity of other symbolic forms. In the wholly different world of moral and religious experience a different language and a different kind of symbols are necessary. The modern reaction against anthropomorphism is, as he recognizes, understandable, but in his opinion is, nevertheless, 'in principle unsound.'

Few critical scientists would, I believe, contest the first part of this statement. To hold that the symbols are the concrete reality itself would for most constitute the fallacy of misplaced concreteness and few would fail to realize it. The second part of Eddington's contention would, however, not be so generally admitted, at least in the form in which it is here stated. But the principle itself would, I believe, be accepted by most of those who have come to understand the implications of modern scientific method. For after exhausting the physical method— and who would deny that it has its limits?—we must indeed return again, if not to the inmost recesses of consciousness (that has indeed a subjective sound!), at least to those non-physical categories and postulates which, if they do not enable us to correlate phenomena, certainly are indispensable for an *understanding*, not only of life and mind, but ultimately of the *omnitudo realitatis* of which they are a part.

Such a return has actually been the inevitable result in modern philosophy of a proper understanding of symbolism as a scientific principle. For the moment science postulated (and it is mere postulation) that concepts, in order to be scientific, must be resolvable into the physical and mathematical, that moment, by virtue of this very postulate, it implicitly recognized that there is that in reality which cannot enter into its conceptual net, and that, therefore, there must be other symbolic forms in which these aspects alone can be expressed. From one point of view it is immaterial how this symbolic form is conceived, whether in the 'organic' terms of a Bergson or a Whitehead, or in terms of the more developed concept of personality, in either case the principle is the same—after exhausting the physical methods they again return to the inmost recesses of consciousness. If we are disposed to shy from the notion of consciousness, let us return to those value categories of the categorial scheme which, for lack of a better term, we call spiritual. In the general categorial scheme the 'lower' or physical categories may be primary for 'explanation,' but the higher or spiritual are necessary for 'understanding.' In other words, all postulate, explicitly or implicitly, the primacy of the axiological for metaphysics, the postulate which, as we have seen, underlies the entire European tradition.

B

Closely connected with this issue is the question of what is called the 'value of science.' The critics of this new epistemology of science, having identified it with 'idealism,' charge it with the devaluation of science. These 'realistic' critics are found among the representatives of both science and religion, but it is the latter that we shall here have chiefly in mind.[1]

It is recognized that the scientists of the last century tended to claim too high an ontological status for their concepts—as representing literal copies of objective reality. Their present-day successors, however, so we are told, often go to the other extreme, and it is now the task of the philosopher to save them from themselves. It is scarcely surprising, however, that scientists have not been unduly enthusiastic in welcoming these efforts towards their own salvation. For the value of science, they are likely to think, can best be determined by those who understand the ends and purposes for which its method has been developed. Nevertheless, there is a real issue here and one the clarification of which is important for our entire argument.

The question of the value of science, like that of the value of religion, or of any other human activity, is, of course, ambiguous and for much the same reasons. The value of science in a practical reference is beyond dispute on any view of its nature. However we may be disposed to feel towards the uses to which the techniques of science have been put, whether beneficent or maleficent, they certainly accomplish their purposes and, humanly speaking, their value in this sense is beyond question. The question here, as elsewhere, is the relation of this value in a practical reference to value in a theoretical reference. It is often argued that to have value in this first sense concepts must correspond absolutely to that to which they refer, and therefore be literally

[1] See Fulton J. Sheen, *Philosophy of Science*, chapter iv.

true. There seems to be little ground for such an inference. For manipulation and control certainly no such literal truth is required, and for the correlation of phenomena the ontological status of our concepts is irrelevant. Moreover, since the function of the scientific concept is not to copy reality but to symbolize it, its truth value no more requires absolute correspondence or literal truth than in any other sphere of human truth. Indeed it can be shown that while the truth notion in science, as elsewhere, starts with the notion of correspondence, more and more science finds it necessary to abandon it for other conceptions.[1]

In so far as the specific issue is concerned, that the new epistemology of science is idealistic and, as such devalues science, the inference is wholly unwarranted. Even if it were idealistic it would not affect the value of science in a practical reference—the idealist may and does make discoveries and invent techniques no less than the realist. But it does not devalue science in a theoretical reference, for any 'concessions to idealism' this epistemology finds itself forced to make do not constitute a denial of a transcendent object to which its concepts refer—idealism no less than realism postulates an antecedent reality—it merely asserts that reality is given as a problem to be solved and can only be constructed by symbols. It merely asserts that truth in science, like truth everywhere, is human truth, and that the concepts of science, while adequate for its purposes, are not absolute. Far from constituting a devaluation of science, this new epistemology only helps us to value it more truly. The surest way to devalue any form of human knowledge is to claim for it objectives which in the nature of the case it cannot realize. What some would call the failure of science arises from just such claims. True science, however, is modest and makes no such claims, and it is this modesty that makes it powerful.

[1] See on this point my article, 'The Dialectic of Meaning and Truth,' *Philosophy and Phenomenological Research*, Vol. IV, No. 3, especially pp. 391-4.

V

What Science Has to Say About Man: Scientific Anthropology.
Nature and Human Nature

A

The pronouncements of science significant for religion comprise what it has to say about man and his relation to the ground of things. They include the historical and anthropological, the cosmological and the metaphysical, corresponding to the pronouncements of religion already discussed. The cosmological and ontological have, to be sure, the more ultimate significance, but it is with man that religion is primarily concerned and it is Christian anthropology, as it has been called, which has been most significant in the culture of the western world and which, apparently, comes into most violent conflict with what modern science seems to say about man. It is to this issue, therefore, that we must first direct our thought.

So far as the explicit statements of religion and science on man are concerned, the conflict between science and religion here seems to be at its height, a fact which was exemplified by the questionnaire some decades ago on the religious beliefs of men of science. It was found, significantly enough, that, whereas many representatives of the physical sciences retained their belief in God (although by many he was conceived as impersonal) it was the representatives of the social sciences, especially the anthropologists and the psychologists, who disavowed such belief.[1] Nor was one left in doubt as to the chief reasons for this difference. For these sciences man is, it would seem, simply not what he is for religion. Viewed as man inevitably must be in the light of their premises, it seems almost ludicrous that to him should be applied such phrases as 'son of God' and as 'little lower than the angels'; and still more ludicrous that, being what he is, God, if there be one, should be mindful of him. Whereas for Christian theology man is a son of God, certainly for a naturalistic anthropology, based on the hypothesis of naturalistic evolution, he seems, at least, to be merely a high-grade simian.

[1] J. H. Leuba, *The Belief in God and Immortality: A Psychological, Anthropological and Statistical Study.*

The question of what science really says about man is, however one of extraordinary difficulty. The nearer science comes to man, the more ambiguous its pronouncements become and the more varied and uncertain its theories. Actually, there is, as Heidegger maintains, no such thing as a science of anthropology, but merely a loose collection of so-called 'sciences the only unity of which is in the name.'[1] There is, however, one aspect of the sciences of man which places our problem in the clearest possible light. Whatever unity there may be in these sciences arises, apparently, out of the postulate of biological evolution which constitutes the thread, however tenuous, upon which they are all strung. The dogma of the unity of scientific method is presupposed. The categories of life mind and value (spirit) although they correspond to different aspects of reality and require different languages for their complete expression, are nevertheless only partly independent of the basal physical categories. It is for this reason that, despite protests and counter-movements, the main trend of evolutionary theory has, on the whole, been towards 'reductionism' and, whatever they may say to the contrary, the so-called anthropological sciences have found themselves driven along the same path.

B

The part of anthropological science in which these methodological issues can be most clearly seen is naturally that of psychology; it is the part also in which the conflict between religious and scientific anthropology is apparently most intense. For the essential of the former is that 'man became a living soul;' the essential thesis of the latter is that the soul belongs to the realm of pre-scientific myth. The oft-quoted saying, that psychology first lost its soul, then its mind, and finally lost consciousness, puts in epigrammatic form the inevitable trend in psychology as a 'science.'

It seems obvious that if concepts to be scientific must be resolvable into the physical and mathematical, what it is science

[1] Martin Heidegger, *Kant und Das Problem der Metaphysik*, p. 199. No period, he tells us, in human history has known so many things about man, ethnology, anthropology, psychology. But also no period has known less what man is. In no time has man become so problematical to himself as in the present. This is the source of his own demand, as well as that of many in the present period, for a 'philosophical anthropology.'

must of necessity say about the mind and soul of man. A modern psychologist, while admitting, perhaps that there is more to man than can be expressed in his language, is nevertheless inclined to insist that progress in explanation, in his sense of the word, has come only by the exclusion of non-physical postulates. Whether he extrudes the soul altogether, or reduces it to subconscious dispositions, however conceived, he must inevitably translate all those characters and values which make man what he is for morals and religion, into a wholly different language, one in which, as we have seen, the idioms of morality and religion have no meaning. If this is so, if this is what science really says about man, then scientific and religious anthropology are indeed wholly incompatible.

'Modern psychology,' so Julian Huxley tells us, 'is giving us an entirely new insight into the phenomena we have been used to describing under the names of revelation, conversion, grace, salvation, demoniac possession, miracles of healing, prophecy, communion with the divine and many others. It is showing us that the phenomena thus described, though perfectly definite facts of experience, need not be interpreted in the traditional way. They do not require us to postulate supernatural beings outside ourselves as their cause; they can be accounted for by the natural workings of the individual mind. But—and an important but—this need not diminish the value of the phenomena.'[1] This amiable illusion can maintain itself only with the greatest difficulty and is already rapidly disappearing. Much truer to the facts is the view of Nicolai Hartmann that naturalistic interpretations of moral phenomena are 'throughout a hopeless undertaking.' Such interpretations 'tend to stultify the person himself.'[2]

I think there can be little question that this is so. And if this is true of moral phenomena it is a fortiori true of religious. If science does tell us that revelation, conversion, grace and salvation are simply names for 'natural workings of the mind,' whether conceived in terms of subconscious or non-conscious dispositions, then indeed are these pronouncements of science incompatible with religion. But they are also incompatible with those of morality or any other activity of the human spirit—

[1] *Religion Without Revelation*, pp. 253 ff.
[2] *Ethics*, Vol. III, p. 175.

even that of science itself. There are theories of man which make not only honour and beauty but also intelligence impossible in any genuine sense. It is doubtless true that 'such explanations do not affect the facts,' but they can denature them and take all the meaning out of them. But it is just as certain, I think, that science, rightly understood, does not say these things at all. If it did, it would stultify its own nature and method and, in doing so, would refute itself out of its own mouth. It is this that we have now to make clear.

C

No one would, I suppose, question the 'facts'—in so far as they are facts—upon which the evolutionary theory rests. That 'speaking and reasoning man did evolve by natural processes from anthropoid ancestors, is,' so it is said, 'not seriously disputed even by those whose deepest sympathies are opposed to the admission.' In a sense this is true. No one would dispute the proposition that between these same anthropoid ancestors and the speaking and reasoning man of to-day successive stages may be interpolated. But that is not the issue; the issue is what these facts really say—what 'evolution' in this sense means. It is admitted that 'mystery still surrounds the manner of this evolution'— and it indubitably does—and we are further told that, because of this mystery, there still remains 'the refuge of ignorance' to which the transcendentalists, with their belief in souls, can always repair. But, as I should insist, it is not to ignorance and mystery that the transcendentalist appeals, but to critical science itself. Fully conscious of the limits of his own method, the critical scientist tells us quite frankly that he will admit only naturalistic postulates, but the fact that he excludes all others does not for a moment imply, as he would be the first to admit, that such postulates may not be necessary for a full understanding of both life and mind. True science does not tell us that anything which cannot be caught in the conceptual net of its evolutionary concepts does not therefore exist.

The philosophical theologian has constantly insisted—and in this he is surely right—that the evolutionary theory is wholly compatible with the postulates of religion so long as it is not applied to the soul. With this no scientist should quarrel, for souls are not objects in his universe of discourse at all, but he would scarcely say that, because this is so, there are no universes of discourse in which they not only have meaning but are themselves the very conditions of meaningful discourse. Few critical scientists, even in anthropology—although they are, alas, much less critical than their fellows in physics—would assert that what the so-called humanities tell us about man is wholly meaningless and without truth, and yet they constantly speak about 'souls' and can, as we shall see, scarcely speak intelligibly at all without using that notion or its equivalent.[1] It is for this reason that, as we shall see, what the humanities tell us is in certain respects more significant than what science has to say. In sum, it is the new conception of the limits of science, which science itself has implicitly accepted as the results of the development of its own method, which makes its postulates compatible with those of religion.

The apologist for man—the true humanist, whether religious or not—is tempted to say that these modern anthropological sciences tell their little truths in the interest of a great lie, and, like Bernard Shaw, in the preface to *Back to Methuselah*, to hurl this great lie back into their teeth. One can sympathize with the Shavian passion—and there are indeed those who merit this lie direct—but science, properly understood, does not, I believe, tell this great lie. The lie which it is supposed to tell— and if told it would be indeed a monstrous one—is that man, with all the attributes which make him man—his ideals of honour, beauty and intelligence—are the products of the merely irrational processes of natural selection and the struggle for existence, and their sole value is their survival value. This lie, I believe, true science has never told. I should not want to say that Shaw was merely tilting at windmills, for what he attacked with such superlative vigour is a conception of man which has had far-reaching influence on the entire social and political culture of our time, but rather that, in attacking it, he has not attacked science as such, but rather those who, not understanding what science rightly and truly says, make it say what it never taught.

[1] On this point see Chapter xi, pp. 403 ff.

VI

The Cosmological Pronouncements of Science. What Science Has to Say About the 'World'

A

The theme of cosmology is, as we have seen, the basis of all religions, and the 'story' of the beginning and end of all things cannot, in the nature of the case, be unaffected by what the cosmological pronouncements of science say, or seem to say. The scientific theories which develop this theme are those of cosmic evolution and cosmic devolution, and what these theories say explicitly or implicitly has long been one of the chief issues of the philosophy of science. A theory of cosmic evolution which should derive value from the non-valuable—the essence of naturalism and atheism—is of course inimical to religion. So also is a conception of cosmic devolution, of a degradation or running down of the universe, which involves, so to speak, a dissipation of values as well as of energy. It is of the utmost importance, therefore, for religion to know just what science really says, if indeed it says anything at all, on these questions of ultimate origination and ultimate destiny.

B

It has long been recognized that of all the 'generalizations' of science which ultimately affect the dogmas of religion that of evolution is the most significant. Evolution—in the limited sense of biological evolution, and, in so far as the organic is the basis of mind, mental evolution—has had, of course, a tremendous effect upon our view of man and his relation to the ground of things. It is, however, when the notion is extended symbolically and metempirically to the cosmos as a whole that the issues become clearest, for it tells us a 'story' of the universe which seems to many a 'more likely and even more noble one' than that which religion has told. Evolution, rather than creation—evolution as a process of gradual self-creation, so to speak—seems the cosmic myth which appeals to the dramatic sense, no less than the intelligence of the present. It is of importance, therefore, to know what evolution in this sense 'really says.'

357

Now the so-called 'facts' of cosmic evolution are, I suppose, no more questionable than those of biological evolution. That the present state of the physical universe is the outcome of 'natural' processes of 'evolution' or development is again not seriously disputed, even by those whose deepest sympathies might conceivably be opposed to the admission, certainly not by any responsible religious philosopher. Whatever differences of opinion there may be as to the factors in this evolution, the notion itself—of a cosmic evolution from star dust to worlds—is accepted in principle by all astronomical physicists. The question is, then, not of the facts, but what the facts really say. Surely they are made to say, by popular science at least, a great deal more than they actually do when properly understood. For evolution here, even more obviously than in the limited sphere of the biological and anthropological, is simply our name for successive phenomena in the time process and the factors of evolution simply concepts for the correlation of these phenomena. Here empirical verification is in principle at least possible. But if we go beyond these 'facts' to some picture of 'evolution of the whole,' no matter what our picture may be, we have entered into the realm of the metempirical where such verification is not possible. From this point of view it is immaterial what our fables are—whether we picture an automatic process in which by some magic something is created out of nothing, or a creative evolution in which an *élan vital* struggles against matter—in every case the situation is the same. Our language becomes dramatic and our pictures take on the character of cosmic myth. I am, of course, far from saying that men should not think and speak in this way. I am inclined to think that 'drama is a cosmic category' also and that even our view of nature depends ultimately upon the dramatic for its rationality and intelligibility. I am merely saying that when we have recourse to such conceptions we are no longer speaking the language of science, and the 'understanding' which such concepts seem to give us is not the intelligibility of science. Science has explicitly and deliberately confined itself to a notion of intelligibility which 'consists exclusively in establishing rational relations between phenomena'; this does not, however, exclude other concepts of intelligibility but, as we have seen, actually presupposes them.

It is for these reasons that the philosophical theologian has constantly insisted that evolution, as a scientific theory, does not exclude creation, and when we see what this theory really is and says, we see that he is right. When he tells us that evolution describes the method of creation, he is really saying that the formulas of evolution are descriptions of processes, whether biological or cosmic, not ultimate explanations. They have to do with proximate, not ultimate, origination. With the scientist who says he is not interested in such questions the theologian should have no quarrel, for he has said what, as a scientist, he should have said. But the scientist is also a man, and the theologian may well doubt whether as a man he can so easily disclaim such interest. He might point out too, that if he understands what the dogma of creation really says and what it involves, it is at least conceivable that he will find the notion, not only more noble but in the end more intelligible, than the cosmic myths with which men would supplant it—at least if he understands what intelligibility in this context means. He will, of course, separate the category of creation from the mythical language in which it has inevitably found expression, but having once come to understand the character of cosmic myths in science he will find no difficulty with the same language when employed in religion.[1]

The second great cosmological principle which has significance for religion is the pronouncement about the physical universe that it is 'running down,' or the application of the principle of increasing entropy to the physical whole called the universe. It would be impossible to exaggerate the effect which this idea has had upon the human spirit and to be deaf to the consequent Cassandra cries which self-appointed prophets of science have felt it their duty to emit. But whether it has or has not this tremendous significance all depends upon what science really says at this point.

As in the case of the other great cosmic generalization of science, namely, cosmic evolution, there is here also, of course, a basis of fact—facts which nobody disputes. There is the second law of thermodynamics, the law of increasing entropy, and this law is empirically verifiable. But what does this law say? What

[1] For a fuller discussion of this entire problem see Chapter ix of my book, *The Intelligible World*, entitled 'Intelligible Evolution.'

it does say explicitly—and that alone is empirically verifiable—
is that the law holds for finite conservative systems with which
we may experiment. Its extension to the whole of the physical
universe is neither explicitly stated nor is it a necessary implication of its verifiable statements. The warning given by Lotze
long ago, against 'crediting as a prophetic announcement with
regard to the future those ingenious calculations which draw
conclusions as to the final state of the world from our experimental knowledge of the economy of heat,' is still constantly
repeated by responsible physicists themselves. In giving us this
warning they are, I think, wholly right. The facts of science, as
they actually are, do not, I believe, warrant any such conclusions about the final state of the world and such prophetic
announcements with regard to the future. At least they are not
a necessary part of science in the sense that they are implicit
in its verifiable propositions.

The extension of the notion of increasing entropy symbolically to the physical universe as a whole, like all such extensions
to the metempirical, has in it the undeniable character of a
cosmic myth. The imagery of the universe running down is a
fable with which we deck our mathematical equations. But
even if such an extension were possible, I do not think that the
consequences for religion would be what many people seem to
think they are. Miss Stebbing thinks that 'no arguments
favourable to Christian beliefs can be drawn, from the law of
entropy either with regard to the beginning of the world or with
regard to its gradual and final degeneration into a condition of
thermodynamical equilibrium.'[1] With this I should, of course,
agree. She also seems to hold that no arguments inimical to
Christian belief can be drawn. She speaks of Professor Millikan's
faith in the Christian religion as 'robust' and, in her opinion
rightly, 'as independent of the outcome of physical speculations.'[1] With this I should also agree. I too admire this robust
faith, I too hold that religion is independent of physical
speculations, but for significantly different reasons. It is not that
faith can be detached from all cosmology but rather that the
pronouncements of science are, when properly interpreted and
evaluated, not inimical to the cosmological pronouncements
of religion. In this specific case it is not because Christian

[1] *Op. cit.*, p. 259 f.

eschatology is concerned only with things above and can therefore contemplate with equanimity the dissolution of the physical
universe, but rather that the dissolution of this universe, which
is, after all, merely physical speculation, does not involve the
dissolution of the universe in the sense of the philosopher.
'There is,' as Simmel, with insight, has said, 'no entropy of
being.'

C

There is in many quarters a curious lack of understanding of
the cosmological pronouncements of science, both as to what
they actually say and as to their status in science. Not only may
they be made to say, as we have seen, a great deal more than
they really say and thus, unwittingly perhaps, made to bear
false witness, but their true nature, as propositions about the
cosmos as a whole, is seriously misconceived.

Of the second law of thermodynamics Bergson has said that
it is the most metaphysical of all the laws of science because it is
historical, but it becomes doubly metaphysical, so to speak,when
it is applied symbolically to the cosmos, for then it purports to
be a history of the whole—and as such is empirically unverifiable as all metaphysical propositions are. But this is equally
true of cosmic evolution. Both are and must be meta-physical
in the sense of the physico-mathematical method of science.
This is true even when we speak of the cosmos in the sense of the
'universe' of physics; it is *a fortiori* true when we understand by
the universe the *omnitudo realitatis*, including life, mind and values.
Neither of ultimate origination nor of ultimate destiny can
science say anything without stultification of the very method
with which it has identified itself.

As the humanist is tempted to say of anthropological science
that it tells its little truths in the interest of a great lie, so the
philosopher may be tempted to say the same of physical science.
When it tells us, or seems to tell us, that the cosmos, including
life and mind, has come from nothing and will end in nothing
this is the great lie in the interest of which it tells its little truths.
But true science, I believe, has never told this great lie, and is
careful not to tell it, for if it did it would stultify its entire
nature and method. It has won its great triumphs by its own
voluntary self-limitation. So long as it remains in the world of
its own choice it says many important things, but actually it

361

does not say much that it is often made to say, and which is supposed to be so significant for our views of first and last things. It is true that some representatives of science have wished to speak with authority in their own field and at the same time with the authority of science on first and last things. But this is a system of double book-keeping which cannot be allowed. Science cannot really have it both ways. It cannot claim all the values of exactness and rigour which come from the extrusion of all 'anthropomorphic' categories and at the same time claim all the meaningfulness which comes from the use of them. It cannot claim all the values which come from a purely operational and phenomenal view of science and at the same time make propositions about the cosmos which, in the nature of the case, are not subject to operational and phenomenal verification. It cannot serve God and mammon, leaving it for science itself to decide, of course, which it will call God and which mammon.

VII

The Ontological Pronouncements of Science: What Science Has to Say About Ultimate Reality

A

The cosmological pronouncements of science, being met-empirical in their reference, are also *ipso facto*, implicitly metaphysical, and as such come into relations with similar pronouncements of religion. But there are other supposed ontological pronouncements which have a special bearing upon the relation of science to religion. What science has to say on the ultimate status of natural law and regarding the nature of matter has, as we have seen, implications which have had great influence on certain modern physicists, leading them to some form of 'idealism' and, since idealism is supposed to be in some way especially congenial to religion, affecting significantly their views on religion. It may be denied that science has such implications. It is doubtless true that, as E. A. Milne tells us, 'strictly speaking, physics has no philosophy; it has method.'[1]

---

[1] E. A. Milne, F.R.S., 'Some Points in the Philosophy of Physics,' an address before the British Institute of Philosophy and published in *Philosophy*, Vol. IX, No. 33.

But if from this very method, and the new epistemology to which reflections upon the method have given rise, there have actually resulted changes in our views regarding the status of natural law and the nature of matter, it seems scarcely possible that they should be without some implications, however indirect, for these more ultimate issues. If the scientist does not draw certain inferences, *qua* scientist, he will scarcely escape them as a man and as a rational being. There are those who are willing to be eunuched for the kingdom of Heaven, but few, I suppose, for the kingdom of science. In any case it is generally assumed that science has something to say, at least implicitly, on these points, and it is important to determine what it is, if anything, that it really says.

B

For nineteenth-century science it was in the main assumed that one of the things science most surely says is that everything is determined—that the 'reign of law is absolute.' It is now maintained, by many scientists at least, that this is not so, and that, if its implications are read aright, science says rather that reality, in so far at least as its microscopic character is concerned, is characterized by a fundamental indeterminancy. Many say, therefore, that 'nature is simply not completely determined,' meaning by nature the whole of reality as conceived by the physicist. Leaving out of consideration for the moment the question of the consequences of this statement, if it is true, let us first see whether science really says either of these things, whether, with the dogmatism of nineteenth-century science, it says all is determined or whether, with the perhaps equal dogmatism of some modern writers, it says nature is simply not completely determined. The specific issue is, of course, the Heisenberg principle and the problem of its interpretation. Into this much-debated question I shall not go in detail but merely try to discover, if possible, what it really says and what bearing it may possibly have on the present issue.

The important point in this context is to distinguish between what it actually says explicitly and what it is often supposed to say implicitly. All that it asserts explicitly—and many physicists are loud in insisting upon this point—is a 'principle of inaccuracy.' It merely tells us that it is not possible by observation to compute the changes in an electron. One may choose either to determine the place of the flying electron or ascertain its speed with precision, but there can be no experiment which will fix the location and velocity at the same time and with maximum accuracy. But what does this peculiar coupling of inaccuracies mean? What, if any, are its metaphysical implications? Surely it is a gross epistemological misunderstanding to suppose that the facts expressed in the principle of inaccuracy even imply, still less verify, a metaphysical principle of indeterminancy. The latter goes far beyond any facts of experience. The merely operational principle of inaccuracy does not 'prove' that reality is undetermined, for the latter is a proposition about an unlimited whole and can not in the nature of the case be verified by any accumulation of empirical facts. If then science can not tell us that all is determined, no more can it tell us, so long as it remains science, that it is undetermined. The status of natural law is different from that conceived by either principle.

It is sometimes argued that, even if our view of the status of natural law in the cosmos as a whole is thus challenged, this does not in the least affect the principle of determinism as applied to the macrocosm and, therefore, to man and all his works which are part of it. But surely this involves a grave epistemological misunderstanding also. It is true that, while denying the application of Newtonian physics, with its implied mechanism, to the world of the inconceivably small, science does hold that so far as we know, it still applies to the world of moderate dimensions or the macrocosm. But even so, it holds only in the sphere of the physical phenomena for the explanation of which the principle was postulated, and if it is extended to the sphere of life and mind—to the unlimited whole of the macrocosm—it becomes a meta-physical pronouncement in the nature of the case unverifiable empirically. This many thinkers of a high order, including James and Bergson, have fully seen. Both tell us, in their different ways, that science does not find man determined, but postulates that he is and then interests itself only in those aspects of human behaviour that can apparently be caught in its deterministic net. In any case—and this is my sole point here—neither determinism nor indeterminism may be asserted of the cosmos as a whole—whether of the macrocosm or the microcosm—as something which science *really says*. If we make such assertions we have passed beyond the range of science and scientific method.

But how, it may well be asked, do issues such as these affect in the slightest degree the problems of religion and science? Certainly, as it has been said, 'we can no more infer the existence of God from the fact that the electrons do not obey mathematical laws than we could infer His existence from the fact that they do.' This is undoubtedly true. Certainly the old argument that from the reign of law we can infer a Divine law-giver no longer carries conviction, for it presupposes a conception of law that no longer holds in science. Does it carry any more conviction to argue that because the cosmos in its microcosmic character is apparently 'lawless,' therefore the ground of the world is God? Surely not. But that is just the point I am making. In so far as science speaks unambiguously it can not be called upon to witness either for the dogmatic determinism and mechanism of the nineteenth century or for the equally dogmatic indeterminism of the twentieth. But precisely this negative conclusion is not without its significance for religion, for in the universe of discourse about first and last things negations are often as significant as affirmations. In sum then, our view of the status of natural law has been changed by natural science but that change is such as to enable us to see that the old contrast between determinism and indeterminism has become a thing of the past.

C

If our changed view of the nature and status of natural law in science has tended, as I believe rightly, to affect men's views of the relation of science to religion and philosophy, still more has our changed view of the nature of matter.

Since Berkeley, to go back no further in the history of western philosophy, it has been assumed in many quarters that the problem of the status of matter is fundamental for a religious philosophy, and in this respect metaphysical 'idealism' is more congenial to religion than any other position. Berkeley, whose main problem was, after all, the issues between the science and the religion of his time, seemed to have believed that if the 'matter' of the physical science could be shown to be but our name for the coherence of sense data—if this thing, matter, were, so to speak, not an object of perception but a construction

365

of the mind—the way would be open for a theory of direct intercourse with God or Spirit and the grounds for materialism and atheism would be removed. The good Bishop was an apologist for religion and that was the reason he used all his wit and subtlety to show that it is 'plainly repugnant to reason' that matter should exist independently of its being perceived and that 'what is said of the absolute existence of unthinking things is perfectly unintelligible.'

Berkeley's argument—and the still more subtle arguments of Kant—had little effect upon the rank and file of the scientists of the nineteenth century. 'When Berkeley said there was no matter, 'twas no matter what he said'—at least for them—and the same held true for the Kantian conception of matter as ideal construction. It was assumed, more or less without question, that the constituents of the physical world—the molecules, the atoms, or what not, are literally existent as represented—in more philosophical terms have absolute ontological validity. The new scientific epistemology, with its necessary 'concessions to idealism,' has, however, changed the situation—sufficiently, at least, to raise the question whether, as it seemed to Berkeley and other philosophical idealists, our view of the nature of matter does not actually have profound implications for religion and theology.

This line of reasoning comes out clearly in the thinking of many physicists. Because of the character of our physical concepts the world to which they refer must surely be of the 'stuff of our own consciousness.' Indeed some would go so far as to say with Eddington that idealism 'is not merely a philosophical doctrine to which intellectual assent might be given but has become part of the scientific attitude of the day, illustrated in the current scheme of physics.' 'We have found,' he writes more poetically, 'strange footprints on the shores of the unknown. We have devised profound theories, one after the other, to account for their origin. At last we have succeeded in reconstructing the creature that made the footprint. And lo! it is our own.'[1]

It is scarcely to be wondered at that, whether rightly or wrongly, many physicists have, like Jeans, felt themselves 'inclined to the idealistic theory that consciousness is fundamental

[1] *Space, Time and Gravitation*, pp. 200–1.

and that the material universe is derivative from consciousness,' or like Schrödinger, have insisted that 'consciousness can not be accounted for in physical terms, for consciousness is absolutely fundamental.' Nor is it surprising that, having gone thus far, they should often feel justified in taking a further step in arguing that since consciousness is thus fundamental, it constitutes the ground of things, and that to this Great Consciousness they should, as men have often done, give the name of God. It is indeed not to be wondered at that men should think thus, but it does not follow that so to think is a necessary inference from science. Certain concessions to idealism the modern scientific epistemology does indeed make necessary; the question is whether these concessions involve the step to metaphysical idealism. I do not think that they do, and it is rather important, I believe, in the interests of both religion and science, that the reasons for this should be made clear.

Against such idealistic inferences it may be contended—and is constantly maintained—that 'natural science must always remain materialistic in the sense that it must always reject explanations of physical phenomena in terms of disembodied spirits.' This is undoubtedly a naïve way of speaking, but it expresses a truth implied in the entire development of modern scientific method and one which we shall do well to consider. It is quite true that, if our concepts, to be scientific, must be resolvable into the physical and the mathematical, certainly science 'remains materialistic' in this sense. The *verae causae* of science do not include spirits, whether embodied or disembodied; and of course none of the physicists mentioned would, in making consciousness fundamental, suppose that they did. But it is true —and this is the point I am making—that if men do argue for idealism in the above fashion, the inferences can no longer be called scientific and can not be viewed as extensions of the scientific method. If, however, science, as science, cannot be made to witness for idealism, it does not at all follow that when its concessions to idealism are duly weighed they are not of significance for the philosophy of religion. For if the epistemology of modern science constitutes a refutation of dogmatic mechanism and determinism, just as surely does it constitute a refutation of dogmatic materialism. Even this, it is true, is sometimes challenged. One philosopher has said that 'the popular notion that materialism has been refuted by the theory that the atoms are composed of electrons is fatuous.' Such a notion is doubtless fatuous, but if it is popular it is certainly not one held by any critical physicist or responsible philosopher. What these really hold is that the electron theory and other developments of modern physics have so changed our conception of matter as to make many of the old problems meaningless and, as Miss Stebbing has said, 'the old contrast of materialism and idealism a thing of the past.'

But here again it may be asked, what, after all, has all this to do with the fundamental issues of religion? Above all, with the very blunt question, Does God exist? Surely we can no more infer the existence of God as creator from the fact that the atoms and electrons are 'manufactured articles' than we can infer His existence from the fact that they are not. To the modern scientific mind they indeed bear all the marks of being manufactured articles, but it is to man rather than to God that their making is ascribed. The strange footprints on the shores of the unknown unquestionably reveal a being who has walked there, but are they God's footprints, as Newton thought, or are they our own? It does indeed appear that *if* there is a God he *is* more like a great thought than a great machine. If there is a God doubtless he is a mathematician among other things, for the fullness of being we call God must include the abstract ideas of mathematics, but from a mathematical picture of the universe surely the God of religion cannot be directly inferred. On this there can be, I think, no doubt. It is enough that the new epistemology of science has challenged the great lies which it was often made to tell in the nineteenth century. Science no longer tells us the great lie of absolute determinism. Nor does it tell us that even greater lie, that 'all is matter and motion, the rest is moonshine.' It is even at great pains to disavow such nonsense. For it knows full well that should it say so, either explicitly or implicitly, it would stultify its own nature as physico-mathematical method, and condemn itself out of its own mouth. It knows full well that to say these things is the veriest dogmatism, in violation of the very principles of verifiability with which as science, it has iden- tified itself. Even more, it knows full well that to transfer notions appropriate to the cosmos of physics to the whole of reality, or the fullness of being, is a fallacy so egregious that, since the critical philosophy of Kant, none but the most naïve have been guilty of it. In sum, to quote the words of Tolstoy on this point, 'the true science, which knows its own place and therefore its subject, is modest and therefore powerful, and has never spoken in this way.'[1]

VIII

The 'Scientific Concept of Nature.' Nature and the Supernatural

A

It is then, what 'true science,' the science that 'knows its place,' really says, which has been the burden of this chapter. The conclusions reached may, perhaps, best be summed up under the notion of 'the scientific concept of nature.' It is of nature and of the 'nature of things' that science speaks, including human nature in so far as this part of nature is at all apprehendable in the categories of science, or expressible in the physical-mathematical idiom in which, in the last analysis, science alone can speak.

It seems obvious that if science is what it claims to be, there are many things about which it cannot speak at all. It seems to have been one of the main misunderstandings of the nineteenth century that scientific method is applicable to everything. It seems equally clear that in so far as we form a concept of nature that shall be 'scientific,' it must exclude many things. If science is really a method and not a philosophy its concept of nature must, in the last analysis be determined by its method. If in applying this method it abstracts from aspects of reality which are significantly there, it follows that its concept of nature can not be identical with the *omnitudo realitatis* of philosophy.

In his *The Concept of Nature* Whitehead rightly tells us, 'that the homogeneity of thought about nature excludes any reference to values,' but he also tells us, with equal truth, that 'these values of nature are the clue to any metaphysical synthesis.' The 'homogeneity of thought' of which he speaks is precisely that unity of science which springs out of its method of

[1] Leo Tolstoy, *On Life*, translated and edited by Leo Wiener, p. 252.

which we have already spoken—that homogeneity, without which science is not science. But it does not at all follow that the values are not there, nor that their presence, however embarassing for science, is not the clue to metaphysical synthesis, the task to which Whitehead applied himself in his later works. Whether his particular synthesis is or is not wholly satisfactory, it cannot be doubted that he has grasped the problem and contributed much to its solution. In the world there are both facts and values and it is precisely the task of metaphysics to interpret the world thus constituted as a unity.

It is often denied that the homogeneity of scientific method, and therefore of its thought about nature, does exclude values. But such denial surely rests upon a misunderstanding both of values themselves and of explanation as understood by science. For what are values when science speaks of them? And what must they be in order to be conformable to scientific method? In order that they may be thus conformable they must, as we have seen, be translated into terms that denature them, just as they 'stultify the person' who apprehends and acknowledges them. No one would for a moment suppose that the categories of physics and chemistry are of a character adequately to express the nature of value. He would be bold indeed who claimed that the nature of human good can be deduced from the facts of nature in this sense. It is only when we come to the biological sciences, and the anthropological as related to them, that such claims are even plausible. But what conception of human good could possibly be related to biological concepts of value? Surely the only conceptions possible are those of adaptation and survival—sustenance for as long as possible for as great numbers as possible. But unless we assume that mere persistence in being, mere biological life, is itself an absolute value, surely there is no possibility of deducing our human values, moral and aesthetic, from this wholly amoral concept of nature. I do not deny, of course, that there are goods, human and subhuman, which may be said to be thus deducible from nature. I am merely saying that there are some that are not and that it is these by which man must ultimately live if he is to be man. I should also say that even the natural values are instrumental and, to be themselves ultimately significant, must presuppose the intrinsic, non-natural values of honour, beauty and intelligence—and that, if separated from these, they lose half if not all their value.[1]

I think we must conclude then that the scientific concept of nature does exclude reference to values when the nature of values is properly understood. But we are driven, it seems to me, to a further conclusion. If these values, thus excluded, are the clue to metaphysical synthesis, they must be there in some sense. Indeed we are explicitly told that they *are* there—'even the mechanist and materialist must acknowledge them.' But if they are there—if the ideals of honour, beauty and intelligence, which make man what he is, are a part of reality—then there is a realm of being which can no longer be called merely natural. For if, as some would wish to do, we include in nature all that is, not only the starry heavens above but the moral law within; not only the moral law but that which even some naturalistic philosophers would wish to include, even the quality of deity itself—then we may well ask with Kemp Smith, 'is not nature when so conceived really revealing herself as Super-Nature, and can she be synoptically envisaged save as so conceived?'[2] To me an affirmative answer to this question is inescapable.

There is, then, I should be disposed to maintain—and it is an important part of my entire argument—a sense in which a scientific concept of nature, if it is really scientific, presupposes the supernatural. Not, to be sure, in the degraded forms which both science and religion find it necessary to repudiate, but in the philosophical sense here employed. It is true that in reply to this many of the so-called 'new naturalists' are wont to say, 'but I mean by nature simply all that is'; but surely, when so defined, the concept becomes meaningless, for it is only through contrast that the term gets any significance. One may call nature what he will—there is no law against such loose speaking —but certainly one cannot call this the scientific concept of nature. The point I am making is, I believe, of considerable importance, for it brings to light a fundamental ambiguity in the concept of nature which certain modern forms of naturalism have exploited 'to the limit.' On the one hand, naturalism is

---

[1] The relation of these two concepts of value will be further discussed in Chapter xi, pp. 413 f.

[2] *Prologomena to an Idealist Theory of Knowledge,* p. 231 ff.

defined in terms of scientific method and thus is secured all the prestige which comes from such identification. On the other hand, when these new naturalists wish to display their humanity and to prove that naturalism is friendly to all forms of the human spirit, sometimes even including religion itself, they soft-pedal if indeed they do not abandon, this scientific concept of nature, and include in their *omnitudo realitatis* all those things which such a concept, by its very nature, excludes. Here we have that 'double talk', that double book-keeping which to all critical minds must appear, if not downright disingenuous, at least fatal to the formulation of any adequate philosophy.[1]

True science does not deny the supernatural. It tells us many great truths but it does not tell them in the interest of this great lie. In including in its method only those things resolvable into the sensible and the measurable it does not deny things not thus resolvable. By the same token, when it forms its concept of nature, as determined by this homogeneity of method, it does not deny that which is beyond nature in this sense. The meaning of things in space and time, it knows well, lies outside space and time. Whether this meaning can be known, by our reason or only by a mystical experience which transcends reason, is of course a question which has exercised the minds of men from the beginning and will doubtless continue to do so. But I am very sure that true science will never say that this meaning is not there or that it can never be known.

A real understanding of the scientific concept of nature forbids us then to deny that which is beyond nature and refuses to allow the complete naturalization of the human spirit. But it forbids also another position equally inimical to religion, namely the identification of natural science and its method with human reason as a whole, and therefore any attempt to found the truths of religion solely on the pronouncements of science. The false assumptions underlying this position, already indicated in the introductory chapter, have now been made wholly clear in the light of what Whitehead tells us about the scientific conception of nature. If, in so far as it is scientific, it excludes all reference to the values which are the initial datum

[1] This fundamental ambiguity runs throughout the entire length of a recent volume of essays entitled *Naturalism and the Human Spirit*, Columbia University Press, 1944, and it is upon this mainly that its appeal rests.

of religion, one may indeed wonder how any religion could be based on this concept. The nature from which men argued to God in the past was a far different thing—one in which the humblest element participated in the good, the beautiful and the true; nature, as science now conceives it, is formed by excluding these *ab initio*, and a nature thus understood could not possibly witness to God. This does not mean that these same values are not a clue to metaphysical synthesis; it is, in fact, only in such a synthesis that the limited truths of science can themselves be ultimately understood. Nor does it mean that the ultimate premise upon which all such synthesis of the past was based—namely that truth is one and indivisible, and the truth of nature and of God are one—is in any way denied. It simply means that the unity and indivisibility of truth raises problems much more ultimate and difficult than men at first think and that, therefore, we must seek other ways than these if we are to achieve any reconciliation of science and religion. This is the task of the following chapter.[1]

[1] These assumptions seem to underlie the argument of my colleague, Professor F. S. C. Northrop, found in many of his writings but developed especially in Chapter vii of his *The Meeting of East and West* entitled 'Roman Catholic Culture and Greek Science.' One can have nothing but praise for his broad view of human culture which emphasizes the necessity of aesthetic and religious components as well as the scientific. One can agree also that religion and theology are inseparable from metaphysics and that the attempt to separate them has had tragic results for both religion and culture. But I do not believe that science, as now understood and practised, can be given the primacy among the components of culture, and still less that any metaphysics upon which religion might be based could be derived exclusively, or even primarily, from the pronouncements of science. However that may be, he is surely wrong in his presentation of the scholastic doctrine of science. To say that for St. Thomas and the scholastic philosophy in general 'the traditional words of Christian doctrine are by themselves quite meaningless noises unless they are identified, or, by the accepted methods of logic, connected with the specific content of scientific knowledge,' can be true only if in science we include the 'science of God and of the blessed.' A much truer picture of the scholastic doctrine of science is presented by Fulton J. Sheen in a chapter so entitled in *The Philosophy of Science*, already referred to.

Waynesburg College Library
Waynesburg, Pa. 15370

Chapter XI

Religion and Science in Contemporary Philosophy. The 'New Understanding of the Limits of Science'

I — A

THE famous saying of Laplace, 'Sire, I have no need of that hypothesis,' is rightly taken as the classical expression of the relation of science to religion, but it is rarely realized just what is implied in this answer to Napoleon's question. When the emperor asked him if he had found God in his astronomy it was the God of religion, the Heavenly Father of prayer and praise and the Most Perfect Being of theology which he had in mind. Laplace saw clearly that the dramatic language and the symbolic form of this universe of discourse afforded no terms nor symbols which could be employed in science. This fact did not, however, for a moment, exclude the possibility that, like Newton and Kant, when as a creature and a man, he looked at the starry heavens above, he too was filled with awe and might feel himself impelled to employ a language for which he could find no use in science.

Suppose Laplace had believed himself to have found God in his astronomy. What sort of a god could 'it' be? Surely it would have been a curious god then, and still more curious in the astronomy of today. Would he not be, according to the astronomical theories men now hold, a cosmic giant blowing up an expanding universe, or watching it run down after he had blown it up? For the physicist he might be a gigantic 'cosmic atom,' for the mathematician he would doubtless appear as a mathematician; for the biologically minded there could be found for him only the curious name of the Vital Force. There is no direct way from science to God, still less from the images of science to the *imago Dei*.

Despite these obvious facts, it is still widely supposed that we should be greatly impressed when a scientist uses the name of God. In the questionnaire already referred to, on the religious beliefs of American men of science, it was found that while a significant number, pre-eminently physicists, believed in the existence of God, by far the larger number of these thought of him

RELIGION AND SCIENCE IN PHILOSOPHY

as impersonal law or force and found it difficult to think of him in any other way. No one should have been surprised. The scientist, as scientist, is not looking for God, and if by chance he should somehow stumble on something to which he felt he must give this 'name' one could be quite sure that, for the religious man, it would be a misnomer. At least no philosopher would be shocked, for this is precisely what he would expect.

B

In a public lecture at Yale, Professor Weyl, whose reflections upon the epistemology of modern science we have found enlightening, said of himself, 'I am one of those scientists who do not hesitate to use the name of God.' And it may perhaps be said that the number of scientists who do not hesitate to employ this name of names is increasing. The theologian may, however, fear the scientist bringing gifts, for it is quite conceivable that the God of the physicist is not the God of religion. Indeed, he rarely is. For the majority of scientists make God, if not in their own image, at least in the images of their favourite science. It is sometimes thought that it is to these that the modern man must go for his idea of God, and that for the dramatic language of religion and its symbolism we must substitute the abstract language and symbolisms of science. In its more childish forms the absurdity of this notion is immediately evident and we can but smile and hold our peace. But should we not also smile when God is spoken of as a mathematician or when to the Divine Being is given the name of Vital Force?

There are those who are rather contemptuous of the theologians who are so ready to welcome any sort of God the scientist is willing to allow them and who, as Mr. Russell says, 'do not seem to mind so very much what kind of God he gives them so long as he allows them to have one at all.' I am not at all sure that such contempt is merited, although I should myself be more suspicious of the scientist bearing gifts. Such over-eagerness on the part of the theologians is indeed doubtful wisdom, for it means too often a lack of understanding of the nature of science and of the real character of its hypotheses, more especially its cosmic speculations. On the other hand, this very eagerness, it must be remembered, is the inheritance of a long tradition of faith in reason. The theologian cannot believe that the scientist is less reasonable than himself and that when he drops the conventions of his craft and becomes a man, his reason will not also take him to God. I doubt whether the theologian is quite as pathetically gullible as here suggested. He would never think of going to science for his idea of God—he gets that elsewhere—but he rightly feels that any idea of God is to be welcomed however impoverished and even grotesque it may be.

But surely, it will be said, you are not denying that the scientist has a right to name the name of God or that he is justified in trying to find some image of the force that made and moves him. Far from it, for if I did I should have to deny the premises upon which this entire treatment has proceeded, namely, the rational basis of religion. I am merely saying in this special context what has been said all along, namely, that from a merely scientific concept of nature no idea of God can be deduced and from the cosmos only a cosmological, not a religious, idea of God can be inferred. The scientist has every right to name the name of God, but only in so far as he is also a man. As mere scientist he cannot name the name of God without taking that name in vain. In so far, however, as he is also a man, even the twentieth-century scientist might catch the music of the spheres, and with the eighteenth-century poet, cry:

> The spacious firmament on high
> With all the blue ethereal sky
> And spangled Heavens, a shining frame,
> Their great Original proclaim.

> In reason's ear they all rejoice
> And utter forth a glorious voice
> Forever singing as they shine,
> 'The Hand that made us is divine.'

II

*The Reconciliation of Science and Religion. A New Version
of the 'Twofold Truth'*

A

The conflict between science and religion, as we have said, reached its zenith at the end of the last century. This was due, in the main, to the fallacy of misplaced literalism which made both religion and science say what they really did not say. On this level of thought conflict was inevitable, and ordinary sincerity seemed to demand a blunt either-or which brooked no compromise. Even at this stage, however, there were many, both men of religion and men of science, who felt that things could not be really so, and who sought earnestly for ways of conciliation between these two forms of the human spirit.

The chief way of reconciliation consisted in distinguishing between the intellectual and emotional sides of man and in assigning the former to science, the latter to religion. Both scientist and theologian seemed often to find this division of labour a satisfactory *modus vivendi*. The scientist felt himself to be most generous towards religion when he associated it with poetry and, while avowing that he did not deny the value of poetry, merely declined to bring its concepts within the sphere of knowledge and truth, where they do not belong. On the other hand many religious men—and even some theologians— seemed ready to accept such a division and, in extreme cases, to be content if to religion were left what was called the world of values.

To the question, Will science destroy religion? the answer was often in the negative. The acids of modernity may have eaten God out of the universe but they have not eaten what we have known as the God-like out of the human heart. It ill becomes us wholly to deprecate such noble sentiments, but the thoughtful man cannot but feel that, noble though they may be as gestures, they are really not very intelligent. The rapidity with which such sentiments have disappeared indicates how untenable this attitude really is. For there is one fact which neither noble sentiments nor critical sophistication can gainsay, namely, that in a universe in which there is no God there is also no human heart as here understood—that, as we have elsewhere expressed it, there are views of the universe which make values impossible and these same views make also impossible man in the sense in which any such appeal can be made to him. In other words any reconciliation of religion and science must rest upon deeper foundations than these.

A second way of harmonizing these two great forms of

human culture was the affirmation of the essentially religious
character of science itself. Men spoke of the 'religion of science,'
and in making science religious, so it was thought, the sting was
taken from the conflicts which inevitably took place on the
lower levels of both religion and science. Science seeks truth and
in so doing it finds itself identical with religion.[1] Men even
went so far as to say that the ethics of Christianity and the ethics
of science are identical and pointed with pride to the comforts
and benefactions brought by science to man as, supposedly,
evidence of this identity.

Here, too, the thoughtful man will not be too contemptuous
of these noble sentiments, however fatuous they have turned out
to be. Actually they are as untenable as the preceding. So far
as the ethics of science are concerned, it has become more and
more clear that it has none. At best it is ethically neutral. It
sells its wares to the highest bidder, whether it be beneficence
or maleficence. Nor on reflection is the first point any more
tenable. It is true, of course, that science seeks truth as its
highest value—and its heroes in the service of truth are note-
worthy—but the question is what the truth is that science seeks
—whether it is the same as the truth of religion, the *veritas
ontologica* which is of the essence of Deity itself, or something else.
The entire development of modern scientific method makes
this doubtful. Although in a sense disinterested, in a more
fundamental sense it is really interested only in certain things,
and truth, as understood by religion, is not among them.

B

It has, accordingly, become increasingly clear—at least to
those who understand the problems really involved—that
reconciliations of this type are as ephemeral as they are superficial. It has become ever more apparent that no reconciliation
is possible which does not, so to speak, go behind the returns of
both religion and science to what they really say, to those
implicit pronouncements which only a philosophical interpretation of both can reveal. This has led to a third way of
reconciliation based upon a recognition of the limits of science.
Even in the nineteenth century this way of reconciliation was

[1] An outstanding illustration is E. Boutroux, *Science and Religion in Contemporary
Philosophy.*

favoured by the more critical scientists and philosophers, especially those influenced by Kant—James Ward's *Naturalism and Agnosticism* being an outstanding illustration. There has, however, come about 'a new understanding of the limits of science,' as Pringle-Pattison calls it, and this new understanding is the fruit of the new scientific epistemology as developed in the preceding chapter.[1]

It is unnecessary to recall the details of this epistemology. It will suffice to emphasize its new understanding of the limits of science. The main point is that science is now seen to be symbolic form—that its function is not to copy reality but to symbolize it; that, moreover, the symbols of science have meaning and validity only in the universe of discourse in which they function and for the specific purposes for which they were constructed. The exploration of the external world by the methods of science leads not to 'concrete reality,' to reality in all the fullness of its being, but to a world of symbols beneath which these methods are not fitted to penetrate. This new understanding of science implies, if it is really understood, other symbolic forms for the expression of other aspects of reality, of which science, by virtue of the very nature of its language and method, is not fitted to speak.

With this new understanding comes also a new understanding of the relation of the pronouncements of science to those of religion. If the explicit pronouncements of both are taken literally they appear to be in conflict. Actually, when examined more closely, they are seen to be not so much in contradiction as to belong to quite different universes of discourse. When one is talking about creation out of nothing, about a last judgment, about sin and redemption, incarnation and ascension, one is speaking a language which is indeed intelligible within the realm of Grace, but for which there are no synonyms in the realm of nature. I think it is quite clear that propositions of this sort cannot, properly speaking, be said to be in contradiction with the propositions of science. No two propositions can contradict one another unless they are answers to the same question—unless they are in the same universe of discourse. As propositions have meaning only in the universe of discourse which gives them their meaning, so also contradictions between

[1] S. Pringle-Pattison, article on 'Mysticism' in the *Encyclopaedia Britannica*.

propositions have meaning only in the same universe of discourse.[1]

But if science and religion are not contradictory can they be said to be complementary, as traditional rational theology has uniformly held? This is a much more difficult question, but I think it may be answered in the affirmative, even if we follow the ways of thinking of modern science and philosophy. Indeed it is the new epistemology of science, with its implications, which makes such an affirmative answer possible.

'There can,' writes Max Planck, 'never be any real opposition between religion and science, for the one is the complement of the other. Every serious and reflective person realizes, I think, that the religious element in his nature must be recognized and cultivated if all the powers of the human soul are to act together in perfect balance and harmony. . . . Science enhances the moral values of life because it furthers a love of truth and reverence—love of truth displaying itself in a constant endeavour to arrive at a more exact knowledge of the world of mind and matter around us, and reverence, because every advance in knowledge brings us face to face with the mystery of our own being.'[2] This statement of the complementary relation which he finds exemplified in 'the greatest thinkers of all ages' may seem to be little more than the superficial reconciliation of mere attitudes which we found as ephemeral as superficial, but it is far from that. It is a conclusion based upon precisely this new epistemology of science and the new understanding of its limits of which we have written. I shall state it in the idiom with which we are already familiar, an idiom, however, which is in principle no different from that used by Max Planck.

Really to understand this epistemology is to understand the limited character of its objectives. If the symbolic constructs of science have meaning and validity only with reference to the purposes for which they are constructed, it follows that in the very recognition of this fact is implied also the acknowledgment of other ends and values and other symbolic forms.

[1] See Chapter iv, pp. 134 f.

[2] Max Planck, *Where is Science Going?* New York, 1932, p. 168. In this most enlightening study of modern critical science, two chapters are especially significant: Chapter iii, 'The Scientists' Picture of the Universe,' and Chapter v, 'Causation and Free Will, The Answer of Science.'

Even the ends and values of science itself, so Planck like other critical scientists sees, are themselves neither discoverable nor justifiable by the methods of science. The scientific concept of nature does not include these values and when understood presupposes that which deserves the name of Super-nature. It is with this world that religion is concerned. It is religion that first discovers and embodies the values not deducible from nature, and it is religion alone that, in the last analysis, can make them intelligible. To the questions asked by religion science has, and in the nature of the case can have, no answer.

This is one aspect of the complementary relation. But such new understanding of science involves a new understanding of religion and its pronouncements. Religion is also symbolic form. If the symbolic constructs of science have validity only with reference to the ends and values for which they were constructed and in the universe of discourse in which they have meaning, the same is true of the symbolic form of religion. If science has no answer to the questions which religion asks, so religion gives no answers to the questions which the methods of science were designed to answer. To attempt to express the original phenomena of the spiritual life in the language of science is to denature them and to stultify the person. On the other hand, to attempt to 'explain' the happenings of nature in the dramatic language of religion distorts nature in the sense of science and stultifies the principles of evidence developed by science.

This complementary relation may then be phrased in the following way. In order to 'explain' in the sense of science, physical categories must be basal and irreversible. But it is equally true that in order to 'understand' in the sense of religion, spiritual categories must be ultimate and irreducible. Can we not say that science and religion are complementary in that, while science requires religion for its ultimate understanding and justification, religion requires science for a valid application of its ideals and principles to life?

I do not think that this way of stating things is far removed, in principle at least, from the relation proposed by classical religious philosophy. For the latter, the truths of nature, while true, are not exclusive and ultimate, for there is that which the inquiry of reason cannot attain—the intelligible

things of God which surpass the whole range of human reason.
On the other hand, the truths of religion cannot be completely
rationalized, for then they would become truths of nature
and not of grace. But while they are different, they are not
contradictory, for they represent diversified applications of
one indivisible truth, and are therefore complementary. They
are relatively autonomous, but not absolutely. Our way of
stating this relation is, I think, little more than a translation
of this ancient insight into a modern idiom, an idiom, moreover,
which has the advantage of affording a common philosophical
universe of discourse in which critical scientist and critical
theologian can, perhaps, better understand one another and
in the end come to speak a common language.

Both theologians and scientists, in so far as they are at all
critical, have, I believe, to a considerable degree achieved
thus mutual understanding and speak a common philosophical
language. No enlightened theologian would any longer defend
religion by 'picking holes in science.' He would recognize that
scientific method constitutes a whole and he would seek rather
to understand that whole. No enlightened scientist would any
longer seek to uphold science as against religion by charging
the latter with anthropomorphism. That would be merely the
pot calling the kettle black. He recognizes the essentially
anthropomorphic character of his own concepts, for he now
knows just how he has made them. He, too, understanding
science as a whole, would try, rather, to understand religion
as a whole. Both know too much about themselves and each
other to resort to such childish practices. Both have come to
maturity and with maturity have learned to understand. I am,
of course, far from saying that this more enlightened standpoint,
as I have ventured to call it, is universally characteristic of
either theology or science. There are still fundamentalists
in both camps who, if they were allowed to dominate, would
make this mutual understanding impossible. But they are, on
the whole, properly evaluated by the theologians and scientists themselves. Their demand for literal truth is understood
and appreciated but their fallacy of misplaced literalism is
constantly exposed. It is the obligation of the philosophic
scientist, no less than of the philosophical theologian, to render
them innocuous.

C

Despite all this the tension between science and religion, of which Archbishop Temple wrote, still exists and is of tragic moment in our modern life. Nevertheless, I am disposed to think that it is neither so intrinsic to the two ways of thinking as he supposes nor is it to be found precisely where he thinks to find it. 'No law of nature as discovered by physical science is,' so he tells us, 'ultimate and therefore a tension exists between philosophy and religion.'[1] The first part of the statement seems to be true enough if we accept as a necessary part of science the changes in our concepts of natural law which appear to have been necessitated by the new epistemology of science. On the other hand, it is not at all clear that religion, any more than science, lays claim to the ultimacy of its pronouncements in the sense here understood. According to traditional philosophical theology, these pronouncements, while true, are not ultimate in the sense of giving us an exhaustive knowledge of God in all the fullness of His being, or of 'divine things' of which it has always been said that 'we now see through a glass darkly.' It is not clear that the tension, although real, is to be found precisely at this point.

We are further told that 'A purely transcendent God who intervenes often to give special direction to the course of events is incompatible with a scientific apprehension of the world, while a purely transcendent God who never intervenes at all, or has done so only once or twice in recorded history, is incompatible with vital religion.' There is thus 'a sharp choice to be made here: the tension between the habit of mind congenial to religion and the habit of mind congenial to science is acute.' The way to mitigate this tension, he adds, 'is to recognize the necessity and origin of these two views so that neither science nor religion may encroach one upon the other.'[2] Here, I believe, we have come upon the real *locus* of the tension and also upon the only way, not only to mitigate but ultimately to remove it. The tension is psychological, between two habits of mind, but the philosopher cannot allow psychological habit to be determinative. It is his business

[1] William Temple, *Nature, Man and God*, p. 267.
[2] *Op. cit.*, pp. 293 ff.

to seek to understand both the origin and the necessity of these two ways of thinking, and if he does, so I am inclined to think, not only will the tension be removed, but the dilemma which it appears to express will be seen not to demand a sharp choice, but to permit of a middle ground. It is precisely the origin and necessity of these two views that we have sought to show in this and the preceding chapters. Only when, as I have expressed it, we 'go behind the returns' of both is there any hope of a permanent understanding between these two fundamental activities of the human spirit.

D

It is natural to say of all this that it is but a modern version of the doctrine of the twofold truth. In a sense this is true, for anyone who seeks to understand the necessity and origin of these two different ways of thinking, 'so that they will not encroach the one upon the other,' presupposes this doctrine in some form. But if it is, it involves a restatement of the doctrine, as new as the new understanding of the limits of science of which it is an expression. Certainly it is different enough from the older forms to enable us to avoid the difficulties inherent in them.

The doctrine of a twofold order of knowledge arose inevitably so soon as men realized the difference between the concepts and symbols of dogmatic and rational theology and thus became an essential part of philosophical theology. A more serious issue arose with the development of modern physical science and scientific method. For it then became clear that between the language of theology, whether dogmatic or rational, and that of science is a yawning chasm which no artifices of dialectic can permanently bridge. It was, therefore, for many but a step to a further extension of the principle of the twofold truth and to maintain, with Duns Scotus, that what is true in religion is not true in science and vice versa—a doctrine which the Church found it necessary to condemn.

It was natural that Giordano Bruno, at his trial at Venice in 1592, should have appealed to this latter interpretation of the twofold truth. Bruno found himself in a dilemma which increasingly presented itself to the scientists of his time and on the horns of which it seemed they must, although unwilling, be impaled. If they spoke the physical-mathematical language which was rapidly becoming the only language of science, they would seem to deny that which was spoken in the language of faith. If, on the other hand, they still continued to speak the language of Grace they must seemingly violate their scientific integrity.

Bruno's scientific conscience demanded of him the assertion of the infinity of physical space and this became one of the eight heretical sentences with which he was faced. Bruno saw that if we conceive of physical reality in terms of Euclidian space, it follows that physical space cannot be limited by a sphere, the sphere of the fixed stars. Consequently he had to deny the Platonic and medieval conception of such a limitative sphere. Spatial limits are by definition boundaries in space, and it is a contradiction in terms to speak of any shape as a limit of space. In this he was undoubtedly right, and since his time the Church has accepted the astronomical views which it condemned in Bruno. This ultimate acceptance, it is commonly held, was the result of sheer necessity and of an implicit acknowledgment of the primacy of science and of its idiom. This is scarcely a true interpretation of the situation. It was rather that the theologian came to recognize the relative autonomy of science and the scientific method. But this is not the point I wish to make here. It is rather that the universe of discourse in which Bruno asserted the infinity of physical space is concerned with a wholly different language and symbolism from those in which the truths of religion are expressed. They constitute answers to wholly different questions, and, as we have seen, contradiction can arise only between propositions that are answers to the same questions and are therefore in this same logical universe of discourse.[1]

Nevertheless, as it was natural that Bruno should appeal to the doctrine of the twofold truth, it was just as natural that the Church should condemn it in the form to which the appeal was made. It is of the utmost importance to understand why the appeal should be denied.

The doctrine of the unity of truth was, for reasons we have seen, both a necessary and a permanent element in Christian philosophy. In this Christian theology reflected revelation—

[1] Chapter iv, pp. 134 f.

'the Truth says that He is the truth'—but it found powerful support in the *sensus communis* of the natural reason. For this common sense, truth can no more be divided than could the child by Solomon's sword. There can be no question of the imperious character of this demand; it is the fundamental demand of integrity. A divided truth is no more possible than a divided self. The argument for the indivisibility of truth is thus *a priori* and for that very reason commended itself all the more strongly to the dialectical mind of theologian and philosopher. Unity of truth does not, however, exclude diversity of expression, although no expression of truth can be completely autonomous.

There was thus every ground, in both common sense and reason, for the denial of Bruno's appeal to the doctrine of the twofold truth. For in this form it involved, as became increasingly evident, not only the absolute autonomy of science but also its primacy, in the sense of embodying in its method most completely the ideal of all knowledge—a position which neither common sense nor reason, in the more ultimate sense, could possibly accept. These difficulties, inherent in the Scotistic conception, the new understanding of scientific method and its limits enables us to overcome. The denial of the complete autonomy of science follows necessarily from the principle of indivisibility of truth, but it seems equally necessary that if there are different orders of knowledge, different symbolic forms in our manner of speaking, some principle of primacy, some hierarchy of symbolic forms is inevitable. This also the new epistemology of science affirms. After exhausting the physical categories of science we must, if we would understand, return to those value categories which men call 'spiritual.' This principle of the primacy of the axiological is, as we have seen, implicit in the new epistemology of science itself.[1] To the further development of this point we must now turn.

[1] Chapter ix, pp. 348 f.

III

The Doctrine of the Twofold Truth and the Problem of the Primacy of the Axiological

A

There seems to be little question, then, that the doctrine of a twofold order of knowledge has always included a principle of primacy. There seems to be just as little question also as to which of the two ways of knowing the primacy has uniformly been given, and why it has been ascribed to it.

That theology should be held to be the queen of the sciences was inevitable if knowledge and science were made identical. But it was also inevitable that this overlordship should be challenged with the development of modern scientific method. When the chief function of philosophy itself was thought to be embodied in natural theology, it was inevitable that philosophy should be held to be *ancilla theologiae*, but it was equally inevitable that this role should be repudiated by philosophy as more and more it attached itself to positive science. But while this formulation of the principle of primacy was challenged the principle itself remained. Within philosophy itself had persisted, from Greek times on, a conception of primacy—of the primacy of the axiological—and it is upon this principle that the modern spirit has fallen back.

The great thinkers of European philosophy, so Nicolai Hartmann rightly tells us, 'have always acknowledged the categorial supremacy of values to principles of being and given precedence in their systems to values.' First of all there is Plato for whom the Good is the apex of the realm of ideas and for whom values are above existence in strength and dignity. Aristotle asserts this supremacy also, identifying the Nous with the highest good. The masters of scholasticism also, in identifying the *ens perfectissimum* with the *ens realissimum*, continued the tradition. St Anselm states it explicitly in his *De Veritate*, for in his mind truth itself is a form of justice. It is implicit in St. Thomas, as we have seen in our examination of his formulation of the theistic argument. This primacy is implicit in continental rationalism, especially in its Leibnizian form, for the principle

of sufficient reason as formulated by him was essentially axiological in character and continued the Platonic tradition in
theology and philosophy. 'Everywhere,' as Hartmann says,
'except with difference of form, the axiological principle is made
the foundation of the whole.'[1]

There has been, as indicated in the introductory chapter,
no break with this tradition in modern times. Indeed Kant
himself sought to make the principle fully explicit in his doctrine
of the primacy of the practical reason. However unfortunate his
expression of the primacy of the axiological—and we have recognized the difficulties which it has engendered—this principle,
implicit in the entire development of European philosophy, was
bound to take this particular form, so soon as the physico-
mathematical method of modern science achieved its relative
autonomy. It is sheer misunderstanding to speak, with Aliotta,
of Kant's 'arbitrary mutilation of knowledge'[2] and to say that
'it banished from the realm of true science to that of aesthetic
contemplation all those forms of judgment and all those categories of which the physical mathematical sciences do not make
use, and that everything which cannot be comprised in these
schemes is therefore not considered true knowledge.' The very
essence of the Kantian critique was precisely the opposite,
namely, to show the limits of what Kant called pure reason, in
the sphere of knowledge as a whole. When Kant distinguished,
as we saw, between the various employments of the reason, it
was for the very purpose of showing the limits of the empirical
employment known as science in the hierarchy of the functions
of reason, all of which are, for him, determined by the axiological
principle of orientation towards the Good.[3]

It is, however, just this sort of misconception that has led to
a misunderstanding of the primacy of the axiological in the
whole of European theology and philosophy. It is this same misconception which, if not removed, would lead inevitably to a
misunderstanding of our present argument. It is therefore in a
sense a crucial point of this entire chapter. This misconception
arises out of the assumption that the primacy of the axiological
constitutes a substitution of value for being. This charge has

[1] Nicolai Hartmann, *Ethics*, Volume I, p. 241.
[2] Aliotta, *The Idealistic Reaction Against Science*, p. 197.
[3] Chapter v, pp. 164 f.

been sufficiently answered in connection with our discussion of the theistic argument,[1] but one point may be recalled in view of its significance in the present context.

According to the classical formulation Being is indeed primary in the order of knowledge, as St. Thomas would say, but in the order of interpretation the Good is logically primary. In terms of our present discussion, the categories of existence are primary for 'explanation' and the categorial scheme irreversible; in the order of understanding and interpretation, however, value categories are primary in the categorial scheme and this scheme also cannot be reversed. There is thus no substitution of value for existence or of existence for value. Substitution of categories of value for those of existence leads necessarily to anthropomorphism and subjectivism, but substitution of categories of existence for those of value leads inevitably to mechanism and materialism. If then the primacy of the axiological does not mean substitution of value for being, what does it mean? It means that, while being and value are ultimately convertible, *ens et bonum convertuntur* being the axiom of all traditional metaphysics, in so far as we seek the meaning of existence, the Good must be primary. For being, abstracted from the Good, is the most empty and meaningless of all concepts. It is only when, so to speak, existence is clothed upon by value that it becomes significant at all. It is this, and this alone, that the principle of the primacy of the axiological affirms.

All this—and this is the significance for our present argument —the new epistemology of science both implies and confirms. In so far as modern philosophy understands this epistemology and presupposes it in its thinking, its solution of the problem of science and religion must be along these lines. The futility of earlier solutions, based upon the exclusive autonomy of science in the world of the spirit, serves only to set in clearer relief the present situation. It was only natural that in the first flush of the affirmation of the autonomy of science, an assertion necessary for its very life, science should have also asserted its primacy as the norm of all knowledge. It was only necessary that it should reflect more deeply on its own methods and objectives to realize that the very limitation by which it achieves its power presupposes that its own objectives, however

[1] Chapter vi, pp. 209 ff.

389

important and relatively autonomous they may be, presuppose still more ultimate objectives of the human spirit. It is only when science becomes one of the humanities, and the scientist, however preoccupied with his own ends, continually calls to mind that he is also a man, that the true relation between science and religion is possible.

B

In concluding this chapter I should like to use the closing words of Eddington's *The Philosophy of Physical Science*, words which to my mind express better than any I could devise this concept of science as itself one of the humanities, and the principle of the primacy of the axiological, acknowledgment of which can alone make science humane.

'In the age of reason, faith yet remains supreme; for reason is one of the articles of faith.' He then continues, 'the problem of knowledge is an outer shell underneath which lies another philosophical problem—the problem of *values*. It cannot be pretended that the understanding and experience gained in the pursuit of scientific epistemology is of much avail here; but there is no reason for trying to persuade ourselves that the problem does not exist. A scientist should recognize in his philosophy—as he already recognizes in his propaganda—that for the ultimate justification of his activity it is necessary to look, away from the knowledge itself, to a striving in man's nature not to be justified of science or reason, for it is itself the justification of science, of reason, of art, of conduct. Of the relation of mysticism and science I have written elsewhere.'[1] Of 'this other problem,' the problem of values, we shall write more fully in the next chapter. Here I should like, for the moment, to dwell on the question of science and mysticism. Since, however, the two questions are closely related, some comment is necessary on the problem of values.

For the ultimate justification of science itself it is necessary, we are told, to look away from science to something that is not to be justified by science. This obviously is an expression, however unsatisfactory, of the principle of the categorial supremacy of values. If this something is not to be justified by science itself, that is validated or verified by the scientific method, properly understood, it follows, almost of necessity, that, in so far as the

[1] *Op. cit.*, p. 222.

scientist accepts the principle of homogeneity of method, the acknowledgment of this other realm will, *from the point of view of method at least,* involve trenching on the mystical. My own view is that the acknowledgment of this other realm is presupposed by scientific epistemology itself, but in any case it is at this point that the question of science and mysticism arises.

There can be little question, I think, that a revaluation of the mystical element in experience is in process, and just as little question that in important respects it is the result of the new understanding of the limits of science. It may not be true that, as Georg Simmel once said, an element of mysticism is a necessary part of every first-rate modern mind, but it is certainly true that an increasing number of scientific minds of the first order confess to this element in their thought. Pringle-Pattison is surely right when he says that 'the changed outlook in physical science and a *new* understanding of its limitations [italics mine] have brought about a rapprochement between mysticism and philosophy.'[1] It cannot perhaps be said that science as such trenches on the mystical, but many scientists, in so far as they are self-critical, certainly do.

It is possible, I think, to be even more specific and to put one's finger on the exact point at which the mystical element appears in science. The meaning of things in space and time, it is said, lies outside space and time. Space-time is the matrix of the existent, the all-pervasive form of all that is, in the sense of science. Of this meaning, outside space and time, science as such cannot speak. But it knows that it is there, and merely because it has no language in which to express it, the true scientist does not try to persuade himself that it is not there.

There is, then, I believe, a 'natural mysticism,' as distinguished from the theological mysticism of religion but, as we shall see, closely related to it. It manifests itself at the limits of all the natural activities of human life, the moral, the artistic and scientific, as well as the religious. In science it manifests itself in the acknowledgment of that which is beyond space and time. In the humanities, in literature and in art, which deal primarily with the life of man in space and time, it manifests itself, as we shall see, in the acknowledgment of a meaning which is 'beyond life.' In religion the mystic *eo nomine* represents

[1] See article on *Mysticism* already cited.

in a superlative degree this mystical element which is present in some degree or form in every truly human soul. The mystical element constitutes then the final problem in connection with our general theme of Humanity and Deity, but before considering this problem we must raise the question of what the humanities say about man and with it the cognate question of Humanism and Theism.

Chapter XII

Religion and the Humanities. Theism and Humanism

I — A

THE seat of the conflict of our present culture with religion is no longer chiefly science, but rather what we may, broadly speaking, call the humanities. The powerful anti-religious tendencies in the cultural and political life of the present are not due so much to the fact that religion is in conflict with science as because it is felt to be in mortal conflict with genuine human values. This is the situation in the world today—not only in those cultures and peoples in which the antagonism is overt and outspoken, but, more secretly and implicitly, in those regions in which the humanistic values, hitherto bound up with religion, are still formally professed. We may call it the conflict of the two humanisms, the naturalistic and the religious or super-naturalistic.

It is true, of course, that this naturalistic humanism was closely related to the natural science of the nineteenth century, and it is with this interpretation of science that it, in a sense, stands or falls. Science, then, especially the sciences of life and mind—but in a sense also the physical science which lies back of them—is undoubtedly the background of naturalistic humanism. But after all the real issue is within the humanities themselves—those objectifications of the spirit in which the nature of the human is most completely revealed. It involves the question, What after all is man? and whether belief in God is a necessary presupposition of the human. To this question two diametrically opposed answers are given. There are those who think that man without God is no longer man, but there are also those who think that with God he somehow has his humanity annulled, and that in trying to love God and to be like Him he becomes less than man.

Our problem, then, is religion and the humanities. The thesis which I propose to argue in this chapter is that it is the humanities alone that give us an adequate understanding of man and that when they are properly interpreted—that is, when we have determined what they really say, both explicitly and implicitly—it will be seen that, far from being in opposition to religion, they actually presuppose it; that no genuine humanism is possible that does not go beyond mere humanism. In other words, to be really human man must have his beginning and his end in God, and for the humanities to be really humanistic they must acknowledge and express that fact. But more than this—we shall also maintain that no genuine humanism is possible which does not presuppose certain ideas about God. The *imago Dei* is so bound up with the idea of the human— Humanity and Deity so inseparably related—that to have a true image of the one requires that we shall have a true image of the other.

B

The notion of the humanities, like the notion of science, is far from unambiguous. It is possible, of course, just as in the case of science, to define it so broadly as to have it say everything or nothing. The essence of humanism, it is sometimes said, is 'the enlargement of comprehension and sympathy,' as contrasted with 'the ideal of exactness and rigor—and verifiability—in the case of science.' But humanism is not primarily this, desirable as in itself it may be. It is, to be sure, the humanistic attitude which says that nothing human is alien to me, but much depends upon what the human is conceived to be, whether this enlargement of sympathy and understanding is real humanism or sentimentality. Doubtless he who thinks of man as merely a high-grade simian has for him a certain sympathy, whether ironic or mawkish, but one would scarcely call it a humanistic attitude.

The humanities are said to comprise, in the first place, 'all that tends to the enlargement of man's range of values.' But since the condition of such enlargement seems to be freedom, the humanities are further said 'to embrace whatever influences are conducive to freedom.' As initial definitions, these pronouncements are not without value, but how much value they will turn out to have depends upon the way in which the theme is developed—upon what the values are, the enlargement of the range of which is desirable, and what the freedom which is to be enhanced turns out to be.[1]

[1] This is the definition of the humanities given by Ralph Barton Perry in his lecture in the recent Princeton lectures on the humanities published in the book

RELIGION AND THE HUMANITES

On one point all humanisms must agree, by implication at least, namely, that that which distinguishes the human from the non-human, both animate and inanimate, is the presence of just this sense of value, the enlargement of which is said to be the criterion of the humanities. This implies, further, the presence in some form of what we call the 'moral.' Nature does not have morals even in the sense of *mores*—not even that part of nature which we call the animal world. Still less does it have the sense of the awareness of values from the acknowledgment of which springs our sense of obligation. Man is not only 'the valuing animal,' as Nietzsche says, but, in so far as we know, he is the only 'bearer of values' in the entire range of nature that is conscious of his burden. Doubtless every created being has its own good, but it is man alone who is conscious, however confusedly, of his natural good and in whom that consciousness becomes part of his very being.

The expression, 'the enlargement of the range of values,' however vague it may be, leads, nevertheless, directly into the central theme of the humanities, namely, that of man as the bearer of values, and of an order of values, the apprehension and acknowledgment of which make him man. Enlargement of our ordinary value spectrum is, doubtless, in itself one of the most precious gifts of the humanities. To have our spiritual senses opened to the lower as well as the upper limits of that spectrum is in itself a boon, but the very presence of the high and low presupposes a scale of values, and there is no real understanding of man until there is revealed the principle of order which gives meaning to the spectrum. There are in this scale, as we have seen, values deducible from nature, but there are also those that are not, and it is precisely the relation of these in the value scale that constitutes the basal humanistic problem. This is not to deny that there is also an external order, a *scala naturae*, of which human nature is in a sense a part, but it is the inner scale, transcending nature, which is the source of all human aspiration

The Meaning of the Humanities. As a starting point, it is well enough, but as the argument proceeds one has the feeling that it does not matter much what the values are—they are anything that fulfils human interest, and that the freedom so highly praised, described as 'enlightened choice,' is little more than a glorified form of the 'enlightened self-interest' which constituted the vague humanitarianism of the nineteenth century. One cannot help feeling that the issues of humanity today lie too deep for any such conception of the humanities.

and endeavour and which, being significant for our under-standing of the human, constitutes the central theme of the humanities.

C

When one speaks of the humanities in contrast to science, one has primarily in mind the fine arts and literature. The painter and the sculptor—even the musician—may express the human, but it is the 'poets,' in the broad sense of the term—the lyricists, the dramatists and the novelists—who are, in a special sense, the protagonists of the human. For their medium is the medium of language; it is only in language that pronouncements about man and his relation to nature and the ground of things are possible, and it is in these alone that the particular 'idiom' of humanism, together with what humanism says, both explicitly and implicitly, can be determined.

Art has been defined as 'the objectification of the inner spirit of man' and whatever else it is, it may for our purposes be so conceived. Such objectification may be direct or indirect. In the lyric, or allied forms of expression in the other arts such as music and painting, the spirit of man, including man's sense of values, is objectified directly and to a degree directly communi-cated, but there are more indirect forms of objectification also. The way in which the novelist or dramatist, even to a degree the painter and the musician, envisage their material is in-directly revelatory of the inner spirit of man, and in so far as man is a part of nature, indirectly revelatory of nature also. I should be disposed to say that the way in which the poet or artist envisages nature tells us truths of nature itself and that no understanding of nature is complete which does not include this element.

It follows from all this—and it is a consequence of the utmost importance—that the language of the humanities is funda-mentally different from that of science. The latter, as we have seen, strives inevitably towards a physico-mathematical language. Its ultimate goal is correlation, control and mani-pulation, and in the service of that ideal develops a language of a definite character. The language of the humanities embodies a wholly different ideal, an ideal which we may characterize as that of expression and understanding. The primary object is to express the nature of man as the bearer of values and as that part of nature or reality in which value is sought and realized. This only a dramatic language, in the sense of our definition, can achieve.

This general thesis may be made even more specific. Whereas the language of science strives towards the ideal of a non-dramatic physico-mathematical language—and consequently tends ever more and more to exclude all so-called anthropomorphic notions of activity and ends as 'pre-scientific' and mythological—the language of the humanities not only retains them but perfects them as essential to its symbolic form. No adequate account of what happens in human life, the central home of action and drama, is possible if relations of the mental type and the dramatic way of rendering them are left out. Even of nature, in so far at least as it is conceived to include man, no wholly adequate account can, I believe, be given except in this symbolic form. Be that as it may, the present issue concerns an adequate account of man and this the humanities alone can give.

D

This distinction between the language of the humanities and that of science brings to the fore again the issues raised in preceding chapters, namely, the character of the language of science and the question whether that language, being what it is, can, in the very nature of the case, tell us what man really is—in other words, whether, strictly speaking, there *are* anthropological sciences, or sciences of the human. The question what science really says about man has already been discussed and I shall not repeat that discussion here, but merely reaffirm the main conclusion in terms relevant to the present discussion.

It is simply impossible, as we have seen, to apply the methods and language of modern science to man without 'stultifying the person' or dehumanizing man, and the consequences for humanism and for the humanities are far-reaching. What is called 'realism' in the modern envisagement of man—a form of realism which has found its way into all the arts, but especially the novel and the drama—simply amounts to saying that this abstraction is what man really is. To say that this is to dehumanize man may, of course, be held to be a begging of the question, but I do not think that it is. It is rather he who calls this abstraction man who begs the question if any one does. Certainly the man thus supposedly pictured by science is not the man which the scientist himself is when in pursuit of science he seeks knowledge and truth. For in this very search for what he believes to be truth about man he himself reveals that he acknowledges certain values and their implied obligations which the scientific construct called man could neither understand nor acknowledge —a fact which proves that he himself is something more than the artificial robot which his so-called artificial anthropology would have him believe.

In thus contrasting science with the humanities, I do not mean to say that science itself may not be a part of human culture and therefore humane, but merely that it must also speak the language of the humanities as well as its own special idiom. What it is to speak this language we have seen in the preceding chapter. In so far as it acknowledges that the problem of values underlies that of science itself, that for the solution of this problem the method of science will not avail, and that finally for the ultimate justification of its own activity it must appeal to other activities of the human spirit, and thus to the humanities themselves—in so far as it acknowledges these things, science has again become humane and become part of the humanities.

II

The 'Poet' as the Protagonist of the Human.
What Poetry Really Says

A

The protagonist of the human, and therefore of all the humanities, is not the scientist but the poet. In the last analysis the language of humanism is always 'poetic,' in our terms, dramatic, with all that this implies. It is of the utmost importance, therefore, for the general problem of the relation of humanism to religion, to understand what this language is and what, when they speak this language, the humanities really say.

This thesis is manifestly absurd unless we undertand by poetry something quite different from what is ordinarily understood in the modern world. If we think of it as the opposite of prose, the thesis is nonsense; if, however, we think of it as the opposite of science, it is full of sense. We have already argued this point at length; it is necessary now merely to expand our thesis.

Poetry, as thus understood, is the essential language of the humanities and its symbolic form the only form in which the human can be expressed. The two fundamental poetic modes are the lyrical and the dramatic—the first the direct, the latter the indirect objectification of the spirit of man. Both are indigenous to human speech as such, and constitute a symbolic form in which alone the human can be adequately expressed. What is said in this language is no less significant and true than that which is said in the language of science; it merely tells us things which science, in the nature of the case, cannot say.

As the language of the humanities is in principle different from that of science, so also are the symbols employed different from the symbolic constructs of science. When, having recognized that there is that in reality into which the symbols of science are not fitted to penetrate, men have recourse to others, it is inevitably to this symbolic form, older than that constructed by science for its special purposes, and from which science itself is derived, namely, the myth—the only form in which the original phenomena of the spiritual life can be expressed—that they turn. This is the original symbolism and, however perfected and spiritualized the symbols of poetry may later become, they never lose completely this primal character.

The symbolic form of poetry, whether of nature or of man, is, of course, anthropomorphic, but the important thing is to understand what anthropomorphic here means. It is the opposite of mechanomorphic, if the term be allowed. The latter is also, as Bergson pointed out, a form of anthropomorphism, a reversed teleology, but a later form developed not for understanding but for control. It might almost be said that in order to control one must renounce real understanding of man, and in order to understand he must cease to control.

B

What then does poetry, so understood, have to say about man and about the world in which he lives? Does it really say anything at all? And if so, has it any significance for philosophy?

It may be said, first of all, that poetry, *as such*, says nothing. If anything significant is said in the poetic form it is the individual poet that speaks—not poetry; the poet objectifies himself, not the human spirit. Now it is undoubtedly true that the three philosophical poets, for instance, Lucretius, Dante and Goethe, envisage life and the world differently. Even more is this true when we contrast the poetry of Dante with that of Ibsen, although the differences may be greatly exaggerated. Yet while this is true, all are *poets*, and the fact that they speak the poetic idiom rather than the scientific, means that they say something, implicitly at least, which is common to them all. That they actually do so, we shall see presently. Here the point is that the very fact that they use the dramatic language of poetry rather than the language of science, involves certain assumptions about man and nature, common to them all, which differ significantly from the assumptions of science. In this respect there is as much unity in the humanities as there is in science.

But there is a second objection, even more serious, in the way of any such interpretation of poetry as a whole, namely, that precisely because the poet is a poet and uses the language of poetry, he really says nothing; he merely expresses emotion. With this issue in its more general form we are already familiar through our discussion of the relation of poetry to religion, but the issue is so fundamental for all that follows that it is desirable to meet it more specifically and more technically at this point.

It seems certain that the poet, the dramatist and the novelist themselves believe that they are saying something significant and true about the reality which they envisage and express. Even to the lyrical poet his poems are not merely 'melodious sighs.' This is, moreover, the working hypothesis, not only of poets, but of all the great artists—painters, sculptors, even musicians. It would seem to follow, then, that we cannot understand them unless we share their belief, for precisely this belief is part of what they seek to communicate; we are perhaps 'enjoying' them to a degree, but certainly not understanding them, if we hear merely melodious sighs or see simply pleasant patterns of form and colour. It is true that the sharing of this belief may be a temporary assumption and may pass

RELIGION AND THE HUMANITIES

with the aesthetic experience. It is also true that the truth they give us may be symbolic not literal truth. But to deny that they say anything at all is to stultify both the artist's activity and our own aesthetic experience.

This does not, however, wholly meet the difficulty raised by the emotive theory of poetry. If we are to talk meaningfully about what poetry says there must be in poetry assertions, propositions, for otherwise it can, strictly speaking, say nothing. Now that there are 'apparent' propositions no one denies; but are they real propositions—real in the sense that truth and falsity are applicable to them? This the emotive and anti-intellectualist theory denies, and this denial is not, on the face of it at least, easy to refute. For that truth in the aesthetic sphere is not wholly the same thing as in the scientific, every one is, of course, aware. It is sometimes called truth of the 'imagination' rather than of the 'reason.' Professor L. A. Reid calls it 'perspected' truth in contrast to propositional truth. 'Art,' he tells us, 'is not true as propositions are true, but, like the knowledge of which propositions are the expressions, art is a revelation.'[1]

There is obviously an element of truth in this position— and a very important one—but it is, I think, only part of the truth. There are clearly no explicit propositions in either painting or music, although I think it can be shown that every work of art expresses or represents in some form an object to which it refers (certainly Cézanne is right when he says that there is no 'picture' in the sense of a painting which does not contain an element of representation); but be that as it may, surely in the case of linguistic art the situation is clear. It contains both explicit and implicit assertions about its objects. The former may, indeed, be symbolic and require interpretation, but the latter are philosophical in their import and, as Professor Reid says, although they arise out of the processes of poetry, have their value also for discursive knowledge. It is these propositions and their status in knowledge with which we are primarily concerned—whether they are what poetry really says, although implicitly, and whether therefore the predicates true and false are properly applicable to them.

[1] L. A. Reid, *A Study in Aesthetics*, Chapter x, entitled 'Art, Truth and Reality', p. 207.

The issue here raised is fundamental for the philosophy of art, yet, curiously enough, many philosophers are ambiguous on this point. In one breath they tell us that art is revelatory and in the next they tell us that it 'says nothing,' which is the same thing as saying that it is not revelatory. For if it is revelatory it must reveal something; if it does, however, that 'something' must be expressible, and if expressible it is, by that very fact, either true or false. This ambiguity which vitiates so much of modern aesthetic philosophy is but a special case of that double talk in which the new naturalisms, in contrast to the old, find it necessary to engage. Here, too, they cannot have their cake and eat it too. They cannot at the same time identify all knowledge with the scientific method and tell us that art 'says nothing,' and by still speaking of art as revelatory seek to retain their humanity.

This is the issue upon which our entire argument largely turns. That art gives us 'perspected truth' many would admit; the real issue is whether there is in any sense propositional truth also. I venture to say that every work of art is an implicit proposition, that all expression includes an element of re-presentation and thus says implicitly that the object is so. I have argued this general position elsewhere, including other forms of art than the linguistic;[1] here I shall confine myself to the implicit propositions of poetry, the language of which, in contrast to the language of science, constitutes a special symbolic form. No one would question, I suppose, that, except in those extreme cases in which poetry is sheer imagery or merely melodious sighs (if indeed there be such which I doubt), all poets try to say something. But there is just as little question, I think that if we wish to understand what they really say—and not merely share their emotion—what they say is potentially propositional and not only can, but inevitably must be taken up into discursive knowledge. Interpretation is as much a part of the understanding of poetry as of religion or science and until the explicit pronouncements of the poet are interpreted we do not know what he really says. The 'philosophy' of a poet, a dramatist and a novelist is no idle figure of speech, and it is this philosophy which is of significance for the interpretation of the humanities.

[1] See my *Language and Reality*, pp. 481 ff., in which illustrations from the various arts are used to substantiate the thesis.

It is my contention that when the varied explicit pronouncements of the humanities are interpreted, what they say implicitly has elements common to them all. It is this that we shall
now attempt to make clear.

C

I think it would be generally agreed except by those influenced by wholly modern prejudices, that what the poet, the
dramatist and novelist tell us about man and human life is a
truer objectification of their real nature—and, therefore, more
representative and more revealing than the representations of
these objects possible in the universals and symbols of science.
Surely, after what has gone before, we may at least say that
while science may indeed describe some aspects of man more
accurately for certain purposes, it is only the poet that can
'objectify' the meanings and values which make him man.
Poetry says certain things about men and women and about
human life explicitly, and it is these explicit pronouncements,
in lyric, drama and novel, which are of interest to the critic and
interpreter, but it also says certain things implicitly, and it is
these which, as in the case of other forms of the human spirit,
are of interest to the philosopher.

Poetry, then, always says certain things explicitly about man
and about human life. What it says explicitly is manifold and
varied and often contradictory; but in so far as it is authentic,
all explicit assertions have one common character—they are
assertions about *persons*. This may seem to be the veriest platitude
but it is, properly understood, of the utmost significance. For
science, rightly understood, never speaks of persons and has no
interest in them as such. 'Scientific' psychology is always psychology without a soul. Poetry, as poetry, always speaks of
'souls,' even when paradoxically, as in naturalistic poetry, it
denies their existence. By this I mean that even the naturalistic
dramatist, let us say, in so far as he is a dramatist, must treat the
personnae of the play *as though* they were persons even if he thinks
they are not.

The one differentia of the person significant in the humanistic
context is, as we have seen, that he alone of all the parts of
nature is conscious of the values of which he is the 'bearer' and
therefore of the 'ought,' or obligation, inseparable from the

awareness of values. In him at least, however it may be of other parts of nature, purpose, finality, 'axiological determination' is its fundamental character and its 'deepest law.'[1] The 'tension' between what is and what ought to be, whether the 'is' be a law of society or a law of nature, is man's deepest character, and to have this character is to be a 'soul.' In his account of motivation —of this axiological determination—the 'poet' may often use the language of science—of psychology and sociology—but he does so at his peril, for the language of the latter fights against the language of the humanities. Not only does he imperil his poetry as poetry, but his poetry as 'truth,' for naturalization of man means his stultification.

The language of poetry is thus even more significant for what it says implicitly and indirectly about man and human life. It says many things implicitly but there is one thing which it always says, whether it knows it or not, namely, that human life and man are unique, free and self-determining parts of nature. The dramatic mode of representation always implies this; it is the necessary presupposition of all drama, and in so far as the poet employs the dramatic way of rendering life, he always says this implicitly.

This is true of all drama, but it is pre-eminently true of tragedy. A naturalistic view of man—one which makes of him merely a part of nature—cannot rise to tragedy. The death of a tree or of a dog cannot be tragic. The 'tragic sense of life' is possible only on the supposition of this transcendence of nature, and the tragic *catharsis* is possible only when the drama expresses that transcendence. Naturalistic drama can only 'depress' us. We have, then, what a recent writer has called 'the dilemma of modern tragedy.'[2] If the modern dramatist writes on the basis of naturalistic assumptions he cannot achieve the tragic; if, on the other hand, he writes on the basis of the transcendental assumptions of classical tragedy, he is not 'realistic' in the modern sense. He must choose between the two. This dilemma runs throughout the whole of the modern drama and, as this writer further points out, is especially patent in Eugene O'Neill, whose

[1] For a complete development of this notion, see N. Hartmann, *Ethics*, Volume I, Chapter xix.

[2] This essay, entitled 'The Dilemma of Modern Tragedy,' is by Allen Reynolds Thompson and is found in *Humanism and America*, edited by Norman Foerster.

vacillations, in both objective and method, are due to a fundamental indecision. In any case, the drama is possible only on humanistic rather than scientific postulates, and in so far as the dramatic mode is used in rendering life, the humanistic view of man is assumed and postulated.

It would, of course, be absurd to say that a dramatist cannot write a play on the basis of a wholly naturalistic view of man. He can and often does. But it is not absurd to say that in so far as his play is really dramatic and his characters speak the language of drama, they will make their creator refute himself out of his own mouth. In like manner it would be absurd to suggest that a poet cannot write poetry which deals with values 'wholly deducible from nature.' He can and often does. Some poetry is written as though the only goods of men were sex and mastication. But even then, the poet tries to tell the truth and to tell it beautifully, and thus implicitly recognizes values of truth and beauty as things that *ought to be*. There are, to be sure, some things which cannot be said beautifully any more than they can be done beautifully—there are limits to the language of art, just as there are to the language of science. Hedda Gabler's charge to Löwberg that he 'do it beautifully' was a sign of perverted sensibility, and the attempt to say things beautifully which cannot be thus said, implies a sensibility no less debased. But this does not in the least affect the main contention that, even if the dramatist does use a language which stultifies the person, in so far as he achieves true drama at all he will deny implicitly all that he has explicitly said.

D

Poetry is, as we have said, primarily an objectification of the life and spirit of man. But this same life and spirit are parts of nature in the sense of reality as a whole. It cannot be directly revelatory of man without, at the same time, being indirectly revelatory of the nature of which he is a part. Now poetry has always had much to say about nature, and it seems fairly clear what it has in the main always said. It has spoken about nature in the dramatic way, in terms of relations of the mental type; in other words it has, as we say, personalized nature, its poetic form has been anthropomorphic.

It is, of course, immediately clear what poetry does and must

405

say about nature explicitly. For the poet the river 'runs,' the brook 'ripples' and even 'sings,' the mountains 'rear their heads,' the sea 'roars.' Even where metaphors are not used, where the merely intuitive language of poetry is employed, this language conjures up a living universe. The first book of Wordsworth's *Prelude*, Whitehead tells us, 'is pervaded with the haunting presences of nature. . . . Of course,' he continues, 'Wordsworth is a poet writing a poem and is not concerned with dry philosophical statements. But it would hardly be possible to express more clearly a feeling for nature as exhibiting entwined prehensive unities, each suffused with modal presences of the others.'[1] I am not sure that these are the right words in which to express philosophically that which Wordsworth says poetically —certainly I should myself want to express it differently; the essential thing is that 'the interfusion of the presences' of which Wordsworth speaks contains implicitly a metaphysic which the philosopher recognizes, but which, as a philosopher, he must express in other words.

What is true of Wordsworth's *Prelude* is true in different degrees of all poetic rendering of nature. It conjures up a living universe and in so doing, by virtue of the very symbolic form in which it speaks, tells us many things. It tells us, implicitly at least, that the picture of nature in terms of matter and motion— the night-side of nature, as Fechner called it—is not its ultimate character; there is also a 'day-side' which the poet apprehends and expresses. As the poet *qua* poet tells us that science, falsely interpreted, dehumanizes man, so he tells us also that, falsely interpreted, it also denatures nature. Poetry in its inmost nature is always the enemy of naturalism in the sense that the picture of nature given us by science is *alone* true and the *whole* truth.

It is what poetry tells us *not* to think of nature that is primarily significant for religion and philosophy. But it has positive implications also. The nature which the poet apprehends is a concrete nature—not the abstract concept of nature which the homogeneity of scientific method demands. It is a nature in which the exclusion of values, inevitable if there is to be scientific method, has not yet taken place. This nature may be little more than the vague animism of the mythical world-view, but it may also be the nature of Christian philosophy in which the

[1] *Science and the Modern World*, pp. 121 f.

lowest of created things has its own good and in which the humblest part participates in that which is above nature in the scientific sense, namely, the transcendentals, the good, the beautiful and the true.

Here, again, it is easy to be misunderstood. It would be absurd to say that a poet cannot write a poem on the basis of a wholly naturalistic, or even materialistic, conception of nature. Lucretius did it in his *De rerum natura*. But it is not absurd to say that in so far as his poem really is a poem, he will refute himself out of his own mouth. He will, whether he likes it or not, inevitably make nature dramatic. He will, like Lucretius, speak of forces of love and of hate, of attraction and repulsion, otherwise the poem will not be a poem. It will not 'march.' It cannot even get started as a poem unless the poet uses this dramatic language, with all that it implies. In so far as he uses that language, however, the conception of nature implied will not be the materialistic one which his poem sought to envisage and to celebrate.

Poetry, then, whether it be the poetry of man or of nature, constitutes a symbolic form in which certain aspects of reality can alone be expressed, and, like science or any other fundamental symbolic form, also presupposes a metaphysic. All art is, in Bergson's terms, *une métaphysique figurée*, and poetry, in the words of Coleridge, a 'covert metaphysic.' Doubtless when this covert metaphysic is uncovered, when the figurative is translated into terms of higher generality, the abstract terms may vary. But one thing they always have in common—they are 'spiritualistic', if we may be permitted to use that much abused term. The metaphysic may be little more than a vague pantheism, whether high or low, but it may also rise to a full and rich theism, in which even the common dandelion has a quality and a glory which takes the thoughtful man beyond nature; the important point is that, whatever its form, it is always a metaphysic in which nature is a symbol of the Divine.

When these facts are duly realized, it is seen that the covert metaphysics of poetry, and of the humanities in general, has much in common at least with the fundamental metaphysics of religion. In other words, the implicit pronouncements of poetry as a symbolic form are similar to the implicit pronouncements of religion. This suggests that there is a close relation between the humanities and religion, and to this relation we shall now turn.

III

Humanism and Religion. The Essentials of
Christian Humanism

A

It is not surprising, then, that we find many interpreters of the humanities arguing that the human, as expressed in the arts, more especially in great literature, can be understood only when it is related to the Divine. That, in the terms of our present discourse, the language of 'poetry' and of religion are so closely akin that they presuppose and embody a similar world-view, similar presuppositions as to the nature of man in relation to the ground of things.

This is the thesis of certain representatives of the 'New Humanism' from whose common pronouncement *Humanism and America* we have already quoted. True, there is difference of opinion on this point, namely, as to the extent to which humanism presupposes religion in the ordinary sense of the word. Some are prepared to go further in this direction than others, but all agree that 'man, to be man, must live by values higher than any deducible from nature' and that in this sense at least the supernatural is presupposed. Certainly, they are all one in their negation of pure naturalism and in the belief that a genuine humanism is incompatible with naturalism, properly understood—that the humanities when they are really understood go beyond naturalism.

These humanists call themselves new because the ancient and honourable term has been stolen and applied to something which they conceive to be its very opposite, namely, a naturalistic conception of man which degrades him and is, in their view, the very opposite of historic humanism. Primarily men of letters, it is in literature and art generally that they chiefly find evidence of this degradation of life, and it is a necessary presupposition of humane letters that a new definition of man be developed. Literature has been defined as the criticism of life, and in the criticism of life which modern literature presents us they find a complete reflection of the modern man's degraded notion of himself. The fundamental characteristic of the modern man is 'his lately gotten sense of the tininess of the human element in the race, the enormity of his animal past.' For us moderns, 'the primeval forest with its thick-spawning life, its ferocious beasts, its brutal phallic worship, is still here.' No one can deny that the moderns have been writing novels, composing music and painting pictures, as men who feel this strongly— Swinnerton has said that 'men even write novels differently since Darwin.' Whether they must so write, as he further suggests, is another question; nevertheless these things are here, and in them the New Humanists see the ultimate source of all the decadence and degradation which they find in so much of modern art.

The older humanism—of the Renaissance—felt itself called to battle against a view of life and of man that it believed to be wholly other-worldly. A Montaigne and a Rabelais fought with weapons none too nice against a notion of man which, while seeking to exalt him, nevertheless, in their view, often subtly degraded him. In demanding of man that he should be more than man, the ascetic ideal often made him less. Today humanism, it is held, must battle with a contrary notion, with a conception of man as animal, a notion which in attempting to naturalize him completely in the physical universe, really denatures and dehumanizes him.

Enough has been said, I think, to show that this battle of ideas is not merely a tempest in the literary teapot, nor merely even 'a conscientious overhauling of our entire attitude towards literature and life', but one rather that goes to the very heart of fundamental philosophical issues. In an article entitled 'Humanism and Value,' Mr. Hazlitt, a critic of the new humanism, recognizes this fact and characterizes it as a battle of theories of value. The new humanism, he tells us, asserts that a sound theory of values cannot be naturalistic; its opponents assert that such a theory can and must be naturalistic.[1] This is indeed the real issue for, as we have seen, a naturalistic theory denatures values and stultifies the person who is their bearer.

[1] In a volume entitled *A Critique of Humanism.*

B

Man simply to be man, so I contend, must live by values higher than any deducible from nature, and any genuine humanism must acknowledge this fact. But if this is true, something else is true. It involves the further notion of 'higher and lower,' of an order or scale of values, and that it is the essential character of man that upon the multiplicity of goods presented to us by nature he imposes a scale of values, a transcendent order; and this also naturalism stoutly denies.

In a sense, of course, any form of humanism recognizes some principle of selection and therefore an order of values in some form. Even the naturalistic theory finds, as Santayana tells us, that 'it is natural to every creature to arrange different perfections imagined by it in a scale of ascending values.' I doubt very much whether it is natural to every creature, but certainly it belongs to the nature of the human creature to do so, and it is that with which we are here concerned. The question is, of course, whether these perfections are *imagined*, and with them the scale in which they are arranged, or whether both perfections and scale are independent of the creature and *found* by him. This is, as every one knows, a central issue, not only in value theory *eo nomine*, but in modern philosophy as a whole. It marks one point at least at which naturalism and humanism come into complete opposition.

The humanist of whatever sort recognizes then, that moral distinctions and comparisons are a necessary feature of the human and with this recognition accepts some order of value. He resents as strongly as any the charge that naturalism leads to indifference and to anarchy of morals. But he believes that he can meet all such charges by accepting the principle of order as merely a *natural* character of the creature. It is sufficient that ideals and orders be merely set up or imagined by the creature and that they need not have any other kind of reality or objectivity. The fundamental contention of naturalism is, he holds, sound. The varied ideals of men are all determined by natural causes, by living dispositions of the biological order, and, as such, are pre-moral. They acquire moral status in man only because the creature, man, arranges these different ends and values in an ascending scale. Once he has done this—even if it is merely a matter of imagination, the entire situation changes for man. For he now acknowledges the obligation following from this order and has in consequence, as Santayana, for instance, curiously maintains, 'as clear and dogmatic a system of ethics as any other.'[1]

This sounds plausible enough, but any one who maintains it is immediately faced, I believe, with a dilemma that no form of naturalism has ever found it possible to escape. Nature, according to this view, is itself indifferent to man's endeavours and ideals and to all distinctions of good and bad, beautiful and ugly—yes, even of truth and falsity themselves—which arise and vary according to circumstances. Values have no cosmic significance. Man is himself the creator of values; he reads them into the cosmos and does not find them there. But if nature is thus indifferent, if the cosmos is a-moral, should not man, in so far as he is a child of nature, be indifferent also? On these premises what justifies the selection of one value or order of values above another? Would not the true humanist, with his ideal of enlargement of sympathy, or enlargement of the range of values, 'love them all'? Are we not back again in that essential parity of all values which is involved in naturalism as it is in pantheism? To set up any exclusive code must in the end involve, not only a dogmatism which is contrary to such a humanism, but also an illusion which is dissipated by natural knowledge. Moral bias is perhaps necessary for life, but viewed *sub specie aeternitatis* all opposing moralities are equally acceptable, and the true humanist, as the true philosopher, will recognize them as such.

It is possible, of course, that this may be the true humanistic attitude—that Walt Whitman, with his cry, 'O to be rid of all distinctions,' with, in short, his dictum of the parity of all values, represents not only the epitome of true humanism, but also, as it has been maintained, the true democratic metaphysics, although I hope that neither is the case. Be that as it may, all that I am contending for here is that we cannot have it both ways. We cannot, as humanists, have that vague wideness of sympathy that results in the parity of all ideals and at the same

[1] This seems to be the argument of George Santayana. See in this connection a discussion of his present views in the book entitled *George Santayana*, by George W. Howgate, 1939.

time that depth and vigour, that 'tragic sense of life,' if you will, which can come only from the transcendent character of the good. For many philosophers this incompatibility of a genuine humanism with a consistent naturalism is becoming increasingly clear. Even Nicholai Hartmann, who is far from accepting the theistic implications thought by many to be implicit in a genuine humanism, nevertheless speaks of a naturalistic theory of value as the *pons assinorum* of all forms of naturalism. In any case, the battle of humanism with naturalism is, as Mr. Hazlitt saw, a battle of theories of value.

C

The issues we have been examining arise, in our western culture at least, chiefly in connection with the Christian doctrine of man. It is what religion says about man which has, as we have seen, the greatest immediate and practical significance. Christianity has had certain things to say about him which, as every one familiar with the facts admits, whether he likes it or not, have entered into the very warp and woof of our entire western social and political thought. The doctrine of natural rights, and of the inviolability of the person presupposed, is historically ununderstandable except on the basis of this anthropology; and modern scientific anthropology, so-called, has, as every one knows, exercised a drastic, and in certain respects fatal critique upon the logical foundations of our democratic order.[1] It is, however, with the problem of religion and the humanities that we are here concerned. We may, I think, speak not only of a Christian anthropology but also of a Christian humanism.

In a suggestive lecture on the subject of 'Theology and the Humanities,' Professor R. L. Calhoun speaks of theology as one of the humanities and he bases his contention on the fact that the need of salvation is part of the essence of the human and that theology deals primarily with this theme. 'All the humanities,' he tells us, 'deal on occasion with this theme, but for theology it is definitive. A discipline approaches theology in the degree to which the theme, "Man saved by God," controls it.' This, I believe, expresses a profound truth, although I should hesitate

[1] See my Rice Institute lectures entitled *The Logical Foundations of Democratic Dogma*, especially Chapter ii.

to call theology one of the humanities; I should rather speak of it as presupposed by the humanities. To place this ancient 'science' of the knowledge of God among our wholly human activities, however exalted, is to start us on a path which if pursued consistently would seem to lead to mere humanism.[1]

The need of salvation is doubtless part of the very essence of the human and therefore the theme of salvation—God, grace and the eternal life—is the fundamental motive of all religions that have permanently satisfied the needs of humanity. The very substance of human life is the tension between the natural values and those not deducible from nature. When this tension reaches a point 'beyond all human power' to resolve, the recourse to that which trancends the human, whether to supermen or to gods, is inevitable. But an essential part of this theme is not only man's need but his value. However weak and sinful he may be thought to be, it is after all his worthiness to be saved as well as his need that is ultimately stressed. In Christianity the *theologia crucis* is the transcendent expression of the theme of salvation, but it has its counterpart and presupposition in the *theologia gloriae*, part of which is the dignity and glory of man. The heart of Christian anthropology is the tremendous pronouncement that man is the son of God, son by adoption to be sure, but no less essentially such. A central dogma of the Christian faith, it has, in the first instance, the tremendous negative significance which all dogmas have. It tells us how not to think of man. We are not to think of him as merely a creature, still less as a simian whether of high or low degree. We are never to think of him as means but only as an end. 'Thou hast made him a little lower than the angels and crowned him with dignity and honour.' This is the Christian doctrine of man and upon this anthropology, for the Christian, a genuine humanism can alone be based.

For this integral humanism man is, first of all, a creature of the natural order and, as such, lives and must live by the natural goods. 'God loves,' it has been truly said, 'the virtues

[1] R. L. Calhoun, 'Theology and the Humanities' in the collection of lectures already referred to, *The Meaning of the Humanities*. I do not know whether Professor Calhoun would accept my emendation of his thesis or not, but I do not think that he would take any fundamental issue with the way in which I have here developed it.

of the natural man and does not desire that they be negated and destroyed, but rather that they should be the basis of a supernatural structure'—a structure in which the transcendentals, goodness, beauty and truth, have their eternal being. In such a structure even the natural goods have more than a merely natural significance, and even the natural virtues, which have their 'utility' in the natural order, contain in them that which is more than this mere utility. Finally any one who apprehends this 'more,' any one who believes in the more than utilitarian worth of prudence, justice and chastity, will also be led to the supernatural virtues of faith and hope, and, above all, of charity. And when a man thinks on these things— on both the natural values and those for which there is no merely natural explanation—he will, like many another, be led to God. For he will not be able to accept any theory of the universe which makes these impossible.

For Christian anthropology, man without God is no longer man. There is a remarkable story told by Maxim Gorki in his marvellous little book on Tolstoy. Gorki was telling Tolstoy of a new writer who had appeared in Russia. Tolstoy had only one comment to make—the question, 'Does he believe in God?' At first sight, this appears to be but an extreme expression of the element of fanaticism in Tolstoy which even his greatest admirers would not deny. But it was a great deal more than this. What Tolstoy meant was that, *as a novelist*—a humanist—he would fail to catch and express the true nature of man unless he believed in the Divine with which the human, to be human, is inevitably bound up.[1]

IV

Humanism and Theism. The Superhuman and the Supernatural

A

That some presupposition of the *more than human* is necessary to the very existence and meaning of the human, is rather

[1] Tolstoy saw clearly what many only dimly sense, namely, that the Divine is a necessary presupposition of the human. But he also saw that to be such, it must be more than a presupposition purely human. However unsatisfactory in many

widely felt and is being reasserted with increasing force and insistence in philosophical circles. But it is also more or less widely held that the superhuman thus necessarily implied cannot be the supernatural and that the religion of the modern man cannot be the religion of theism in the historic sense of the word. This 'old-fashioned theism,' as it is called, is no longer tenable and the newer fashions in theology, whether they be modern forms of pantheism or a doctrine of 'a god in the making,' are, it is held, not only necessitated by modern 'science,' but even afford a better understanding of the relation of the human to the Divine. This is the general thesis of a recent book entitled *Beyond Humanism*, and since it represents in certain important respects the movement I have in mind, it may be with advantage taken as a point of departure for our present study.[1] I shall not want, however, any comments I may make to be considered a critical study of the book itself, but rather merely as the basis of the positions developed.

Those who recognize the insufficiency of mere humanism follow a line of thought with which this chapter has already made us familiar. They not only acknowledge the dehumanization of man involved in naturalism, but hold, as we have also maintained, that the humanistic and naturalistic components are ultimately incompatible. Indeed Professor Hartshorne's own argument consists partly of a criticism of well-known forms of naturalistic humanism, among them those of Dewey and Santayana; and whatever one may say of the details of the criticism he makes it quite clear that, although these positions are often separated from atheism by words, they constitute a virtual atheism with all that it implies. Some sort of theism, as opposed to such mere naturalism and atheism, is, he holds, necessary for any genuine humanism.

With this part of the argument we may, therefore, find ourselves in substantial accord. There is also much in the positive aspect of the argument that calls for no serious disagreement. It proceeds, in the first place, from an explicit denial

---

respects his argument for God's existence, and still more unsatisfactory his conception of the nature of such a God, on these two essential points his insight amounted to genius—an insight which made him the greatest novelist of our times.

[1] Charles Hartshorne, *Beyond Humanism, Essays in the New Philosophy of Nature*, 1937.

that the concept of nature developed by scientific method is the whole of nature. It accepts the well-known criticism of the billiard-ball theory of earlier physics, and recognizes that the mechanism and materialism associated with this conception have been disposed of by the new scientific epistemology. The idiom in which the argument is couched is that of Whitehead rather than of the physicists whose views we have chiefly examined, but the position is in essentials the same. Hartshorne recognizes the symbolic character of physical constructs, the fallacy of misplaced concreteness which inevitably follows upon a misplaced literalism, and finally—and most important of all—having recognized the inability of the symbols of physical science to penetrate into the ultimate nature of reality he, too, following Whitehead, returns to the 'inner recesses of consciousness.' A more adequate analysis of concrete experience leads to the belief that every actual occasion, every event, is seen to have a psychical aspect, including that of value. He too makes concessions to idealism which lead to a panpsychism, concessions which Whitehead has said lead to a conception of reality which he himself has ventured to describe as 'an objective idealism transformed unto a realistic basis.'

With all this, I repeat, we need be in no substantial disagreement. It is rather the character of the 'new theism' which creates difficulties for us—the thesis, namely, that while the God thus presupposed by a genuine theism must be superhuman, He cannot be supernatural. It is with this, I think, that we must take issue. We must ask ourselves whether this new theism —and the *imago Dei* which it includes, corresponds with a genuinely religious conception of God and, more specifically, with the idea of God demanded by a genuine theism. To both these questions the answers must, I believe, be in the negative.

I confess to considerable embarrassment in my attempt properly to evaluate all such proposals for what are called new theisms. I admit, first of all, a profound initial prejudice against the use of the terms new and old in connection with such fundamental matters—as though fashions, whether new or old, have anything to do with timeless issues! But my embarrassment goes even deeper than this. It arises from the fact that those of this way of thought can still repeat so uncritically the stock charges of the naturalists and the pragmatists against the old-fashioned theism, namely, that its supernaturalism is an 'escape philosophy', and that those who believe in the supernatural lose their interest in the human and the natural—charges which I have thought had long since been seen for the tragic misconceptions they are. I am still more embarrassed by the uncritical fashion in which the theistic proofs are described as things of the past whose unsubstantial ghosts still return to plague us. But these are, in a sense, minor matters. The real issue, and indeed the sole issue at this point, is whether the position here developed deserves the name of 'theism' and, secondly, irrespective of what we may call it, whether such a philosophy constitutes an adequate basis for a genuine humanism.

The first of these questions may, perhaps, be thought to be merely a matter of definition, but I do not think that it is. Surely it is not wholly without significance that Professor Hartshorne himself constantly vacillates between the two terms with which he seeks to characterize his position, namely, the 'new theism' and the 'new naturalism,' and that it is largely a matter of context whether he uses the one or the other. It is the new theism when he is speaking the language of religion and criticising those elements in naturalism against which he revolts; it is the new naturalism, however, when he is criticising the old-fashioned theism, and conceding elements to naturalism of which he approves. Can it be that he is trying to run with the hare and hunt with the hounds? If so he is merely doing what many protagonists of humanism are constantly attempting to do. I should not labour this point were it not that it is just this ambiguity which not only vitiates so much of modern naturalism, but equally a large part of modern 'liberal religion.'

For myself I doubt whether such a new naturalism can be properly called a form of theism, whether old or new, and it can only confuse the issue so to call it. It seems to be assumed that it is enough for religion, and even for a theistic theology, to show that values and mind are in the world, no matter how primitive these aspects are, and that a vague panpsychism such as here presented constitutes a sufficient basis. Now it is undoubtedly a great thing—at least from the standpoint of the present argument—to find mind and values in the universe at all. That is the Alpha of a philosophical theology, although it is not its Omega. It is true also that such panpsychism is also the covert metaphysics of much of nature poetry, and the philosopher does well to listen to the poets at this point. But the poet and the humanist are not concerned wholly, or indeed primarily, with nature, but rather with human nature. When we take into account what the humanities have to say about man—especially the moral element which creates all the struggle and drama of human life—a theism such as this seems singularly inadequate. What the humanities say about man, if indeed they are to be listened to at all, is that persons alone are the conscious bearers of values and that the values, the acknowledgment of which constitute man a person, presuppose for their very meaning the coimplicate of perfection, and a metempirical reference to a Perfect Being of which they are, so to speak, the reflection. In a human context at least, it seems also inevitable that 'the concept of personality should dominate,' that this Perfect Being who is God should possess the character of person with an absolute possession. This does not exclude the possibility that, as we have seen, personality conditioned by the way in which it appears in creatures is a symbol when applied to Deity, although an inadequate symbol, for it embodies an intuition which is itself non-symbolic.

The point I am making is a simple one, but, as it appears to me, as inescapable as simple. It is not enough, I repeat, for true religion and for an adequate theology to show that values are all-pervasive in the cosmos, no matter how primitive these aspects are. As against certain forms of naturalism this is a significant negative argument, but as a basis for any form of theism it is insufficient. There is, indeed, a 'higher pantheism,' as Tennyson wrote, and, in contrast to some forms of pantheism, very near the kingdom. There is perhaps also a higher naturalism which, in contrast to lower forms, is greatly to be preferred. But whether high or low, neither pantheism nor naturalism is enough for a genuine humanism, as we have come to understand it. It may be that this is all science permits, although I do not think so, but in any case that is another matter and in this context irrelevant. The only question here—and it is one which we have every right to ask—is whether such a theism, if it may be so called, affords an adequate basis for a genuine humanism. Surely not. A genuine humanism does not well consort with any and every conception of God. When once we understand what man is and what it is that makes him truly man, we certainly get little backing for a genuine humanism from ideas of God that make him merely the Life Force, still less from those which see in God merely a name for an all-pervasive energy, however that energy be conceived. Any idea of God derivable solely from science must be a misnomer.

V

Humanism and the Imago Dei. *What the Humanities Have to Say About God.*

A

There can be little question, I think, that when we speak of God in a specifically human context, we always have in mind the idea of a Perfect Being—perfect in the sense of possessing perfect knowledge, perfect power, perfect goodness or holiness—yes, also perfect beauty in so far as we are developed enough to put beauty among the higher values. It has been maintained that 'the idea of God must mean at least these things to be of any moral value whatsoever.' This is perhaps an exaggeration in that lesser ideas of God have been, and still are, of value to the human race. An imaginative and understanding interpretation of what we call the lower levels of religion may even lead us to love these *idola* which other men have so greatly loved and adored. And yet, when all is said, an idea of God adequate for us can be only that of a Perfect Being and it must remain so if it is to be of highest and enduring value.

And yet it is against this very idea of God that many of the new theisms and new naturalisms have set their face; it is the very essence of the old-fashioned theism which they attack. The idea of a finite God or of a god in the making seems to many, not only the *imago Dei* alone permitted us by science, but also the idea of God really presupposed by our moral and religious experience. This has led to a widespread 'redesigning' of the idea of God—streamlined, so to speak, in the sense that from it are eliminated all characters and predicates which are thought

419

to be superfluous in the pragmatic sense of their functional character in the practical and social life of man. What William James has to say of the metaphysical predicates of Deity indicates perfectly the character of these new designs.[1]

It cannot be denied that, at first sight at least, the motives for thus redesigning our ideas of God are at least partly humanistic and in a certain sense even religious. It is often argued that the God of religion—of human prayer and praise—cannot be the Absolute, and again that the need of salvation, which is apparently part of the human as such, demands, for some inexplicable reason, that to be a saving God, God must be a fellow struggler. Above all, it is argued that to keep the goodness of God in face of the manifest evil in the world is the first requirement, and that this can be done only by abandoning His omniscience and His omnipotence. It is not my intention to meet all the issues raised by these motives but merely to recognize their humanistic character and, in so far as possible, evaluate them rightly in the present context. I do not deny their force, but I do deny that they are valid when the problem of God and the humanities is rightly understood.

One can understand how the simple can love and adore finite gods—and the poet and the dramatist often picture such devotion—but it is difficult to see how the enlightened soul can continue to love and worship such gods. One can understand how the simple can say of his god, 'he is a good fellow and all will be well'—and to many the goodness of God means little more than this—but it is difficult to see how to the enlightened believer such goodness can be divine goodness at all. But hardest of all to understand is how salvation by such a god could be salvation in any significant sense. It could be little more than that which simple men have constantly and pathetically sought from saviours among themselves and by whom they have just as constantly been left in the lurch. A salvation worthy of the name could come only from that Perfect Being in whom goodness and power are one.

Be all this as it may—and I think it is true—the real issue is much deeper than this. The doctrine of the Perfect Being and of the divine attributes is at once a metaphysics and also a

[1] Chapter iv, pp. 150 f.

theory of the nature of ultimate value, the conception of God being thus at the same time the definition of the goal or object of human life. Thus the final good not only for the religious but for almost all western philosophers consisted for more than a millennium in some mode of assimilation of or approximation to the Divine nature, whether the mode was defined as imitation, or contemplation or absorption. In other words, the very integrity of our human values—of honour, beauty and intelligence—is bound up with the *imago Dei* as *ens perfectissimum*. Deny all the attributes which God possesses with an absolute possession, and in the same breath you have denied ultimate meaning to our human notions of the Good. Make of God a finite being like ourselves, and you have · accepted a theory of the universe which makes honour, beauty and intelligence, in any genuinely valid sense, 'impossible.'[1]

B

It does not become us, to be sure, to be too captious of any philosophy which proposes to take us beyond mere humanism. As it is a mistake to be contemptuous of the theologian for seeming over-ready to welcome any idea of God which the scientist permits him, so it is a mistake also to be over-critical of those humanists who still wish to use the name of God, however forlorn and impoverished their idea may seem to be. But we do have the right, as well as the duty, to be critical in the philosophical sense—to raise the question whether in using that name they have not taken God's name in vain. We may recognize that it is natural that men, inspired by what they call the

[1] Hesketh Pearson in his book on Shaw (*op. cit.*, p. 254), tells us that Shaw sent a copy of his *The Showing-Up of Blanco Posnet* to Tolstoy, with a letter in which he wrote:

'To me God does not yet exist; but there is a creative force constantly struggling to evolve an executive origin of god-like knowledge and power; that is to achieve omnipotence and omniscience; and every man and woman born is a fresh attempt to achieve the object. . . . We are here to help God, to do his work, to remedy his old errors, to strive towards Godhead ourselves.'

Brave words these but, as I believe, as futile as brave. I wonder whether Shaw would say these things with quite the same conviction as in earlier days. Would the Shaw who, on meditating upon the possibilities of the atomic bomb, wrote of the blowing up of our civilization, if not indeed of the universe, as an eventuality which he 'would not be expected to deprecate,' now hope very much from a 'god' among whose 'errors' are the atomic bomb itself, still less from a god that 'does not yet exist'?

scientific spirit, should, if they seek to retain the idea of God at all, seek also to mould it to the scientist's heart's desire. It is natural also that, inspired by the legitimate motives of the humanist, men should also seek to mould our image of God to what seems to them to be the deepest demands of the human. It is, however, only just that we should ask of them, scientist and humanist alike, that they realize what they are doing and to face the consequences, both practical and logical, of their daring.

In the first place both must realize that the idea of God as thus redesigned is not the *imago Dei* as it functions in any genuinely religious context. Dean Inge is perhaps over-severe in his strictures upon these modern notions of God, but surely he is right in pointing out that 'no theist, whether Christian, Jew, or any other kind, would recognize them as identical with what they mean by God.'[1] It is scarcely possible that they should be able to say to such believers, 'Him whom ye ignorantly worship, declare I unto you,' for they would immediately know that such a God is not the God whom they worship, whether ignorantly or not.

In the second place, they must recognize that all talk of a God who is superhuman but not supernatural, of a theism which is both theism and naturalism, is to play fast and loose with words. I suppose few who really name the name of God at all would doubt that religion presupposes at least the superhuman—some 'power, *not ourselves*, which makes for righteousness.' But really to take the notion of the superhuman seriously is also to imply the notion of the supernatural. If, as we found, there is in man that which transcends nature in any sense intelligible to science, then, *a fortiori*, that which transcends the human must also transcend nature and be supernatural in the proper sense of that word. If, on the other hand, we include in nature 'all that is,' even that which many so-called naturalists would wish to see included, namely, the quality of deity itself, then nature, so conceived, becomes a Super-nature and cannot be viewed synoptically save as so conceived. We may still call it nature if we will—there is apparently no limit to the magic men may work with that blessed word—but we shall not long deceive others however much we may deceive ourselves.

[1] *Op cit.*, pp. 230-1.

C

Humanity and Deity thus remains the fundamental issue of the philosophy of religion. There are those who say, Where there is no God there is no man. Man without God is no longer man. There are those, on the other hand, who challenge this conception of humanity and tell us that to be men we must disavow God and give glory only to man. Man with God has often become less than human. Man's inhumanity to man, including himself, is not an idle word, and while much of this inhumanity may result from his thinking of his fellows as mere animals and as merely means to ends, much of his inhumanity comes also, it is affirmed, from his thinking of himself as more than man, and by sacrificing his humanity to the Moloch of the Absolute.

We are familiar enough with this issue on the practical level of morals, politics, and even art, but this practical opposition of the two humanisms has its basis in a much more fundamental opposition of which we have become increasingly aware throughout this discussion. Naturalistic humanism contends that 'theism' involves a humanization of the cosmos and that this humanization of the cosmos 'means the moral annulment of man.' It is not my purpose to re-argue this issue here—the entire chapter contains a refutation of the argument. He who says that theism in its classical form humanizes the cosmos understands neither the classical argument itself, nor the doctrine of analogy of being which is based upon it. He who says that theism means the moral annulment of man understands neither the moral character of man as exhibited by the humanities nor the conception of Deity which is supposed to annul him. Supernaturalistic humanism, on the contrary, contends that, far from annulling man, this theistic conception of the cosmos is the only one which makes man as man possible, for it embodies in a supereminent degree the values which make him human. Here we have the great divide which separates the two humanisms and, with them, the two ideologies which battle for supremacy in the cultural and political life of the present. So far as the philosophical side of the question is concerned, it is sufficiently answered, I believe. On the practical side, it seems patent, to me at least, that a humanism divorced from supernatural conceptions tends more and more to end in

nihilism and sub-human naturalism. This the entire development of modern life and thought makes ever more and more
clear.

In concluding his Gifford Lectures, *Theism and Humanism*,
Earl Balfour thus sums up the object of his lectures: 'My desire
has been to show that all which is best in human culture,
whether associated with beauty, goodness or knowledge, requires God for its support, that humanism without theism loses
more than half its value.'[1] This, too, is in a sense my desire,
but my argument goes further than this. Humanism without
theism loses not half but, in the end, all its value. For there are
theories of the universe which make our human values impossible. I have sought to show also that any true portrayal of
the human, any objectification of the spirit of man (such as we
find it in the humanities)—at least of man when he is at his
highest stretch—witnesses to God.

VI

Humanism and Mysticism: Life and 'Beyond Life'

A

That which above all negates a merely naturalistic humanism
is the mystical element in the humanities. An essential part of
the humanities, and a part, moreover, which is above all
significant for their complete understanding, is the mystical
element present in all literature—and indeed in all art—
whether specifically religious or not.

'Mysticism in English Literature' is the title of a suggestive
study of this element, and such a book might be written about
the literature of all the great cultural peoples.[2] In addition to
the 'devotional and religious mystics' there are studies of what
are called the 'love and beauty mystics' and the 'nature
mystics.' It is of man and nature that the poet sings and about
which, directly or indirectly, the novelist and the dramatist
write. Of man it is love that forms the principle theme, of
nature the 'presences' which make it more than the shell which

[1] *Op. cit.*, p. 248.
[2] C. F. E. Spurgeon, *Mysticism in English Literature*, Cambridge, 1914.

appears to our physical eyes; of both it is the beauty which the poet seeks to express, that beauty which is at the same time truth. One cannot long dwell upon these themes without being driven, in greater or lesser degree, to that act of the soul which can be described only as 'trenching on the mystical.'

As the meaning of things in space and time, even for the scientist, lies outside space and time, so the meaning of our life, as lived in space and time, lies beyond this life. This appears most clearly in that greatest of all themes with which poet, dramatist and novelist are so greatly preoccupied, namely, what men call love. Our life in space and time is both initiated and consummated in acts of love. As a 'biological urge,' the way in which science can alone speak of it, it is a meaningless repetition in space and time, as all the pessimists, pre-eminently Schopenhauer, have rightly seen. But all love—in its lowest as in its highest forms—'seeks eternity,' and it is in this seeking that its meaning alone is found. Wherever there is love, there are, for all men, moments also when they trench on the mystical.

Art, and above all poetry in the sense of our definition, is an objectification of life and of the inner spirit of man, but just in so far as it becomes an objectification, it becomes also, implicitly, a criticism of life. Such criticism involves inevitably a transcendence of life and thus leads us, as the subtitle of the section suggests, Beyond Life.[1] If for the critical scientist the meaning of things in space and time, if indeed there be any meaning at all, must lie outside space and time, even more to the poet is it clear that, if the life lived in space and time— and with it the loves that make it life—are to have any ultimate meaning at all, that meaning must be found beyond life. It is at this point that the mystical element enters into literature and art as it does into science.

This element of mysticism in literature we may, in contrast to the specifically 'theological' mysticism of religious devotion, describe as natural mysticism, natural, to be sure, not in the sense of the nature mystics, nor still less in the sense of 'naturalism', but in the sense that the mystical is, in the words of von Hügel, 'something in the soul of every man,' part of

---

[1] This is the title of a book by James Branch Cabell in which all this is beautifully said.

human nature as such. It is accordingly only to be expected that natural mysticism should appear when the poetry of love and of nature are at their highest pitch, that the language of poetry should insensibly pass over into the language of religion, and that nature mysticism and the mysticism of love and beauty should become devotional and even philosophical mysticism.

'There are,' writes Plotinus in a letter to Flaccus, 'different roads by which this end' (apprehension of the Infinite) 'may be reached. The love of beauty which exalts the poet, the devotion to the One and that ascent of science which makes the ambition of the philosopher, and that love and those prayers by which some devout and ardent soul tends in its moral purity towards perfection. These are the great highways conducting to that height above the actual and the particular, where we stand in the immediate presence of the Infinite which shines out as from the depths of the soul.' Of these three ways we have now considered two, the ascent of science and the love of beauty which exalts the poet. We may now turn to the third way, to that love and to those prayers by which the devout and ardent soul tends towards that Perfection which is God.

Chapter XIII

Religion and Mysticism. What the Mystics Tell us about Divine Things

I — A

IT IS impossible to understand religion, much less to evaluate it adequately, without including in it that element which is known as the mystical. From the most primitive religion, with its sense of the *mysterium tremendum*, to the most developed form, with its sense of the mystery of the Divine love and grace, mystery in some form is an integral element; and where there is mystery there is always also a mystical way of apprehending and also of expressing the intuition of the Divine.

Every religion has not only its mystical element, but its mystics *eo nomine*—those who having found this unique way of apprehension make of these supernal experiences the be-all and end-all of life. Whether this 'exclusive mysticism,' as von Hügel calls it, this excessive concentration, with its technical exercises and its ecstasies, is a disease of religion, as some profess to believe, or its superlative form, I shall not attempt to say. In any case it is not with this aspect of mysticism that I am principally concerned but rather with its character as an essential element in all religious experience and its expression. For as it is impossible to understand religion itself without this element so also is it impossible to understand theology without taking into account the points at which it inevitably trenches on the mystical.

Taken in the broadest sense, the mystical experience is not only the mother-sea and fountain-head of all religion, but also an essential element in all discourse about God. Every dogma of religion has, therefore, in addition to its practical and intellectual elements, its mystical character. Of the two fundamental types of theology, the positive and the negative, it is with the latter that the term mystical theology is usually associated, but both presuppose an element of mysticism. If God cannot be named at all, then, obviously, to know that he cannot we must also know what it is in Him that makes our names inapplicable; and such knowledge, if it be such, can be only of a mystical character.

On the other hand, if God can be named, if by analogy we can apply to Him, the unconditioned, our predicates as humanly conditioned, we must also know, in some fashion at least, what it is in Him that makes possible their ontological sublimation and therefore their application in a supereminent degree. To know this surely involves trenching on the mystical; and therefore a positive no less than a negative theology involves an element which may fairly be called mystical.

B

This then is the general situation out of which the problem of mysticism arises for the philosophy of religion. But it may be made still more specific by emphasizing the point at which the issues become especially clear, namely, the problem of religious symbolism and its correlate the notion of non-symbolic knowledge. Doubtless theology is not merely 'a dialectical development of symbols,' but it is none the less true that the language of theology, like all language, contains a symbolic element. Negative theology would dispense with all symbols and seek a wholly immediate oneness with the Divine, while a more positive theology seeks, in and through the symbol, that which transcends all symbolic representation. In either case the concept of symbolism is central in mysticism.

True mysticism, it is sometimes said, has nothing to do with analogies and symbols. 'The believer must suppose that there is with and through all images some direct noesis of the supreme noumenon, God himself. In so far as mysticism is a privileged heightening of the noesis it is a fuller grasp of Him who is eternal.'[1] True enough in so far as the last sentence is concerned, but the question about which the main problems of mysticism revolve is, as we shall see, whether this heightened noesis is with and through the images and symbols, or whether the fuller grasp of the Eternal is possible without them. Mysticism has everything to do with symbols. In this life we have no other experience of the Absolute than through symbolic representation. The real issue is whether we have 'this heightened noesis' at all.

The knowledge value of the mystical experience is, accordingly, an inevitable problem in any philosophy of religion, as

[1] Austin Farrer, *Finite and Infinite*, p. 56.

indeed the more general problem of the mystical element in all knowledge is an inevitable problem in any philosophy. Even if, with the French positivist, we say, 'Mysticisme c'est l'ennemi,' mysticism must be there in order to be an enemy. If, on the other hand, we accept mysticism not as an enemy but as a friend, even if we are not mystics ourselves (or think we are not)—if we recognize the mystical experience as real—we must seek to understand it and evaluate it in the context of our human knowledge as a whole.[1]

II

Definitions of Mysticism. Natural and Theological Mysticism

A

Like religion itself mysticism is difficult to define and for much the same reasons. Definition is not wholly futile but we must recognize that the same dilemma—between the narrower and broader notions—is present here as elsewhere.

'The best definition' of religious mysticism, according to Miss Underhill, is the following: it is 'in essence the concentration of all the forces of the soul upon a supernatural object conceived and loved as a living person.' That this defines a highly specialized form of religious mysticism, and one characteristic of many Christian mystics, is undoubtedly true, but there are two difficulties in the definition, even as a definition of religious mysticism.

The conviction of supernatural realities is, of course, necessary to religious mysticism, as it is to religion itself, but this reality is not necessarily conceived as a living person. Even in Christian theology, for which, as we have seen, person is a name which is applicable to God in a supreme degree, there is still that in the fullness of His being which cannot thus be named, and many Christians have felt this deeply. It is true that in

---

[1] In contrast with the richness of well-recognized works on mysticism such as Baron von Hügel's *The Mystical Element in Religion*, Dean Inge's *Christian Mysticism*, Evelyn Underhill's *The Mystics of the Church*, Dom Butler's *Western Mysticism*, and Rudolf Otto's *West-Oestliche Mystik*, this chapter will appear thin indeed. I can only hope that, despite its manifest inadequacy, it may be without serious misunderstandings.

the main Christian mystics tell us that God is love and the Being who thus loves is conceived by them as a living Person. But even among them are found those who feel person to be an inadequate symbol and recoil from the word love unless it be sublimated into that intellectual love of God which, as Spinoza said, is God's love for Himself.

Nor is it wholly true that mysticism is that concentration of the soul of which this definition speaks. Such concentration is, indeed, a characteristic of mysticism as a specialized way of life. But the mystical element in religion, as such, does not seem to require it. The mystical experience does indeed come when man is, so to speak, 'at his highest stretch,' but that stretch is rarely forced. If the kingdom of Heaven itself is not to be taken by violence, neither, we may well believe, are any anticipations of the heavenly vision likely to come when we seek to summon them by force.

A much more satisfactory definition of mysticism, even in the religious context, is, so it seems to me, that of Récéjac. 'Mysticism,' he tells us, 'is the tendency to draw near to the Absolute in moral union by symbolic means.'[1] It is true that if the former definition seems too narrow, this may seem too broad. While the term Absolute avoids the limitations of the preceding definition it seems also to exclude what is certainly an essential element in some forms of mysticism. But this, I think, is only in appearance. For while the mystic may conceive and love the supernatural reality as a living person, he never, if he is a true mystic, doubts that He is person in a supereminent and absolute degree. The expression, 'in moral union' seems to exclude the cognitive aspect, but this too is only apparent; it simply emphasizes the fact that the union is one of feeling as well as thought. Finally, the expression, 'by symbolic means' seems to offer some difficulty. It is true that in some forms of mysticism the symbol is in the end negated, but it is by means of the symbol that the mystic, in the first instance at least, always 'draws near,' and in the major forms of mysticism the symbol is never completely abandoned. Even in the mystical experience the symbol is part of the intuition itself.

This definition does not, however, really go to the heart of

[1] E. Récéjac, *Les Fondements de la connaissance mystique.* English translation 1899, p. 70.

the matter, as Récéjac himself recognizes. The really fundamental character of all mystics, of whatever type, is, as he tells
us, that they are able to make certain syntheses which the non-
mystical find impossible. It is impossible 'without an act of
mysticism actually to make in one's self a synthesis of freedom
and determinism.' But there are other syntheses equally fundamental which the mystics claim to make—of unity and plurality,
of the monistic and the personalistic concepts of God, of being
and becoming, of perfect activity and perfect repose. Above all,
there is the synthesis of the One and the Good—of the *ens perfectissimum* and the *ens realissimum*. The essence of mysticism is then
the *coincidentia oppositorum* which, on the intellectual side at least,
has been the *sine qua non* of mysticism of all times and all places.

It is sometimes charged that this conception of mysticism
is really nothing more than 'a protest against the limitation of
experience to the data of the senses and pure reason' and that it
'is not describable as mysticism in any recognizable sense.'[1]
With this I cannot agree. True, it does express such a protest,
as all mysticism must, but it is much more than a protest. The
term mysticism is, indeed, used by writers of a positivistic turn
of mind for all philosophies which do not so limit experience and
therefore are transcendental or 'spiritual,' but this element in a
philosophy does not in itself make it mystical. All mysticism
presupposes the transcendental and the spiritual, but the latter
type of philosophies, although they tend, as we shall see, to
trench on the mystical, are not, as such, forms of mysticism.

B

There is little question, then, that it is these 'acts of synthesis'
that distinguish the mystical from other forms of experience and
just as little question, I think, that of all these syntheses it is
that of the One and the Good about which all the others revolve.
It is the fusion of the Good or Value with Being which, while it
is never possible by wholly intellectual means, is, nevertheless,
the essential element in all that the mystics really say. The identity
of the sovereign Good with absolute Being is the postulate of
dogmatic theology; the logical necessity of this identification
is the burden of rational theology, and the actuality of this
identity is the essence of the beatific vision.

[1] A. S. Pringle-Pattison, article on 'Mysticism,' *The Encyclopaedia Britannica*.

The source of this element in western thought, and therefore in the major forms of Christian mysticism, is, of course, Plato and the Neo platonism stemming from Plotinus. 'You have been told,' says Socrates in the *Republic*, 'that the essential form of the Good is the highest object of science and that this essence, by blending with just things and all other created objects, renders them useful and advantageous.' It is this blending, this fusion of value and being, that constitutes the final insight, the essential *Einheitsschau* of all great religion and great philosophy alike. The 'One or the Good,' the title of the Sixth Ennead of Plotinus, represents the highest expression of natural mysticism and the identity of the Good with Being the highest form of theological mysticism. The deliverances of reason may indeed lead us to the insight that *ens et bonum convertuntur*, but the full realization of the actuality of the synthesis is itself possible only by trenching on the mystical.

This is then the central synthesis upon which all the others depend. Of these others, one stands out as of primary importance in the mystical experience and of equal significance for mystical theology, namely, the synthesis of the temporal with the timeless. 'Mysticism,' writes Dean Inge in his volume *Christian Mysticism*, 'is the attempt to realize in thought and feeling, the immanence of the temporal in the eternal and of the eternal in the temporal.' The dualism of time and eternity with which that of value and existence is so closely connected, is for thought alone perhaps unsolvable. Yet nothing is clearer than that the great mystics have been able to make this synthesis and have found, as we shall later see, a language in which to express these deepest of ontological realizations. The synthesis of the temporal and the eternal is, moreover, the point at which pre-eminently religion and philosophy come together, for the problem of the relation of temporal process and timeless being and value is the ultimate problem for both.

C

The synthesis of Value and Being—of the One and the Good—remains then the fundamental synthesis of mysticism. The realization of this synthesis—in both thought and feeling— implies of necessity the two points between which all mystical experience moves—the subjective pole of love and emotion and the objective pole of intuition and insight.

What I have in mind corresponds, of course, to the distinction made by Rudolf Otto between the two great types of mysticism—between the way of *Selbstversenkung* and the way of *Einheitsschau*. For the former God or the Super-reality is thought of as primarily the being whom the mystic finds by sinking into the centre of his own being (the subjective pole); for the latter God or the Super-reality is thought of as the being whom the mystic finds by going to the One behind the phenomena of the world (the objective pole).[1]

These two poles are present in some form and in some degree in all types of the mystical experience. The experience of union may be subjectively toned, the emphasis put upon the *soul* and its union with God or its *absorption* in the Absolute. In this case the descriptions of the mystical experience are 'psychological' in character and it is this aspect which the psychology of religion inevitably exploits. On the other hand, the emphasis may be upon the object with which the union is achieved, in which case we have the beatific *vision*, and it is the content of this vision which the mystic describes. There is no question in the present context of evaluating one aspect or pole of the mystical experience more highly than the other—both are necessary and both significant—but for our present purpose it is the objective pole, the *Einheitsschau* that is of pre-eminent importance. An agreement of the mystics with regard to the subjective 'transport,' while significant, tells us little or nothing of import for knowledge. It is the descriptions of the vision, not its beatific character, which, being predominantly theological and metaphysical, are therefore chiefly significant for the problem of the knowledge value of mysticism.

D

In all discussions of mysticism a distinction is made between natural and theological mysticism, and since it is upon the existence of a natural mysticism in man that the argument of the present chapter largely rests, it is necessary that these notions be clearly defined and their relations definitely shown.

[1] Rudolf Otto, *Mysticism, East and West* English translation, Chapter iv.

Mysticism, as Baron von Hügel tells us, 'consists precisely in being not everything in any one soul but something in every soul of man; and presenting at its fullest amplest development, among certain special natures with the help of certain special graces and heroisms, what in some degree or form is present in every truly human soul.'[1] Or, again, as Miss Underhill tells us, theological mysticism 'is merely a specialized form of the heightened and completed life which is the constant characteristic of the human consciousness.' That 'every one who wakens to a world that is more than the world of sense and intellect is, of necessity, started on the road that follows at low levels, and among many illusions, the path which the mystic and the mystical philosopher travel at high levels.'[2] This 'something in the soul of every man,' this 'constant characteristic of the human consciousness,' I shall call natural mysticism in contrast with supernatural or theological mysticism.

The recognition of this universal and natural mysticism is, I believe, the *sine qua non* of any understanding of the specifically religious mysticism and of the mystical theology which grows out of it. 'Only thus' (because of this something in the soul of every man) 'does mysticism' (in religion), as von Hügel further tells us, 'attain its full dignity.' It is only because mysticism *eo nomine* is but a specialized form of a constant character of all human consciousness that what the mystics tell us can be understood, and what they say can be judged to be either true or false. The philosopher is, indeed, often criticized for not making an absolute distinction between natural and theological forms of mysticism. He supposes, it is said, that man, left to himself, provided he makes the required effort, is competent to reach the mystical experience. This, however, the theologians maintain is the gift of Grace. But the fact that, as von Hügel puts it, 'among certain natures, and with the help of certain special graces and heroisms,' a vision of God is vouchsafed, does not exclude the fact that there is something in all of us which enables us to recognize it when it is told. In this respect the situation is similar to that of natural and supernatural faith. If we envisage the latter as something wholly unrelated to the natural and primary acknowledgments of value characteristic of the

[1] *The Mystical Element in Religion*, Volume II, p. 284.
[2] *The Mystics of the Church*, especially pp. 14 ff.

434

moral consciousness, we end in making it wholly unintelligible. The same is true of any complete divorce between natural and theological mysticism.

There are, to be sure, those who deny this relation. Thus Paul Elmer More takes issue especially with Miss Underhill's formulation of this thesis. Her view of the mystics 'simply as people who see and experience more vividly a Reality which is there for us all', while applicable to devotional forms of mysticism is, he holds, 'false if extended to such writers as Ruysbroeck and John of the Cross. Her method of interpreting the bolder mystics may be defended on the ground that it alone can bring us into brotherly relation with them and so help us in our lives, but it will do so only by ignoring a large portion of the facts.'[1] I am, of course, not unaware of this bolder mysticism, although St. John of the Cross in my view hardly represents it. It is rather the greater boldness of a Tauler, of a Meister Eckhart, of a Boehme which cuts them off, not only from brotherly relations with us, but also, as I believe, from such relations with the majority of Christian mystics. It consists in taking a final step the precise significance of which it is all important to understand in determining the knowledge value of mysticism.

This final step, associated with what is known as negative theology, consists in denying all predicates to God and, finally, when carried to the limit, in denying also the subjective characters of love and feeling in the believer which certain attributes of Deity alone can evoke. Thus both poles of the mystical experience tend to collapse, leaving indeed only the darkest night of the soul in which all distinctions disappear.

The negative mystics, western as well as eastern—generally agree that God is not an object of human understanding at all. He utterly transcends all predication and everything said of Him is untrue. 'Be still,' Eckhart says in a sermon 'and prate not of God [i.e. of the Godhead] for whatever you prate in words about him is a lie and sinful. If I say God is good it is not true; for what is good can grow better, and what can grow better can grow best. Now these three things [good, better, best] are far from God for he is above all,' that is above all distinctions. No

---

[1] Paul Elmer More, in his chapter on 'Christian Mysticism' in *The Catholic Faith*, 1931, p. 286, note.

word that voices distinctions or characteristics may be spoken of the Godhead. Eckhart's favourite terms are: 'the Wordless Godhead; the Nameless Nothing; the Naked Godhead; the Immovable Rest; the Still Wilderness where no one is at home.'[1] God is not only beyond the Good but 'beyond all existence.'

There can be little question that mysticism as bold as this cuts itself off from brotherly relations with us, but it also constitutes a break with the main stream of Christian mysticism. If, as it has been said, the fanatic is one who redoubles his efforts when he has forgotten his goal, surely the epithet is not wholly inapplicable here. The object of all mysticism is the vision of the One or the Good and, on the subjective side, the union of the soul with the Sovereign Good as the love of God. In seeking this goal the mystic seeks to annul every barrier between himself and the Divine and to realize everything revealed in scripture as an 'eternal now.' In this effort it is only natural that he should seek to transcend the mythical and the mythical categories of positive religion. It is even understandable that he should seek to interpret the historical pronouncements of religion in terms of that which is beyond all time and history. But once started on this path, it is possible to forget the goal and to deny the very things which the vision of the One and the Good implies, namely, the 'existence' of the One and the Good themselves, and thus follow the dialectic into nothingness. If this is the essence of mysticism it is not surprising that to the pious it should seem a disease and to the theologian anathema. A God who is a 'naked Godhead' and a 'nameless nothing' is no God at all. This is, however, not the way of the devotional mystics. That which above all distinguishes them is their ability to combine the God of prayer and praise, the loving Father in Heaven, with the God of the philosopher, the most perfect Being. This is true even of St. John of the Cross, cited as one of these bolder mystics who, while he may warn us against the 'letter that Killeth,' never doubted that the symbol was a way to the Absolute.[2]

I should not of course deny that many mystics, both of the East and the West, have, in fighting the literal, ended in this negative

---

[1] Quoted from Rufus Jones, *Studies in Mystical Religion*, London 1909, pp. 225 f.
[2] See in this connection Robert Sencourt's *Carmelite and Poet, A Framed Portrait of St. John of the Cross, With His Poems in Spanish*, 1944.

mysticism. Even in Christianity there are those who, as Cassirer has said, have 'fought this fight' and followed this road. It is true also that, as F. S. C. Northrop holds, the philosophical mystics of the east have found their 'reality' in a wholly 'undifferentiated continuum' which is indeed a nameless nothing. I should merely contend that it is not the main road of religious mysticism, and not the road that mysticism must necessarily take.[1] If, as some hold, such mysticism is a disease, it is not a disease of religion but of philosophy. That which makes the truly devotional mystics immune from this disease is love, which is always a prophylactic against the cancerous growth of logical nihilism. 'Logic is love', Bosanquet tells us with an unwonted daring, but if it is love, it is not that logic which is sufficient of itself, but one which gets both its justification and its drive from that which is beyond itself, namely the oneness of the good and the true.

III

The Language of Mysticism. Mystical Insight as Communicable and Intelligible

A

On certain views of mysticism there should be, strictly speaking, no language of mysticism. It is the very inadequacy of human language—and of the intelligence bound up and conditioned by that language—that gives rise to mysticism. But here we face a paradox, for it is the mystics who, above all, seek to express the ineffable. They tell us to be still and not prate of God, and then proceed to speak, and often in no modest fashion. There are the silent mystics, it is true, but there are also the garrulous, if we may use the term without offence, and it is from the latter that we must learn if we learn at all. Studies of the specifically Christian mystics, such as those of James, Evelyn Underhill and von Hügel, make it abundantly clear that there is a special language of mysticism and it is this form of speech that we must learn to understand.

[1] See in this connection, Ernst Cassirer, *Die Philosophie der Symbolischen Formen*, Volume II, pp. 303 ff. Also F. S. C. Northrop, 'The Complementary Emphasis of Eastern Intuitive and Western Scientific Philosophy,' being Chapter viii of *Philosophy—East and West*, already cited.

The language which the mystics speak is, in the first instance
at least, the language of poetry, as all religious language is, and,
as we are told, 'wholly concrete.' Its images and symbols are
taken, in the main, from sources so deep in the human heart that
they are understandable to all those for whom the heart has a
language which the intellect knows not of. There is, first of all,
'that craving which makes man a wanderer and a pilgrim, that
longing to go out from his normal world in search for a lost home,
or a better country, an Eldorado, a Heavenly Syon, a city that
hath foundations; that craving of heart for heart, of the soul for
its perfect mate,' and finally 'the craving for inward purity and
perfection which makes men ascetics and in the last resort
saints'—it is in language such as this that the experience of the
mystics is expressed and in such terms that the seeking and finding of the Absolute are described.[1]

The love of the creature for 'its perfect mate' has always been
considered a natural analogue of the most obvious sort of the
supernatural love of the mystical experience. *The Song of Songs*
has for the Christian mystic become the supreme image, con-
secrated by scripture, for the trials and progress of the mystical
experience of the love of God. It was the inspiration of St. John
of the Cross, as M. Robert Sencourt tells us, no less than of St.
Theresa who was closely associated with him in the great
Carmelite reformation. But there is also the love of the creature
for all created things and this also may be a natural analogue.
The glory of the simple dandelion—of weed and grass—is a
revelation of the love of God. 'The flower garden of the world'
is, for the mystic, 'the veritable clothing of God.' 'Well, I wrote,'
says Mother Juliana, 'that heaven and earth and all that is
made, is great, large, fair and good; the full head of joy is to

---

[1] The 'psychological resemblances of poetry and mysticism,' so often commented
upon in studies of the mystics, are, as Récéjac says, 'very close. Francis of Assisi
loved nothing so much as the songs of the troubadours and Theresa of Avila was
absorbed in the poetry of Spanish chivalry before either of them entered into the
contemplative life. That which separates them,' he continues, 'perhaps all that
separates them, is faith. While the poet is far from identifying himself with his
creations, the mystic identifies himself with his symbols.' (*Op. cit.* p. 94.) The close
relations are undoubted but we may well question whether the difference is properly expressed. Doubtless the poet does not identify himself with his symbols, but
neither does the mystic, and both believe that they convey truth. The real difference lies in the fact that mysticism is a heightened noesis of the numinous and this
expresses itself in a language which, while poetic, is more than poetry.

behold God in all and truly to enjoy Our Lord is a full and loving thanksgiving in his sight.' 'This completely unmanichaean attitude, so Christian when held as ultimate among the divers sad and joyful, strenuous and contemplative moods of the soul' is, as von Hügel tells us, 'as strongly present in Clement of Alexandria in the Sts. Catherine of Siena and Genoa, in St. John of the Cross, and indeed in all the recollective thoughts of the great mystics.'[1]

There is one aspect of the language of mysticism of unique importance. As a protest against the abstractions of theology and philosophy mysticism is primarily concrete. But for the mystic the very universals and essences have the power of themselves becoming concrete and thus a vehicle for the communication of the numinous and ineffable. Thus, we are told, 'the love of the frail and sinful soul is not only for God as Providence and Saviour, but as Absolute Perfection, Absolute Love.' All the great words, Goodness, Beauty and Truth, at once universal and individual, become transfigured in the language of the mystic. They are 'stung to life', as it has been excellently said, and it is this bringing to life of 'dead words' which partly at least constitutes the new element which mysticism brings to consciousness. All these 'words of splendour that exhilarate the soul' are, indeed, in a sense man-made, conditioned in their signification by our creaturely existence, but they are infinitely more than that. In the mouth of the mystic they become the medium of expression of that intense and eternal life which is hid with God. It is this 'more,' this excessivity, as we shall call it, which constitutes the unique quality of the language of mysticism. The language of religion is itself numinous poetry, but when it issues from the mouth of the mystic it has a quality all its own.

B

If there is one thing above all, then, that distinguishes the language of the mystics from all other forms of human expression it is what we may describe as its exuberance. 'Exuberance is beauty,' cries Blake, and for him as for the mystic in general, it is truth also. The Infinite, The Absolute, cannot, it is true, be 'represented' in language, but can be 'shown forth,' in the very spirit and substance of our utterance. Speaking of Shakespeare,

[1] *Op. cit.* Volume II, p. 305.

Cardinal Newman writes, 'a narrow critic will call his language verbiage when really it is a sort of fullness of heart.' How much less is the exuberant language of the mystic verbiage when, in the fullness of his heart, he seeks to show forth that fullness of Being which is God. This quality of the language of mysticism is fully understandable only when we realize what it is out of which this exuberance springs. It is the joy in the Lord of which they all speak, but it is a joy of a special kind—that supernal bliss which arises out of the vision of the identity of the One and the Good, which, as we have seen, is the fundamental synthesis of mysticism of every type.

In illustrating this point I shall take preferably not a passage from the language of specifically religious mysticism but from a mystical poet, Blake. I do it for two reasons: first, because, at first sight at least, it seems most removed from the universe of discourse of the religious mystics; but, secondly, also because it expresses both the excessivity of mystical language and the fusion of value with being which is the essential note of mysticism:

> 'The pride of the peacock is the glory of God.
> The lust of the goat is the bounty of God.
> The wrath of the lion is the wisdom of God.
> The nakedness of woman is the work of God.'

In these magnificent lines Blake has 'gone to the limit' of this fusion. Pride, lust, wrath, nakedness, these things of nature, are one with the eternal goods, the glory, the bounty, the wisdom and power of God. We know that it is excessive, yet we understand.

The extravagance of Blake's language may distress the faith of the simple, and even the more serene intelligence of the theologian, but the Christian mystics are not far behind in the daring of their affirmations. They too often embarrass us. They have indeed been able to bring together things which to our little souls seem impossible. But this coincidence of opposites in the Absolute is an essential part of Christian theology, and among these magnificent syntheses is that of the 'high and the low' also. In Jacopone da Todi's 'Lode,' from which St. Catherine of Siena derived, as von Hügel shows, many of her ideas and idioms, illustrations of this superb synthesis are to be found. 'Waters, rivers, lakes and ocean, fish within them and their swimming; airs, winds, birds and all their flying; all these turn to jewels to me.' But in the light of certain very different experiences of the soul—'Moon, Sun, Sky and Stars—even these are not among my treasures; above the very sky those things abide which are the object of my song.'[1] For Mother Juliana also, to whom, as we have seen, 'heaven and earth and all that is made, is large, fair and good,' these qualities of nature of which Blake sings would be included, and she would, we may well believe, 'enjoy our Lord in them all.'

The *theologia gloriae* which, in contrast with the *theologia crucis*, has perhaps constituted the chief inspiration of the great mystics, always expresses this attitude. The language of the mystics represents in very truth the culmination of the *theologia gloriae*. The subjective pole of the mystical experience speaks the language of love and of the *Agnus Dei*. The objective pole—and it is to this, as I believe, the greatest mystics in the end naturally gravitate—speaks the language of the *Sanctus*, for Heaven and Earth are full of His Glory.

C

This study of the language of mysticism brings to the fore two questions which have always been raised in connection with mysticism, namely the communicability of the mystical experience and the intelligibility of that which is communicated.

'The incommunicability of the transport is the keynote of mysticism,' writes William James, and for this reason, probably, he also denies the character of knowledge to the mystical experience. On the other hand, Dean Inge speaks of the mystical intuition as directly communicable and also of its evidential character. How can two philosophers, both of unusual insight in such matters, say two such opposite things? An answer to this question, if such an answer be possible, will, I believe, help to solve one of the most fundamental problems not only of mysticism but of the entire philosophy of religion.

The incommunicability of the transport is the point emphasized by those who have their eye on the subjective pole of the mystical experience, but even then this is only partly true. For there are many things which 'cannot be said' which can

[1] *Op. cit.*, Vol. II, pp. 102–10.

nevertheless be 'shown forth'—in the very exuberance of the language itself. Language has, so to speak, a double function. It describes or represents its object in picture and symbol, but it also shows forth in its very drive and immanent spirit that which cannot be directly expressed. There is intoxication of the spirit as well as of the senses, and, while most of us prefer the latter, we are not witless enough to deny the former. It is the objective pole, however, which, as we have seen, is really significant for the philosopher—that identity of intuition, despite variety of subjective form, which Dean Inge and all of like mind have in view when they speak of the communicability of the mystical experience. This identity of intuition is the vision of the One as the Good, from which all other syntheses, including that of the temporal and the eternal, ultimately spring.

As the mystical experience is communicable so also is it intelligible. Miss Underhill does not exaggerate when she tells us that 'the great mystics of history are above all things definite. In some cases they have been ridiculously intelligible. They are almost childishly concrete and, like the Hindu mystic, can abstract Brahma from a millet seed.' This childish concreteness we all know. Who in reading St. Francis has not often smiled, yet understood? The ridiculous excessivity of the mystic we also know and have even been embarrassed by it, but who, in the very moment of embarrassment, has not also fully understood? For we remember that we also 'are most ridiculous when we try to express the glory that is in us.' There are those, to be sure, for whom the language of the mystics is mere verbiage and what they tell us unintelligible nonsense, but I do not think that we should be unduly impressed. For they say the same things about all that is most significant in our human discourse, our 'babble,' as they would call it, about the good, the beautiful and the true.

IV

The Veridical Character of the Mystical Experience:
'The Creature Sees True'

A

The fact that there is a language of mysticism, that the mystical experience somehow gets itself expressed, brings it within the range of truth and falsity. If all the mystics of the world were to remain silent their visions could be called neither true nor false—they would simply be. It is only because there is real communication, only because one can say, Yes, I know what you mean, for I in my small way have had them too—that it is possible to speak of their truth or falsity.

For the common man, as well as for the elect, there are then these moments of insight and realization. They come at the chief points of concentration of life—when, so to speak, the soul is at its highest stretch and the sense of reality is most intense. Even one of the mutest and most inglorious of mortals, as Zona Gale describes him in her novel *Birth*, saw things at times 'in that delicate haze which, in love, is poured over all. As if then, alone, the creature sees true, in a light which would lie over all, if he but knew how to perceive it.' The creature 'sees true'— and in that divine lucidity comes the assurance that all will be well. 'Only but this is rare,' as Matthew Arnold tells us in his poem *The Buried Life*—in many respects one of the best expressions of natural mysticism. Can we not live as though we always loved? cries Maeterlinck. So we might ask, can we not live as though we always saw? Apparently the latter is as impossible as the former. Even the very elect themselves, those who by the help of special graces have come near to achieving constancy of both love and vision in this life, have learned that for them also great moments must alternate with little, fullness with emptiness, and the contemplative life with a life of action— that an exclusive mysticism, like all extreme concentration, has its own nemesis. This is true of natural no less than of theological mysticism.

It is, however, with the latter that we are chiefly concerned— with what the mystic tells us about God; whether here the creature also sees true and whether he speaks truly when he speaks of divine things. This is, I believe, a fundamental question not only for religion itself but for the philosophy of religion. What, if anything, so we may phrase this fundamental question, can the philosopher learn from the mystic? Is this heightened noesis, this insight which comes when the soul is at its highest stretch, genuine knowledge, and what is its place in knowledge as a whole?

In raising the question of the veridical character of the

mystical experience I do not, of course, have reference to those phenomena of supernormal psychology (presentiments, sensorial impressions beyond the range of the senses, visions of past events or prevision of the future) which sometimes accompany it; these may or may not be true but with them we have no concern. It is conceivable, of course, that where there is super-sensitivity of the spirit there should be supersensitivity of the senses also. It is conceivable also that the heightened noesis of the mystical experience should express itself in heightened emotion and should lead to forms of excessivity which have been called the 'degradations of mysticism.' However this may be, whatever supernormal phenomena may accompany mysticism, they are not the mystical insight itself, as all competent students of mysticism now realize. At the most they are secondary accompaniments, perhaps the phantasms of which the theologian speaks, for if men know the essence at all, it is only through sense imagery without which, in this life, contemplation is not possible. In any case, the veridical character of the mystical experience itself does not depend upon the veridical character of these phenomena, but rather on the intrinsic content of intuition and whether there is that in the soul of every man which recognizes and acknowledges this content.

B

'What,' asks Bergson, 'can the philosopher learn from their [the mystics'] experience?' He learns that God is there and that the human soul is in Him. God acts by the soul in the soul. The love by which it is consumed is not merely the love of man for God but the love of God for all humanity.' The agreement of the mystics on these points indicates that there is an identity of intuition which can most simply be accounted for by the real existence of the Being with whom they believe themselves to be in communion. 'The existence of God, moreover,' we are further told, 'which philosophy makes it possible only to con-jecture, the mystical experience compels us to accept un-conditionally.'[1]

Now I shall not deny that this is what many of the mystics tell us, and that from this we may learn much, but I am inclined to believe that such a description narrows the mystical experience

[1] *Les deux Sources de la Morale et de la Religion*, p. 268.

unduly. The mystic does tell us that God is love, but he tells us even more fundamentally that God and the Good are one. This more fundamental insight places the value of mysticism, as knowledge, on a plane far beyond the merely personal and subjective aspects of the mystical experience and emphasizes the *Einheitsschau* which is the element constantly present in the recollective thoughts of all the great mystics. I should even be disposed to say that, despite appearances to the contrary, this is true not only of the mystics of the West but, *mutatis mutandis*, of the East also, for in the last analysis the categories of value and being, and their relations, are the same for both.[1]

Of this agreement itself, and of the identity of intuition to which it witnesses, there can be, I think, little doubt, and just as little that it has evidential value, but I doubt very much whether it extends quite as far as Bergson would have us believe. It is true that sceptics and atheists tell us that 'the mystic is the one person who makes them consider sometimes that there may be some sort of a god,' but I cannot see why the mystic should make them thus consider unless they themselves had some experience in terms of which the deliverances of the mystic could be understood, and unless, moreover, they themselves had already considered the grounds for a reasonable belief. The knowledge value of mysticism, as I see it, consists rather in the fact that this identity of intuition confirms a belief already existing implicitly, whether the result of the intuitions of faith or of the demonstration of reason. I should put it in this way. If there is a noesis that can fairly be called mystical it can be only a 'heightened noesis'—the fullest development in certain special natures of a knowledge present in some form and in some degree in every soul. If there is this 'fuller grasp of the eternal' it can be only the deepening of an intuition which already exists. Privileged as this heightened noesis may be in special natures, it can only be one which does not cut them off completely from their less favoured fellows. If such heightened noesis exists it is still noesis and cannot be unrelated to other forms of knowledge— to the intuitions of faith and the evidence of reason. The simple believer may believe by faith but in order to live his faith sincerely he must know that it is true for his reason also. The mystic may have intimations of the beatific vision, but in order

[1] Chapter viii, p. 257.

445

that the vision may be really beatific it must include the knowledge that the truth of that vision must ultimately be true for his
reason also. The identity of the Sovereign Good with absolute
Being is the postulate of dogmatic theology; the logical necessity
of this identification the burden of rational theology; the actuality of this identity the essence of the beatific vision of mystical
theology. Without these three elements the knowledge of
divine things remains for ever incomplete.

It is true that many students of mysticism take issue with this
account of its knowledge value. The real issue, they tell us, is, in
the words of Abbé Bremond, whether 'beyond and outside the
knowledge properly called intellectual, which ends in abstract
concepts, does there or does there not exist a real knowledge,
a direct intuition which, without the intermediation of images
and concepts, would establish between the real, whatever it may
be, and ourselves a kind of immediate contact amounting to
complete adherence and possession?' And, having more in
mind the theological aspect, he continues, 'Can it happen, does
it in fact happen that the reality itself, if I may so express myself,
and not the idea of God offers itself to this kind of knowledge,
deigns to descend to this contact, so impressing itself in the
depth of the soul, taking possession of it, purifying and sancti-
fying it?' And he adds: 'Tout le reste est verbiage.'[1]

I do not believe that this is the real issue, but, if it were, I am
quite sure it never could be settled. For even if there were this
'immediate contact,' this complete adherence and possession,
the fact could not be known, even, I am disposed to say, by the
one who had it; and certainly not by any one else. Even the
heightened noesis which is the mystical experience is still noesis
and really can be expressed, like any other knowledge, only in
the language and categories in which statements about reality
are possible.

The rest is verbiage? Perhaps. But it is most important
verbiage. All that the mystic contributes to the fact are, perhaps,
the words in which he enunciates it, but without this enuncia-
tion there is no 'fact,' whether in scientific or any other knowledge; there is no immediacy in this life that is wholly unmediated. Speaking of the vision of Jacob, St. Thomas said

[1] Quoted from Paul Elmer More's *The Catholic Faith*, p. 206. The passage is
found in *Le Sentiment religieux en France*, VI, p. 175.

certain very memorable words. 'For, as stated, Jacob said, I have seen God face to face and my soul has been saved. . . . But these words of Jacob, I saw God face to face, do not imply that he saw God's essence, but that he saw some shape, imaginary of course, wherein God spoke to him. In the present state of life human contemplation is impossible without sense imagery because it is connatural to man to see the intelligible species in the phantasms.'[1] Without entering into the general theory of knowledge which underlies this manner of expression, we may be sure that in principle the contention is sound. In the present state of human life knowledge of God is impossible except as conditioned by the way in which knowledge appears in creatures, and no expression of that knowledge is possible save in language so conditioned. Even mystical experience of God cannot be wholly unmediated.

C

The question of the knowledge value of mysticism is often presented in the following way. What value, it is asked, is to be attached to such experience in our general evaluation of religion? Those who stress the practical or philosophical sides of religion are likely to tell us that the rarity of the mystical experience, in its intense and exclusive form, makes it impossible that it should furnish grounds for belief for the majority of those who believe in God. On the other hand, there are those who find in the experience of the mystics, because of its rarity and uniqueness, in its exclusive form, its great noetic value. We must, as Bergson tells us, believe them when they tell us of God as we believe the physicists when they tell us of matter.

Neither of these positions, it seems to me, quite expresses the truth of the situation. It is not on the authority of the mystics, whether, because of the supposed rarity of the mystical experience, we consider it slight, or, because of its transcendent character, we consider it great, that the witness of the mystic is significant. It is only because what the mystic says corresponds to something in the soul of every man that we either understand him or believe him. Here, as elsewhere, there is no wholly solipsistic knowledge, none that does not presuppose communicability in some form and in some degree. Mediated

[1] Quoted from M. C. D'Arcy's *Thomas Aquinas: Selected Writings*, p. 206; the section on 'The Contemplative Life.'

immediacy here as elsewhere is the condition of all verifiable knowledge.

Many have asked, with John Laird, 'Why should we deny that religious experience and particularly mystical experience is a fundamentally new way of knowing?' There is no reason, I believe, why we should deny that the mystical is *a* way of knowing, but we should be cautious in thinking that it is *wholly new*. The denial of its knowledge value on the part of philosophers has various motives. Kant did not dare to trust the mystics because he feared lest human indiscretion should bring God down from the kingdom of ends, where we know that he exists, and place him among our own interior events which belong as much to passion and imagination as they do to reason; and, as Récéjac remarks, 'Kant was not wholly wrong here as we know from the degradations of mysticism.' But this was not Kant's sole reason—nor even his main one. It was rather the claim of mysticism to be wholly new and therefore wholly unamenable to any *criteria* of knowledge known to man. For, after all, knowledge is knowledge wherever found, however different the ways of knowing, and to be knowledge must conform to the basal requirements of all knowledge, communicability and verifiability. It is just because the mystical is not a wholly new way of knowing, but corresponds to something intrinsic to human knowledge as such, that it has its place in religious knowledge. It is because it is the natural culmination of faith and reason in the heirarchy of knowledge that it is significant for the philosophy of religion.

'The severe schools,' writes Sir Thomas Browne in his exquisite idiom, 'shall never laugh us out of the view that this visible world is but a picture of the invisible.' They certainly shall also not be able to laugh us out of the view that the invisible may be expressed, if not fully and adequately, yet truly in terms of the visible. Finally they will never be able to laugh us out of the view that the visible and the invisible are continuous and that the Good and the existent are one. In so far as the mystics tell us this they will never be laughed out of court, for while what they tell us can never be completely 'proved,' it can nevertheless be known.

The severe schools today are in principle the same as in the days of Sir Thomas. If they do not seek to laugh us out of these larger views they at least call them 'logical nonsense', which in the end amounts to much the same thing. Logic and mysticism is accordingly an inevitable topic in philosophical discussion. Logic is by its very nature severe, and rightly so. It demands logical analysis of terms and propositions and insists rightly that anything we say, to have meaning, must have reference. It insists upon the law of parsimony and is again right, from its standpoint, in excluding all unnecessary hypotheses. It is severe finally in giving absolute validity to the law of contradiction and, from its standpoint, right in excluding the synthesis of opposites, the *coincidentia oppositorum* which is an essential of mysticism. But this is but one side of the truth. For even the logician knows, if he is also a philosopher, that this very strictness and severity is merely *die moral des Denkens*, not thought itself; that logic can give us merely correctness and not truth and that unless thought conceive from some other source it remains lifeless and barren. There have always been these minute philosophers, but there have always also been the magnanimous, those who simply will not have themselves laughed out of these larger views, and who have therefore always insisted that without the inclusion of an element of mysticism, thought and knowledge cannot complete themselves. In passing thus, for the moment, from mysticism in religion to mysticism in philosophy we shall be but making a temporary *détour* which will ultimately bring us back, with greater understanding, to the main road.

V

Mysticism and Philosophy. As far as Thought Can Reach

A

If, as we have contended, mysticism is a constant characteristic of the human consciousness, it would seem to follow that it is an essential element not only in religion and theology, but in the life of reason which we call philosophy—that here too thought must ultimately trench on the mystical. It was this element, already present in Plato, which made possible the explicit mysticism of Plotinus and of the Christian tradition.

It was a similar element in Aristotle which made possible the inclusion, in a sense, of a mystical element in Thomism. What Plato had to say on the love of the Good afforded in part the language in which the mystical element in theology was expressed. What Aristotle had to say on 'the life of God' afforded the idiom in which much that the mystics tell us about God was said. I shall not repeat these facts known to all, but rather turn to certain modern philosophers by whom this necessary element in philosophy is explicitly recognized.

In his book *The Realm of Ends* James Ward finds that there are certain points in philosophical thought where we inevitably 'trench on the mystical and ineffable and can only speak in parables.' Again Bosanquet confesses in an article entitled *Idealism and Realism*, 'with the strongest predilection for rationalistic simplicity, and after the most resolute effort to follow out a realistic empiricism, I have not, in the long run, found it possible to construct a philosophy without an element that might be called mystical.' These confessions are in themselves enlightening, but still more so are the precise points at which, to use Ward's terms, trenching on the mystical becomes necessary. They are precisely those points at which, as we have seen in our definitions of mysticism, the act of mysticism occurs, and the act itself is again just that synthesis or fusion of apparent opposites without which the mystical experience is impossible. This mystical element is in principle the same for both philosophers, but Ward has formulated the situation in a way most usable in our present context, so we shall let him speak.

'God, Spirit, Will, the Idea,' as he says, become inevitably the ground of the world. But we trench upon the mystical when we attempt to envisage this ground—'to picture the divine immanence, closer to us than breathing, nearer than hands and feet.' At yet another point philosophy inevitably trenches on the mystical. 'We have,' says Ward, 'been contemplating the universe as a realm of ends. If we were asked what is the end of the realm of ends, we might answer rightly enough that its end can only be itself; for there is nothing beyond it and no longer any meaning in beyond. It is the absolutely absolute.' But in it we still find the oppositions of the One and the Many, the conflicting values of the individual and the overindividual. 'Can we not transcend,' he asks, 'these one-sided extremes and find some sublimer idea which shall unify them both? We can, indeed,' he answers, 'and that idea is love.'[1]

There are then limits to thought and it is the chief function of thought—indeed its chief glory—to know its limits. It is also its glory, as well as its obligation, if it is honest, to confess that when it has reached these limits, it must trench on the mystical. We have seen the specific points in science at which these limits are reached; let us now put the notion into more general form. I shall discuss it under the caption, 'As Far As Thought Can Reach.'

This phrase is the title of the last act of Bernard Shaw's *Back to Methuselah*. In this extraordinary play the author has cast his thought imaginatively backward to the 'Garden of Eden,' and far beyond that to the beginning of all things, to the creative act itself, and finds, as we all do, that there he can speak only in parables. At the close of the play he casts his thought forward, far beyond all the utopias that men may devise, to the end of all things, and here he also finds that thought approaches a limit and that we can speak only in parables. And the parable or fable he himself tells is one of rare beauty and suggestion. This is the cosmological meaning of the phrase, but there is also a still deeper meaning which we may call metaphysical or ontological. Cosmological thinking takes place within the framework of space and time and is concerned with first and last things in this sense. Metaphysical thought, although also concerned with first and last things, is concerned with them in the ontological sense. Here too we must use the phrase, as far as thought can reach. Both of the philosophers we have been considering find this limit of thought precisely at the point at which we have found it, namely in connection with the basal metaphysical issue, the relation of value to being.

Thought alone, it is important to reiterate, can take us only so far—to 'God, Will, Idea'—but of these we may well ask, as did Royce in an eloquent passage, are they only thoughts? 'Truth is indeed valid, but is it only valid? The forms are eternal, but are they only forms? The universal truths are true, but are they only universal? The moral order

[1] *Op. cit.*, p. 452 f.

is genuine, but is it only an order? The concept of God is a necessary and valid idea, but is it only an idea?' To this Royce of course answers, No!—as indeed must any competent philosopher. But argument, even such argument as that of Royce, can never demonstrate this completely. The identity of the One and the Good, of value and being, remains, as we have said, the 'sacred mystery' beyond which thought, as pure thought, cannot go. It can be shown that 'value is no stranger to being.' It can be shown that to make the God-idea, however necessary and valid, only an idea, is not only to make the life of religion an illusion, but the life of reason also. All this thought can indeed show, but that is the limit of its showing. The fusion of the two, the blending of which Plato speaks, can be realized only in experiences that trench on the mystical and can be told only in language which bears the indelible mark of such experience. Perennial philosophy is not itself mysticism, as Aldous Huxley would perhaps maintain. Still less is it that fanatical mysticism which cuts itself off, not only from the *sensus communis,* but from the common reason of its fellow men. But there have been certain points at which philosophy has always trenched on the mystical, and this its supreme exponents have always known.

VI

What Is Said of God in Its Mystical Interpretation.
Mysticism and the Imago Dei

A

All of which brings us back to one of the main themes which has underlain our entire treatment of religion, namely, the question of 'what religion says' and how its pronouncements are to be interpreted and evaluated. That these pronouncements are to be interpreted symbolically we have already seen, but, as Abelard said, they must also be interpreted mystically.

The mystics, as we are told, always followed in the path of symbolic interpretation. They sought 'to annul every barrier between themselves and the content of scripture and strove to realize everything set down in scripture as an eternal now.' They have always known, with St. John of the Cross, that 'he who will rely on the letter of the divine locution will necessarily fall into delusion, for the letter killeth, the spirit maketh alive.' The mystics have always spoken with perfect understanding the lyrical and dramatic language of religion but how different it sounds on their lips: They have spoken the language of classical theology with equal understanding, but, again, with what a significant difference! This difference, we are told by Höffding, consisted in the fact that, 'whereas the scholastics attempted to maintain the principle of analogy in respect to the concept of God, the mystics rejected it. This, however, is only in part true, as we have seen. Rather, as von Hügel has pointed out, with respect to St. Catherine of Siena, they in the main accepted it, but only to transcend it.

To recognize in the symbol a genuine means of drawing near to the Divine—not to discard it, but to interpret it mystically—is, then, the way of the greater mystics. Thus have they always understood the historical and cosmological pronouncements about the Divine operations in time. It is, however, their symbolic interpretation of the temporal predicates as applied to Deity—of all the problems of philosophical theology the most fundamental—which is most significant for the philosophy of religion. Of this problem they have always been keenly conscious, and how fundamental it is not only for our concept of God but for the entire spiritual life.

B

What is said of God 'in bodily form' is necessarily said in spatial terms, whether in the language of religion or the language of theology, and, as such, must obviously be interpreted. But how about the temporal terms, so closely related to the spatial? Are these terms also symbolic—symbolic of a non-temporal reality?

That there is an important difference between the spatial and temporal predicates is realized, not only by the religious consciousness itself, but also by theological and philosophical thought. So far as practical religion is concerned the language of religion must apparently be a temporal language. God speaks to man, but there is no speech of gods or men that

does not have its tenses, the forms of the verb which indicate
the time of action. God loves; but there is no form of loving
known to man which does not include the yearning for that
which is loved—which is the very essence of time. God knows;
but there is no knowledge known to men which is not, in part
at least, discursive, which does not move from idea to idea,
which movement is, again, of the very essence of time. Time
seems, therefore, to be of the very essence of life, whether
of man or of God. How far then is it conceivable that temporal
predicates, when applied to the life of God, can really be symbolic of that which is timeless?

That these temporal forms of expression are symbolic of
a life that is timeless has been maintained by the major part of
Christian theology. 'There is but one living and true God,
everlasting, without parts and passions, of infinite wisdom and
goodness, the maker and preserver of all things, both visible
and invisible.' So speak the *Thirty Nine Articles* of the Church
of England, as indeed all traditional theology. Without passions
as well as without parts—non-temporal as well as non-spatial.
Nor is there any question what has driven religious thought
to this belief in the Divine impassibility. It is the underlying
assumption that a Being must exist to whom nothing may
attach which could present itself to thought as an imperfection;
only a most perfect Being can, for religious thought—and
ultimately for religious feeling also—be called God. For
similar reasons the main stream of European philosophy, so
closely bound up with theology, has also been moved to deny
the ultimate reality of time as well as space. For, as Bergson
says, 'for this philosophy space and time have the same origin
and the same value.'

The classical expressions of this thesis are eminently clear on
this point. 'The three times, past, present, and future,' so St.
Augustine tells us, 'are certain three affections in the soul. I
find them there and nowhere else. There is the present memory
of past events, the present perception of present ones and the
present expectation of future ones.' God, however, possesses
the splendour of ever-tarrying Eternity, which is 'incomparable
with never tarrying times,' since in it 'nothing passes, but the
content of everything abides simply present.' And in the next
life, 'perhaps our own thoughts will also not be flowing, going

from one thing to another, but we shall see all that we know simultaneously, in one intuition.' St. Thomas is even more positive, 'All things will' in Heaven, 'be seen simultaneously and not successively.'[1]

C

This then is the traditional position and it constitutes the theological and philosophical framework within which the mystical interpretation of the spatio-temporal language of religion has in the main taken place. Opposed to this interpretation there are more modernistic conceptions of God and of His life which proceed from a fundamental distinction between space and time and which, while recognizing the symbolic character of the spatial attributes of Deity, insist upon the literal character of the temporal. A similar distinction between space and time within philosophy marks off also a large part of modern philosophy from that of the past. It may be epitomized by Bergson's comment on Kant's space-time doctrine, to the effect that while Kant was right with regard to the subjective and human character of space, he was wrong with regard to time.

We are told by many modern theologians and philosophers that no spiritual life, at least no significant life, can be imagined apart from time. It is pointed out that for the life of will as we know it, and for the intelligibility of all our moral values connected with the will, time is essential. Purpose is the time-form of values and without this time-form they are meaningless. It is similarly argued that scholastic theology, in adopting from Neoplatonism the doctrine of God's life as being a *nunc stans*, a *totum simul*, not only claims to know more about God's life than man without absurdity can claim, but sets up a wholly unimaginable notion of the Divine Life. 'Timelessness,' says Fawcett, 'is a favourite term of the philosophers. There is a voice in the study, but no answering experience shows in the vasty deep.'[2] Finally—and this is perhaps the strongest argument of all—this acceptance of the ultimately temporal character of reality is necessary not only in order 'to save our human values,' but speculatively also in order to save

[1] St. Augustine, *Confessions*, Lib. XI, Chapter xxvii, 3; Chapters xx and xi. St. Thomas, *Summa Theol.* I, qu. 12, art. 10.
[2] *The Divine Imagining*, p. 107.

455

philosophical intelligibility. 'The moment,' so writes one philosopher, 'I try to reduce time to a logical category in an eternal and unchanging universe, that moment I am forced to abandon outright my every-day descriptions, and since I am not compensated for my loss by an increase of intelligibility, I hesitate to make the change. All efforts to rationalize the non-temporal are,' he adds, 'complete failures.'[1]

All this sounds plausible enough. Nevertheless, I believe it to be in the main untrue and, in so far as it contains any element of truth, wholly irrelevant to the present issue. We are told that no significant spiritual life can be imagined apart from time. But who would for a moment doubt this? Certainly neither St. Augustine nor St. Thomas, nor any of the great representatives of classical theology. Imagination is in its very essence imagery and any image of God—even if it is an image of the Divine life and love is precisely what it says—an image. It is inconceivable that we should be able to form a *picture* of a timeless life which would not be both ugly and meaningless. It is said that when travellers describe the blue eyes of northern peoples to the black-eyed primitives of warmer climes, they seem unbeautiful and monstrous, because the latter see vividly in their imagination that unheard of blueness, but not at the same time the flesh and hair tints which alone harmonize with the blue eyes. Similarly, any life *imagined* as timeless but including elements taken from the temporal life of creatures, is bound to have an element of the monstrous also. But it does not at all follow that although the Divine life cannot be *imagined* apart from time, it cannot, and must not, be *thought* as timeless. We are also told that the notions of the *nunc stans* and the *totum simul* are merely empty words for which there is no corresponding sense experience. Who would deny this? Certainly not St. Augustine nor St. Thomas. But it does not at all follow that we have, even within the sensible and temporal experience itself, no analogies through which the timeless may be understood. Finally we are told that all efforts completely to rationalize the non-temporal are failures. Who again would deny this? Certainly neither St. Augustine nor St. Thomas. But it does not at all follow that because it is impossible to reduce time to a logical category there is no

[1] A. K. Rogers, *What is Truth*, pp. 175 ff.

basis in knowledge at all for the assertion of a timeless mode of being. In sum, all these arguments are irrelevant because, while true with respect to imagery and imagination, they are not true with respect to thought. Traditional philosophy has always distinguished between what can be imagined and what thought, and this distinction is fundamental.

D

The crucial problem for any philosophy that proposes to 'take the timeless seriously' is, then, as Dean Inge has told us, 'whether the human mind has any knowledge of such a mode of being. If not, we can say nothing about it. '[1] If it has, we may use this knowledge, as do the mystics, in the interpretation of the Divine Life.

This mode of knowledge is, I believe, an essential part of that natural mysticism without which theological mysticism would be neither communicable nor intelligible. One thing is certain; men constantly talk as though they had experience and knowledge of the timeless. *Dem Glücklichen Schlägt Keine Stunde*, cries the poet, and the happiness which he has in mind, while not the same in every respect as the beatitude of the heavenly vision, is yet sufficiently analogous to enable those who experience the former to understand something of what is meant by the latter. If in the higher forms of human love the creature sees true, the truth he sees may at least be a foretaste of the deeper truths revealed in the love of God. If 'with respect to the highest poetry' it may be said that, 'as relates to his (the poet's) conceptions, time, place and number are not,' surely with respect to that numinous poetry which constitutes the language of religion, time as well as place and number are not. In sum, even the human mind has 'natural' knowledge of a mode of being which is timeless, and it is because of this element in natural mysticism that the mystical interpretation of what is said of God is both understood and validated. The immanence of the eternal in the temporal and of the temporal in the eternal is a form of experience not denied to any son of man, still less to any son of God.

With respect then to the highest poetry, there is a language in which 'time, place and number are not,' and this is one of the

---

[1] *Op. cit.*, p. 272.

chief characters of the language of mysticism—that language which, as we have seen, has as one of its major characters the power to 'sting to life' those absolute qualities and essences which are timeless and to make of them the medium of communication of the intense and eternal life which is hid with God. What, asks Dean Inge, could we do with a Plato or a St. Paul if we did not have knowledge of this mode of being and understand this language? What indeed, he also asks, with Shelley's *Alastor* or with Wordsworth's interpretation of nature? Literally nothing. Unless we ourselves are able to make, however imperfectly, this synthesis, and thus understand the idiom in which it is expressed, it would all be nonsense, as indeed it is to some.

The assertion that the human mind has knowledge of such a mode of being is in no way in conflict with the earlier contention that there is no mode of knowledge, even the mystical, which is wholly immediate. Even the timeless, so far as we know, is realizable only as immanent in the temporal, and all our descriptions of this mode involve an element of analogy and symbol. This raises the question of the significance of a form of temporal experience which has seemed to many philosophers preeminently fitted to enable us to understand this mode of knowledge—namely the musical. A man listening to music, as for instance a great symphony, is so absorbed in its unity as to lose himself in the durational flux. In such experience, it is aptly said, we ourselves are 'on the way to escape duration and so are capable of understanding in some degree God's eternity.' What is the value of this instance?

What value we shall give to it depends, to some degree at least, upon our general type of mind, and we are not surprised to find that philosophers differ as to its significance. If we are prosaic—and, without any intention of depreciation, we are, therefore, scientific—we shall tend to minimize it. If, we shall be disposed to say, to abstract from duration is to approach eternity, this intimation of God would be nothing very significant; and if we are not over scrupulous we might even suggest that drug addicts and maniacs seem to have this privileged approach to Deity. If, on the other hand, we are of a more aesthetic type we shall be likely to value it differently. We shall be disposed to say that this is a privileged approach to Deity and perhaps value unduly the aesthetic element in religion. Both ways of valuing the experience, I am inclined to believe, misconceive the significance of the illustration. The real issue is not whether such a form of consciousness is actually an approach to Deity, but rather whether in this form of human experience we have something by analogy with which we may understand what an experience of the timeless would be, *were there such*. The musical experience does not prove the veridical character of the *nunc stans* and of the mystics' experience of God—that, as we have seen, is a problem of a wholly different order—it simply gives us an analogy in terms of which it may be imagined and symbolically expressed. However this may be, there seems to be little question that such a mode of knowledge—of a timeless intuition—has been assumed in Christian theology from St. Augustine on, and that it is on the basis of this assumption that the mystical interpretation of what is said of God has proceeded. True, it is only in Heaven that 'our thoughts will not be flowing' and 'all things will be seen simultaneously and not successively,' but it is also held that we are not without intimations of this mode of knowledge in our creaturely existence and that these enable us to express, in figure and symbol at least, what the beatific vision will be.

E

All this, however, it is now held by many philosophers, our modern theories of space and time have made no longer possible. I refer to what is called temporalism in philosophy and in general to the so-called process philosophies. These tell us in more general terms what modernist theologians say specifically about the life of God. As no life or love can be imagined without temporal process, so no reality or being can be thought which is not ultimately process. In this respect time is different from space. To be is to change, and the intuition of duration or process is the intuition of ultimate reality. I do not believe that this contention can be maintained.

For traditional philosophy, as we have seen, space and time have necessarily the same origin and the same value. The same diminution of being is expressed both by extension in space and detension in time. Both are but 'the distance between what is and what ought to be.' Having the same origin and ultimately the same value, they cannot be separated, and what is said of

459

the one as applied to God must be said of the other also. The modern contention is that they can be separated, the ground of the separation being the fact that the time that is conceived as thus inseparable is already spatialized—and not real time, duration. The time which the Christian philosopher denies as an ultimate attribute of Deity or ultimate reality is, it is held, already this spatialized time. If we despatialize this time, what is said of God in terms of process can be said of Him truly, for from an ultimate standpoint God and the time process are one. In the terms of Whitehead, who, with respect to the fundamental issues here involved, speaks the same idiom as does Bergson, 'neither God nor the world reaches static completion. Both are in the grip of the ultimate metaphysical ground, the creative advance into novelty.' And, whatever he may say about 'eternal objects,' at all critical points in his philosophy, as in the case of Bergson, time and flux are given the last word.

The technical issues here involved are too difficult and too far-reaching to permit of any extended discussion in this context.[1] It must suffice to suggest the one point about which the entire problem revolves, namely the question of the necessary linkage of space and time in traditional philosophy, a linkage which made it inevitable that, if we cannot speak of God in spatial terms, neither can we in temporal terms also.

The essential point, of course, is that both space and time are indissolubly linked with body or matter and that if we speak of God as temporal we have of necessity spoken of him in bodily form. This linkage of time with space, and ultimately of both with matter, is fundamental in classical philosophy, in both Plato and Aristotle. The scholastics also taught that both space and time are bound up with matter in some way, although they would not hold, of course, that all knowledge is of space and time existents. For Kant this indissoluble linkage holds also. Space is linked with matter and similarly time is linked with matter; hence both, as functions of knowledge, being related to the sensuously manifold, are necessarily linked with each

---

[1] Elsewhere I have discussed this fundamental problem of both religion and philosophy. In Chapter vii of *The Intelligible World*, entitled 'Space, Time and Value,' I have argued this position in detail. Also in *Language and Reality*, Chapter xiv, pp. 705 ff.

other. But Kant, no more than either the Greeks or the Scholastics, held that all knowledge is of space-time existents.

I do not think that modern physical science has changed our views significantly on this fundamental point. It continues to link space and time together and both with matter. It is true that the modern physicist does not link them together in the same fashion as either traditional philosophy or Kant, but the results for our present problem seem to be the same. For the modern physicist, as for Kant, space and time are functions of knowledge, tools of the understanding enabling it to achieve an objective correlation of phenomena.[1] But in that function they are inseparable and any primacy given to time—any genesis of space out of time—is not science but a part of a scientific mythology. It is for this reason that for science, no less than for religion and philosophy, the meaning of things—if they have any meaning at all—'lies outside space and time.' Here too, as we have seen, science also trenches on the mystical.

This necessary linkage of space and time, so we contend, makes it inevitable that in so far as theology and philosophy are concerned, they do have the same origin and the same value, and cannot be separated in our interpretation of what is said of divine things. This comes out pre-eminently in Aristotle's description of God as *purus actus*, and what he had to say on this point was naturally of great influence on later Christian theologians and philosophers. When the medieval theologians taught that God is pure activity they were making use of Aristotle's concept of *energeia* or actuality, as opposed to that of genesis or becoming. They saw no difficulty in applying the term activity to God in reference to creation and his relation to the universe of creatures, while reserving the term actuality for the nature of Deity itself. Like Aristotle, they could not think of God's essence except as *purus actus* or sheer actuality, but this did not prevent them from speaking of the life of God—his activities or 'operations' in terms conditioned by the way in which life appears in creatures. But the essence of Deity is another matter. To Deity as such nothing can attach which can present itself to thought as an imperfection. Only a most perfect being can for religious thought be called God. The

[1] See on these points C. B. Garnett, Jr., *The Kantian Philosophy of Space*, Chapter ix, especially pp. 243 and 261.

complete despatialization and detemporalization of the *Imago Dei* thus becomes the supreme instance of the *analogia entis*.[1]

It is, therefore, only to be expected that the Christian mystics, like the mystics of all times and all places, should have witnessed, implicitly at least, to a God that transcends both space and time. Like their brothers everywhere, they have known how ruinous for the spiritual life would be the triumph of the category of time. In this they but witness to something that is known deep down in every heart. We not only know that time must have a stop if life itself shall have meaning, but even more that the category of time must stop when we come to God. For who of us does not really know that for feeling, no less than for thought, only a most perfect being can really be called God? All of us have tried in various ways to temporalize the Absolute, but have we not always found that the Absolute will then no longer bear the weight of our immortal souls?

VII

Humanity and Deity and the Mystics

A

There are many things that the philosopher may learn from the mystics, but of them all the greatest, perhaps, is a true understanding of the relation of the human to the Divine. They have taught us how to love Deity without losing our humanity.

In so far as the main stream of Christian mysticism is concerned, the humanity of the mystics is their outstanding quality. It is not merely that his fellow friars enjoyed the company of St. John of the Cross because he made them laugh. Not merely that St. Theresa of Avila, in company with St. John and many of the great mystics, speaks of the love for God with an audacious humanity that puts to shame our childish prudery. There is something more fundamental as it is more significant, namely, their ability to combine in one magnificent synthesis the most truly human with the most truly divine.

The dominant attitude of the great mystics has always been,

---

[1] On the concept of *purus actus*, see Aristotle, *Metaphysics*, A. 5–7, and St. Thomas Aquinas, *Summa Theol.* I. q. iii, aa 1, 2, and *Summa contra gent.* I, c. xvi.

as von Hügel tells us, that of acceptance and transcendence. They have been able to use the language and symbolisms of simple faith and at the same time to speak a language that transcends it immeasurably in beauty and truth. The love of God to which they witness is the transcendent thing it is just because it is at the same time the love of the Father in Heaven and the self-diffusion of the Sovereign Good in whom there is no variableness neither shadow of turning. In the mystical experience more than in any other, men know that the two Gods are one. Earl Balfour has put in unforgettable words a truth that has reaffirmed itself over and over again in the long story of Christian mysticism, and we shall do well to take his words to heart. 'I must admit,' he confesses, 'that I have never succeeded to my own satisfaction in fusing the two conceptions. Yet I do not profess to be content with their separation. The attribution of personality, though much truer I think than the denial of it, is manifestly inadequate to the full reality we are struggling to express. Some of the greatest religious teachers, Christian and non-Christian, that the world has seen, have more or less explicitly held both, or at least have leaned towards neither exclusively . . . *Nor, so far as I know, has Christian mysticism ever felt the least difficulty in bridging the chasm by which, in the eyes of discursive reason, the two conceptions seem to be divided*' (italics mine).[1] This may well represent the highest wisdom in these matters. It is well to allow those to whom Divine grace has been vouchsafed in special measure to speak with corresponding authority.

B

So fundamental is this principle—of acceptance and transcendence—that it is sometimes argued, even by the most thoughtful, that since some 'anthropomorphism' is inevitable, the cruder anthropomorphisms are in a sense the better. Since man cannot escape the 'snares of metaphor', as they would call them, is it not well, they ask, that he should use the crudest and the homeliest? Is it not just such crying disproportion between the image and the reality it represents that warns him that his words are indeed humanly conditioned? Does not their very poverty help him the more to realize the unsearchable riches of God? There is much to be said for this way of thinking,

[1] *Theism and Humanism*, p. 35.

but it is safe for us men only because we have the mystics to rescue us from the delusions of the literal mind against which St. John of the Cross constantly warns. One can have only the deepest reverence for the great souls of both East and West who have been able to combine these two ways of thought—who have found it possible to seek Deity without losing their humanity.

There are two types of religious philosophy which have little place for the mystics and for which the mystical experience has little significance. They are the religion of mere humanity and the religion of mere Deity, of which we spoke in the Introduction. For mere humanism the sense of the infinite refers not to God but to humanity, not to the supernatural but wholly to the natural. The claim of the mystic to know God is a delusion, for there is no God, in his sense, to be known. For the religion of mere Deity, the claim of the mystic is denied for an opposite reason. Since religion can be grounded on nothing human, but only on God, the mystics who, as creatures, claim to see God, are also under a delusion. The source of this depreciation of the mystics is the same in both cases—namely the denial of natural mysticism, and therefore of the theological mysticism which is its flower and fruit. As it is only on a doctrine of a natural knowledge of God—including the *analogia entis*—that any adequate conception of revelation can be based, so also a recognition of the natural mysticism present in every soul alone makes possible a real understanding of the mysticism of Grace.

Against both of these heresies, a religion of mere humanity and a religion of mere Deity, the mystics stand as an eternal witness, and in our hearts we know that their witness is true. We learn from them, indeed, that the love of man for God is also a love for all humanity, but we also learn from them that our human love, both for God and man, is also a witness of the love of God for us. In this love divine, all loves excelling, we know the oneness of the Good and of Being which our human reason, while it can demonstrate it as a reasonable belief, can never completely prove. And in this knowledge all our other knowledge finds its fulfilment and its crown.

APPENDIX

The Word of God and the Word of Man. Revelation and Reason

I

A

How is Divine revelation possible? For theology, perhaps, the question does not exist, for to God all things are possible. For the philosopher, however, it is a genuine problem and one which arises, in the first instance at least, out of the nature of language. It is with this aspect that we shall be mainly concerned, other issues being considered only as related to it.

The language of religion—of its 'stories,' its prophecies and its songs—is always the language of men. But this same language is also held to be the language of God—at least in all forms of religion which contain the notion of revelation—and a religion without revelation, Plutarch might well have said, does not exist. The relation of the Word of God to the word of man thus becomes a basal issue of the philosophy of religion and gives rise to problems never absent from any religion which has reached the level of contemplation and self-understanding.

The very conception of the voice of God—of a Divine locution—is itself at least partly figurative and symbolic. It is not necessary to doubt the voice in the burning bush or that after the whirlwind there was a still small voice; it is necessary for our purpose merely to recognize that whatever the voice was it was in human language that it spoke. The Divine locution is always conditioned by the way in which language appears in creatures. As such, it is not only a sensuous language of things, but also a particular language in which this sensuous and bodily form is also conditioned by its origin and development in a specific speech community.

It goes without saying that when we speak of the word of man in this context, in that notion is included not merely language in the sense of terms, grammar, syntax, etc., but in the broader sense of the 'philosophy of language,' for which ideas, meanings and values are not separable from the speech forms in which they are embodied. Men speak varied languages in the sense of linguistics, but they also speak different languages in the sense of spiritual dialects and of the moral idioms which they embody. How then can the word of man be the Word of God? How can the language of men, conditioned as it is by the way in which experience appears in us creatures—how can this language be the idiom in which God speaks to human souls? In general there is, and indeed can be, only one possible answer to this question, namely, some conception of Divine revelation which enables us to combine the variety and particularity of human speech with the universality and unity of the Divine locution—some doctrine of mediation which shall combine historical relativity with the timeless validity of the Eternal Word.

This notion of revelation has been stated in various forms. I shall attempt to put it in a way which will fit into the general development of the argument of this book.

B

A necessary historical, and therefore relative, element in religion is recognized by most philosophical theologians. The Christian theologian would realize that his own experience of religion is bound up with, and conditioned by, the words of men. It was only through the media of his boyhood home, and the Christian community, with its sacred stories, its hymns and prayers, that he had any religious experience at all. This is simply a matter of fact, but it is also a matter of fact that it was through these very media that God revealed Himself to his soul. This same theologian would also admit that there are other words of man in which this same Divine presence is felt, other stories, prayers and hymns than those of his own sacred Book, which for other men have been the media of the realization of the Divine. This also is a matter of fact; for it is also a matter of fact that if God speaks to man at all it must, in the first instance at least, be in his own 'tongue,' for truth, even the truth of divine things, to be spoken at all in any age, must be spoken in that age's own dialect, with all that this implies of moral and spiritual idiom.[1]

[1] For an excellent statement of this aspect of religion and for the theory of revelation which it involves, see John Baillie, *Our Knowledge of God*, 1939.

Now whether in this endlessly mediated experience there is an element of immediacy, and whether that immediate experience is authentic, has already been discussed in Chapter IX (*The Problem of Religious Knowledge*); here our concern is solely with the relation of the *words* of man to the *Word* of God. How, so to speak, man knows that the two are one.

There is, I think, in principle, only one possible answer to this question, an answer, moreover, already implied in our examination of the language of religion. The criterion of the Word of God is, and indeed must be, found, first of all, within the language of religion itself; the Divine presence, the quality of Deity, must be immanent in the numinous character of the Divine locution itself. Those who are the mediators of the Divine locution speak as other men *do not* speak, and when we ask what this unique way of speaking is, we can only say that, while the words are human, while the emotions, ideas and values these words express are also human, often all too human, they are transposed to another scale—a scale so transcendent as to give them a new quality, so wholly other as to make them uniquely revelatory of the Object towards which they are directed.

It is of the utmost importance that the philosopher should be clear on this point. It is sometimes maintained that the Divine presence is revealed not so much in the words as in the ways of God with man, in the Divine behaviour rather than the Divine locution—in Christian terminology, the fullness of the Godhead is revealed bodily in the face of Jesus Christ. Let us suppose, however, that Jesus went about doing good, but remained speechless—said nothing about himself or his Father—what would such a revelation be? Surely as he was dumb, so also would all his followers be deaf. It is only in the logos, as the word of God, that the Logos, the Divine reason before all worlds, can be really known. The principle remains, that it is only to the word that adequacy of expression can ultimately be ascribed.

C

There are then 'divine sentences,' sentences with the quality of Deity, that numinous quality which makes of the language of men also the language of God. Mohammed, as A. E. Taylor reminds us, expressly disclaimed all appeal to miracle in support of his own revelation. His appeal was apparently to the inimitable intrinsic divinity of his own verses or sentences and his followers were to expect no other sign. This doctrine of the inspired word is, in principle at least, the only possible answer to the question, how is revelation possible. It is the doctrine of the Divine presence in the word, namely a quality of Deity in the words of man themselves which makes them no longer human but divine, no longer things of nature alone, but revelatory of that which is itself beyond nature.

It is the insistence upon this aspect of the answer to the question, how is revelation possible, which constitutes the element in Protestant Neo-orthodoxy which gives it at once its power and its element of truth. In the face of that 'modern liberal self-deception,' as Barth calls it—which not merely seeks, as did the men of the Enlightenment, to base religion on natural theology alone, but attempts to go a step further and to base it upon pure naturalism without a theology of any kind— this emphasis on revelation, and on the supernaturalism it implies, is not only inevitable but, in a sense, welcome. One can feel a certain sympathy even with the 'extreme revelation-ism,' as it is called, which, piling paradox upon paradox, maintains even that all that God has to say to man is contrary to human nature and human reason. For one knows how desperately evil human nature may be and how perverse human reason in its extremes of rationalization may become.

All this we may admit, and freely acknowledge the mystery of the Divine initiative. But we also know that this answer to the question will not of itself alone suffice. There is a second aspect to revelation, without which this first element cannot be made intelligible, namely the presence in man of that which enables him, *as man*, to hear the Word of God and to recognize it in the words of man. Only with this postulate is it possible to form any objective criterion, any canon for deter-mining the Divine presence in the word. This criterion must be internal, not only in the words themselves, but also within him who hears them. This double criterion is, I believe, implied in any theory of revelation.

In formulating this double criterion I should like to make use of the words of Professor D. C. Macintosh, whose views on religious realism I found it necessary to criticize in an earlier context. 'The criteria of the Divine,' so he tells us, 'is subjectively the numinous and objectively the realm of absolute values, the worshipful.' The Divine presence is in the word itself, but that which constitutes the objective criterion of this presence is the intuition of perfection which in the last analysis alone can tell us what is Divine. This criterion is, I believe, already implied in the classical expression of the fundamental relation between the human and the Divine. Not only is there an analogy between the Divine Perfection and the perfections conditioned by the way in which they appear in us creatures, but also, if I may so put it, an analogy between the language in which our human perfections are expressed and the Divine locution which tells us of perfections which far transcend our own. This analogy, I shall attempt to show, is really presupposed in *any* philosophical theory of revelation.

D

In any case this double criterion is presupposed, either explicitly or implicitly, in all classical theories of revelation. The notions of Holy Writ, of the sacred scriptures, do indeed imply something uniquely intrinsic to these writings which makes them holy and sacred. But in order to distinguish them from other writings there must be a canon of Holy Scripture and this canon, however it be formed historically, cannot be merely one of external authority but must be in the last analysis an internal one; internal moreover, not only in the sense that the Divine presence is in the locutions themselves, but in the sense also that man has in him the capacity to hear the Word of God in the words of men—in theological terms, the *testimonium internum Spiritus Sancti*.

Much depends, of course, upon how this testimony is conceived. It may be thought of as possible only as a special gift of Grace. It may be thought of as belonging to every individual in his own right or as a special possession of the beloved community, the Church—or indeed of both together. Finally it may be thought of as an illumination that lighteneth every one that cometh into the world—in every case, however, any criterion of Holy Scripture presupposes this double aspect. For however it functions, it requires both that men shall

recognize the Word of God in the words of men and secondly
that there shall be some objective criterion for their interpretation.[1]

However this *testimonium internum* may be conceived by the
theologian, it must, I think, in the last analysis, be for the
philosopher that light which lighteneth every man, that sense
of perfection which arises from and conditions the analogy
between the human and the Divine.

For the Christian tradition the grounds for the canonicity of
the *Song of Songs* is a case especially in point. Why, so one might
ask, should God have gone to the writer of this highly erotic
poem to speak to us, and why should its oriental language become the medium for the expression of the most exalted experiences of man's relations to the Divine? Its canonicity, we are
told, has never been doubted, the evidence in its favour being
as strong as that of the other books of the Old Testament. Both
Jewish and Christian tradition has considered it allegorical or
figurative, the former holding that the ode portrays the yearning of the bereaved Israelite Church towards the Holy Temple
on Mount Zion after the separation of the ten tribes, the latter
holding the language to be figurative of the union between
Christ and His spouse, the Church. Is the Divine presence, we
may well ask, in this poem of love? The only answer that we
can really give is that men have found it there. They are, indeed,
human emotions that the poem portrays, some would say,
human all too human, but they are emotions transposed to
another scale—a scale so transcendent as to give them a new
quality, a quality so wholly other as to make them as unique
as the Object towards which they are directed. So at least the
mystics have always found. If, however, men have found the
Divine presence there it is also only because there is such an
analogy between the love of man and the love of God, that from
the perfections of the former we may rise to the perfection of the
latter.

[1] The Papal Encyclical *Providentissimus Deus*, which has to do with the study of
sacred scripture, recognizes this double criterion in principle. The words themselves are divine, although the interpretation (Hermeneutics) is necessary. Even
this, however, is inadequate to determine the complete sense of the scriptures
because of 'religious obscurity,' and such interpretation must ultimately rest with
the Church.

APPENDIX

II

A

The foregoing answer to the question, how is Divine revelation possible? includes also, by implication, an answer to a specific question invariably and inevitably raised in all discussions of revelation, namely the relation of revelation to reason. This question, already raised in connection with the problem of the relation of dogmatic to rational theology, may now be further examined in connection with the problem of the Word of God and the word of man.

For reasons which we have seen, in whatever form God may reveal himself to man, it is only to the word that adequacy of expression can ultimately be ascribed. Since therefore all statements of revealed religion are expressed, and must be expressed, in language, and since this language, like all language, is ultimately drawn from the finite world of things, it must, because of the 'religious obscurity' inevitably involved, be interpreted. No doctrine of revelation, however absolute, can, for this reason, suppose that these statements are perfectly literal. God is not man—and for this very reason, human language requires to be read with certain qualifications before it applies to Him. Such qualifications can be justified, however, only on some theory of the relation between the human and the Divine, and that can be determined only by reason. Moreover, any supposed revelation must be thought about to be received and it can be thought about only in language conditioned by the way in which it appears in creatures. These finite words can not signify the Divine to men unless the proper mode of signification functions in their minds, and what this proper mode is can be asserted only on the basis of some theory of the relation of the Divine to the human, and such a relation can be determined only by reason. In sum, prior to any particular revelation, and its interpretation, is the postulate of the relation of finite words to the Eternal Word. The dogmatic theology of revelation presupposes, as we have already seen, a natural theology of reason and the two can not ultimately be completely separated.

The 'extreme revelationist' as we have also seen, often denies this fundamental relation of the Word of God to the word of

471

man. He believes that he can retain the uniqueness of the Divine initiative only by denying the relative and human. But surely such denial is vain and carries with it its own nemesis. For even if it were true that God and man stand over against one another as Absolute and relative, and consequently religion can not be grounded on anything human but only on God, it still remains true that if God is to speak to man at all, he must be understood by man. Even if it were true that all that God has to say to man is contrary to human nature and human reason, one might well ask how is it possible that man should really understand what He says. Communication of whatever kind, whether human or Divine, has of necessity two poles—the one is not intelligible without the other—and no miracle of Grace can make it intelligible. If we conceive revelation as 'a bolt out of the blue' and refuse to relate it to the primary and original intuitions and valuations of men, we end in making the process by which revelation is received wholly ununderstandable. More than this, if we insist upon the uniqueness of our own revelation to the extent of refusing to relate it to the revelatory element in the faith of others, we end by making it impossible either to understand their faith or to communicate the essence of our own. If the Word of God is completely separated from the word of man there is no way, short of the most unintelligible miracle, by means of which they can be brought together again.

B

The problem, how is Divine revelation possible, is then, in the first instance, a problem of language—how can the word of man be the Word of God? But this question involves problems of a still more far-reaching character, although, as I believe, they can be answered only in the light of the preceding considerations. I shall not go into these questions here but rather refer to a discussion of revelation which is more adequate than any I should be able to offer.[1] There is, however, one comment I should like to make which may be viewed as of the nature of a corollary of the preceding discussion.

[1] 'I propose,' writes A. E. Taylor in his chapter 'Reason and Revelation,' *op. cit.*, 'to offer some reflections on the cogency of such a destructive *Kritik aller Theologie die als Offenbarung auftreten will.*' I should say that I agree in principle with the outcome of these reflections, and should accept without any serious reservations the view of revelation here developed.

APPENDIX

Unless one proposes, in terms of a recent book, a *Religion Without Revelation*, one must fall back, it is held, upon the notions of a general revelation with which the particular revelation is related, and of a progressive revelation in which the unique and once-for-all character of the special revelation is viewed as its culmination. Indeed it is maintained that only by means of such notions can a doctrine of revelation be saved at all. Properly understood, these contentions are, I believe, sound.

The historical, and therefore relative, character of all religion is, we have seen, implied in the nature of its language. If every man must hear the voice of God in his own 'tongue,' this in itself implies that presupposed in any special revelation is that more general revelation which makes the special understandable. Not only has God spoken in sundry times and places, but, humanly speaking, he would of necessity have had so to speak if the word of the latter days is to be understood. If truth, even the truth of God, must be spoken in an age's own dialect, with all that this implies of moral and spiritual idiom, then if there is in any sense progression of the ages, there must be progressive revelation also. It is true the idea of a general revelation may be made so general as to become meaningless. There are those who, including all poetry art and science, tend in the end to wipe out all distinctions between revelation and reason, between nature and Grace. There are those also who, in the same spirit, make progressive revelation in religion but one aspect of that deterministic secular theory which, denying the providential theory of history upon which alone such a progressive revelation could be based, again wipe out all distinctions between nature and Grace. But neither of these consequences is necessarily implied in the notions of general and progressive revelation.

Nor do such conceptions necessarily detract from the uniqueness, the one-for-all character which we ascribe to the specific revelation. Rousseau asked, so Professor Baillie reminds us, why God should have gone and found Moses to speak to Jean Jacques Rousseau, and this question really goes to the heart of the matter. Why, indeed, should God have found Moses or even Jesus and St. Paul, to speak to us? If he speaks at all, why not in the idiom of the present? There is only one answer to such questions, namely the immanence of the timeless in the temporal. The 'divine sentence' is divine simply because it is

473

timeless; the numinous quality of the Word is such because those who have been uniquely near to God at any time are nearer to us than our contemporaries, however remote they may be in the far reaches of time. Not only are they our real contemporaries, but they also speak a language which, far from being archaic, is one which, because it is dateless, is always up-to-date. Religion has its *Urwörte*, its essential idiom, which, in so far as the original intuition is concerned, the original phenomena of the spiritual life, age can not wither nor custom stale. All this, however, is another story, involving the entire question of the historical and the supra-historical in religion, a theme sufficiently discussed, I suppose, in Chapter VIII.

INDEX OF SUBJECTS

INDEX OF NAMES